DATE DUE

DEMCO 38-297

The Dark Sides of Virtue

David Kennedy

The Dark Sides of Virtue

Reassessing International Humanitarianism

Illustrated by Doug Mayhew

PRINCETON UNIVERSITY PRESS
Princeton and Oxford

Published by Princeton University Press, 41 William Street, Princeton, New Jersey 08540

In the United Kingdom: Princeton University Press, 3 Market Place, Woodstock, Oxfordshire OX20 1SY

ISBN: 0-691-11686-5

British Library Cataloging-in-Publication Data is available

This book has been composed in Sabon and Didot

Printed on acid-free paper. ∞

www.pupress.princeton.edu

Printed in the United States of America

10 9 8 7 6 5 4 3 2 1

FOR MY PARENTS

Contents

Human Rights Occupies the Field of Emancipa-
tory Possibility • Human Rights Views the Prob-
lem and the Solution Too Narrowly • Human
Rights Generalizes Too Much • Human Rights
Particularizes Too Much • Human Rights Is Lim-
ited by Its Relationship to Western Liberalism
• Human Rights Promises More Than It Can
Deliver • The Legal Regime of "Human Rights,"
Taken as a Whole, Does More to Produce and
Excuse Violations Than to Prevent and Remedy
Them • The Human Rights Bureaucracy Is Itself
Part of the Problem • The Human Rights Move-
ment Strengthens Bad International Governance
• Human Rights Promotion Can Be Bad Politics
in Particular Contexts

Preface

When you land on an aircraft carrier — even on the mail run, strapped in backward, wearing a crash helmet and goggles — they tell you it will feel like a "controlled crash," and you do decelerate fast. Coming down hard can be disorienting, but it is also thrilling. When the plane pulled off the braking cable, the rear cargo door opened and a young man in a flight suit and life vest stepped across the deck, yelling into his helmet mike. Through earplugs I heard that Dr. Kennedy would be the first to deplane. It was March of 1998, two weeks after Kofi Annan shortcircuited a threatened strike against Iraq. I had flown from Bahrain to the U.S.S. *Independence* in the Persian Gulf to spend some time with the command staff who would have coordinated and executed the strike. My host, Admiral Charles ("Bill") Moore, at that time Commander of the U.S. Fifth Fleet, was waiting to greet me. His attorney would take me to my quarters, just under the flight deck, where I would spend the better part of a week with something like five thousand men, one woman, and no windows.

Twenty-six years before, I had registered for the draft as a conscientious objector. My childhood milieu was broadly liberal, my own political impulses loosely internationalist, progressive, and humanitarian. To be humanitarian and progressive in the American suburbs of 1972 meant opposing the military — its war in Vietnam, its "culture of death," its "military-industrial complex." Strictly speaking, my friends and I had missed the sixties, if only just. But the rhetorics of peace and protest still hung in the air. Through the seventies, my generation went to school and entered the professions, pulled in the wake of the sixties semitrailer.

I became an international lawyer, trained to promote the international rule of law as a humanitarian, progressive, and cosmopolitan project. The military seemed all that international law was not, violence and aggression to our reason and restraint. We began to take power just as the greatest generation prepared to give way to the baby boom in the person of Bill Clinton. Many of my age cohort would get their first chance in government as junior players in his administration. The Cold War was over, and Vietnam suddenly seemed a long time ago. International humanitarianism had begun to change its spots. I knew something was up during the Gulf War when I found myself rushing from the ski slopes to catch the latest intelligence photos.

By the early 1990s, the most liberal of my students embraced each new American military deployment with enthusiasm. In Somalia, Haiti, and Bosnia, a new alliance of humanitarian and military interests was being forged. When Madelaine Albright asked Colin Powell, "What's the point of having this superb military that you're always talking about if we can't use it?" she knew her constituency. Those of my students who argued most vigorously for U.S. military intervention in Kosovo or Rwanda had not been born when I had registered for the draft or protested what I still thought of as "the war." These young professionals, assertively humanitarian and progressive in their politics, had largely lost faith in government as an agent of social change at home. But the military seemed newly capable of saving failed states and mending broken societies abroad. In the early nineties, my students resisted the military in matters of culture and individual expression — this was the time of Tailhook and "don't ask/don't tell" — but not in strategy, except when the military seemed squeamish about humanitarian-mission creep.

Like others my age, I found myself reevaluating. It was time to revisit my aversions — the military profession no longer seemed so alien. I hung out with students who had seen military service, read up on military history and strategy, taught a course about war. In June of 1997, I joined a team of American military officers in Dakar to train the Senegalese high command in international law, human rights, and the rules of engagement for coalition operations. Back home, I spent time with people who found pleasure in military uniforms and the controlled application of force. A year later, a friend got me invited to the carrier *Independence,* and I jumped at the chance to assess the relationship between the routines of maintaining a "no-fly zone," the uneasy thrills of planning a first strike at Iraqi "weapons of mass destruction," the pleasures and power of military life — and my increasingly perplexed humanitarian sensibility. I report the results of these investigations in chapter 8 — one well-meaning civilian professional, internationalist and humanitarian in sensibility, takes another look at American military culture.

But my appetites needed as fresh a look as my aversions. Experience with the legal institutions and professional practices of international humanitarianism had led me increasingly to question their virtues. The international human rights movement, the legal and institutional system for the protection of refugees, the campaign to establish the rule of law as a strategy for development, the effort to bring the societies of Central and Eastern Europe into the orbit of Western market democracy after the fall of the Berlin Wall, the campaign for a gentler globalization of labor rights and environmental protection — all these provided settings in which a vague humanitarian yearning could become a concrete institutional or professional project. I had been attracted to them, had participated in them, had sometimes succeeded in making them my own. But I had come increasingly to feel these projects could be as much part of the problem as of the solution. This book sets out to explain how that can happen and what might be done to avoid it.

The international humanitarians I have known rarely place the darker sides of their endeavors center stage, where they can be assessed and either refuted or taken into account in future work. The negatives are discussed privately, often cynically, but rarely strategically. With so much evil out there to fight, it hardly seems worth it to focus on the downsides of the few humanitarian practices which have been set in motion. But these darker sides can swamp the benefits of humanitarian work, and well-intentioned people can find themselves unwittingly entrenching the very things they have sought voice to denounce. Still, it is terribly hard to know, and there is no doubt that raising critical voices can itself weaken important ventures. In this book, I propose a posture or sensibility for humanitarian work which I hope will make it easier to navigate these issues — to recognize and engage the dark sides of our work, to work through them strategically and pragmatically, and to act on our humanitarian yearnings, even when our analysis leaves us uncertain.

HUMANITARIANISMS

The impulse to do good, to remake the world more fairly, to strengthen the hand of tolerance and understanding takes shape for each of us in the available cultural and professional vocabulary. Humanitarianism begins as an impulse — and becomes known as a practice. These chapters explore the movement of humanitarian desires into action — often first as ideas, and then as practical projects, professional practices, modes of expertise, and broad vocabularies for policy making and advocacy.

All of us who have felt a humanitarian impulse also know the satisfaction which comes from affiliating with others who share our intuitions about justice in order to make our yearnings real as projects and practices. Coming together to exercise power on behalf of our commitments, or simply to affirm our commitments to ourselves, can be thrilling. And, of course, when such a project ceases to inspire, no longer connects you with people you respect, or runs out of steam as a vehicle for making a difference in the world, you can also come down hard.

This book explores the enchantments and disenchantments which accompany the expression of international humanitarian sentiments. Support for an institution like the United Nations, for a cause like nuclear disarmament or nonproliferation, even for a slogan like "World Peace through World Law," can come to express the impulse to make the world a better place. Opposing the military in Vietnam had been like that for many people. So had supporting military intervention in Bosnia. At one point or another, well-meaning international humanitarians have worked for U.S. membership in the League of Nations, for nuclear disarmament and nonproliferation, for Atlantic federalism, self-determination, international refugee protection, decolonization, development assistance, "coexistence," "convergence," "cooperation" with the Soviet bloc, and for detente. They have supported the work of the International Labor Organization, the Red Cross, and the nongovernmental organizations of an emerging global "civil society." They have lobbied for women's rights, for international environmental protection, and for higher labor standards. They have extended markets to former socialist states, promoted law reform abroad, fought corruption in the third world, and exported the "rule of law" and democracy. They have opposed excessive intellectual property protection and regulation of the Internet. And, of course, they have fought wars.

International humanitarian sentiments have inspired different projects in different places. Bombing Belgrade to save Kosovo can seem like a humanitarian triumph or a catastrophe, depending on where you sit. There have been humanitarianisms of the left and the right, of the establishment and the margin, and everything in between. There are humanitarianisms of Europe, of Africa, of the global, and of the local.

My focus here is on the humanitarian work I know best—the efforts of well-meaning people, usually in the United States, to express their humanitarian yearnings on the global stage. The humanitarians most familiar to me are professionals—international lawyers, political scientists, economists, development specialists, international civil servants, human rights activists, and academics. Their work has spawned a wide range of institutions and professional practices which are now associated with international humanitarianism—many affiliated with the United Nations, the global human-rights movement, and the work of nongovernmental organizations. In the last decades, their activities have generated whole new vocabularies for policy making and statecraft.

I know these humanitarianisms well enough to have felt the pleasures of engagement and the disappointments of a faith betrayed. I have written these reflections to capture both the significance I continue to feel the effort to make humanitarian desires real can have, and the disenchantment I have experienced with our routine humanitarian practices and professional vocabularies. Undoubtedly, these institutions and practices — human rights, refugee protection, development policy, humanitarian law — will look different, will seem to generate different costs or benefits, engage different yearnings, and engender different dark sides for other humanitarians in other places.

The first part of the book focuses on the international humanitarian as an *activist,* primarily in the field of human rights. I write from my experience as a human rights advocate seeking to represent political prisoners in faraway locations and as a participant in launching a new institutional platform for advocacy. Activists typically see themselves outside the centers of power in global affairs, and seek to speak to those powers — to advocate — in the name of humanitarian ideas and causes. They give voice to humanitarian norms and values, articulating a humanitarian vision, demanding compliance with humanitarian commitments. They seek, in short, *to speak as truth to power.*

Humanitarian activists often speak to power as representatives of others — human rights victims, for example. The advocate is something of a translator — representing people outside the political process to those within it. In doing so, the advocate occupies a liminal position, and speaks neither the language of power nor the language of one particular interest against another. The humanitarian activist speaks rather in the language of universal commitments and interests. The powerful must respect human rights not to protect the interests of these victims, but to respect the universal significance of rights themselves.

This work can be done by individuals, and it can be done by civic groups, churches, foundations, and grass-roots movements of all types. International human rights has become by far the most common vocabulary for humanitarian activists. I focus on the growing network of activist individuals and institutions in the international human rights movement. The first chapter develops a list of arguments about the possible dark sides of this work, and the next two narrate experiences of my own which raise these themes.

The second part of the book focuses on the international humanitarian as a *policy maker,* participating in a campaign for legal or political reform. I write from my experiences working with the United

Nations High Commissioner for Refugees, with the European Union as it sought to integrate the economies of Central and Eastern Europe into the West after 1989, and as a participant in debates about the appropriate role for lawyers in economic development and the effort to render "globalization" more humane. These chapters consider the humanitarian in postures we associate more readily with governing. Unlike activists and advocates, humanitarian policy makers see themselves participating in the institutions of global governance. They speak the language of strategy, of problem solving, of getting things done — less speaking truth to power than providing the expert voice of power itself, deployed for humanitarian ends. These short studies illustrate how routine professional practices and vocabularies can limit and misdirect the humanitarian policy maker's best efforts to make the world a better place.

Of course, activism and policy making are not always so distinct. The activist aspires not only to articulate what the universal requires, but also to make that articulation effective. The humanitarian policy maker is not simply governing to solve problems or please constituencies, but to foster outcomes which vindicate humanitarian values and objectives. We might see activists and policy makers as partners in governance. Increasingly, they share a common vocabulary. Perhaps the most familiar is the international law of force, whose terms — proportionality, self-defense, military necessity — have become common to military strategists, statesmen, and humanitarians alike.

It can be unsettling to think of humanitarians, whether activists or policy makers, as participants in the world of power and influence. It is difficult to think of humanitarian vocabularies — human rights, humanitarian law — as idioms of statecraft. Humanitarians are used to thinking of their efforts as marginal, weak, barely able to be heard. Those who develop humanitarian policies often see themselves giving advice rather than making policy, formulating proposals which others — the real rulers — will need to implement.

But our work, our ideas, our institutions, our professional practices of advocacy and policy making do have consequences. State power is now routinely exercised in the vocabularies of these helping professions. As is economic power. We should own the uses made of the institutions and professional practices we have set loose in the world. We should come to see humanitarians less as people outside looking in than as participants in governance. Their truth is also power.

DARK SIDES

Once we see international humanitarians as participants in global governance — as rulers — it seems irresponsible not to be as attentive as possible to the costs, as well as the benefits, of our work. International humanitarian efforts to rebuild societies, to reproach and shame the unjust, or to protect the vulnerable can all be swamped by the opposition and inattention of others, or undone by lack of resources and commitment among humanitarians themselves. Making humanitarian headway is almost always harder, more expensive, and more time-consuming than we expect.

These quite formidable problems of implementation are not my focus. I am concerned about the difficulties which our *best* efforts themselves may bring, and with the unacknowledged costs of routine humanitarian endeavors on the international stage. I do not propose a unified theory for the dark sides of international humanitarianism. My sense, rather, is that things can go wrong in all sorts of different ways. We promise more than can be delivered — and come to believe our own promises. We enchant our tools, substitute work on our own institutions and promotion of our own professional expertise for work on the problems which gave rise to our humanitarian hopes. At worst, we can find our own work contributing to the very problems we hoped to solve. Humanitarianism tempts us to hubris, to an idolatry about our intentions and routines, to the conviction that we know more than we do about what justice can be.

This book aims to develop a catalog of such possible difficulties, unforeseen bad consequences, routine blind spots, and biases of humanitarian work. The first chapter catalogs criticisms which have been made of human rights activism, and is followed by two chapters exploring the dark sides of human rights advocacy and institution building. Chapter 4 compiles a similar list of general criticisms made of humanitarian policy making. The three chapters which follow develop these observations in the context of particular policy making projects. All these chapters argue for a pragmatic renewal of humanitarian activism and policy making. Chapter 8 considers the limits of humanitarian pragmatism, exploring the difficulties which arose as humanitarians came to join hands with statesmen and military planners in a common pragmatic—and humanitarian—vocabulary to limit the incidence and violence of war. It builds on what I learned about the authority of humanitarianism by spending time with the U.S. military and observing the influence of humanitarianism in promoting and criticizing the recent war in Iraq.

All governance projects have dark sides, costs, unacknowledged risks, unanticipated losers. Numerous clichés help us become accustomed to the dark sides of rulership—"you can't make an omelette without breaking some eggs," "if you can't take the heat, get out of the kitchen," "it's two steps backward for every one step forward." In my experience, humanitarians have a hard time thinking about their own work in these familiar terms. We have a hard time focusing on costs in part because we do not think of ourselves as rulers. *Other* people govern, and it is our job to hold *them* responsible. It seems perverse to blame the humanitarians—the good guys, the ones trying to make things better. That people get hurt and pay a price for humanitarian initiatives is routinely underestimated or left unseen. Even the clichés seem to push the other way—"better to light a single candle than to curse the darkness."

My hope is that bringing the costs of humanitarianism to the surface will encourage an attitude of responsibility for the difficulties our endeavors inevitably bring. Perhaps we will learn to disenchant our routine humanitarian practices and understand the damage we sometimes do. If we do, we may also find ways to avoid or minimize these costs. But we may not—there are limits to what we can foresee, to what we can understand about the effects of our power in the world. For all our good intentions and careful attention to costs and benefits, dark sides, blind spots, biases all will remain with us. As we come to see the dark sides of our work, we will also need to develop new habits of mind, become more able to accept responsibility for the unforeseen and unknowable costs of making our humanitarian visions real in the world. The most interesting test for humanitarianism comes precisely when we realize we must remain uncertain about where virtue lies and what costs we impose — but when we nevertheless step forward to govern. In the last chapter, I propose that those who share my impulse to make the international world a more just and humane place join in building a humanitarian practice which embraces the freedom and responsibility that come with an ongoing awareness of the dark sides of humanitarian governance.

RENEWING HUMANITARIANISM: SOME HELPFUL TRADITIONS

Three quite different intellectual traditions have influenced my own thinking about the dark sides of humanitarianism and what might be done about them. None is new to the humanitarian tradition. Indeed, each has been the foundation for important prior efforts to renew humanitarian practices. Rather than offering an integrated program of my own for renewing international humanitarianism, I draw on these traditions in various ways, in the hope that those who wish to keep the humanitarian impulse vigorous in the world will add to our toolkit of diagnostic and remedial vocabularies.

A Pragmatism of Intention

A pragmatism of intentions encourages a clear-eyed focus on the purposes of our work and a relentless effort to avoid being blown off course as we seek to make our humanitarian impulses real. The focus is on the gap between our good impulses and their bad expression. A central idea is betrayal — of an original impulse, purpose, or objective — by the work we do to fulfill it. Our ends can be foiled by the means we use to pursue them. Our ideals can be compromised by the words we use to express them, just as our deeds can in turn betray our words.

It is common for humanitarian purposes to be overtaken by the institutions and professional practices which express them. Work to build the movement can substitute for work on the problem. We can enchant our tools and abandon our ideals. At our most well meaning, we can pay more attention to compiling documents than developing solutions, to proclaiming rights than fashioning remedies. Procedures to enforce human rights can become rituals which substitute for effective human rights enforcement.

As circumstances change, it is tempting to avoid the difficult work of ascertaining what our commitments now mean or how they can best find expression. Our canonical expressions can substitute for our best humanitarian ideas and fealty to a "correct" position can substitute for the political or ethical concerns which motivated its adoption. Conventional expressions — "right to life" — can take on a life of their own, migrating to other applications and uses.

We can also betray our best intentions by our unconscious desires and hidden ambivalence, by bad faith and hypocrisy, or by blind spots and biases in our institutional practices and professional vocabularies. We can get wrapped up in our own advocacy and lose track of the biases and desires we each bring to humanitarian work. And, of course, our best intentions can also be betrayed out in the world, when our ideals are misunderstood or when our initiatives run into frictions and resistance from the institutions we hoped would implement them.

A pragmatism of intention encourages renewed fealty to purpose and intention, enforced by habits of analytic vigilance and skepticism about the forms these purposes have come to take. We think this way most clearly when we select rules and standards most likely to render our humanitarian ideas real. Over the last century or more, international humanitarians have struggled repeatedly to reaffirm their commitments in effective terms — think of the tremendous effort put into the codification of human rights and the restatement of humanitarian law. They have fostered professional skepticism about entrenched rules and shopworn institutions which purport to express humanitarian objectives in definitive terms. The return to virtuous intentions can lead one to reaffirm important rules and normative formulations, just as it can demand that rules be set aside where they would impair fealty to humanitarian ideals.

Most of the criticisms I develop to encourage a pragmatism of intentions will be familiar to humanitarian activists and policy makers. The best humanitarian professionals struggle constantly to bring their advocacy and policy making back in line with their humanitarian ideals. It is a good part of what we mean when we say humanitarian work is pragmatic and purposeful. This spirit is particularly familiar to advocates and activists, who must remain vigilant about the purity of the truth they speak to power.

However helpful, a pragmatism of intentions also has limits. Our humanitarian yearnings are often too vague to guide our action. Circumstances change. In the name of recapturing our original impulse, we are easily tempted to substitute one false idol, one fetish, for another. Humanitarian purposes often diverge and give no guidance in the struggle over which to pursue. Habits of vigilance can themselves go awry — careful comparison of different routes to our goal can further mystify the goal itself. In some sense, what we "meant" is inaccessible — we know it only after we get going. These are common and well-known problems — the dark sides, if you like, of efforts to renew humanitarian practice through a pragmatism of intention.

A Pragmatism of Consequences

These limitations are often addressed by shifting attention from goals and purposes toward assessment of outcomes. A pragmatism of consequences seems more hard-boiled, focusing our attention on good outcomes rather than good intentions. Innoculate this child, and don't worry so much about the precise entailments of the "right to health," or about your original desires for and fantasies about what doing good might mean. When activists think in instrumental or functional terms about their advocacy — when they make strategic choices about which rule or standard to invoke, which institution to engage — they focus on the consequences. The best humanitarian policy makers think this way all the time — in many ways policy making is precisely the effort to ask as carefully and rationally as possible who would win and who would lose from proposed governmental action. The decision to set up a rule system or institutional structure to address an international humanitarian problem is similar.

Focusing on consequences takes us into the social sciences, with all their technologies for measuring and predicting the results of governance. Will the inoculation actually protect the child? How can we compare a campaign of inoculation with a campaign to cleanse the water supply? Or a campaign to protect children with a campaign to protect rural workers? Problems of measurement and prediction will limit our ability to assess consequences accurately.

When the data are uncertain, humanitarians are guided by hunches, inferences, past experience, and conceptions of best practice. Much humanitarian expertise consists of broad ideas and shared arguments about the likely consequences of various policy or advocacy initiatives. International lawyers think multilateralism will generally produce more humanitarian results than unilateral action — and have developed a series of expert reasons for thinking so. We generally expect the establishment of monitoring institutions to strengthen observance of human rights norms, or the ratification of human rights conventions to strengthen the hands of those who would seek compliance with their terms, and have developed expert accounts of why and how this could happen.

A pragmatism of consequences runs into difficulty when expertise of this type substitutes for careful analysis of long- and short-term consequences. Like other experts, humanitarians can get caught by the blind spots and biases of their professional vocabularies and misestimate the costs and benefits of what seems the best policy or activist strategy. It is all too easy to misjudge reactions to humanitarian endeavors, or fail to appreciate the costs our work imposes on other projects and groups, or to substitute assertion that things will work out for any careful weighing of probabilities. The desire to work from expertise can lead us to underestimate what expertise cannot tell us — or to mistake ideological preferences for shrewd hunches about best practice. Our professional vocabularies can narrow our appreciation for the stakes of our humanitarian work and still the experience of deciding aware that we cannot know how things will turn out. The client can get lost in the shuffle or be created in the image of the grievance we understand.

Humanitarians are particularly susceptible to these difficulties because they tend to be uncomfortable thinking of themselves making the kind of distributional choices among winners and losers which seem required by a pragmatism of consequences. An inoculation program will place resources here and not there, will target these diseases and not those. Translating humanitarian commitments into choices among winners and among losers takes us to a terrain more familiar as politics than as expertise. For activists, this can seem inconsistent with the ambition to speak in universal terms — as truth, rather than as choice. For policy makers, proposals which cannot be defended in general terms raise the specter of choices among humanitarianisms — of the left and right, labor and capital, men and women, rich and poor, urban and rural, children and the elderly, or first world and third. It can be unsettling, even scary, to translate humanitarian commitments into these more political terms, or to accept that we make choices which create losers. It is not surprising that we so often prefer to rely on best practice, or to defer reckoning with hard consequences until some future date when our favorite institutions have all been built and our practices will have become routine.

Beyond Pragmatism — Uncertainty, Responsibility, and Decision

International humanitarians have long understood the difficulties of remaining true to their best intentions and careful in their assessment of consequences. Campaigns to renew the traditions of international humanitarianism have quite regularly been launched as efforts to return to pragmatism in one or another of these two senses. As international humanitarians have become more pragmatic about their advocacy and their policy making, they have come to participate ever more successfully in governance. The rules and standards they chose to make real their intentions blend with the institutional strategies and ideas about best practice their instrumental calculations have developed as expertise. The result is a regime — a professional language and practice of pragmatic humanitarianism.

But dark sides remain. Too often, we have become rulers in flight from rulership. The pragmatic expertise we have developed seems to take us ever further from the responsible exercise of power. Humanitarians are also people with projects, confronting as many blind corners and confusions as possibilities. Our motives remain obscure, our best intentions conflict — and no amount of careful analysis will suffice to make known the consequences of our humanitarian work. Our work is often tawdry and uncertain, and we approach it with ambivalence. Humanitarians have all sorts of attitudes and ambitions — they seek to affirm their commitments, affiliate with others who share them, be effective in the world on their behalf. They want to express their aversions, to disaffiliate from those they scorn. Alongside their will to power runs a will to submit, to remain marginal to rulership. This human side of the story takes us to the difficult terrain of desire, power, knowledge, and responsibility. We are all uncertain, unknowing, about our own motives and purposes, and about the results of our action. But our humanitarian impulses can be made good only by doing things with rules and procedures, crafting remedies, building institutions — and when we do, people will get hurt.

The last chapters of the book develop these themes, raised most starkly by the story of humanitarianism's engagement with the military. Perhaps surprisingly, international humanitarianism has been at its most pragmatic when seeking to limit the violence of warfare. These humanitarian projects have been altogether more successful than one might have thought. Humanitarianism has become an increasingly dominant vocabulary for thinking about military strategy and tactics. But the story of what I found onboard the *Independence* will need to wait.

Let me say here simply that I have written this book in the hope that well-meaning people, people who hope to make the world a more humane and just place, will find better ways to make those yearnings real. I end the book with a series of suggestions for those who seek to move beyond pragmatic renewal in their search to understand and manage the dark sides of international humanitarianism. Our challenge is to develop professional habits — a style or posture, if you like — for taking responsible action as a ruler where expertise cannot be perfected. My hope is that we will come to embrace the human side of humanitarian practice, including its dark sides, uncertainties, and ambivalences. Responsible humanitarian action in a cloud of uncertainty — my hope is that humanitarian advocates and policy makers will develop an appetite for this most basic experience of rulership. Perhaps the word *grace* will capture something of what I have in mind — I propose we rethink our humanitarian traditions as the search for grace in governance.

Acknowledgments

There are too many people to thank. The inspiration for this book comes from the love, the faith, and the habits of intellectual inquiry and honest skepticism my parents, Nancy Kennedy and Paul Kennedy, nurtured — both in our family and among the close circle of friends with whom they founded a small church in the 1950s and in whose congregation I was raised. My thanks also to my grandmother, who never failed to ask as I recounted a childhood triumph whether I thought it was "a good thing or a bad thing."

This book emerges from my own congregation of friends, colleagues, students, and fellow humanitarians. My thanks to you all for supporting my efforts to face the dark sides of humanitarianism without losing faith. Philip Allott, Helena Alviar, Antony Anghie, Marie-Claire Belleau, Jim Bergeron, Nathaniel Berman, Yishai Blanc, Patrick Breslin, Anne Marie Calareso, Deb Cass, Hilary Charlesworth, David Charny, Maxwell Chibundu, Robert Chu, Dan Danielsen, Catriona Drew, Ioannis Drossos, Claus Ehlermann, Karen Engle, Jorge Esquirol, Guenter Frankenberg, Jerry Frug, Marge Garber, James Gathii, Richard Goldstein, Ryan Goodman, Denise Grey, Janet Halley, Helen Hartnell, Barbara Johnson, Duncan Kennedy, Paul Kennedy, Karl Klare, Karen Knop, Outi Korhonen, Martti Koskienniemi, Matt Kramer, Mike Lewis, Alejandro Lorite, Pat Macklem, Susan Marks, Bob Meagher, Ed Morgan, Rose Moss, Athena

Mutua, Vasuki Nesiah, Joel Paul, Scott Newton, Joel Ngugi, Ileana Porras, Balakrishnan Rajagopal, Annelise Riles, Kerry Rittich, Phillipe Sands, Alvaro Santos, Hani Sayed, Natalia Schiffrin, Amr Shalakany, Thomas Skouteris, Leopold Specht, Henry Steiner, Mackay Taylor, Ruti Teitel, Chantal Thomas, David Trubek, Detlev Vagts, Jean-Francois Verstrynge, Robert Wai, Judith Walcott, Glenn Ware, and David Webb have all had a hand in these pages. My thanks to each of you.

Portions of several chapters have been published previously, and are included in amended version, by permission. Illustrations by Doug Mayhew, courtesy of Mayhew Orion Inc. and Glitterati Incorporated, NYC.

Parts of chapter 1 were originally published as "The International Human Rights Movement: Part of the Problem?" in *European Human Rights Law Review* 3: 245–67 (2001) and *Harvard Human Rights Journal* 14: 101–25 (2001). Chapter 2 was originally published as "Spring Break," *Texas Law Review* 63 (1985): 1377. The essay was reprinted, with a new introduction, in *Knowledges: Historical and Critical Studies in Disciplinarity*, edited by Ellen Messer-Davidow, David R. Shumway, and David J. Sylvan, 422 (Charlottesville: University Press of Virginia, 1993). The names of prisoners have been changed. An extended version of chapter 3 was published as "Autumn Weekends: An Essay on Law and Everyday Life," in *Law and Everyday Life*, edited by Austin Sarat and Thomas R. Kearns, (1993), 191. An excerpt was reprinted as "An Autumn Weekend" in *After Identity: A Reader in Law and Culture*, edited by Dan Danielsen and Karen Engle, 191–210 (New York: Routledge, Chapman, Hall, 1995). That excerpt appeared in French as "Weekends d'automne" *Droit international* 4 1999–2000: 133–78. An early version of chapter 4 was published as "The Politics of the Invisible College: International Governance and the Politics of Expertise," 5 *European Human Rights Law Review* (2001). A version of chapter 5 was published in *Law and Development: Facing Complexity in the 21st Century*, edited by Amanda Perry and John Hatchard, London: Cavendish Publishing (2003). I first published reflections on my time with the United Nations High Commissioner for Refugees, the topic of chapter 6, in "International Refugee Protection," *Human Rights Quarterly* 8 (1986): 1. An earlier version of chapter 7 appeared as "Turning to Market Democracy: A Tale of Two Architectures," *Harvard International Law Journal* 32 (1991): 373.

PART I The International Humanitarian as Advocate and Activist

ONE

The International Human Rights Movement: Part of the Problem?

There is no question that the international human rights movement has done a great deal of good. It has freed individuals from great harm, provided an emancipatory vocabulary and institutional machinery for people across the globe. It has raised the standards by which governments judge one another, and by which they are judged, both by their own people, and by the elites we refer to collectively as the "international community." A career in the human rights movement has provided thousands of professionals a sense of dignity and confidence that one sometimes can do well while doing good. The literature praising these, and other, accomplishments is vast. Among well-meaning legal professionals in the United States and Europe — humanitarian, internationalist, liberal, compassionate in all the best senses of these terms — the human rights movement has become a central object of devotion.

But are there also dark sides? This chapter develops a short list of hypotheses about the possible risks, costs, and unanticipated consequences of human rights activism. These are all familiar to human rights activists; they circulate in the background of conversations as worries, cynical doubts. The best human rights practitioners often assess their work in just these terms. Sometimes, of course, critical reflection can itself become part of the problem. If the costs turn out to be low or speculative, any time spent fleshing them out is time lost to the project of using human rights for emancipation — although having "been through" criticism might also strengthen the movement's ability to be useful. Periodic hand-wringing might do more to stabilize the humanitarian's confidence than to undermine it, even where it turns out the costs far outweigh the benefits. But in the end, one cannot think pragmatically about human rights work without some such list of possible costs in mind.

In the first instance, thinking pragmatically about humanitarianism means taking care that humanitarian intentions are realized — that the purposes of human rights are achieved. This chapter focuses on pragmatism in this sense — assuming the goals and intentions of humanitarian action are clear, how can we improve our ability to assess whether humanitarian work in fact contributes more to "the solution" than to "the problem"? Doing so requires careful evaluation of the benefits and the harms of our humanitarian endeavors. The list of hypothetical harms developed here might serve as a checklist.

Difficult as such assessments can be to make, they get us only partway. The problem and the solution will not look the same to everyone. Nor will the costs and benefits of humanitarian action. For those who feel the death penalty deters, its abolition is a cost which effects a distribution from victims to criminals. Although I speak in this chapter of costs and benefits (or the "problem" and the "solution") as if we shared the aspiration for a more humanitarian, progressive, and egalitarian global society, it would be more accurate to think of these "benefits" as distributions of power, status, and means toward those who share these objectives and away from those who don't.

A pragmatic assessment of humanitarian activity also requires attention to these distributional consequences. Doing so will take us to the special difficulties of representation — advocacy *on behalf of* particular groups or individuals — and of political commitment in humanitarian work, as well as to the intensely human problems raised by the ambivalent and contradictory feelings we bring to assessing these choices. The chapters which immediately follow address these human and political difficulties more directly. The politics of international humanitarianism preoccupies the later chapters on humanitarian policy making. Here, I develop a list of possible costs, as a first step toward pragmatism about humanitarian action.

A checklist of possible downsides is not a general critique of human rights. Benefits and harms must be analyzed in particular cases, under specific conditions, at particular times. The cases and conditions may be extremely specific (pursuing this petition will make this magistrate less likely to grant this other petition) or quite general (articulating social welfare needs as individual "rights" makes people everywhere more passive and isolated). Indeed, benefits are often cast in immediate and local terms — these people out of this prison, those people provided with housing, this country's political process opened to elections, monitored in this way, these individuals spared the death penalty — while costs tend to be expressed more generally, as indictments of the human rights "idea." Most likely, however, these general costs will also be more or less intense in different times and places.

Toting up the costs and benefits is no simple thing. It is as easy to give human rights too much of the blame for costs as it is too much credit for benefits. Sometimes, of course, the costs of human rights — as a vocabulary and as a movement — arise when they are *misused, distorted,* or *co-opted.* Or the benefits and burdens of human rights might, in the event, be swamped by the effects of other powers. That said, we should be suspicious if costs are *always* attributed to people and forces outside the movement, just as we should be suspicious of claims that everything bad which happens was somehow always already *inherent* in the vocabulary used by unwitting human rights advocates. And it will be terribly hard to isolate the effects of "human rights" — humanitarians will also speak other languages, or use the human rights movement and its vocabulary to get in the door before speaking instrumentally or in more exclusively ethical terms. Ultimately, we must also compare whatever assessment we make of the human rights vocabulary against the costs and benefits of *other* emancipatory vocabularies which might be used to the same ends.

In the end, of course, different observers will weigh the costs and benefits of human rights activism in different ways. Imagine an effort to use the vocabulary and political capital of the international human rights movement to end capital punishment in the Caribbean. It might well turn out that leading corporate lawyers acting pro bono in London define the problem and solution differently than do lawyers working with nongovernmental groups in London, and differently again from lawyers and organizers in the Caribbean. For some the anti–death penalty campaign might seem a distraction from more pressing issues, might occupy the field, might, if the campaign is successful, even legitimate other governmental (in)action or other social conditions which kill more people in the Caribbean. There might be a struggle within the movement about the usefulness of the vocabulary, or within the vocabulary about the conditions and costs of its deployment in particular places. Some people might use the death penalty and the human rights vocabulary to generate interest in other issues or other vocabularies — others might use it to close off broader inquiries. Wherever you are located, if you are thinking pragmatically about devoting scarce institutional resources to furthering or limiting the effort to bring human rights to bear on the instance of Caribbean death penalty, it will be necessary to come to some conclusion, however tentative and general, about how these conflicts and divergent effects will net out.

And the factors influencing the pragmatic humanitarian making such an assessment will not, by any means, all be empirically proven, or even provable. To count as a cost (or benefit), effects must be articulated only in terms plausible enough to persuade people seeking to pursue human rights to take them into account. People will evaluate risks, costs, and benefits differently. Some people are most influenced by ethical criticism, others by political, philosophical, even aesthetic objections. Others focus on the bad effects not so much of what the human rights movement does, as what it leaves undone. Costs might include what happens to potential victims and violators of human rights, or to innocent bystanders. They might include what happens to other elites — people doing good things weakened, doing bad things strengthened — or which affects participants in the human rights movement itself: professional deformations of various kinds which might be subject to ethical, political, or philosophical criticism and then count as a cost of the endeavor.

For some people, it matters (ethically, politically, philosophically, aesthetically) what the human rights movement *expresses*. If the human rights movement increases the number of descriptions in legal decisions or elsewhere of women as mothers-on-pedestals or as victimized care givers, that, for some people, is already a cost — ethically, aesthetically, politically. It is bad if women have been represented in too narrow or stereotypical a fashion, even if the only consequence is to pry lose some resources for redistribution to women. A number of the criticisms I have included here are of this type.

For other people, and I must admit, for me, nothing goes in the "costs" column until the human rights movement has a bad *effect*. A bad effect means influencing someone to act (or fail to act) or to think in a way which counts as a cost (again, ethically, politically, philosophically, aesthetically) for the person making the argument. Intensifying stereotypical representations of women might be thought to have an effect on at least some women, encouraging them to *become* narrower and more stereotypical or to think of themselves more narrowly than they otherwise might. We might imagine this happening to plaintiffs, to women using the human rights movement as a vehicle of self-expression and freedom, or to others who learn who they are from what the human rights movement says women are. And, of course, such representations would have an effect if they encouraged people in some positions of authority — judges, men, legislators, other women — to exclude women not meeting this stereotypical profile from benefits they would otherwise receive.

In building my own checklist of downsides, I have tried to eliminate criticisms that are altogether disconnected from effects — for example, the debate about whether human rights "really exist" or are "just" the product of efforts to articulate and use them. Although I find it hard to take too seriously the idea that rights *exist* in some way, let us assume that they do, and that the human rights movement is getting better and better at discovering and articulating them. If it turned out that doing so caused more misery than it alleviated, because human rights turned out to be more part of the problem than the solution, then, as a good-hearted legal professional, I would advocate our doing all we can to keep the existence of rights a secret. In a similar way, if it turns out that rights are "just" a fantasy, a social construction, and so forth, that tells us nothing about whether they are useful or not. If they are more useful than not, more power to the society which constructed them.

Traditional debates about whether human rights do or do not express a social consensus, in one society or across the globe, are similarly beside the point. Indeed, we could see them as updated ways of asking whether human rights really exist. Let us say they do express a social consensus — how does this affect their usefulness? Perhaps being able to say they express consensus weakens them, thins them out, skews their usefulness in various ways; perhaps it strengthens them. To decide, as my grandmother used to ask, "whether that's a good thing or a bad thing" we still need to know whether once strengthened or skewed or weakened or whatever they are useful, and if so for what and for whom.

Or take debate about whether human rights "talk" is or is not coherent. Let's say the human rights vocabulary, institutional apparatus, even the soul of the human rights advocate are riddled with contradictions which would not stand up to logical scrutiny for a minute. Knowing only this does not move us any closer to an understanding of whether they are part of the problem or the solution. Perhaps ambivalent porosity is their secret strength — to the extent human rights is useful, we should then be grateful for the contradictions. Perhaps incoherence is a fatal weakness, but if human rights creates more problems than it solves, this would be all to the good.

I have also left out criticisms which could be answered by intensifying our commitment to the human rights movement — that rights are not adequately enforced, that the list of rights is underinclusive, that participation in the movement or in rights enforcement could be broader, that rights are poorly or unevenly implemented because of opposition from people outside the movement or the movement's own lack of resources. Criticism of this sort is certainly important, but it sheds less light on whether the human rights idea and movement themselves are causing harm — unless it appears that these deficiencies will not, in fact, be solved by more commitment and resources and will have bad effects.

Here is my short list of pragmatic worries.

HUMAN RIGHTS OCCUPIES THE FIELD
OF EMANCIPATORY POSSIBILITY

Hegemony as Resource Allocation

The claim here is that this institutional and political hegemony makes other valuable, often more valuable, emancipatory strategies less available. This argument is stronger, of course, when one can say something about what those alternatives are — or might be. But there may be something to the claim that human rights has so dominated the imaginative space of emancipation that alternatives can now be thought only, perhaps unhelpfully, as negations of what human rights asserts — passion to its reason, local to its global. As a dominant and fashionable vocabulary for thinking about emancipation, human rights crowds out other ways of understanding harm and recompense. This is easiest to see when human rights attracts institutional energy and resources which would otherwise flow elsewhere. But this is not only a matter of scarce resources.

Hegemony as Criticism

Human rights also occupies the field by implicit or explicit delegitimation of other emancipatory strategies. As an increasingly dominant emancipatory vocabulary, human rights is also a mode of criticism, affecting other emancipatory projects which, by comparison, can seem "too" ideological and political, insufficiently universal or objective. Where this is so, pursuing a human rights initiative or promoting the use of human rights vocabulary may have fully unintended negative consequences for other existing emancipatory projects, including those relying on more religious, national, or local energies. Of course this takes us directly to a comparative analysis — how do we compare the gains and losses of human rights to the (potential) gains and losses of these other vocabularies and projects?

Hegemony as Distortion

To the extent emancipatory projects must be expressed in the vocabulary of "rights" to be heard, good policies which are not framed that way go unattended. This also distorts the way projects are imagined and framed for international consideration. For example, it is often asserted that the international human rights movement makes an end run around local institutions and strategies which would often be better — ethically, politically, philosophically, aesthetically.

Resources and legitimacy are drawn to the center from the periphery. A "universal" idea of what counts as a problem and what works as a solution snuffs out all sorts of promising local political and social initiatives to contest local conditions in other terms. But there are other lost vocabularies which are equally global — vocabularies of duty, of responsibility, of collective commitment. Encouraging people concerned about environmental harm to rethink their concerns as a human rights violation will have bad consequences if it would have turned out to be more animating, for example, to say there is a duty to work for the environment, rather than a right to a clean environment.

The "right to development" is a classic — and well-known — example. Once concerns about global poverty are raised in these terms, energy and resources are drawn to developing a literature and an institutional practice of a particular sort at the international level. Efforts which cannot be articulated in these terms seem less legitimate, less practical, less worth the effort. Increasingly, people of goodwill concerned about poverty are drawn into debate about a series of ultimately impossible legal quandaries — rights of whom, against whom, remediable how — and into institutional projects of codification and reporting familiar from other human rights efforts, without evaluating how these might compare with other deployments of talent and resources. Meanwhile, efforts which human rights does not criticize are strengthened. For example, neoliberal players who do not see development as a special problem may find it easier to take over international economic policy affecting global poverty.

HUMAN RIGHTS VIEWS THE PROBLEM AND THE SOLUTION TOO NARROWLY

Narrow in Many Ways

People have made many different claims about the narrowness of human rights. Here are some: the human rights movement foregrounds harms done explicitly by *governments* to individuals or groups — leaving potentially more severe harms brought about by private groups or indirect governmental action largely unaddressed and more legitimate by contrast. Even when addressing private harms, human rights focuses attention on *public* remedies — explicit rights formalized and implemented by the state. One criticizes the *state* and seeks *public* law remedies, but leaves unattended or enhanced the powers and felt entitlements of private actors. Human rights implicitly legitimates ills and delegitimates remedies in the domain of private law and nonstate action.

Insulating the Economy

When combined, these ideas about human rights often define problems and solutions in ways unlikely to change the economy. Human rights foregrounds problems of *participation* and *procedure*, at the expense of distribution. As a result, existing distributions of wealth, status, and power can seem more legitimate after rights have been legislated, formal participation in government achieved, and institutional remedies for violations provided. However useful saying "that's my right" is in extracting things from the state, it is not good for extracting things from the economy, unless you are a property holder. Indeed, a practice of rights claims against the state may actively weaken the capacity of people to challenge economic arrangements.

Whether progressive efforts to challenge economic arrangements are weakened by the overwhelming strength of the "right to property" in the human rights vocabulary or by the channeling of emancipatory energy and imagination into the modes of institutional and rhetorical interaction which are described as "public," the imbalance between civil/political and social/economic rights is neither an accident of politics nor a matter which could be remedied by more intensive commitment. It runs deep in the philosophy of human rights, and seems central to the conditions of political possibility that make human rights an emancipatory strategy in the first place, and to the institutional character of the movement.

Foregrounding Form

The strong attachment of the human rights movement to the legal formalization of rights and the establishment of legal machinery for their implementation makes the achievement of these forms an end in itself. Elites in a political system — international, national — which has adopted the rules and set up the institutions will often believe and insist that they have addressed the problem of violations with an elaborate, internationally respected and "state of the art" response. This is analogous to the way in which holding elections can come to substitute for popular engagement in politics. These are the traditional problems of form: form can hamper peaceful adjustment and necessary change, can be overinclusive or underinclusive. Is the right to vote a floor — or can it become a ceiling?

Backgrounding the Background

The emphasis on human rights can leave unattended the wide array of laws that do not explicitly condone violations, but that certainly affect their frequency and may in fact be doing more harm than the absence of rights. These background laws, left with clean hands, can seem more legitimate. Moreover, to maintain the claim to universality and neutrality, the human rights movement pays little attention to background social and political conditions which will determine the meaning a right has in particular contexts, rendering the evenhanded pursuit of "rights" vulnerable to all sorts of distorted outcomes.

Even very broad social movements of emancipation — for women, for minorities, for the poor — have their vision blinkered by the promise of recognition in the vocabulary and institutional apparatus of human rights. They will be led away from the economy and toward the state, away from political and social conditions and toward forms of legal recognition. It has been claimed, for example, that promoting a neutral right to religious expression in Africa without acknowledging that traditional religions and imported evangelical sects have sharply different cultural, economic, and political authority will dramatically affect the distribution of religious practice. Even if we limit our thinking to the *laws* which influence the distribution of wealth, status, and power between men and women, the number of those laws which *explicitly* address "women's issues," still less "women's rights," would form an extremely small and relatively unimportant percentage. However much the human rights movement reaches out to address other background considerations affecting the incidence of human rights abuse, such "background" norms remain, well, background.

HUMAN RIGHTS GENERALIZES TOO MUCH

Universal Goods and Evils

The vocabulary and institutional practice of human rights promotion propagates an unduly abstract idea about people, politics, and society. A one-size-fits-all emancipatory practice underrecognizes particularity and reduces the possibility for variation. This claim is not that human rights are too "individualistic." Rather, the claim is that the "person," as well as the "group," imagined and brought to life by human rights agitation is both abstract and general in ways which have bad consequences.

Sometimes this claim stresses the loss of a preexisting diversity of experience — human rights limits human potential as the plurality of experience is poured into the mold of its terms. Others who make this argument worry less about the loss of a prior, more authentic or diverse *real* experience. They worry about limiting our picture of emancipation to that provided by this particular vocabulary as compared to others which generalize less or differently.

Becoming Free Only as an Instance of the General

To come into understanding of oneself as an instance of a preexisting general — "I am a 'person with rights' " — exacts a cost: a loss of awareness of the unprecedented and plastic nature of experience, or a loss of a capacity to imagine and desire alternative futures. We could term this "alienation." The human rights movement proposes itself as a vocabulary of the general good — as knowledge about the shape of emancipation and human possibility, which can then simply be "applied" and "enforced." As an emancipatory vocabulary, it offers answers rather than questions, answers which are not only outside political, ideological, and cultural differences, but also beyond the human experience of specificity, against the human capacity to hope for more, and in denial of the tawdry and uncertain quality of what we know and dream about justice and injustice. Rather than enabling a discussion of what it means to be human, of who is human, of how humans might relate to one another, it crushes this discussion under the weight of moral condemnation, legal adjudication, textual certainty, and political power.

Not Just Bad for Victims

The articulation of concrete good and evil in abstract terms is limiting not only for victims. The human rights vocabulary makes us think of evil as a social machine, a theater of roles, in which people are "victims," "violators," and "bystanders." At its most effective, human rights portrays victims as passive and innocent, violators as abnormal, and human rights professionals as heroic. Only the bystanders are figured in ambivalent or uncertain terms. To enter the terrain of emancipation through human rights is to enter a world of uncivilized deviants, baby seals, and knights errant. There is a narrowing here — other evils and other goods receive less attention. Privileging the baby seals delegitimizes the suffering of people (and animals) who are, if anything, more typical in the complexity of their ethical and political posture, and renders the broader political culture less able to understand and engage with more ambivalent characters. But this vocabulary also exacts a cost from those who fit most easily into its terms. However many carefully elaborated "rights" we offer to violators, we — and they — will find it difficult to recover a complex sense for their human possibility and ambivalent experience. Differences among "victims," the experience of their particularity and the hope for their creative and surprising self-expression, are erased under the power of an internationally sanctified vocabulary for their self-understanding, self-presentation, and representation as "victims" of human rights abuse.

Even Bad for Advocates

To come into experience of oneself as a benevolent and pragmatic actor through the professional vocabulary of human rights representation has costs for the advocate. Coming into awareness of oneself as the representative of something else — heroic agent for an authentic suffering elsewhere — mutes one's capacity for empathy or solidarity with those cast as victims, violators, and bystanders, and stills the habit of understanding oneself to inhabit the world one seeks to affect. This claim is often put in ethical terms which focus on the advocate's character: human rights promotes emancipation by propagating an unbearably normative, earnest, and ultimately arrogant mode of thinking and speaking about what is good for people, abstract people, here and there, now and forever. This is bad for people in the movement. It can demobilize them as political beings in the world while encouraging their sanctimony, shrinking their sense of the potentially possible and desirable to fit a uniform size.

HUMAN RIGHTS PARTICULARIZES TOO MUCH

Emancipating the "Right Holders"

The specific way human rights generalizes is to consolidate people into "identities" on the basis of which rights can be claimed. There are two issues here: a focus on *individuals* and a focus, whether for individuals or groups, on *right-holding identity*. The focus on individuals and people who come to think of themselves merely as individuals blunts articulation of a shared life. The focus on discrete and insular right-holding identities blunts awareness of diversity, of the continuity of human experience, of overlapping identities. Together these tendencies inhibit expression of the experience of being part of a community.

Again we find two types of claims. For some, the key point is that human rights reduces and distorts a more promising *real* experience, of more malleable, less-bounded identities. A focus on right holders may blunt access to a general will or foreclose our access to identities and social arrangements which have no corresponding right or privilege. For others, the point is that compared to other vocabularies, human rights renders those who use it inarticulate about and less capable of both solidarity and more open-ended possibility. Either way, the human rights movement intensifies a sense of entitlement — the stable sense that one is what one is and has what one has — at great cost to collective political life and the sense that one's life is part of a more diverse community.

Strengthening the State

Although human rights advocates express relentless suspicion of the state, human rights places the state at the center of the emancipatory process, structuring liberation as a relationship between an individual right holder and the state. However much one may insist on the priority or preexistence of rights, in the end rights are enforced, granted, recognized, implemented, and their violations remedied by the state. By consolidating human experience into the exercise of legal entitlements, human rights strengthens the national governmental structure and equates the structure of the state with the structure of freedom. To be free is . . . to have an appropriately organized state. We might say that the right holder imagines and experiences freedom only in the role of *citizen*. This encourages autochthonous political tendencies and alienates the "citizen" from both his or her own experience as a person and from the possibility of alternative communal forms.

Encouraging Conflict and Discouraging Politics among Right Holders

Encouraging each person and group wishing to be free to tally the rights he/she/it holds so that they may be asserted against the state reduces intergroup and interindividual sensitivity. A right or entitlement is a trump card. In emancipating itself, the right holder is, in effect, queue jumping. But recognizing, implementing, and enforcing rights is distributional work. Encouraging people to imagine themselves as right holders, and rights as absolute, makes the negotiation of distributive arrangements among individuals and groups less likely and less tenable. There is no one to triage among rights and right holders — except the state. The absolutist legal vocabulary of rights makes it hard to assess distribution among favored and less-favored right holders and forecloses development of a political process for trade-offs among them, leaving only the vague suspicion that the more privileged got theirs at the expense of the less privileged.

"Refugees" Are People Too

For fifty years, the human rights movement and the legal departments of the great international institutions have struggled for legal recognition of the status of "refugee." As we will see in chapter 7, by certifying individuals as refugees, they have helped to generate millions of people who think of themselves precisely as "refugees." Certification formalizes the person's disconnection from both the state of origin and the state of ultimate destination, cutting the international refugee establishment itself off from engagement with the causes of refugee flows and from participation in their ultimate and lasting solution. The thirty-year stillborn effort to codify a "right to asylum" as an entailment of refugee status illustrates the difficulty of using a legal entitlement to guarantee a satisfactory solution — illustrates it so strikingly that we should question whether the effort to define the identity and rights of "the refugee" is more part of the problem than the solution.

HUMAN RIGHTS IS LIMITED BY ITS RELATIONSHIP
   TO WESTERN LIBERALISM

Tainted Origins

Although there are lots of interesting analogies to human rights ideas in various cultural traditions, the particular form these ideas are given in the human rights movement is the product of a particular moment and place: post-Enlightenment, rationalist, secular, Western, modern and capitalist. This strand of Western liberalism has marked the ideology, ethics, aesthetic sensibility, and political practice of the human rights movement. From a pragmatic point of view, of course, tainted origins are irrelevant. That human rights *claims* to be universal but *is really* the product of a specific cultural and historical origin says nothing — unless that specificity exacts costs or renders human rights less useful than something else. The human rights tradition might itself be undermined by its origin — be treated less well by some people, be less effective in some places — just as its origin might, for other audiences, accredit projects undertaken in its name. This is the sort of thing we might strategize about. Perhaps we should downplay the universal claims or look for parallel developments in other cultural traditions.

The movement's Western liberal origins become part of the problem (rather than a limit on the solution) when particular difficulties typical of the liberal tradition are carried over to the human rights movement. The global expression of emancipatory objectives in human rights terms can narrow humanity's appreciation of these objectives to the particular forms they have taken in the nineteenth- and twentieth-century Western political tradition. One cost would be the loss of more diverse and local experiences and conceptions of emancipation. Even within the liberal West, other useful emancipatory vocabularies (including those of socialism, Christianity, the labor movement, and so forth) are diminished by the consolidation of human rights as the international expression of *the* Western liberal tradition. Costs would be incurred whenever the human rights tradition seemed to carry with it particular downsides of the liberal West.

Downsides of the West

That the emancipations of the modern West have come with costs — alienation, loss of faith, environmental degradation, immorality — has long been a theme in critical writing. Criticizing human rights as part of the Western liberal package is a way of asserting that at least some of these costs should be attributed to the human rights tradition. This might be asserted in a variety of ways. If you thought secularism was part of what is bad about the modern West, you might assert that human rights shares the secular spirit, that as a sentimental vocabulary of devotion it actively displaces religion, offering itself as a poor substitute. You might claim that the enforcement of human rights, including religious rights, downgrades religion to a matter of private and individual commitment, or otherwise advances the secular project. To the extent human rights can be implicated in the secular project, we might conclude that it leaves the world spiritually less well off.

Critics have linked the human rights project to liberal Western ideas about the relationships among law, politics, and economics. Western Enlightenment ideas which make the human rights movement part of the problem rather than the solution include the following: the economy *preexists* politics, politics *preexists* law, the private *preexists* the public, just as the animal preexists the human, faith preexists reason, or the feudal preexists the modern. In each case, the second term is fragile, artificial, a human creation and achievement, and a domain of choice, while the first term identifies a sturdy and natural base, a domain outside human control.

Human rights encourages people to seek emancipation in the vocabularies of reason rather than faith, in public rather than private life, in law rather than politics, in politics rather than economics. The human rights vocabulary helps draw the lines between these spheres. In each case, it underestimates what it takes as the natural base and overestimates our ability to instrumentalize what it takes as the artificial domain of emancipation. Moreover, human rights is too quick to conclude that emancipation *means* progress forward from the natural passions of politics into the civilized reason of law. The urgent need to develop a more vigorous human politics is sidelined by the effort to throw thin but plausible nets of legal articulation across the globe. Work to develop law comes to be seen as an emancipatory end in itself, leaving the human rights movement too ready to articulate problems in political terms and solutions in legal terms.

The posture of human rights as an emancipatory political project which extends and operates within a domain above or outside politics — a political project repackaged as a form of knowledge — delegitimates other political voices and makes less visible the local, cultural, and political dimensions of the human rights movement itself. As liberal Western intellectuals, we think of the move to rights as an escape from the unfreedom of social conditions into the freedom of citizenship, but we repeatedly forget that there can also be a loss — a loss of the experience of belonging, of the habit of willing in conditions of indeterminacy, of innovating collectively in a way unchanneled by an available program of rights.

The West and the Rest

The Western/liberal character of human rights exacts particular costs when combined with the highly structured and unequal relations between the modern West and everyone else. Human rights has been an overwhelmingly one-way street — criticism of the periphery by the center. It is not clear that the problems addressed by the human rights movement are or should be at the top of the third world's agenda. Neither is it clear that an interventionist international human rights movement is or should be at the top of the first world's agenda *for itself*.

Moreover, the form of legal and political modernization promoted by the human rights movement in third world societies is too often based only on a fantasy about the modern/liberal/capitalist West. The insistence on more formal and absolute conceptions of property rights in transitional societies than are known in the developed West is a classic example of this problem — using the authority of the human rights movement to narrow the range of socioeconomic choices available in developing societies in the name of "rights" which do not exist in this unregulated or uncompromised form in any developed Western democracy.

At the same time, the human rights movement contributes to the framing of political choices in the third world as oppositions between "local/traditional" and "international/modern" forms of government and modes of life. This effect is strengthened by the presentation of human rights as part of belonging to the modern world, but coming from some place outside political choice, from the universal, the rational, the civilized. By strengthening the articulation of third world politics as a choice between tradition and modernity, the human rights movement impoverishes local political discourse, often strengthening the hand of self-styled "traditionalists" who are offered a commonsense and powerful alternative to modernization for whatever politics they may espouse.

HUMAN RIGHTS PROMISES MORE THAN IT CAN DELIVER

Knowledge

Human rights promises a way of knowing—knowing just and unjust, universal and local, victim and violator, harm and remedy—which it cannot deliver. Justice is something which must be made, experienced, articulated, performed each time anew. Human rights may well offer an index of ways in which past experiences of justice achieved have retrospectively been described, but the usefulness of this catalog as a stimulus to emancipatory creativity is swamped by the encouragement such lists give to the idea that justice need not be made, but can be found or simply imported. One result is a loss of the habit of grappling with ambivalence, conflict, and the unknown. Taken together, belief in these various false promises demobilizes actors from taking other emancipatory steps and encourages a global misconception of both the nature of evil and the possibilities for good.

Justice

Human rights promises a legal vocabulary for achieving justice outside the clash of politics. Such a vocabulary is not available: rights conflict with one another, rights are vague, rights have exceptions, many situations fall between rights. The human rights movement promises that "law" — the machinery, the texts, the profession, the institution — can resolve conflicts and ambiguities in society by resolving those within its own materials, and that this can be done on the basis of a process of "interpretation" which is different from, more legitimate than, politics. And different in a particularly stultifying way — as a looser or stricter deduction from a past knowledge rather than as a collective engagement with the future. In particular, the human rights movement fetishizes the judge as someone who functions as an instrument of the law rather than as a political actor. This is simply not possible — not a plausible description of judicial behavior — given the porous legal vocabulary with which judges must work and the likely political context within which judges are asked to act.

Many general criticisms of law's own tendencies to overpromise apply in spades to human rights. The absoluteness of rules makes compromise and peaceful adjustment of outcomes more difficult. The vagueness of standards makes for self-serving interpretation. The gap between law in the books and law in action, between legal institutions and the rest of life, hollows promises of emancipation through law. The human rights movement suggests that "rights," rather than people taking political decisions, can bring emancipation. This demobilizes other actors and other vocabularies, and encourages emancipation through reliance on enlightened, professional elites with "knowledge" of rights and wrongs, alienating people from themselves and from the vocabulary of their own governance. These difficulties are more acute in the international arena, where law is ubiquitous and unaccompanied by political dialog.

Community

The human rights movement shares responsibility for the widespread belief that the world's political elites form a "community" which is benevolent, disconnected from economic actors and interests, and connected in some diffuse way through the media to the real aspirations of the world's people. The international human rights movement promises the ongoing presence of an entity, a "community," which can support and guarantee emancipation. This fantasy has bad consequences not only when people place too much hope in a foreign emancipatory friend who does not materialize. The transformation of the first world media audience, as that audience is imagined by the media, into the "international community" is itself an astonishing act of disenfranchisement. This submerges alternative political sites — diplomacy, national legislatures, grass-roots movements — and vocabularies which may be more useful, more likely to emancipate, more likely to encourage habits of engagement, solidarity, and responsibility, more open to surprise and reconfiguration.

Neutral Intervention

The human rights vocabulary promises Western constituencies a neutral and universalist mode of emancipatory intervention. This leads these constituencies to unwarranted innocence about the range of their other ongoing interventions and unwarranted faith in the benign nature of a human rights presence. Thinking their interventions benign or neutral, they intervene more often than they otherwise might. Their interventions are less effective than they would be if pursued in other vocabularies.

Emancipator as Emancipation

Human rights offers itself as the measure of emancipation. This is its most striking — and misleading — promise. Human rights describes itself as a universal/eternal/human truth and as a pragmatic response to injustice — there was the holocaust and then there was the genocide convention, women everywhere were subject to discrimination and then there was the Convention on the Elimination of All Forms of Discrimination Against Women. This posture makes the human rights movement *itself* seem redemptive — as if doing something *for human rights* was, in and of itself, doing something *against* evil. It is not surprising that human rights professionals consequently confuse work on the movement for emancipatory work in society. But there are bad consequences when people of goodwill mistake work on the discipline for work on the problem.

Potential emancipators can be derailed—satisfied that building the human rights movement is its own reward. People inside the movement can mistake reform of their world for reform of the world. What seem like improvements in the field's ability to respond to things outside itself may only be improvements in the field's ability to respond to its own internal divisions and contradictions. Yet we routinely underestimate the extent to which the human rights movement develops in response to political conflict and discursive fashion among international elites, thereby overestimating the field's pragmatic potential and obscuring the field's internal dynamics and will to power.

Think of the right to development, born less in response to global poverty than in response to an internal political conflict within the elite about the legitimate balance of concerns on the institutional agenda and to an effort by some more marginal members of that elite to express their political interest in the only available language. The move from a world of "rights" to "remedies" and then to "basic needs"and on to "transnational enforcement" reflected less a changing set of problems in the world than a changing set of attitudes among international legal elites about the value of legal formalism. The result of such initiatives to reframe emancipatory objectives in human rights terms is more often growth for the field— more conferences, documents, legal analysis, opposition and response—than decrease in violence against women, poverty, mass slaughter and so forth. This is harmful when it discourages political engagement or encourages reliance on human rights for results it cannot achieve.

THE LEGAL REGIME OF "HUMAN RIGHTS," TAKEN AS A WHOLE, DOES MORE TO PRODUCE AND EXCUSE VIOLATIONS THAN TO PREVENT AND REMEDY THEM

Treating Symptoms

Human rights remedies, even when successful, treat the symptoms rather than the illness, and this allows the illness not only to fester, but to seem like health itself. This is most likely where signing up for a norm — say, against discrimination — comes to substitute for ending the practice. But even where victims are recompensed or violations avoided, the distributions of power and wealth which produced the violation may well come to seem more legitimate as they seek other avenues of expression.

Humanitarian Norms Excuse Too Much

We are familiar with the idea that rules of warfare may do more to legitimate violence than to restrain it — as a result of vague standards, broad justifications, lax enforcement, or prohibitions which are clear but beside the point. The same can often be said about human rights. The vague and conflicting norms, their uncertain status, the broad justifications and excuses, the lack of enforcement, the attention to problems which are peripheral to a broadly conceived program of social justice — all these may, in some contexts, place the human rights movement in the uncomfortable position of legitimating more injustice than it eliminates. This is particularly likely where human rights discourse has been absorbed into the foreign policy process.

Humanitarian Norms Justify Too Much

The human rights movement consistently underestimates the usefulness of the human rights vocabulary and machinery for people whose hearts are hard and whose political projects are repressive. The United States, the United Kingdom, Russia — but also Serbia and the Kosovar Albanians — have taken military action, intervened politically, and justified their governmental policies on the grounds of protecting human rights. Far from being a defense of the individual against the state, human rights has become a standard part of the justification for the external use of force by the state against other states and individuals. The porousness of the human rights vocabulary means that the interventions and exercises of state authority it legitimates are more likely to track political interests than its own emancipatory agenda.

Background Norms Do the Real Damage

The human rights regime, like the law concerning war, is composed of more than those legal rules and institutions which explicitly concern human rights. The human rights movement acts as if the human rights legal regime were composed only of rights and of institutions for their implementation. In fact, the law concerning torture, say, includes all the legal rules, principles, and institutions which bear on the incidence of torture. The vast majority of these rules — rules of sovereignty, institutional competence, agency, property, and contract — facilitate or excuse the use of torture by police and governments.

THE HUMAN RIGHTS BUREAUCRACY IS ITSELF PART OF THE PROBLEM

Professionalizes the Humanitarian Impulse

The human rights movement attracts and demobilizes thousands of good-hearted people around the globe every year. It offers many thousands more the confidence that these matters are being professionally dealt with by those whom the movement has enlisted. Something similar has occurred within academic life — a human rights discipline has emerged between fields of public law and international law, promising students and teachers that work in the public interest has an institutional life, a professional routine, and status. Professionalization has a number of possible costs. Personnel are lost for other humanitarian possibilities. As the human rights profession raises its standards and status to compete with disciplines of private law, it raises the bar for other pro bono activities which have not been as successful in establishing themselves as disciplines, whose practices, knowledge, and projects are less systematic, less analogous to practice in the private interest. Professionalization strengthens lawyers at the expense of priests, engineers, politicians, soothsayers, and citizens who might otherwise play a more central role in emancipatory efforts. At the same time, professionalization separates human rights advocates from those they represent and those with whom they share a common emancipatory struggle. The division of labor among emancipatory specialists is not merely about efficient specialization. We need only think of the bureaucratization of human rights in places like East Timor that have come within the orbit of international governance — suddenly an elaborate presence pulls local elites away from their base, or consigns them to the status of local informants, the elites turning their attentions like sunflowers to Geneva, New York, to the Center, to the Commission. To the work of resolutions and reports.

Downgrades the Legal Profession

Sometimes the concern here is for the legal profession itself. The human rights movement degrades the legal profession by encouraging a combination of both sloppy humanitarian arguments and overly formal reliance on textual articulations which are anything but clear or binding. This combination degrades the legal skills of those involved, while encouraging them to believe that their projects are more legitimate precisely because they are presented in (sloppy) legal terms. Others have argued that human rights offers the profession, particularly at its most elite sites, a fig leaf of public interest commitment to legitimate the profession's everyday contributions to global emiseration. This legitimation effect is strengthened to the extent that other legal fields — and particularly commercial legal fields — come to seem outside politics by contrast. For this, the sloppiness of human rights practice is itself useful — marking a line between the politically redemptive profession of human rights advocacy and the apolitical workaday world of other legal professionals.

Encourages False Solidarity

Of course there are many different types of people in the human rights movement and bureaucracy — different generations, different nationalities, different genders. To be a male human rights lawyer in Holland in your thirties is to live a different life altogether from that of a female human rights lawyer in Uruguay in her sixties. The human rights vocabulary encourages a false sense of the unity among these experiences and projects. As a vocabulary for progressive elite solidarity, human rights is particularly hamfisted, making it more difficult to articulate differences in the projects of, say, male and female Palestinian human rights lawyers, Americans and Nigerians, or intergovernmental civil servants and grass-roots activists.

Promotes Bad Faith

One thing these professionals do share, however, is a more or less bad faith relationship to their professional work. Every effort to use human rights for new purposes, to "cover" new problems, requires that they make arguments they know to be less persuasive than they claim. Arguments about their representative capacity — speaking for a consensus, a victim, an international community — and about the decisiveness of the vocabularies they invoke. Professional bad faith accumulates the more the movement tries to torque its tools to correct for its shortcomings — to address background conditions which affect the incidence of abuse as if they were themselves violations, for example. We need only think of the earnest advocate redescribing torture or the death penalty or female genital mutilation as a problem of "public health" to feel the movement's characteristic professional deformations at work.

Speaking law to politics is not the same thing as speaking truth to power. The human rights professional's vocabulary encourages an overestimation of the distinction between its own idealism and the hard realpolitik motivations of those it purports to address. Professional human rights performances are, in this sense, exercises in desolidarization. One intensifies the "legal" marks in one's expression as if one thought this would persuade an actual other person who one imagines, paradoxically, to inhabit an altogether different "political" world. In this, the human rights intervention is always addressed to an imaginary third eye — the bystander who will solidarize with the (unstated) politics of the human rights speaker because it is expressed in an apolitical form. This may often work as a form of political recruitment — but it exacts a terrible cost on the habit of using more engaged and open-ended political vocabularies. The result is professional narcissism guising itself as empathy and hoping to recruit others to solidarity with its bad faith.

Perils of "Representation"

The professionalization of human rights creates a mechanism for people to think they are working "on behalf of" less fortunate others, while externalizing the possible costs of their decisions and actions. The representational dimension of human rights work — speaking "for" others — puts the "victims" both onscreen and off. The production of authentic victims, or victim authenticity, is an inherently voyeuristic or pornographic practice which, no matter how carefully or sensitively it is done, transforms the position of the "victim" in his or her society and produces a language of victimization for him or her to speak on the international stage. The injured-one-who-is-not-yet-a-victim, the "subaltern" if you like, can neither speak nor be spoken for, but recedes instead before the interpretive and representational practices of the movement. The remove between human rights professionals and the people they purport to represent can reinforce a global divide of wealth, mobility, information, and access to audience. Human rights professionals consequently struggle, ultimately in vain, against a tide of bad faith, orientalism, and self-serving sentimentalism.

Irresponsible Intervention

The people who work within the human rights field have no incentive to take responsibility for the changes they bring about. Consequences are the result of an interaction between a context and an abstraction — "human rights." At the same time, the simultaneously loose and sanctified nature of the vocabulary and the power of the movement itself opens an enormous terrain for discretionary action — intervening here and not there, this way and not that, this time and not that time. There is no vocabulary for treating this discretion as the responsible act of a person, a situation creating intense psychic costs for human rights professionals themselves, but also legitimating their acts of unaccountable discretion. Belief in the nobility of human rights places blame for whatever goes wrong elsewhere — on local politicians, evil individuals, social pathologies. This imposes ethical, political, and aesthetic costs on people in the movement — but also on those elsewhere in the elite who must abide them, and in those who, as the terrain of engagement and the object of representation, become the mirror for this professional self-regard.

THE HUMAN RIGHTS MOVEMENT STRENGTHENS BAD INTERNATIONAL GOVERNANCE

Weakest Link

Even within international law, the modes of possible governance are far broader than those most familiar to human rights professionals. The human rights movement is the product of a particular moment in international legal history, which foregrounded rules rather than standards, and institutional rather than cultural enforcement. If we compare modes of governance in other fields we find a variety of more successful models — a standards-based environmental regime, an economic law regime embedded in private law, and so forth. The attachment to rights as a measure of the authenticity, universality, and above all as the knowledge we have of social justice binds our professional feet, and places social justice issues under the governance of the least effective institutional forms available.

Clean Hands

More generally, international governance errs when it imagines itself capable of governing, "intervening" if you will, without taking responsibility for the messy business of allocating stakes in society — when it intervenes only economically and not politically, only in public and not in private life, only "consensually" without acknowledging the politics of influence, only to freeze the situation and not to improve it, "neutrally" as between the parties, or politically/economically but not culturally. The human rights movement offers the well-intentioned intervenor the illusion of affecting conditions both at home and abroad without being politically implicated in the distribution of stakes which results, by promising an available set of universal, extrapolitical legal rules and institutions with which to define, conduct, and legitimate the intervention.

Fantasy Government

International governance is often asked to do globally what we fantasize or expect national governments to do locally — allocate stakes, constitute a community, articulate differences and similarities, provide for the common good. The human rights movement, by strengthening the habit of understanding international governance in legal rather than political terms, weakens its ability to perform what we understand domestically to be these political functions. The conflation of the law with the good encourages an understanding of international governance — by those within and without its institutions — that is systematically blind to the bad consequences of its own action. The difficulty the human rights movement has in thinking of itself in pragmatic rather than theological terms — in weighing and balancing the usefulness of its interventions in the terms like those included in this list — is characteristic of international governance as a whole. The presence of a human rights movement models this blindness as virtue and encourages it among other governance professionals by presenting itself as insurance of international law's broader humanitarian character.

Governing the Exception

Human rights shares with the rest of international law a tendency to treat only the tips of icebergs. Deference to the legal forms upon which human rights is built — the forms of sovereignty, territorial jurisdictional divisions, subsidiarity, consensual norms — makes it seem natural to isolate aspects of a problem which "cross borders" or "shock the conscience of mankind" for special handling at the international level — often entrenching the rest of the iceberg more firmly in the national political background. The movement's routine polemical denunciations of sovereignty work more as attestations to sovereignty's continuity than as agents of its erosion, limiting the aspirations of good-hearted people with international and global political commitments. The notion that law sits atop both culture and politics demobilizes people who come to understand their political projects as "intervention" in a "foreign" "culture." The human rights vocabulary, with its emphasis on the development of law itself, strengthens the tendency of international lawyers more broadly to concern themselves with constitutional questions about the structure of the legal regime itself rather than with questions of distribution in the broader society.

HUMAN RIGHTS PROMOTION CAN BE BAD POLITICS IN PARTICULAR CONTEXTS

It may be that this is all one can say — promoting human rights can sometimes have bad consequences. All of the first nine types of criticism suggested that human rights suffered from one or another design defect — as if these defects would emerge, these costs would be incurred, regardless of context. Perhaps this is so. But so long as none of these criticisms has been proven in such a general way (and it is hard to see just how they could be), it may be that all we have is a list of possible downsides, open risks, bad results which have sometimes occurred, which might well occur. In some context, for example, it might turn out that pursuing emancipation as entitlement could reduce the capacity and propensity for collective action. Something like this seems to have happened in the United States in the last twenty years—the transformation of political questions into legal questions, and then into questions of legal "rights," has made other forms of collective emancipatory politics less available. But it is hard to see that this is always and everywhere the destiny of human rights initiatives. We are familiar, even in the United States, with moments of collective emancipatory mobilization achieved, in part, through the vocabulary of rights. If we come to the recent British Human Rights Act, it seems an open question whether it will liberate emancipatory political energies frozen by the current legislative process and party structure, or will harness those political possibilities to the human rights claims of depoliticized individuals and judges. The point of an ongoing pragmatic evaluation of the human rights effort is precisely to develop a habit of making such assessments. But that human rights promotion can and has had bad consequences in some contexts does seem clear.

Strengthens Repressive States and Antiprogressive Initiatives

In some places, human rights implementation can make a repressive state more efficient. Human rights institutions and rhetoric can also be used in particular contexts to humanize repressive political initiatives and co-opt to their support sectors of civil society which might otherwise be opposed. Human rights can and has been used to strengthen, defend, legitimate a variety of repressive initiatives, by both individuals and states: to legitimate war, defend the death penalty, the entitlements of majorities, religious repression, access to (or restriction of) abortion, and more. The recent embrace of human rights by the international financial institutions may serve both functions—strengthening states which will need to enforce harsh structural adjustment policies while co-opting local and international resistance to harsh economic policies, and lending a shroud of universal/rational inevitability to economic policies which are the product of far narrower political calculations and struggles. As deployed, the human rights movement may do a great deal to take distribution off the national and international development agendas, while excusing and legitimating regressive policies at all levels. These difficulties are particularly hard to overcome so long as the human rights movement remains tone deaf to the specific political consequences of its activity in particular locations, on the mistaken assumption that a bit more human rights can never make things worse. This makes the human rights movement particularly subject to capture by other political actors and ideological projects. We need only think of the way the move to "responsibilities" signaled by the Universal Declaration on Human Responsibilities of 1998 was captured by neoliberal efforts to promote privatization and weaken the emancipatory potentials of government.

Condemnation as Legitimation

Finally, in many contexts, transforming a harm into a "human rights violation" may be a way of condoning or denying rather than naming and condemning it. A terrible set of events occurs in Bosnia. We could think of it as a sin and send the religious, as illness and send physicians, as politics and send the politicians, as war and send the military. Or we could think of it as a human rights violation and send the lawyers. Doing so can be a way of doing nothing, avoiding responsibility, simultaneously individualizing the harm and denying its specificity. Thinking of atrocity as a human rights violations captures neither the unthinkable nor the banal in evil. Instead we find a strange combination of clinically antiseptic analysis, throwing the illusion of cognitive control over the unthinkable, and hysterical condemnation. Together, they assert the advocate's distance from the quotidian possibility of evil. Renaming Auschwitz "genocide" to recognize its unspeakability, enshrining its status as "shocking the conscience of mankind" can also be a way of unthinking its everyday reality. In this sense, human rights, by criminalizing harm and condensing its origin to particular violators, can serve as denial, apology, legitimation, normalization, and routinization of the very harms it seeks to condemn.

So that is the list. As I said at the outset, some of these worries seem more plausible to me than others. I would worry about some of these costs more than others. The generation which built the human rights movement focused its attention on the ways in which evil people in evil societies could be identified and restrained. More acute now is how good people, well-intentioned people in good societies, can go wrong, can entrench, support, the very things they have learned to denounce. Answering this question requires a pragmatic reassessment of our most sacred humanitarian commitments, tactics, and tools.

Whatever the history of human rights, we do not know its future. Perhaps these difficulties will be overcome, avoided. But we will not avoid them by avoiding their articulation, discussion, and assessment — by treating the human rights movement as a frail child, in need of protection from critical assessment or pragmatic calculation. At this point these remain suspicions, intuitions, hunches by people who have seen the human rights movement from one or another point of view. Each person involved in international human rights protection will have his or her own view about which, if any, of these doubts are plausible and worth pursuing. As a profession, we would do ourselves good by opening conversation about worries of this sort, and thinking further about how they should affect our understanding of the human rights project as a whole.

TWO

Spring Break:
The Activist Individual

INTRODUCTIONS

At 10:00 A.M., March 22, 1984, as guards led Ana Rivera into the small white clinic at Punta Rieles prison, Dr. Richard Goldstein, Patrick Breslin, and I became the first outsiders to speak privately and unconditionally with any of the roughly seven hundred political prisoners held in Uruguayan prisons at that time. We shook her hand, invited the prison officials to leave, and sat down at small table. She was a small woman, about twenty-three years old, her auburn hair pulled awkwardly back in a child's yellow plastic barrette. Around each wrist hung a red and white string bracelet. Under her prison overalls, stenciled boldly with her identification number, she wore two layers of clothing. Fearing transfer to another prison or judicial proceeding when officials had come for her some moments before, she had worn her wardrobe to our brief meeting. Her hands trembled.

Patrick's explanation of our presence was calming. Worn smooth by repetition before numerous officials, his introductory litany of our professions and affiliations was reassuring, factual, and brisk. I'm a writer, he's a doctor, and he's a lawyer. We're from the United States and we represent five scientific and medical institutions—the New York Academy of Sciences, the American Public Health Association, the Institute of Medicine of the National Academy of Sciences, the National Academy of Science, and the American College of Physicians. These became my first one hundred words of Spanish. His next sentence was too long to remember, something like: We have come to Uruguay because our institutions are concerned about the general health situation among political prisoners in Uruguay and in particular about four medical students arrested in June of 1983 on charges of "subversive association" and a number of other political prisoners reported to be in poor health. Patrick was careful to summarize his point: "In short, Ana, we have come to speak with you." Dr. Goldstein will also be happy to discuss any health problems you may have and to examine your body, if you so desire. I think now what I thought as he finished: this moment could be savored if only it would last.

As I tell this story, our moment with Ana seems well structured and meaningful. North meets South, the climax of an adventure which needs to be introduced, retraced, and concluded. Where did they come from? How did they find her? What happened to Ana after they went home? Her trembling and Pat's soothing writer-doctor-lawyer speech seem to fix a point between two worlds: native and foreign, authentic subject and objective role, the agents and their mission's object, cultural life and the law.

But in Montevideo, when Pat stopped talking, things seemed much less clear. Although we seemed to have gotten going, Ana trembled less and the three of us shifted in our chairs, relaxing, it was hard to see where things were headed, hard to figure out exactly what we should do next. As we moved forward, interviewing first Ana and then other prisoners, returning to our hotel to plot our next moves, we wove these moments into stories about our institutions, our professions, the changing Uruguayan political scene, our mission, and ourselves, developing stories about the experience in order to continue it.

In this story, I want to explore both our confusion about these experiences and our efforts, in Montevideo and Boston, to make sense of them. I want to evoke the activist's sense of not knowing what things mean or where they are going in human rights work by exploring the ways our search for the right tactic produced results we could not evaluate, and the ways our inability to know what was intrusive in a situation we had defined as foreign left us confused about our connections and responsibilities. By doing so, I want to explore the sense in which efforts that are often described in a way that makes them seem either noble and important or misguided and trivial are experienced more directly as tawdry and uncertain. In all these ways, I want to examine the situation in which we find ourselves as human rights workers. My hope is that doing so will open the way to speaking more forthrightly about the dark sides of human rights activism developed in the last chapter.

My sense is that telling about a human rights mission and undertaking one are not as different as they sometimes seem. Both activities seek to transform the ambiguity and confusion of moments like ours with Ana into comprehensible narratives. I would like to tell the story of this human rights mission so as to expose the similarity of analytic and activist work in the field of human rights as well as the differences between them. Normally, we are careful to distinguish the muddle of practice — experienced as a mix of intuition, confusion, and quick thinking — from the remove of analysis. We imagine that the confusions of action can be clarified by analysis, and indeed, that the analytic capacity of the mentally agile human rights activist contributes to his success.

Despite this sense of difference, however, analysis often seems simply to relive the experience, digging its confusion more deeply into wisdom. Many of the stories that we characteristically tell ourselves about human rights missions have a similar plot: a knight bursts forth from his domain, has a number of adventures crossing borders, foiling enemies or bonding friendships, and eventually reaches the land beyond the pale, returning with tales aplenty. Stories like this are good fun. But they also reinforce a particular set of ideas about potent actors and their terrain, placing the calculating activist in center stage, bringing reason and justice to the land of the unjust, the victimized. Through these stores we construct our activism in the image of cultural stereotypes about men and women, avengers and victims. It comes as no surprise that as the moment marked by Patrick's words and Ana's behavior came to be acted upon and analyzed, his words took precedence over her suffering.

Patrick opened our story with Ana by reciting our professional roles and institutional affiliations, showing her our coats of arms. In a very real sense, for Ana, these identities and origins explained our surprising presence inside her prison, a response to her desire for an explanation. As I write this now, facing the demand of an audience for a comprehensible story about human rights, rather than Ana's for my credentials, our roles no longer seem so important. To begin where Patrick began, to recount our meeting with Ana just as it was, obliterates a great deal of the moment's originality and complexity by situating the story in an ongoing tradition of human rights disclosure.

I could tell a story about "human rights abuses in Uruguay and the work of private institutions to combat them." Such a story might be about strategies. Our moment with Ana would be given meaning by reference to earlier tactical calculations and later evaluations of our "success." Thought of as a moment in the evolution of law, our mission might be placed in a narrative about evolving human rights norms and machinery. Uruguayan social and political life would be rendered as the rhythmic ebb and flow of the rule of law. The process of Uruguayan "democratization," underway by the time we arrived, might enable, limit, or determine the pace of our efforts. Even an American presidential election might appear as a "factor" influencing the developing interests of our sponsoring institutions in a variety of ways. Alternatively, our mission might be thought of as a moment in some political or historical unfolding, placed in a narrative about social struggle or foreign relations. Our professions, institutions, and norms would be factual intrusions in a narrative about processes beyond their ken.

For all this potential narrative variety, however, it seems that no matter which story I tell, our moment with Ana is bound to be rendered too lucid, its own ambiguity lost to history. The difficulty is that both the analysis and the activism respond to narrative demands. Both enterprises struggle against the confusion of moments like ours with Ana, continuously creating new ambiguities and confusions. Although one point of a story like this one is to remember what was put aside in our moment with Ana, the telling reinforces a deeper social practice of conflict management: we defer coming to terms with the confusion of the moment by embroidering it into the fabric of numerous comforting stories.

THINKING AHEAD

Six days before meeting with Ana, I had left Boston amid the half-joking admonitions of friends to stay out of trouble. Driving through the Callaghan Tunnel to Logan Airport, our mood was jocular. Uruguay seemed far away: dangerous, exotic, exciting. So long as we kept it as distant, Uruguay seemed able to bear the burden of our excitement. As spring vacation approached, I had felt drawn by anything elsewhere, by the prospect of new people and different problems, by the possibility that in Uruguay I would feel more like an international lawyer than I did grading midterm papers on the living room floor. I might be respected differently than in my habitual workplace environment. Although I would be gone only two weeks, I knew time would move differently, more intensely, more quickly, and, lost in new details, I would break sharply the semester's continuity. With luck, I might even return tanned. Uruguay occupied a difficult position; it would need to remain foreign to excite me and to sustain my identity as an American and a human rights lawyer, and yet disclose to me its secrets to satisfy the attraction that brought me there.

Waiting at Logan for my flight to be called, I described my plans to friends who would remain behind. Despite the rush of adrenaline these fantasies produced, I felt a nagging doubt. The more remote I imagined Uruguay to be, the more I doubted whether I had anything to offer it. This doubt surfaced first as a political question of standing. What "right" did I have to do this to "them?" So long as I pictured Uruguay and myself as different enough to sustain my excitement, I worried about becoming an agent of "cultural imperialism." Yet if I were not so different, I would never have been invited. If I could believe that I had a right to go, or even a duty, a formula from which I could derive some limit and basis for my interference as well as some expectation about my effectiveness, my doubts would fade. I could at once respect and contain our mutual difference in a familiar framework of rights and duties.

The complement of this noble doubt, of course, was fear. I worried that I would find Uruguay disorienting, unsettlingly different, outside both my competence and my legitimate involvement. Sitting aboard our Varig flight, Richard and I carefully memorized and shredded background documents detailing the Uruguayan human rights scene from various legal and political perspectives. We hoped that the information from these documents would arm us in Montevideo, would keep us from being duped and would empower us to confront, interrogate, and understand. But we did not want to take them with us. Who knew what might jeopardize our intention to float through the official scene buoyed by our reasonable demeanors and institutional affiliations? The documents might disarm us, marking us foreign, dangerous interlopers just as we sought to assimilate. By destroying the documents while preserving their power for us, we reassured ourselves that we could remain sufficiently innocuous to establish common ground with Uruguayan officials without sacrificing our ability to oppose their regime. Finding a way to seem unthreatening yet potent adversaries would be a recurring problem.

By our fourth day on the ground, as we approached Punta Rieles, Richard, Pat, and I thought we knew each other pretty well. If Uruguay still seemed foreign, we seemed to have become a close team. On the one hand, in three days of intense negotiations, we had developed a comfortable division of labor. The writer introduced us, translating, explaining, clarifying. The doctor spoke for our institutions, enunciating our compassionate concerns, setting forth our objectives. I tried to make sure that the agenda for each meeting was completed and our demands were clearly presented. On the other hand, the more smoothly we worked together, the more comically reductionist it sounded to hear Patrick described as a "writer from Washington," or Richard as the "doctor from New York."

CROSSING OVER

Puenta Rieles prison stands on a slight rise at the end of a long driveway, somewhat off a main highway out of Montevideo, behind a poor settlement. As it became visible some distance behind a low fence, it resembled a small red brick sanatorium near my hometown in southern Michigan. We passed smoothly through the checkpoints despite our early arrival. Guards checked our documents, more formally and seriously than thoroughly. Someone looked in the trunk. Gates opened, and we drove up a freshly raked white gravel drive toward the main entrance. Off to the left stood a small barracks with eighteen or twenty off-duty soldiers gawking at us from its front steps. Two junior officers walked smartly to the gate to meet our car.

For me, we seemed to have reached the final boundary separating our mission from its object. Our passage into Uruguay had taken us across a series of boundaries. Each ritual of entry, through a customs portal at the Montevideo airport or into the office of a government official, had both strengthened our sense of solidarity and reassured us that we were making contact with Uruguay. Each time we were confronted with a man who emerged from the background of Uruguayan life, cast suddenly in the role of gatekeeper. Often as we crossed such a boundary we found common ground with him by momentarily suspending our identities. Sometimes we argued, pleaded, or tricked our interlocutor into letting us pass. Usually we simply presented documents. When we presented and imagined ourselves as our passport identities, as generic professional and procedural conformists, we normally felt no particular relationship to the men who emerged to usher us in. Nor, it seemed, did our identities shift as we passed from one side to the other.

This time, however, as we stepped from the car in front of the prison gates, the boundary crossing seemed threatening and confusing. To our bemusement, the government had provided us with a blond, miniskirted guide in addition to a blue Peugeot and driver. As she emerged from the car to curious stares from the barracks crowd, I realized that she was the only woman in sight. Surrounded by men with machine guns, the women's prison secreted its female charges from view. Standing in the sun watching our guide step gracefully from the Peugeot, I feared that my desire to see the women prisoners, to cross the boundary guarded by these men, shared something with their prurient fascination for our guide.

Pat and I shed our professional accouterments: legal documents, cameras, notepads. Richard tucked his medical bag beneath the car seat, but turned back to slip a stethoscope into his pocket. I wanted to be inconspicuous and open to whatever might confront us on the other side, and Richard wanted to prepare.

Both young officers greeted us warmly. The leanest, who was clearly in charge, ushered us past a statue of Artigas, ubiquitous sign of Uruguayan nationalism, and into the warden's office, where we received smiles, handshakes, and coffee. Smartly pressed but curious soldiers milled outside the door. We sat down for an exchange of formalities.

Across the black leather arm of my chair was draped a leopard skin antimacassar topped with a copper ashtray. As I fingered its tassels, Pat identified us: names, professions, institutional affiliations. The warden seemed unsure how to treat his first international delegation, but was visibly proud of his office, its order, his officers' demeanors. Pat described our object: we want to confirm the health of one medical student "in whose case our sponsors are interested" and of five other prisoners "reported to be in ill health." Does the warden believe that this is really our object? Is it slightly plausible — to him, to us — that five American institutions would "become interested" in particular prisoners? Although I realize that defining interests this way might free us from anything but professional detachment, I wonder whether Pat has put the assertion too matter-of-factly. Perhaps he should tell a story about how institutions like ours get interested in cases like this and send delegations such as this to prisons like his. Despite my doubts, the younger officer has been nodding as if he were checking the text of Pat's speech against his delivery. I am relieved. Maybe we all share a comfortable distance from Pat's remarks and the officer understands that this is merely our handle. Perhaps he talks about his prison's having "taken an interest" in this or that when he is downtown. Maybe these "interests" are what we and they care about.

In any case, everyone is determined to play this script to the hilt. We explain that our concern is scientific and our motivation humane. We are interested in public health, not public policy. (I wonder as I make this bald assertion what it could mean in such circumstances to say that public health and public policy are distinct. On the other hand, if our institutions did not think we could keep them separate, would they have sent us on this mission?) Richard agrees with the warden that we will see the medical student for a substantial period of time, the other prisoners only long enough to ascertain their health. The duration of our contact with each prisoner will be determined by the theory we have used to justify interest in her case and access to her presence. But does a physical exam really take less time than a symbolic interrogation? Although it might scare the warden off to do otherwise, I wonder whether we are right to deny interest in other prisoners, treating our Washington-based list of the sick as definitive. Perhaps we could ask for more: more prisoners, more access, more time. But it appears that the hollower the story of our institutional motivation sounds, the easier it is to get the warden's cooperation and the smoother our relations seem. His superiors have authorized him to grant these specific requests, and he is relieved when we press on him no other demands.

As the warden takes over the conversational initiative, he builds upon the common ground that Pat has established. He describes the prison clearly and proudly. He appears to assume that everyone appreciates a well-run detention facility. I nod sincerely. I picture him, reduced to a stereotype, expounding this story to his wife over dinner. He explains that we must understand that these are violent prisoners, threatening the Uruguayan community. I hope he knows that our conversation is ceremonial and that my acquiescence signals only my foreknowledge of the text he is reciting. As he continues, I begin to fear that we may betray the prisoners before we see them by associating ourselves too completely with his authority. But surely they will understand that I recognize that he must say this, accept that he wants to say it, that he believes it, and that our silence is in their interest. This is just trickery, just a ceremony, men's talk. I think, "When it's over, ladies, I will be true to you." Because they are violent, the warden continues, these individuals have been segregated in this more secure facility. I recognize that he is reversing the violence, projecting it into the prisoners. I notice the nineteenth-century military portraits behind the warden's desk, signs of institutional continuity in this comfortable office. One of the portraits resembles the gaunter of the two junior officers. There is indeed no violence here. These men are managers.

I begin to suspect that he must be convinced not that we buy his arguments, but that we will respect his assertions, taking them without challenge. This is his office, and his characterization of the situation will stand. We are merely passers-through, far from our offices. My nodding becomes vigorous, even understanding. Perhaps our institutions understand their institutions. As I nod persistently, Richard sits forward and begins to interrupt the warden's lecture. The initiative passes to us. My instinct now is to spar with the warden. Assuming a demeanor of factual curiosity, I ask how violent prisoners are selected for segregation here: on the basis of their crime, their particular acts, or in other ways. The warden explains, as we already knew from our shredded documents, that only those accused of crimes against the state are here, even if they have not been convicted or are accused merely of association or spoken criticism. We let the contradiction pass. The warden reclaims the initiative by playing upon our insecurity about interfering in Uruguayan affairs. In our alienage we, the interlopers, remain obsequious while he explains that in the Uruguayan context, political criminals are the dangerous social threats. He recommends two books on national security and the role of the Uruguayan military in case we have any questions. Our turn. We have heard that the prison routine at Punta Rieles and Libertad is intended to break down the prisoner's personality structures. I expect that he will rebut these charges by protesting that the routine is necessitated by bureaucratic considerations. This protest would allow him to feel justified while underscoring the banality of the prisoner's suffering, thus permitting us each to feel satisfied by the exchange. To give him this chance, I ask our host about running a high-security prison — how does he determine the measures necessary to deal with such criminals? Without hesitation he breaks the cultural barriers between us by acknowledging with pride that he learned what he knows from the American military that trained him.

PROFESSIONAL ROLES

In a way, edging toward Punta Rieles, we were just actors playing parts in a tale made familiar by hundreds of childhood fantasies. We were grounded in fealty to our sponsoring institutions and bounded by the oaths of our professional service. We hoped that, like knights abroad, we would band together warmly in foreign territory, our friendships tested and forged. But in another way we were more than just actors in familiar cultural drama. Whether in remaking our institutional sponsorship, redefining our professional roles, or developing our team spirit, we were also narrators and directors, creating our roles and casting others as we wished in a production staged against the backdrop of Ana's imprisonment.

There seem few human rights activists without sponsors. Activism is, in this sense, a representational activity. But not every potential institutional patron is anxious to send would-be activists charging into battle. The scramble for the credentials of patronage and the processes by which institutions come to sponsor activists mean that action, even when guided by the activist's intuition or inspired by his faith, refers back to the institution's motive and forward to its goal. In this sense, the activist merely implements.

Transforming Pat, Richard, and me from Writer in Washington, Doctor in New York, and Lawyer in Boston to writer-doctor-lawyer in Montevideo required imagination on the part of our sponsoring institutions, which initially regarded sending missions to Montevideo as somewhat outside their normal portfolio. Their long-standing concern for the plight of foreign colleagues needed to be translated into an "interest" in four specific Uruguayan medical students and a willingness to send three activists on their trail. Our institutions were somewhat uncomfortable becoming involved in human rights work for several reasons. Scientific institutions often resist engaging in human rights work because they fear it would diminish their scientific neutrality — ironically, the very neutrality that might enable and legitimize their human rights work. Often they resist this work because they fear they have little to offer — it seems counterintuitive, if not a little perverse, to think of political surveillance and imprisonment as threats to the confidentiality of the doctor-patient relationship, of systematic torture as a deterioration in the public health system. Moreover, in my experience, scientists and professionals in institutions normally removed from politics sometimes seem to fear that they will appear naïve and out of place in the hurly-burly of human rights work.

Overcoming these doubts was not simply the triumph of action over the passive habits of professional fuddy-duddies, however attractive that image might be. These doubts were overcome primarily by relying on the well-worn norms of professional responsibility and human rights ideology. As a result, we moved to action by learning to think about Ana and her compatriots as fellow professionals and objects for our moral outrage. My own employer, the Harvard Law School, had moved over the preceeding years toward a public commitment to "international human rights," which facilitated my own involvement in the Uruguayan mission considerably. This commitment is a bit difficult to explain, particularly given our widespread sense that any institutional participation in advocacy threatens the academic freedom that gives the faculty faith in its prerogatives. In part, I suppose, foreign advocacy seems a neutral defense of the "rule of law" rather than a partisan choosing up of sides. As a result, we tend, oddly enough, to use the rubric of "human rights" to refer to everything from foreign investment to cultural revolution. Partly, international human rights work seems to promise safely distanced contact with the certifiably barbaric. Partly, this work seems the natural modern extension of an institutional commitment to civil rights and social responsibility.

Taken together, these images render institutional support for human rights activism possible. They also give that activism a certain structure. The activists will be dispatched professional, individual advocates deployed upon a foreign context in service of human rights. Thinking of ourselves as deployed professionals created a double sense of Uruguay as client and abuser, familiar and barbaric. These contradictory images of Uruguay could be stabilized, controlled, tamed by the language of human rights, our professional language. We render the exotic familiar by scripting the barbarian as "rights abuser" and the victim as our "client." We now have a role in Uruguay: to "represent" the client against the abuser. Our mandate channeled our concerns about violence into a rhetoric of health, our interest in Uruguayan politics into a physical examination of Ana's body, our outrage into a dispassionate recounting of rights violated, remedies not provided.

An activist's mission is shaped by the oaths of his professional service as much as by his institutional origin. There seem few human rights activists who do not enter the field as something: as Christian witness, concerned citizen, public health worker, lawyer. To feel at home in human rights work and to become successful in the field often require only that an activist become better at playing such a role. As a result, action occurs through the prism of these identities. It is, after all, the "activist" who acts.

In the warden's office, our roles seemed like stepping-stones across the cultural divide, simplifying our relations, rendering them possible, closing out the distracting issues raised by unstructured thinking about our situation. We could communicate as Doctor to Lawyer through Writer-Translator to Warden. But our roles produced new walls between us as well as intimacies and complicities. Often I feared that our roles would trap us in wooden sterility or render us complicit in our prisoners' dilemma, even as I counted on them to facilitate direct human contact.

Yet even when I tried to cast aside my professional identity, I could not avoid the prism of my activism. It would be a mistake to think of an edifice of roles simply as a prison for our imagination and to romanticize confronting one another more directly. When I pictured the warden dining at home I was trying to give voice to the desk plaque which announced his name: Kleber Papillon. David and Kleber relaxing around the piano. Sherry. Wives lounging on couches. Servants spreading dinner. For all my effort, I found myself picturing the scene from a television movie aired the previous fall, reducing him to a stereotype precisely because I, the foreign lawyer, would never find him revealed, no longer the warden. The best I could do was to write a soap-opera husband into the script in his place. Now matter how many Klebers I imagined and how different they seemed from the warden, none existed outside my imagination.

As warden, Papillon had to defend his prison while letting us in, an admission that belied his defense. As doctor, Richard had to cast his concerns in the language of medical ethics, an identity his presence in this remote political prison belied. But these scripts were much more open than these structural tensions suggest. To me, Papillon's name and title were more repositories than identities. When I spoke to "Kleber Papillon," I placed his violence elsewhere, in his profession, his institution, his service. On the other hand, when we connected as professionals sipping coffee across mahogany, I placed the violence in Papillon or his men, in the rough edges of his silken intention to help us. Working with this ambiguity — now Papillon, now the warden — I avoided both blaming the prisoners for the violence against them and openly rebuking Warden Papillon's account of their suffering. One might analyze our coffee-klatsch flirtation as complicity or shrewdness, measure it against the greater complicity of accord or the greater opposition of rebuking him directly, but the play was simply more ambiguous, more tenuous, more shifting than such accounts suggest.

If relations with the warden seemed wooden, getting to know one another as a team seemed unambiguously human. Indeed, it was by contrast to our own solidarity that relations with the Uruguayans seemed satisfactorily distanced and professional. But banding together on foreign soil, like relating to our Uruguayan counterparts, was a far more ambiguous affair than it seemed. We became friends, but that friendship developed out of a fluid role-play.

Our delegation had been constructed around our diverse professions, and indeed, we fell easily into a stereotypical division of labor. I, the lawyer, became responsible for aggressive formality; Richard, the doctor, for compassionate bedside manners. Patrick, the writer-translator, mediated, interpreted, and explained. After a while we joked about the writer who refused to travel without his doctor and lawyer. This joke, by reducing our roles to mere tools to be taken up and discarded as we thought fit, released some of the discomfort we felt about behaving in such stereotypical professional ways. Although we were glad for the release, we were still unable to transcend our roles completely. As it turned out, the simple opposition between roles and selves did not capture the complexity of our relationships. We came to know one another by playing with our sense of one another as Patrick-Richard-David and as writer-doctor-lawyer.

This play required that we each posit the others as roles and as differences from roles. I came to know Richard as "Richard" by contrast to "the Doctor," yet the characteristics associated with each seemed fluid. Sometimes Richard seemed firmer than my image of the compassionate Doctor, and I knew him by contrast to his role.

Sometimes, when he seemed too nice, I knew him as a Doctor, whose compassion was required for the triad doctor-lawyer-writer. But my image of doctors was fluid — they seemed both compassionate healers and dispassionate scientists. Which was Richard? Whichever he was, both were projections of my own interpretive imagery. And I am sure he came to know me by interpreting my behavior both within and against his notions about lawyers. Repeated in all the permutations three people and three roles can generate, these experiences were what "becoming friends" meant.

In relating to each other and to the warden, we thus shifted in and out of various identities. Now I was the lawyer, now David; now he was the warden, now Papillon. Throughout, we deferred the moment at which we would settle our identities. Indeed, our ability to relate both to one another and to the warden depended upon our ability to defer the moment at which we would choose to be just the doctor or to treat our opposite number as simply a warden. Usually, telling stories about our activities is supposed to settle issues left open in the experience. In analyzing my time with the warden, however, I seem able only to decide whether he was a dutiful warden or a nice guy by treating some detail of our interaction as dispositive: he offered us coffee, or grimaced menacingly, for example. In this way activism avoids ambiguity by reference to an analysis that treats the ambiguity as having already been resolved in action. Yet, just as the patterns we embroider onto our relations are undone when the ambiguity of the experience is recaptured, so the ambiguity of our analyses is belied by the felt authenticity of our experiences.

Oddly, this work — weaving meaning into our lives only to rip out the cloth — is forgotten, and the story seems simply to unfold, to progress. Propelled forward by our practice and reimagined by our analysis, time seems to move forward independent of our activities. Moreover, as we forget the ambiguity of our play, the results of our activities come to seem real. Papillon was and had always been a warden when our team arrived. What began as a play that we made came to seem like life itself. As a result, while playing with one another's identities, we came to feel that we were manipulating real boundaries and transcending real differences that preexisted our play.

For all its ambiguity, as both lived and told, our story seemed to have direction and meaning—both provided by Ana. The promise of access to Ana gave significance to our work, and the prospect of meeting Ana shaped our relations with each other and with the Uruguayan officials. When we found ourselves connecting emotionally, rather than just professionally, with Papillon, it was fealty to Ana that made us reassert our difference from the warden. When we differentiated ourselves from the warden, it was a sense of our shared difference from Ana that rejoined our team to Papillon. Ana shaped our relations, ordered our experience, gave our mission significance and meaning.

DIRECT EXAMINATION: TELLING ANA'S STORY

After our introduction, Ana asked Pat what we wanted to know. A moment of fumbling silence. Pat, Richard, and I had planned our interrogation. We had known that time would be short and conditions uncertain. We had worried that the prisoners might have been too well briefed or too frightened to speak freely. We had thought that we would need to "establish trust" and move quickly to get what we needed. Richard was a doctor: he needed some health history, and we needed to leave time for a brief physical exam. I was a lawyer: I needed details of the arrest, incarceration, and defense. Our interrogation would have to pass through Pat's simultaneous translation. We acknowledged, of course, that the client-patient-prisoner should be able to tell his-her-its own story. That was sometimes necessary, we knowingly reassured one another, before one could get a direct response to questions, and it might uncover something we would not have thought to ask. Thinking like a lawyer, however, I realized that open-ended questioning, like other luxuries of a relaxed interrogation, would have to give way to direct questioning under difficult conditions such as these. But despite this fairly clear sense of the professionally necessary, doubt seeped into my demeanor as we began. Perhaps because I was uncertain about our standing—we were, after all, only the self-styled "doctor" and "lawyer" for these people—I wondered whether we might not need a relaxed interrogation. I felt apprehensive that this ambivalence might combine with difficult interviewing conditions to sabotage our ability to obtain the information that later would turn out to be important.

Richard told Ana we had about an hour together and asked her to begin by telling us about her arrest and the subsequent events that led to her arrival at Punta Rieles. Good approach, I thought; chronological. With so little time, her story has to make sense. If it rambles, she might not cohere. Ana, calming now, seems to know exactly how to proceed. As she picks up Richard's invitation, she seems to me to have prepared several stock cassettes for such an interview, dry factual renditions of her arrest, treatment, prison life, student politics, and Uruguayan militarism. My fears about reticent or inarticulate prisoners, which Ana's trembling hands had rekindled, now faded. I stopped staring and listened.

She had been arrested on June 13, 1983, while walking on the street alone near her boyfriend's flat. I start taking notes. Officers put her in a car and took her to the police station at about 4:00 P.M. She relates some details about her boyfriend. He too is a medical student. They met . . . I steer her back: what did they tell her when they put her in the car? Did they take any documents or possessions? She responds nicely—nothing, no, but they ransacked her boyfriend's flat, picking up some literature from the medical school student council. What happened at the police station? I inject the questions softly through Pat, recording her responses seriously. Smooth so far. Her boyfriend is now in prison at Libertad. I realize that we will be seeing him later in the day. I begin to think of Ana as a student activist; her calm willingness to speak seems to reflect a self-assured politicization. She says that she never advocated violence and renounces it, contrary to charges made at the police station. As her demeanor reassures, my mind wanders from her words. Although I suppose I called forth this stereotype, it begins to bore me. I think about her boyfriend, wonder how they got together, whether they discussed the possibility of imprisonment, separation. But I ask about the police station again: who said what when?

Richard, less bored than impatient, interrupts—perhaps we should just let her narrate. I stop, but feel a bit uneasy about abandoning my campaign for the legally relevant facts. Our need for this specific information stemmed more from our desire to be their doctor and lawyer than from something intrinsic to our representation. Perhaps our institutional sponsors needed to have certain information to remain interested in the cases in the mission, to feel successful. Perhaps they even had a right to certain information, having sent us so far. Luckily, my insecurity gives way to resignation. Maybe it's hopeless to get all the information we want. I'm not really their lawyer, after all. Her own story, I imagine, will at least be more interesting.

Ana skips ahead to her first days of incommunicado incarceration. The chronology is broken, although her story remains familiar from background reports. But suddenly there is no cassette. She reports being blindfolded, doused in cold water, forced to stand in unheated and drafty surroundings, arms and legs outstretched. An electric prod is applied to her fingers, toes, eyes, nose mouth, and genitals. She is tied to a metal bed frame, electrodes are fastened to her face, genitals, and extremities. Someone cranks a hand operated generator. She can hear it. The cranking resumes. Her hands, wrapped in cloth, are tied behind her back. She is hoisted by her wrists and suspended. As she hangs, they strike and prod her. She wakes up on the ground near a stair. Still blindfolded, she hears a medic cautioning the torturer about head injury. The hanging, the electricity, the torture are repeated.

On June 28 the torture ends and she appears before a judge, charged with membership in the Communist Party. She has signed a confession and statement that she has been well treated. The police return her to the police station and allow her to contact her family for the first time. On August 4 she is brought to Punta Rieles, where she remains awaiting trial.

We have spent forty-five minutes together and still have not discussed the prison, her health, or her defense. But somehow in the last few minutes I have lost interest in the case; I find her personal story too intimate and shocking to relate to. Ana stops talking, and Pat looks to me for more questions. I am fascinated by the strings around her wrists, stare at them, want to admire them, inquire about their origin.

Richard asks about her health. They discuss several medical complaints. Ana describes the prison regimen. Her tone is flat, matter of fact. My mind holds and cannot release the image of electrodes on her wrists, tries, but cannot visualize 200 volts surging on her lips as she speaks. As Richard begins a physical exam, I leave the room. I have become the lawyer again. The doctor will view the body. Outside, in the hallway, the young officer who had accompanied us to the examining room stands chatting with a group of female infirmary personnel. His uniform is smart beside their sacklike smocks. I straighten my tie. The autumn sun lights the group through the bars of an open window. The officer flirts with a nurse. She touches his cheek. They laugh.

We spoke with five other women that morning, all of whom had been at Punta Rieles longer than Ana and had been reported to have had health problems. All reported torture. The wrists of one young woman showed the scars of a recent suicide attempt. Another, whom I had taken for sixty as she described her fourteen years in prison, her cardiac difficulties aggravated by years of hard labor, the ear infection and deafness induced by torture, told us she was forty-four. It was Pat's forty-fourth birthday. "Different lives," she remarked. Pat, a boyishly handsome Washingtonian, tried to bridge the gap. "Same gray hair." He said.

The women's stories began to blend together, a parade of sick and mutilated people. At one point depression overcame the group. Silence, four people staring at the Formica tabletop. One of us said something about there being people outside, in America, who knew she was here and would not forget her. Our institutions would remember. Several of the women wanted to make specific pleas, usually on behalf of nine prisoners purportedly confined in scattered places throughout Uruguay who had not been seen in over a decade. We discussed the psychological pressure of incarceration, the food, the exercise or visitation privileges that guards often irrationally withheld. Often the lull of such normal prison conversation distracted me from empathy. Sometimes, when I remembered that many of these people had been imprisoned under ex post facto laws or for crimes of speech or association, my lawyerly sensibilities made me angry.

Here on my word processor, as I put our experiences in Punta

Rieles together, I want to respond to the worries that we had before going in to Uruguay, about being pawns in an Uruguayan propaganda show, about finding prisoners suspicious, about being unable to tell the true from the false in an environment that promised to be so foreign and exotic. I am tempted to declare that the prisoners' stories seemed by and large credible by all recognized indicia of demeanor, but to make this judgment — to enter into a debate about credibility — is to reduce and denigrate our experience at the prison. I want to make our time in Punta Rieles seem beyond assessments of credibility, out of reach of reason. I want to have been part of the crude solidarity and witness that seemed so endearing among the prisoners. At one point we hear shouts from the cell block below us. Ana explains: whenever anyone is removed from her cell, she yells her number so that others can keep track of her and know if she has disappeared. I want our visit to have been like that. Sometimes, of course, it seemed so. Ana wanted us to write down our names and the names of our organizations so that she could tell the others who knew they were there. In the face of such experiences of solidarity, assessments of credibility would seem insignificant and beside the point.

But our experience at Punta Rieles was not simply one of solidarity and witness, as might be suggested should I now give in to the temptation to rebuke these earlier doubts and flatten our time with the women into a single unambiguously true experience, thereby constituting us as those who went, saw, and returned, having seen something too true to be described or proven in the worldly, lawyerly language we, so removed from grace, are used to speaking. As a result, such a refusal to analyze our prison experiences in the language of credibility and doubt seems no more faithful to Ana than doing so. Although the refusal captures something of our solidarity, it threatens to suppress the many ambiguities of our experience with the women. Similarly, although assessing credibility seems removed from the immediacy of our sense about the truth of Ana's experience, it seems the only way to avoid placing her on a pedestal of untouchable authenticity. Analyzing our experiences from the remove of my Cambridge study, I feel trapped between the necessity and the danger of assessing the truth of Ana's story.

One response to the difficulty of thinking truthfully "outside" the prison about an experience "inside" might be to acknowledge that the boundaries which divide Cambridge and the prison or which separate my experiences from my analytical reflection may be quite permeable. Now that I think about it, this permeability had some basis in our experience. As we left the warden's office in the other direction at 1:00 P.M. and returned to the gaze of the militia outside the prison, the women hidden in one cell block were singing "Happy Birthday." As the officers glanced nervously at one another, we smiled at Pat.

CROSS-EXAMINATION: THE DOCTOR'S TALE

Both within and without the prison walls, our meetings with Uruguayan officials seemed purposive and deliberative, lacking the easy give-and-take of our meetings with the prisoners. As activists avenging our prisoners' honor, we wanted our relations with Montevideo officials to be, first and foremost, effective and official relations, and we embraced the rhetorics of human rights and medical ethics enthusiastically. From the start, however, we had a hard time finding the right mix of lawyerly aggression and medical compassion with Uruguayan officials, and it was difficult to release the full force of our concern effectively.

We got our first chance to practice while still inside Punta Rieles. After speaking with the women prisoners, we met with the prison doctor. He was a small and somewhat ugly bureaucrat, the perfect central casting prison doctor. We had stalled him off all morning, brushing aside his offers to sit in on Richard's examination, to spend time going over each medical record in detail, really, he kept repeating, to help us any way he could. Finally, as the last prisoner left, I asked him to come into the examining room. Richard was completing the notes of his medical examinations and skimming the prison medical files. Interrogation fell to me. After meeting with the prisoners and hearing their medical complaints, I wanted to cross-examine him to the wall. Two general problem areas seemed promising for interrogation: lack of patient confidentiality and the high incidence of torture-related complaints among the prisoners. After getting him to produce evidence confirming these charges, I would be able to force his acknowledgment of the newly adopted United Nations standards on participation by health workers in torture. I had a copy in Spanish and wanted to work through its terms with him.

I started with a setup question: Could you describe your responsibilities at Punta Rieles? Your staff? Female doctors? Psychiatrists? Are they military officers? I figured I had about twenty minutes, including translation. So far the facts looked good: the psychiatrists were military. In describing the range of medial complaints, the doctor emphasized an abnormal incidence of psychological distress of various sorts, spinal problems and other "functional" complaints related to hypertension and digestive irregularities — almost too good to be true for my case about torture. I pressed on. We went through procedures for access to medical care. I circled around, increased the pace and had him on the run about patient trust. The next step was confidentiality. Richard looked up and slipped me the UN Code. One of his institutions had been instrumental in drafting it, and he wanted to make sure we spread the word. My time was short. I switched to torture.

Did he know that charges had been made that the Punta Rieles prisoners had been systematically tortured. Yes. By wrist suspension? Yes. What might be the medical results of such treatment? I would need to hurry. He couldn't speculate. Spinal dislocations? My mind flashed to our forty-four year old and the extra struggle ill prisoners confronted enduring the Punta Rieles regime. I was furious with him for not easing their burden. Suddenly everything was upside down. The more he confirmed our worst suspicions, the better my interrogation seemed. I pulled out the UN Code. Did he know that international standards had been adopted governing medical personnel working in political prisons? He did. Did he know what they said? Yes. About torture rehabilitation? No. Had he seen this document? No commanding officer had ever put pressure on him to act unethically, he offered. I sensed a slip, and restated the question: Did he know what was required of medical officers regarding torture rehabilitation? Richard stepped in.

Surely the doctor sensed the importance of such standards for the profession as a whole, Richard soothed. Suddenly there were two doctors in the room. Solidarity. Mutual respect. He sprang for the escape. Yes, and he shared Richard's pride. It was an honorable calling. I was relieved but also frustrated. My anger had not yet found its outlet, although, as we reconstructed it later, the combination seemed defensible, both effective and authentic. Nonetheless, I was left hanging, an enraged interrogator without a subject.

In part, confusion about the goals of our interrogation made our exchange with the prison doctor difficult. At times I could focus only on a desire to affect him, to imprint our visit on him one way or another — but why not just punch him out? Sometimes I wanted him to admit responsibility for Ana's suffering. I wanted someone to blame, and I wanted him to assume the role of the blameworthy and the stance of subjugation before our witness to their deeds. More often, we sought to induce the doctor to change his ways, perhaps by getting him to recognize a shared professional sense of the "reasonable" or some external legal-ethical standard. We also thought of being effective in ways that did not relate so directly to the object of our interrogation and, in particular, did not require him to change his behavior: by bearing witness to his complicity, monitoring his activity, expressing solidarity with his victims, and reinforcing the human rights norms and institutions with which we confronted him.

Sometimes these goals seemed to conflict or to suggest divergent tactical mixes of lawyerlyness and medical compassion. Getting the doctor to acknowledge a common professional norm seemed, at least to Richard, to require tactics softer than those I was employing to force admission of his complicity and show our solidarity with his victims. Similarly, when I thought a complacent tone might best induce acceptance of a legal norm, Richard hoped to bear witness with firmness. Nor could we face our sponsors if we seemed to have sold out. Even when we could resolve these dilemmas by imagining, as we did with the doctor, that our roles "complemented" one another, we often felt a bit unsatisfied.

Often we tried to structure these ambiguities as personal choices between doing good and doing well. Thinking of things this way channeled my confusion and anger into a set of calculations manageably informed by my sense of my own moral agency. How, I asked, might I combine success and virtue, recognizing that neither authentic human relations nor instrumental effective encounters would alone be satisfying. After all, just as "effective" interrogation kept getting in the way of my relations with Ana, so a desire for "authentic" feelings, to express my anger, kept intruding on my talk with the doctor. By imagining that we wanted to be "effective without compromising our true beliefs," we could make authenticity seem like either a limit on being effective or a goal of secondary importance. I used this approach when one official described his pleasant days at Harvard. I considered whether to respond with a tone of common or divergent experiences in tactical terms: how far could I go in appearing complicit before I would jeopardize his sense of our commitment to the prisoners? In the end, we traded a few anecdotes about how Harvard Square had changed.

Once we started thinking this way, we became adept at formulating strategies (one might even call them doctrines) to accommodate our instrumental interest and our moral position. Sometimes, for example, we distinguished our reasonableness from the hard-heartedness of our sponsors, or our professional reasonableness from the shocking facts of these particular cases. It was more difficult to arrive at a satisfying resolution when our problem was to choose either among conflicting moral values or among conflicting tactics: how far, for example, might I empathize with the prison doctor before denying my sense of his injustice? Despite these strategic resolutions, moreover, our confusion about goals never fully disappeared.

To a certain extent, this fluid confusion served a purpose. It often allowed us to differentiate our moral and our instrumental selves — our retrospective sense of the authenticity of our relations with the prisoners and our more purely instrumental relations with Uruguayan officials — without abandoning our sense that these two dimensions of our personality and activity were integrated in some way. Indeed, we pursued these official relations in part precisely to reconnect us with the authenticity we now imagined ourselves to have experienced with the prisoners.

As Richard asked the Punta Rieles doctor a series of questions about the general health among the prison population, my mind turned to another doctor, on a podium in Paris four months before.

As I had pushed through the crowd of leftists and luminaries gathered in the Assemblé Nationale for a conference on the application of humanitarian law to the conflict in El Salvador, an American physician was finishing his report on the health situation in the area of conflict. It was a numbing litany of statistics: birthweights, arm circumferences, and calorie counts. The crowd milled. I looked to see who I might know in the hall. I wondered how this Manhattan internist had found his way to this motley conference, or to El Salvador for that matter. Probably some UNESCO tour. As his account came to a close he concentrated on a family he had interviewed in the hills—a woman with four children, husband presumed dead or at war. The imagery is strong, of shrinking babies and sagging breasts, low birthweights and the dirty faces of sickly children. He has the audience. Disease gives way to a rhythmic incantation of pharmaceutical shortfalls: wounds that cannot be sutured, sores that cannot be salved. He knows we share his shame, his outrage, his intensity. He has taken us to El Salvador with him. He entreats us to make this conference a success, to respond to the wounds to which he is witness, to find—he pauses for breath before the climax—and to declare a right to health within the annals of humanitarian law. Applause. He is coming down, wiping sweat from his hands. We will respond, the law that is empty will be filled. He will not have gone, and we shall not have come, in vain. Two extra words have crept into his medical diction, promising to transport our concerns to the sick and the needy: not health, but a right to health; not engagement, but declaration.

After we had left the Punta Rieles doctor behind, I wondered how I, trying to release my emotions through the rhetoric of medical ethics or the device of cross-examination, differed from my Paris doctor, titillating us with barbarism while promising a successful, if disengaged, response. For my strategic planning and my tactics, like his, had been constructed to revive images of prisoners bound, and to bring our unresolved and perhaps voyeuristic feelings about being with Ana and others safely into our normal lives.

Sitting with officials, we tended not to think about this. We were with them, after all, precisely because we had left the prisoners firmly behind. If we did wonder, as we projected as much self-assurance about the naturalness of our presence as we could muster, we did so in the language of standing: what right had we to be there, asking these questions? Why should the Punta Rieles prison open its files to us? The issue of standing—the question of our right to intervene in Uruguayan affairs—seemed to trouble the Uruguayans less than it bothered me. I think now that my concern about standing sprang in part from my perception of our relations with Uruguayan officials as purely instrumental rather than as personal and human. These concerns were the products of our unresolved feelings about the chasm we were opening between our moral and our professional selves. In the context of instrumental relations, the intermeddler needs a basis for his intermeddlery. He needs a doctrine—like "standing." My worries about standing arose from my desire to deny that my relations with the Uruguayans had a personal and human dimension. Yet my experience with the doctor, as with other officials, was not an impersonal ritual. It was a complex social and personal crossroads in which dozens of desires, emotions, and roles found expression. My worries about standing arose from my desire to deny that relationship because it was the product of a continuing barbarism, our secret desire to take one more look at the wound.

THE MEN OF LIBERTAD

Back in the blue Peugeot, we speed to Libertad, prison for male politicos. The car is hot. Food and five minutes to relax with one another would be fine. If it weren't for the driver and the guide we would go over our Punta experiences. Behind schedule, we sit silently in the backseat, trying to turn our minds to the longer list of male prisoners awaiting us. I close my eyes. Libertad prison is in the countryside on the other side of Montevideo, in another military district. We see the massive rectangular building long before the sign reading "Rehabilitation Center #2." Just outside the inner grounds, in the military recreation area, healthy young soldiers are playing handball. In a cruel joke on parents who drive this road for brief telephone contact with their children, the last government billboard before the prison depicts a small boy and girl, beside them the words "our hope." As we approach, I notice more uniforms, more check-points, more serious expressions, more guns.

There is no rite of passage into the prison here. Indeed, we never make it to the prison proper. As we step from the car, I can't make out the outline of the prison itself, obscured by too many watch-towers and outbuildings. Someone hands me a red identification badge as we step from the car, surrounded by gun-toting soldiers on a hardscrabble parking area. We trot between two walkie-talkie sol-diers across a compound toward a small brick building. We step through the side door into an office labeled "Director." Inside, an officer in well-worn fatigues confronts us. There are no portraits here. On the walls are blurred black and white photographs of man-gled bodies, victims of the Tupamaro terrorists.

The officer seems ill at ease with an international delegation. He plays it tough and close. State your business. We offer no elaborate introduction. Still standing, Richard hands him our list of names. We may see the three medical students. As to the other ill prisoners, that will not be possible. His orders from Montevideo include only three names. Our list lies limp on the table.

I assure him that this must be a misunderstanding, not to say an error. I suggest that we will gladly wait in his office while he straightens it out. No, he says, we will see the students now. In the meantime he will check with his commanding officer. This seems unlikely to clear anything up — the communications gap must lie be-tween our political contacts in Montevideo and his superior, com-mander for this military district. I think Papillon would have said that he would have liked to help us, if only . . . A truly malevolent director might have relished the rejection. This guy simply hands his list to someone and opens the door.

Guards take us to the visiting rooms. One wing of this outbuilding is partitioned into small chambers by walls of steel and glass. Inside each chamber are fifteen or twenty visiting posts, each with a tele-phone. Around the outside walls are phones for the prisoners. The wing is empty. The atmosphere beneath the bare bulbs is tense. Our voices echo as we protest the unacceptability of such a location for a medical exam. I invoke medical confidentiality: Richard cannot ex-amine a patient under such exposed conditions. Although we will be able to speak privately with the students within one visiting chamber, the glass walls are lined with open telephones. There must be another room. No dice. We are being neither let in nor kept out. I can't seem to build a relationship with these men; there are too many of them, they all look alike. Everything is moving too quickly; we can't sort out who is who. We confer briefly and decide to go ahead on their terms, more resignation than strategic bargaining concession. Still, we hope our acquiescence will advance our attempt to see the ill prisoners. We are to have about twenty minutes with each student.

A steel door opens behind us and through the glass I can see a young prisoner being brought across a barren field into the building. Head bowed and shaven, he stands with his hands clasped behind him, facing away from the guards who escort him. In a gray uniform, number stenciled across his chest, he is the image of subjugation. He catches my eye and winks while the guards slide the door closed.

Ramon Hernandez shakes my hand. His eyes brighten, and I realize that he may not have touched someone from the outside since last June. As Pat races through our introduction, I notice new running shoes beneath his drab overalls. He is Ana's boyfriend. We convey her greetings. We admit there is nothing in particular that we want him to tell us, nor that we have to tell him. We are here, we explain, to see that he is all right and to be with him for the few minutes available.

Ramon puts our visit in political context: our presence here, he reasons, is an opening, a sign of the democratization process, the more significant when viewed in light of the recent release of two well-known political prisoners. He has heard of their release from a comrade who spoke with the Red Cross. We add as an afterthought that Richard will be glad to discuss any medical concerns Ramon may have. He nods. Ramon's political analysis has brought us together, no longer doctor-patient, lawyer-client, but four whisperers, talking politics. There seem no artificial boundaries here, no artificially imposed violence, no hidden mysteries.

Ramon seems to know that he is supposed to tell his story, the story of his arrest and imprisonment. He tells it as though he were in a film: prisoner is brought to meet foreign delegation, describes prison conditions, tells some gory bits, seems in good spirits, complains about the food, scene change. I enter his script and take some ritualistic notes. He warms to his subject. After his arrest, Ramon was charged with membership in the student council of the medical school, a charge he admitted in a declaration signed after torture. He was beaten, doused in cold water, forced to stand with his arms spread, deprived of sleep, and hung by his wrists, tied behind his back. He demonstrates each position with quick gestures. I notice that he stutters. He touches his eyes, lips, ears, and nose where the electric prod was applied. Also his toes and genitals. Sitting cramped on wooden benches in this drab chamber, I picture him being tortured, his face smashed against the cement floor. The police sanctum in which Ana had been violated had seemed distant from the Punta Rieles clinic. Although we had been admitted to the prison, the site of the violence had receded into mystery. Ramon's story seems more violent, his environment tougher, less subtle. He seems to have used his body, deployed it, spent it. He is also an activist. By contrast, Ana's pain seems extra, gratuitous, imposed. They tied Ramon to an iron bed and attached electrodes to his extremities and penis. He could hear the generator too. I find myself recording the details in shorthand, hiding the references in my notebook. My emotional resistance has diminished. I feel as if I understand what has happened to Ramon.

Francisco Zelaya told a similar story, focusing slightly more on the details of time and place than had Ramon: eighteen hours of standing, two hours electricity, nine hours suspended by his wrists, and so forth. There had been a radio playing at the locations of his torture. Francisco is an animated boy; his eyes joke with us. We are all at a dinner party, and he is describing the antics of an opposing soccer squad. I try to picture him with hair. He tells us the posters and documents they found in his apartment he had received unsolicited in the mail and never distributed. I think about the similarity of all alibis, world round.

Libertad is a harsh regime: strict discipline, silence, poor food, infrequent visits. But Francisco seems in good spirits. He thinks medical treatment in the military hospital is fine, but complains about routine health care: waiting days for aspirin, et cetera. His problems begin to sound trivial. He seems just another tortured youth, giving what he had in a battle with many fronts. Libertad's main terror seems to be punishment cells. Prisoners apparently begin their stay in these single unheated cells some distance from the main prison. There, without water, toilet facilities, or furniture beyond a bucket and mattress brought in at night, newcomers learn what can happen at Libertad. Francisco spent eleven days there. As he tells it, the worst seems stripped of mystery. I don't think it could happen to me, and, I suspect, neither does Francisco. Our connection has reaffirmed the gulf between us.

Victor Guerra, our last medical student, is different from the others. A veterinarian graduate, he seems a naïve and sensitive man. Where Ramon and Francisco had focused on the political context of our visit and told of their torture rather matter-of-factly, Victor seems more interested in pleading his defense, more embarrassed to be seen. He describes his arrest and initial appearance before a judge, explaining plaintively that the charges were exaggerated, the process defective. I am not a Communist. His soft eyes melt. Sheepishly, he describes his only political acts: attending a rally, voting against the military in a recent referendum.

Victor reengages me, in his case and in our mission. He explains that the whole group of medical students arrested the preceding June has yet to be sentenced. As I tumble to the fact that none of our students has been either tried or sentenced, hope returns that his incarceration and our visit might be creatively linked. Gone is the mutually resigned solidarity of our conversations with Ramon and Francisco.

Ramon and Francisco seemed to carry themselves as temporarily defeated warriors in a greater political struggle, and that is how they seemed to view their own stories of capture, torture, and imprisonment. Imprisoned warriors like Ramon and Francisco seemed our equals; they needed no rescue. To them we were comrades, coparticipants in a political struggle. The connection we had felt when in their presence — achieved by contrast with our experiences at Punta Rieles — diminished my sense of purpose. Like Ana, Victor, the passive victim, awakens my indignation and motivates me to act. Suddenly, our meeting the next morning at the court might be more than a formal plea for pardon. We might be able to do something. Victor, pleading legal procedure and propriety, rekindles our involvement, which had been somewhat dampened by our abstract political solidarity with his fellows.

Victor describes his torture as if to convince us that it had really happened to him, telling against doubt and strangeness. If Ramon and Francisco had spoken of torture ritualistically — three hours, two blows, 150 volts — Victor's pain comes through plainly as he details the familiar mix of blows, shocks, and torture. Victor, a man without politics, suffers under the harsh prison regime. As the guard returns for him he resumes the stance of subjugation, back to his captor, head bowed, hands behind his back. He cocks his head toward me and says softly in English, "The position."

The three interviews have gone quickly. We are exhausted and drained and have learned nothing new about prison health care or about their legal cases. We seem to have forgotten about being a delegation. These interviews, each emotionally charged — the wink, the touch, the words, the eyes — have disintegrated our difference, our special team spirit, and made me feel subject, for the first time, to the Uruguayan regime. When Pat slips Francisco a cough drop it seems both natural and furtive, pressed by the prison atmosphere. We glance apprehensively at the guards walking on the other side of the glass. We hear them talking down the hall. No flirtation here. I compose myself. As we walk back to the director's office, I straighten my posture and, somewhat foolishly I think, try to look severe.

We were not to see the other prisoners. In part, I was relieved. I wanted out. But I was also angry and wanted revenge. Victor's parting comment had unhinged me somewhat. Richard began a firm but respectful dialogue with a junior officer. Snapped back into our delegation, anger and revenge were again our tools, deployable emotions. We huddled in the hall to talk tactics. I wanted the director to feel threatened with responsibility for the failure of our mission if we were kept from seeing the ill prisoners. Richard thought the main players were in Montevideo and that anger was likely to be wasted here. Besides, he was satisfied with what we had done. He suspected that the institutions would think it sufficient. I insisted. Faced with a malevolent opponent, I argued, we must be especially careful to see the one thing hidden from us: there will be secreted the smoking gun. Very lawyerly. Richard was unimpressed. Back in the office a second time, I expressed anger. Richard expressed disappointment. Pat mediated. We walked briskly to the car and left for Montevideo. It was 6:20 P.M.

TRANSITION: PREPARING TO ACT

Sitting in the car on the way back to Montevideo, my mind turned eagerly to the tasks ahead. Unlike the drive from Punta Rieles to Libertad, this trip was animated. We had come out. Discussing what we were to do in the coming days, we talked a bit too insistently, too loudly, anxious to ignore the heat and dust. In a way, we wanted to forget the prison, and I was struck by the strength of my desire to put it behind us, to break forward from it, as if the memory were pornographic. Just as the temptation in writing about our prison experience with Ana was to analyze the moment's ambiguity into recognizable patterns, responsive to preexisting doubts, so driving back to the city was itself a plunge forward into meaningful action, and the temptation, for us then and for me now, is to get on with the story of our Montevideo follow-up. First, however, I want to suspend this flight briefly to explore the ways in which the rush to move from one place to the other helped to create a system of images ordering the progress of our mission.

Driving back to Montevideo, we differentiated our time inside the prisons from activism outside their walls in two ways. First, we felt the intensity of "the moments we're all in this business for," as a fellow human rights junketeer termed them, those times when you seem able to see it like it really is and in the face of which all else can be merely preparation or follow-up. This sense of difference makes it seem only natural that activists returning from adventures tend to think wistfully of their time away. At the same time, we thought that our prison visits needed — in fact, demanded — expression and completion. Despite their apparent authenticity, as the products of our preparation or the origin of our response, they seemed hollow. Suffering seemed meaningful only when rendered productive. Of these two differences, the second was more useful; it motivated the response we felt able to give. For all these differences, however, the complicated play of identities, roles, and names that had characterized our relations with the warden and the prisoners, as well as with one another, would be intensified rather than set aside in Montevideo.

The mystery is that we experienced the drive not as an active analytic process but as a natural transition from the country to the city. We sustained this sense of spatial and temporal difference by relying upon notions about gender. We distinguished a sphere of violation to be witnessed from a field for active response. In prison we had been with the women, the victims, and we were returning to the men, victimizers in Montevideo. This spatial difference was partly sustained by contrasting the sacred woman with the profane man and partly by contrasting the female victim with the male avenger. In Montevideo, our will, reason, and action could redress the horrors we experienced in prison. These divisions helped us feel we, the men, were moving, first toward, then on behalf of, and finally away from the women. We had kept our relations with Papillon purposive and fluid by holding before us the promise of access to Ana. Coming out, these contrasts made us feel we were back on familiar ground, activists with a cause. Taken together, these two mechanism of differentiation structured our sense of progress, of moving meaningfully forward with our mission. My sense of connection with the male prisoners was achieved by contrast with our experiences at Punta Rieles. Once we had reimagined Ana's torture as an abomination, forgetting our elaborate efforts to connect with her as a person, a political sympatica, it became possible to relate more objectively to Ramon's tales. Ramon seemed subjugated, not violated. His pain was instrumental, his body political. Ana had been trespassed upon, Ramon punished. We repeated this contrast within Libertad between Ramon-Francisco and Victor, the victim. Thinking about it now, I suppose we saw our forty-four-year old as a spent warrior, different from Ana.

It was by manipulating this gender distinction that we got the feeling of simultaneous engagement and distance, of having touched the forbidden and of being able to respond to it, both within the prisons and in relating the prisons to our response. This basic contrast accommodated violence to the vocabulary of calculation and barbarism with which we had prepared our visit and which we would use to complete it. Both inside the prison and en route to Montevideo, the incomprehensible violation of woman's body kept something hidden and mysterious, so that something else — intentional knightly deployment — could seem familiar. In rethinking the trip, this motion, this break between female and male, experience and action, seems its crucial feature. The odd thing is that we experienced only a rush to move on with the show.

Thursday evening, back in Montevideo after a day at the prisons, we sat around a quiet table at a bar near our hotel, reveled in our success, and strategized our remaining thirty-six hours in the country. The next day we were to appear before the Chief Judge of the Supreme Military Judicial Court to plead for the early release of the prisoners who had become subjects of our concern. There were meetings with families, human rights groups, political parties, and government officials. We would return to the U.S. Embassy to brief rather than to be briefed. There were press releases, reports, and law review articles to be written. We had to confirm our onward flight to Santiago, where we would begin again. Our success in getting into the prisons burdened us. We wanted to be sure to maximize our positive impact, paying our debts and finishing what we had started. As we headed out, the pace of the trip quickened dramatically.

It may have been wishful thinking or tired excitement, but by Thursday afternoon we suspected that the hearing at the Supreme Military Judicial Court set for Friday morning might be more than a formality. Government moderates had surprised us by hinting that our four students might be released after our visit. Perhaps contending government factions had struck a deal, and our visit would be the occasion for a demonstration of largesse. We had discovered that, procedurally, no judgment had been entered. It would not be too late to drop the charges. The sentences, due in three weeks, might at least be reduced to time served. I began to hope that our presentation, if done right, might increase the likelihood of such an outcome. At the very least, I didn't want to jeopardize a deal, should one have been struck, and I had professional pride in presenting a good oral argument.

But should I be easygoing or formal? Present myself as an attorney pleading four cases or as a humanitarian interloper representing five North American institutions? Should I plead our clients' naïveté? Rehabilitation? Minimizing the chances of error if a deal had been struck seemed to require more role fidelity and formality—a more ritualistic presentation, a greater emphasis on official Uruguay—than did effective adversarial advocacy. More than just tactical choices, these seemed to pose a conflict between honest witness and ceremonial advocacy. Was it time to come out of the closet, or should we wait until we left Montevideo? Until our prisoners were finally released?

In all these scenarios, invoking international law seemed the least-promising strategy, in part because the court would need to repudiate a good bit of its autonomous and legal self-image to find international law relevant. Nevertheless, I thought that mentioning international law might in some fuzzy way strengthen international norms. More importantly, this approach seemed most closely connected to any theory of our standing (and my competence) that I could devise. Perhaps, I theorized, once a state violates a widely accepted norm of human rights, it loses the right to oppose jurisdictional interference, if not legally, at least in terms of perceived cultural legitimacy. This exchange theory seemed comforting, for it grounded our presence in their conduct, if not their direct consent. In the end, I decided to abandon international law and not to worry about standing. If they had any objection to my appearance, I would try to answer it on other grounds, perhaps agreeing to argue in general on humanitarian terms if the judge would hear no argument on the specific cases. Looking at it now, this shift from a formal standing doctrine to one based in humanitarianism seems fragile. At the time, however, I felt I was escaping doctrine for the bravado of a more direct advocacy style. In any case, having abandoned legalism, I became obsessed with the idea that I needed more information about the Court, the judges, the law, the advocacy practices, the cultural norms of humanitarianism, about Uruguay.

Thursday evening, Pat and I phoned everyone we could think of to set up meetings with attorneys who had represented prisoners before Judge Ledesma. We came up with three, including the attorney of record for one of our students, and arranged appointments for Thursday night and Friday at breakfast. I sat down at an old portable typewriter to draft a press release and oral argument for the next morning. Afterward, we taxied from lawyer to lawyer to pin down the details of Uruguayan military court procedure and test-run my evolving argument.

In a nicely appointed apartment twenty minutes outside Montevideo, we found the attorney for one of our students. She was a thin, upright woman in her middle fifties who had been representing these "youngsters" for several years. As she spoke, my building hope for the following day shrank. Yes, she condescended, the fact that the judge would hear us might mean something. Anything might mean something. But I should realize, she stressed as I questioned her about the Court's jurisdiction and procedure, that these were not trials, but the imitation of trials. She was cynical about newfangled human rights concerns. Where had the political parties been, and where, for that matter, had we been, during the long Uruguayan political silence? She had been driving to the prisons to seek access to her clients, supporting their families, filing habeas corpus petitions as witness to their incarceration. To represent these prisoners had nothing to do with their release, or with sentence reduction. To represent them was not to forget them when nothing could be done.

She addressed me in English. She had seen no files, had not been permitted to discuss the charges with her clients, had been interrogated and searched upon reaching the prisons. To have challenged the Court's procedure would have been to risk professional sanction. At my insistence she outlined the typical case history — arrest, summary process, first instance, decision, sentence, review — in a distracted and distant manner. Here, in her middle-class sitting room, bending stiffly forward in her chair, she described the paperwork of prosecution and defense abstractly, without meeting my gaze, as if she were describing some embarrassing, though fortunately distant, family scandal. But for all her distance, I felt she was teasing us, holding out the promise of something, something beyond cynicism. We were not like her, not Uruguayan, yet she kept hinting, if only we asked the right question, showed the right solidarity, she would release her secret.

Finally, I asked her what she, a lawyer, would do if, like me, she were to face Judge Ledesma ten hours later. Colonel Ledesma, she corrected me, adding somewhat incongruously that I should "not challenge his assertions about procedure and about the Court's fealty to law." He will say he can do nothing: that the case is not yet before him; that military law is punctilious about procedural regularity. She scoffed. Stress, she advised, that these are young prisoners, awkward victims of tough political times, without records, who were picked up for pursuing the natural student curiosity about ideas. I wondered whether this story bore any relation to the cases. She didn't know, not having yet been able to see their files. A factual plea for mercy on fabricated facts seemed risky to me. Yet as she settled on this course, she warmed to our inquires.

This was a technical, professional problem: fashioning an oral argument. She gave it her best shot, and as our adrenaline began to flow in the hopeless late-night aura, we found professional solidarity. Nevertheless, as we left her on her porch at 12:30 A.M., I felt a bit foolish for having imagined there to be any point to my efforts in Uruguay other than the working out of professional courtesies. Yet for all her tragic demeanor, before we left she took my notepad for a moment and, in a rigid block script, printed the names of the three other clients: Gonzalo Mujica Benoit, five years, six months; Ricardo Cohen Pappo, twelve years; Dr. Guillermo Dermit Barbato, five years. Like others whose names would be pressed upon us in the coming hours, these too had a "medical angle," had suffered, deserved our attention.

A MOMENT OF ADVOCACY

At 9:00 the next morning, the Peugeot dropped us at a modest building of stone, identified only by the most discreet chiseling beside the door: Supreme Military Judicial Court. The door opened onto the tiled entrance court of a nineteenth-century city villa. We were ushered up a lavish central oak staircase beneath a stained glass skylight. In and off the courtyard sat military clerks and guards. Around the second floor lobby were the judicial offices. One, crammed with files on open shelves, showed the only sign of business. I felt the European aristocracy debased, their court, still noble in service of a democracy, overrun by the philistines. To the left, an ornate office — head of the Supreme Court — brocade, leather, oak, and books reduced to signs of the law, and of the tradition.

A large man with an open collar approaches us. Car salesman turned judge. His very severe aide introduces him. She, her mouth a penciled formality beneath rouge cheeks, will translate. I thank her, but we have brought our own. Although we know Ledesma speaks English, the rituals of power and respect have taken over. The aide ushers us in. Four chairs have been arranged before his desk, three upright black, one of elaborate red brocade. As we shuffle around the room, I sit decisively in the red chair, perhaps only to befuddle our would-be translator. Ledesma, after some hesitation, produces a second red chair from behind his desk and sits.

Richard introduces us, politely, firmly, and presents thick written appeals from our five sponsoring organizations. I am grateful for word processing. Ledesma interrupts. As this is legal business, and he is a lawyer, he will deal directly with the lawyer, lawyer to lawyer in a court of law. The word *law* festoons his every phase. The Spanish word for lawyer sounds like "avocado." The avocado will speak.

I speak slowly, in a tone that I hope will secure ten minutes without interruption. The translation pauses heighten the drama, phrase by phrase. I don't want to impinge upon these prisoners' proper defense, nor prejudice their legal claims, nor interject any inappropriate considerations into his formal and legal deliberations. I want to speak to him only as one lawyer to another. I think: what does this mean? Why would we be here if not to introduce pressure beyond military law? He nods, and seems satisfied. We have given a sign that we will stay within the protocol assumptions about his dignity as an independent judicial officer. He will reciprocate.

We have come, I intone, to appeal for the earliest possible release of four medical students arrested last summer on charges of subversive association. I have not had access to their files and cannot speak as their counsel, but I speak on behalf of the many thousands of

American scientists who have been concerned about these students. Of course, we seek no special treatment for medical prisoners, or for these individuals, beyond what the law allows. The contradictions mount. This appeal is grounded in general considerations, considerations of international concern, international law, and political democratization that apply to other cases, to be sure. But it is also an appeal specific to these individuals. With his permission, I would like to go over these specific cases. He nods. I am glad I have remembered my opening set of points. The tone seems O.K. The sergeant-translator looks uneasy. I proceed.

I portray our students as naïve children, refer to our visit with them, itself an important signal of Uruguay's political openness. I describe their eyes. Their offenses are nonviolent, crimes of curiosity. They renounce violence; their punishment has already been severe. I do not mention how hard it is for the international community to comprehend such punishment for crimes of association, for Uruguay's friends to hear of physical abuses that contravene international obligations. Perhaps this omission is a mistake. He breaks in.

The judiciary is independent and will follow the law. Why does he keep saying this? He delivers an elaborate discourse on the independence and procedural formality of the military judiciary, a speech oddly incongruous with his availability to hear an extraordinary appeal from five U.S. scientific institutions before the trial court has even convicted our medical students. Superfluous protestation. But he is just warming up. These are dangerous, violent criminals with years of hardening political experience. Can that be right? Although he is merely repeating Papillon's story, it throws me off momentarily, feeds directly my doubts about my standing, my oral strategy. I say nothing. I am reassured to remember that a judge is not supposed to deliver, before conviction, a speech one might expect of a warden.

The country is in danger. Families have lost members to political violence. He can never forget that. His contradictions mount. He, of course, cannot comment on specific cases. He pulls four files from his desk. Which was the veterinarian? Victor Guerra. These individuals have been involved in ten years of political work — work which was, I think, but do not say, legal at the time. He will, of course, review these cases when he receives their files. He will certainly take what we have said into account. Despite his legal demeanor, he seems unaware of such basics of legal protocol as no ex post facto laws, individual guilt and innocence, no associational crimes, innocent until proven guilty, and judicial restraint in discussing cases before the court.

Our presence presents him with a classic dilemma. He must defend his regime, yet any defense will derogate from the propriety that is his best defense. I am also in a bind. Once in his court, I must speak to Ledesma's self-image, yet to do so betrays the ground of our presence. We are each insecure about the ground for the meeting, and as contemptuous of the other's naïveté about the law as of our own gullibility. We embrace the lawyer's role and language to speak in contradiction, but are cynical about it. Polite, respectful, and cynical — it is even a cynicism we can share in a chortle about the protocol of the chairs.

As he stands up, signaling our imminent departure, I begin to suspect that something lurks beneath this cynicism, some rage or fear or tactic that sustains and justifies the pretensions. I think, if only I can keep going, it will emerge. But the audience, a formal success, in which we have seemed reasonable, articulate, and firm, is over. Although I am glad that I haven't blown it, I measure my performance against this hidden image. Having not thrown off my role, having not really spoken my heart, I feel I have failed to touch him. He has neither admitted complicity nor told me what he really thinks. Ledesma relaxes and points to a chair in the corner of his office, owned by a Uruguayan Founding Father. He exclaims proudly, with a sweeping gesture, that the tradition ends here, in this office. We descend the stairs, Ledesma behind us. Clerks snap straight. Heels click. Doors swing open and we step in to a waiting car. As we pull from the curb, Ledesma smiles broadly, waving until we have pulled around the corner, out of his sight.

THE AFTERMATH

We spent our remaining twenty-four hours in Uruguay with human rights groups, political party members, the press, and with the relatives of the disappeared, of political prisoners, of our medical students, and of victims of Argentinean repression. We tried to be supportive and to share our experience, that we might release our emotions of solidarity and frustration, and, perhaps, that they might be released from isolation. We tried to be informal and empathetic, without breaking the confidences of our prisoners and government contacts. Sometimes we connected, but, I fear, more often we failed.

Those with whom we spoke often seemed to refuse emotional connection with us, transforming us into something foreign and exotic, the responsible and incapable. Why, they sometimes asked, had we chosen these prisoners when others, their lovers, sons, and mothers, had suffered so much more? Often, on the other hand, they were respectful, treating us as foreign professionals, from whom nothing personal could be expected. We felt gratitude more often for our official than our personal presence. They thanked us as the representatives of our institutions, and the thanks seemed heartfelt.

Some of those we met seemed politically informed and able to locate our visit quite concretely in their stories about social conflict and suffering in Uruguay. Others seemed bewildered by their situation, by our presence. The mother of one prisoner seemed to have been plucked from her middle-class bridge game and plunked down amid young radicals, press oppositionists, and now foreign delegations, fully without preparation or premeditation. As we managed the flow of one delegation after another through our hotel bar Friday afternoon, we moved in and out of our professional roles and changed the level of political neutrality we projected. Sometimes we struck a formal pose, hoping that its improbable rigidity would signal our true sympathy. I remember declaiming quite piously to a sympathetic young journalist and his microphone when asked to comment on upcoming Uruguayan elections that "our concern has been with public health, not public policy." He nodded, and I thought he understood what I felt and why I did not say it.

There seemed no way to share the facts of our prison visits with the students' parents. They wanted to know too much and could hear too little. At one point, wrapped in my best demeanor of foreign authority, I assured some mothers solemnly that "yours are children to be proud of." We seemed to connect. At times the tangle of expectations rankled. As Richard set me up to interview one group about their legal cases because he thought they would feel better, tempers flared. By 11:00 P.M., sitting down to dinner, the three of us needed to release the day's tension. At a gaudy restaurant around the corner from our hotel we found ourselves laughing giddily, imitating ourselves promising, cajoling, reassuring. We slept well.

Rituals. We talked again to U.S. officials at the Montevideo embassy. One man described such engagement as the U.S. government has with the Uruguayan military around human rights issues this way: "We do what we can, send them up to Panama, and tell them about constitutions and so forth, but it doesn't seem to stick." As if the Uruguayans had not simply learned something else from their American sponsors, something about running a military prison. But we knew what he meant, or why he said it, and I was glad when he put the rest of our talk off the record. We, like they, had heard it all before.

Although nothing we reported had not been repeatedly documented, as we spoke about torture in Uruguay, there was a sense in which these political and human rights officers seemed to be hearing about it for the first time. They were hearing it from Americans, we who had crossed to the other side, and they could hear it anew. Still, just as we in talking with the prisoners had oscillated between a nauseous fascination and a vacant sense of ennui, so these embassy officials seemed both fascinated and bored by our story. It all seemed so familiar, so jading, so tragic.

At the end of a trip such as this, I always feel a little guilty. As I realize that I am leaving, returning to my classes and to my library in Cambridge, I feel I am betraying those I came to serve and will be unable to respond successfully or completely to their problems. As we packed our bags in Montevideo, these feelings came over me quite strongly. I felt it would be impossible for me, a marginal American lawyer, to discharge the obligations I felt to those we had met in Uruguay. So many people had told us their stories, looked at us for help, asked us to take on their struggle, to work when we got back. Even those who understood the limits of our context spoke with both resignation and hope about "international public opinion," whose symbol we three became if only for an instant. We kept saying that our institutions would "remain concerned," that we would write a report, that we would carry their story back. But three individuals cannot fulfill the promise implicit in the words *foreign, American, professional, authority,* and *witness.*

Preparing to leave, I felt corrupt, as if we had deceived the Uruguayans for our own professional and personal reasons. The true price of constituting Uruguay as foreign and exotic was not, as I had feared while leaving Boston, to be paid in Montevideo. It was to be paid upon my return, as I became once more foreign to them, disconnected and out of touch. No amount of immersion in an international human rights bureaucracy seemed likely to discharge the taint of our distance from those we had come to know, for that bureaucracy is the machinery of our mutual estrangement as much as of any connection.

Despite these thoughts, I felt buoyant as we drove along the beach out of town. I considered our latitude. With good fortune, this autumn sun would have brought spring to Boston when we got back. We would continue what we had come to do back there. Our work in Montevideo completed, we enjoyed the tourist paradise this coast must have been. I was glad we would be able to stay in touch when we got home and was thankful that we would be able to count on a network of human rights activists for institutional support. In a way, I was glad to be a human rights bureaucrat.

When we came to Uruguay, our identities as professionals and our affiliations with the institutional machinery of human rights protection had been reassuring. We had felt prepared. Patrick, armed with the analysis of political science, would be able to open up the complexities of a shifting social and cultural environment, taming the foreign power struggle. Richard, bringing the ethical conventions and special talents of the medical profession, would be able to render that most dispassionate of compassions, medical assistance, rendering suffering as diagnosis, if not cure. I had compiled the relevant treaties to which Uruguay was signatory and read up on military court procedures. I hoped to provide a point of access, a justification and normative basis for our involvement, orienting us to a right and wrong, permissible and impermissible, where everything would be different. As we returned to our American identities, we were reassured by these points of connection. They promised us continued access to the land we were escaping.

But medical, political, and legal science can only partly redeem this promise. They provide continued access to foreign situations in part because they seem objective, neutral, scientific, above the differences that divided us from Ana and Ramon, from the warden and the Embassy. This dispassionate image helps us feel connected to Uruguay in part by reassuring us that we can retain our difference and distance. International human rights law reassured me that I could think of concrete moral outrages while remaining safely distant from them.

International human rights law is self-consciously about foreign violence and distant human suffering. Modern human rights advocacy was born in a burst of energy after the Second World War to people who wanted to respond to nonmilitary atrocities that seemed unthinkable, incomprehensible, even banal; who wanted to know them, tame them, redeem them as civilized, name them "genocide," bring them into polite parlance. These people began the process of treaty-drafting and bureaucracy-building that has been carried on by subsequent enthusiasts, bureaucrats, and politicians until one can now speak of a "network" or "community" of international human rights advocates.

Activists in the international human rights community try to develop a "right not to be tortured" or a "right to health" in order to reach out with empathy, assistance, and protection to people who are tortured and sick. They think of their work as a response of civilized society, the response of reason to that which it cannot comprehend. Although it seems obvious to think of human rights work as responsive to a preexisting irrationality, it is far from clear that the world presents itself to human rights advocated neatly divided into realms of reason and chaos. Indeed, human rights discourse plays an important role in sustaining the very image of irrationality to which it purports to be merely responding.

The possibility of not getting into the prisons, of torture remaining beyond our influence, heightened the trip's urgency. And yet, in all

facets of our human rights work in Uruguay, the processes by which
we responded to Uruguayan violence led us to push the barbarism
out of our minds. Papillon's violence remained ahead of us, out of
reach within the prison itself. Driving toward Montevideo, the violence receded behind the prison walls. Even with Ana, our interrogation tamed her story, placing her pain safely in the past at some
distant police station. I remember discussing the Uruguay mission
with a human rights bureaucrat friend of mine who said, "Even if
you don't get inside the prisons, you'll have struck a blow for human
rights." My mission was, it seemed, independent of any actual contact with any actual torture. It only required that torture be out
there. As a human rights advocate, I relied upon exclusion, upon the
untouchability, the unknowabilty of violence, as much as upon a
theory making it seem instrumentally approachable, comprehensible
as a "violation."

The shared practices of those in the human rights community em-
bolden us, reassure us about our ability to know, react to engage,
and actually control phenomena that we want to imagine to be beyond civilization and reason, foreign to our own lives. As human
rights activists, we can touch the barbaric and return unscathed. As
"lawyers" pursuing "remedies" for "abuses" of "human rights," we
find an articulation joining our images of civilization and our understanding that many suffer in its hands. We find a way to acknowledge
their suffering without abandoning our commitment to the system
that produces it; indeed, we give ourselves a role in its elimination. But
meanwhile, torture and violence remain "out there," like the prisoner-
victim, perceived only dimly, in a domesticated, civilized form—the
body, the self, remaining excluded, imprisoned.

But for all this fancy talk, human rights discourse does not seem
limited or narrow to those of us who work within it. Quite the contrary, we seem able through, and perhaps only through its devices to
achieve our object. We thought it was difficult at times for a doctor
and a lawyer to relate to one another. We thought it was hard to get
through to Ana. We wondered about our effectiveness. But we did
not wonder whether we contributed to the sense of estrangement
that we felt in Ana's presence, or whether our approach to one another was perhaps only one way of being together. We were too busy

trying to do as well and as much as we could; we just did not have the time.

And so our professional habits reassured us about the significance of our endeavor and the possibility for its successful conclusion, about returning to America and finding both a continuation and a meaningful stopping point, the possibility of going on to other things. So long as we imagined ourselves to be essentially distinct from Uruguay, able to relate only through our roles, our coming and going would be to cross and reconstitute the barrier of estrangement. We would need a bureaucracy and a discourse of connection. We needed human rights to take us there and bring us back. We needed to reduce the variety of human cultural experiences to spheres, delimited and conjoined as human rights and duties: rights to eat, to work, to develop, to live in peace, to be free from torture—somewhat different from food, jobs, social change, peace, release, but as close as we could come.

Still, for all its promise, for all our need, this discourse keeps congealing, fixing patterns where we felt movement, channeling us, excluding them, and, above all, proliferating itself. As human rights advocates, our discourse is not our tool; we are its property, and the price of our fealty nags at our conscience. What seemed noble comes to seem tawdry and voyeuristic. We were in the discourse, of it, and yet kept resisting its terms. But resistance was heavy, and compliance kept us buoyant.

In the plane to Santiago, we dictated a bit, plunging through the Scandinavian Airlines tunnel across Latin America. Later on, the three of us got together and began to get ready to go in again.

EPILOGUE

February 11, 1985, Pat writes from Washington:

"Other than writing news, we've got a new baby girl, named Glenna (By the way, in case Richard didn't mention it: Ramon Hernandez was released New Year's Eve. All the others were out in September. That gray haired woman who was only 44 was released in August.) And Silva Ledesma, when I saw him in November, to make yet one more pitch for Ramon, was thinking about the future, remembered that I was an *escritor*, and wondered whether perhaps I might be able to give him some advice about New York publishers. Seems he's been writing short stories. Ciao."

THREE

Autumn Weekend:
The Activist Community

My spring break in Uruguay was almost twenty years ago. Younger, relatively new to human rights activism, I was preoccupied with my own role and with the shifting expectations and relationships which emerged as I carried out a mission largely scripted by others. I should confess, however, that the uncertainty, the tawdry feelings of illegitimacy and ineptitude did not recede much with experience. Whether visiting prisons in the Middle East or attending dissident trials in pretransition Eastern Europe, I remained intensely ambivalent about the work, suspicious of my own engagements. But it has also become clear how rarely humanitarian activism takes the form of a one- — or two- or three- — man show. Humanitarianism is a far broader social activity, and international activism has developed an intense culture of its own. Most of the work is institutional and bu-reaucratic — not knights riding out against an evil world at all. International humanitarianism is staged on a field of institutions great and small — a networked culture of reports, funding, lengthy studies, bureaucratic struggles, and litigation. This culture is relatively new — a sprawling global web of nongovernmental organizations, intergov-ernmental committees, corporate responsibility initiatives, and citizen groups has emerged in the last decades to pursue the work of international humanitarianism.

My relations with Ana in prison became, at least for me, a small imagined community of activist and victim, lawyer and client, figure and ground. As I struggled to build a team with my American colleagues on the mission, we came to know one another through our professional roles, our relations tempered by our engagement with victims and violators. Speaking with Uruguayan officials presented interpersonal dilemmas of whom to criticize or court. Our strategic concerns focused on issues of affiliation, and disaffiliation. Parallel, if less personal, worries about representation and illegitimate intervention have also bedeviled efforts to build a world of humanitarian networks and advocacy institutions. As humanitarian activists build networks to support and carry out their work, sustaining an international plane of action and commitment requires a similar imaginary community among international activists, and also with the world of victims whom they claim to represent and into whose world they seek to intervene. The imaginary community which sustains the international humanitarian network is also shaped by its *remove* from the world of victims and violators, as well as from the normal professional everyday of those now "in" the network. To be networked on the international plane is to be lifted up, set apart, from one's quotidian — and to become part of an establishment of humanitarian activists whose relations with what we might call the "governing establishment" are also marked by tense ambivalence, affiliation and confrontation.

In the fall of 1991, I was present for the establishment of the International Platform of Jurists on East Timor and had the chance to see the birth of a humanitarian nongovernmental organization up close. The Platform — IPJET, as we came to call it — became a participant in the global struggle to bring democracy and independence to East Timor. East Timor had been a Portuguese colony for four centuries until 1975, when Lisbon lost control to a decolonization process that spiraled into a civil war and ultimately into an Indonesian invasion and annexation. It was a brutal occupation — some estimate that in the occupation's early years almost one-third of the population was killed. Beginning in the late seventies, the United Nations passed resolutions calling for talks, and successive Secretaries General held talks with Indonesia and Portugal on the status of the territory. By the early nineties the issue began to be taken up by the nongovernmental humanitarian community as well. A dramatic massacre on November 12, 1991, filmed by foreign journalists, sparked a global outcry and a flurry of grass-roots activism and diplomatic initiative.

By the end of the decade, Portugal and Indonesia had signed a UN-sponsored set of agreements calling for limited autonomy in East Timor. After UN-sponsored elections set off further violence, a peacekeeping force arrived under Security Council mandate in September of 1999. They would lead the territory to independence on May 20, 2002.

During the years of Indonesian rule in East Timor, an ever larger circle of international institutions, national governments, and private humanitarian activists became involved in the effort to do something on behalf of the East Timorese people. That independence was achieved after a period of UN administration counts in most eyes as an enormous success for international humanitarian action and multilateral diplomacy. Whether a better result might have been obtained — less suffering and violence, fewer dead, greater economic progress, lower cost — had other strategies prevailed will require the hindsight of history. It is also very difficult now to share out credit — and blame — among the various political initiatives which together produced this result.

My interest is another one. The early efforts to build a network of international humanitarian institutions capable of participating, in one or another way, in the campaign "for East Timor" offers a window into the process by which the activist community organizes itself for action. The conference to establish an international "Platform" for activism by international jurists concerned about East Timor was a weekend of earnestness about justice and cynicism about politics and the bureaucratic form, a weekend in which all the difficulties of representation and doubts about effectiveness I experienced in Uruguay were given institutional shape, sharpened by awareness of the great distance between law's promise for East Timor and what then seemed its likely performance.

SETTING IT UP

The establishment conference for the Platform, a smudged Xerox affair from the start, unfolded as a cantilevered jumble of lawyers and activists, local and international. As I understand it, the project began with Pedro, a Portuguese lawyer working in the Netherlands as an academic of some sort. Pedro had been interested in East Timor since his days at law school in Lisbon, had written about the human rights violations that had taken place there since the Indonesian occupation, and had identified a network of human rights activists committed to East Timorese self-determination. A former Portuguese colony, East Timor continued to figure in the political imagination of the Portuguese as a nonpartisan and rather distant test site for the nation's honor and humanitarian commitment. It seemed that the struggle for East Timorese liberation might somewhat redeem Portugal's colonial experience, both confirmed (it was the boundary between Dutch and Portuguese administration which distinguished East Timor from the hundreds of other cultures and islands within Indonesia) and cleansed by righteous defense of self-determination and international human rights.

In an elaborate bank shot, Portugal had recently sued Australia in the World Court over Indonesian treatment of East Timor. The legal issues were probably too procedural to ignite the imagination: did Portugal, as the former colonial power, have standing to bring a claim on behalf of the East Timorese? did Australia's entry into a treaty with Indonesia to divide the seabed resources lying between East Timor and Australia give rise to a claim against Australia for recognizing an illegal occupation? And so forth. Nevertheless, it seemed reasonable to establish the Jurists' Platform as a legal person in Portugal, in part to situate international legal work on such issues in a knowledgeable cultural milieu. I quickly discovered that everyone in Portugal, like longtime activists, knew to drop the "East" when referring to Timor. In Portugal, moreover, Pedro could implement his plan for an international institution among old friends.

Pedro's idea for a Jurists' Platform borrowed a leaf from the international nongovernmental human rights community, an assortment of nonprofit foundations, research centers, advocacy groups, and religious organizations. Some of these groups are general, some issue focused, some academic, some litigious, and many are focused in the Netherlands. All circle around the large intergovernmental organizations of the UN system to one degree or another, and most share a number of institutional features: an international membership, an international board, an executive director, a small staff, and so forth.

There is a great deal of overlap among the players in this community — the members of one organization may well be the staff of another and so on. The Platform of Jurists for Timor, as Pedro imagined it, would replicate these features to provide a focal point for what would become "our" activity on behalf of Timor.

To inaugurate the effort, Pedro had worked for over a year to identify potential participants and fund an opening conference. I first heard about his efforts from a former doctoral student of mine at Harvard Law School who had returned to Lisbon to teach international law. Paula had called some months before to ask if I and a colleague from Boston would be willing to come to Lisbon to participate in a conference on East Timor. I had said yes in large part out of friendship and respect for Paula, although I suppose also at least partly because I had never been to Portugal. I should report, in a where-are-they-now spirit, that Dr. Escarameia has gone on to a remarkable career in the international legal profession, recently becoming the first woman to join the International Law Commission.

I had not participated in the institutional network of the international human rights movement for some time, frustrated as I was by the oscillation between private cynicism and public piety that characterized many of the international lawyers and bureaucrats I had met there. My expectation that shared private cynicisms be made public when the solemn declarations were not fulfilled was disappointed often enough that I lost interest. I agreed to go to Lisbon partly to see whether things had changed. Substantial criticism of human rights had reached the academy from the Left and the Right, and I wondered whether it had also reached the activist community, whether there was, or might come to be, a different form of activist culture in the international law. My friends kept telling me the most sophisticated network players were hip to all my doubts — but were they? And if so, might one join with them to raise a more pragmatic and more skeptical voice about the ongoing practices of the movement? As for Timorese self-determination, there seemed many reasons to favor it and little to be said on the other side.

From the vantage point of my Cambridge everyday, there is always, of course, an element of fantasy in such events. For activist missions, there is the fantasy that trips to the site of law's deployment will be magic journeys, full of fabulous characters and novel engagements, escapes from the routines of everyday life in the academy. Establishing an international humanitarian "Platform" might also seem exotic, of course, however routine such moments may in fact have become as international "civil society" adjusts its internal affiliations to accommodate new players and problems. More likely, we all projected the fantasies of exotic engagement forward from the establishment of a Jurists' Platform toward the advocacy for which it was the intended vehicle.

For the advocate, law relates to the "Timor situation" as norms to facts, a simple program for action: international human rights norms are to be translated into everyday practice in Timor. The Platform is intended as the link, the site for advocacy which can bring norms established elsewhere — by a yet wider network expressing the commitments of "the international community" — to bear on the very particular site of their ongoing violation. Here, "Timor." However vague the stilted language of "self-determination" or "human rights" might sometimes seem, the fantasy of law's application in places like Timor frames this abstract vocabulary as something fabulous, even magical: words that can become deeds.

The constitutional moment is always a mystical one, and this fantasy of linking law to life touches the institutional work of establishment whenever it occurs. Thinking about going to Lisbon, I couldn't help feeling that even if I did not participate in the normative mopping up operation of later advocacy, I would have been part of, prior to, the very "Platform" for, whatever activism ensued. At the very least, I must admit, this sort of thing can sometimes be cashed in for political correctness points with students and colleagues.

There is a chronology and a geography to establishment. From the past clarity of normative consensus toward the future of their interpretation, application and enforcement. From the international community, incidentally present by reference in Lisbon, to the very specific location of Timor, incidentally globalized by our work. Lawyers who participate in such work remain divided between the transcendent idealism of their normative vision and the institutional grind of legal practice as well as between the programmatic aspirations of legal institutions and the tedium of doctrinal interpretation or document drafting. And like other professionals, the international lawyer is also a ventriloquist, throwing his legal idealism forward from the realism of his everyday.

Characters in a Jurists' Platform might stabilize these internal fantasies by reference to the ground of a "Timor," the client, the base, the terrain of interpretation, application, sanction, and struggle, perhaps especially to the touchstone of visible violence. This can be prurient, it can be pornographic. The activist arranges his polemics and tactics, his righteousness and his realism, to assure the transparent representation of a struggle at another site, the site of the Timorese everyday. For this, St. Timor in agony must be seen. And we imagine a Timor who returns the gaze, disciplining our work. For the lawyer, the mystically receding client operates as a reader of last resort.

As I look back, the Platform seems a kaleidoscope of form and fancy: lawyers and activists, doctrines and institutions, dreamers and tacticians, all refracted against the backdrop of another country and culture, a Timor beyond the exchange of word and deed. Of course, all this was a bit unfocused on Saturday morning when I arrived in Lisbon. Having had tickets for Natalie Cole the preceding Thursday, I left only on Friday and arrived in Lisbon, after a somewhat disorienting stop in the Azores, just as the conference was starting Saturday morning. The meeting was held upstairs in a downtown religious cinder-block kindergarten from the sixties—ubiquitous papal insignia, institutional walls and food, dozens of Portuguese children. Inside were perhaps a hundred jurists and activists.

THE ENTRANCE

Although Paula reassured me with a wink from the dais, I had the uneasy feeling of arriving in an ongoing conversation among strangers. My cross-cultural anxiety was probably heightened by the fact that they were already there and I was arriving a bit late—and by the unexpected presence of so many Catholic children in what was to have been a project of secular professionalism. As a law professor new to Timor, I imagined the others as committed lawyers and activists, sharing a canon of histories, doctrines, and atrocities that I would come at best to recognize, if not learn, by the end of the conference.

As I walked in, I knew it would have been hard for those already in the room reporting their "work" on Timor not to have had a more immediate and ongoing relationship to Timor-the-conference-topic than I. Although I had asked some students to pull together a packet of legal literature on Timor for me to read before dozing on the plane, I was still pretty vague on the whole issue. In a way, this relative ignorance came naturally to me as a lawyer. Blind justice distinguishes the law from everyday plays of power, passion, and prejudice, and I have often been asked to participate in things because I don't know much about them or haven't written about them. Human rights delegations to places like the Mideast are always looking for someone who appears neutral but whose sympathies can be predicted.

In such events, professionals typically start off serious about roles, loosening ties or removing jackets only later. But what roles exactly? Although the institutional effort was to take place among lawyers, establishing a platform for our future work, and would become in its own small way a bureaucracy, in one way or another we were all also activists, for human rights, for Timor. At the start, roles are uncertain and overlapping. Everyone came from work in other platforms, on other issues. Here they could also network for other causes. I could recruit students for Harvard, meet scholars in whose work I had been interested, do research for an article on the institutionalization of human rights activism. If there turned out to be any Timorese in the room, perhaps I could be their lawyer.

For all that, standing at the threshold, I constituted the group as a whole against my identity as a lawyer, a generalist, an internationalist, above all, someone who legitimately didn't know much about what was to go on. This posture — the general arrives in the specific — brings with it some predictable, even clichéd, resentments: the lawyer not as midwife to justice, but as formalistic distraction from activist passions, agnostic in his commitments, apologetic for imperial power, complicit in things mundane. The first thing we do is kill all the lawyers, et cetera. In defense, of course, one can always just assert the power of the objective, the scientific, the broader reality of an international community, of a law that renders any everyday petty. The lawyer as stand-in for everyone else who is not yet onboard. Or, and hopefully simultaneously, one may search for common ground with activists and specialists in an earnestly shared commitment to our clients in Timor.

As things opened, these potential tensions and alliances remained latent. If things went well, once established, the Platform—like the broader network—would become a skein of differentiated responsibilities, labor divided among activists of many sorts. The keys to smooth future institutionalization seem two: interpersonal connection and shared commitment. It would be the work of the establishment conference to offer us opportunities for both. The difficulty—and the challenge for a well-oiled establishment conference—is the quite different vocabularies in which these take place: interpersonal connection in the key of private cynicism, shared commitment in the key of earnest affirmation. And of course, these vocabularies will not be evenly distributed in the room. Should things go wrong, they might well clash.

The next morning, when I thought we had long since put such things behind us, a peach-skinned activist responded acidly to a lawyer's description of the local disco by mentioning her own evening at a "solidarity meeting." It was a bit rude. But we lawyers could always think of this as naïve, and I suppose they could always think of us as cynical or parasitical. At the outset, anyway, I was reassured that the lawyers were thought needed and had been invited. This was after all to be a Jurists' Platform, constructed as a focal point for legal work on behalf of the Timorese, a site for representation rather than solidarity.

If such differences usually fade only after roles have given way to interpersonal reconciliations that merge private cynicism with shared polemics, sometimes, if only briefly, a more public reconciliation may seem possible. I felt that flicker in the person of Pedro—a charismatic activist-lawyer, mobilizer of the metropolis, link to the periphery, Portuguese and Dutch, at once lawyer and client. He was more than just a role and seemed to yield no purchase for cynical connection. Could we ever be that committed, that certain of our direction? In a way he seemed to have achieved personally what we

hoped to achieve as a group over the course of the weekend together—to become one with our mission and with one another. Perhaps, together in a Platform, we might find the determination and
clarity that eluded us alone.

It seemed right that he should be extremely busy, somehow always
just a bit unavailable, attending to some detail that would keep the
conference afloat, to some dignitary who would grace our meeting
with meaning. It wasn't necessary to speak with him; it was fine that
he was kept busy. It was enough that he was there, had brought us
there, that we were all his guests, his friends. I knew Pedro only as a
name at the end of a fax machine when a good friend of his from the
Netherlands picked me up at the airport. Pedro provided a first conversation for any two arrivals: how had we come to know him?
what was he really like? If he had conceived the Platform to multiply
his advocacy, our goal in joining was also clear: to become more like
Pedro.

THE EARLY WORK OF ESTABLISHMENT

That first morning in the main conference hall, numerous plenary
speakers eloquently described our project as linking Timor with the
outside world by narrowing the gap between the law, with its norms,
and the world of political and social life, with its violations. There
was not yet much talk of the Platform itself—and I was not entirely
clear if it would be a set of propositions as well as an institution. As
activists, with or without a platform, "our" work was to take law to
Timor, while bringing—not Timor itself, of course, but knowledge,
awareness, concern for Timor to the international community. By
about 11:00 A.M. on Saturday morning there seemed to have been
enough speeches along these lines, and speakers turned naturally to
more practical points. It was in this spirit that we would move to our
working groups.

The plenary established a quite general activism as our shared and
public agenda—we had put it on grant applications to fly to Portugal, and we would each promise at least ourselves to do something
about it later. Home, writing up our reports, we would remember

our work at the conference in the terms of these opening flourishes, as itself an instance of law's application to fact. Our common language was not only English. The narrative conventions common to our professional disciplines imagine a world of ongoing pragmatic debate among myriad actors speaking the vocabulary of international law, legitimating and delegitimating one another's claims in a thousand disaggregated moments of persuasion. By having been to Lisbon, talking like this to one another, we had played a part. To talk to one another about law, in the vocabulary of law, to call earnestly for law to be applied elsewhere by other people is to have been part of the transnational legal process itself, in our own small way.

I had come in and sat off to one side just as this first plenary broke into groups to "work" variously on litigation, human rights, education, drafting a constitution for the Platform, and a forgotten fifth topic. Having done the constitution drafting at another such conference some years before, I joined the litigation group, thinking, in the light of the ongoing International Court of Justice case, that it might be more interesting. Besides, the constitution-drafting group seemed a distinctly earnest crew of Pedro's Portuguese acquaintances. The human rights and education groups seemed full of activists who had been on the Timor issue for some time in other contexts and knew one another well. Perhaps I was also shy, and hesitant to get too involved. In any event, I went for litigation.

A few minutes after we started, Pedro pulled me out of my working group for an interview with Portuguese television. Through the authority of expertise, I would establish the Platform in the media somewhat in advance of our own constitution by reference to two vague alternative sites: world public opinion and Timor. A charming reporter said she would have a few questions about the U.S. position on Timor and my sense for the legal issues underlying Portugal's position in the ICJ. Such an interview at this stage would have to be a very generic performance. It would only be later, much later, late the following afternoon at the closing press conference that nuanced expertise, the formal opinions of the Platform, and results of our deliberations would be available to be voiced.

Her cameraman turned on the lights. What was my assessment of the U.S. position on Timor? Looking back on it, I should admit that I had no idea what the U.S. position on Timor might be — where were we on Indonesia these days anyway? I flashed rather unhelpfully on nuclear ships and New Zealand. But even if a lawyer is supposed to be neutral, he is not supposed to be totally in the dark.

I said I had, of course, wished for a more forthcoming attitude from the State Department on Timor (don't they always disappoint), but that in light of the newfound enthusiasm for international law and institutions in Washington (brief invocation of Kuwait, the Berlin Wall, the New World Order) we might see more. This is what made initiatives like that of Portugal in the ICJ all the more timely and important. Did I expect Portugal would win its case? There were certainly a number of crucial procedural hurdles, and the case would need to be pursued diligently, but the importance of the norms involved could hardly be overstated. And so on.

We had to repeat the whole thing with the camera pointing the other way and without sound, so I asked her a number of questions about life in the media, in Portugal. And later that evening, there I was, a talking head — not savvy, it was really too early in my Timorese immersion for that, but on television all the same, dubbed into Portuguese and discussing, somewhat prematurely, the work of the International Jurists Platform for Timor.

I took a quick tour of the working groups — each reflected our activist sentiment. The litigation group was hoping to assist with the ongoing litigation, devising tactics to enforce compliance with legal norms. Perhaps we could get an injunction, or start a shareholders' suit involving some oil company. In the education group, they talked about harnessing the great sanction of public opinion, and they debated the fine points of strategy for public relations. The human rights group would feed the machinery of institutional reporting on human rights. In each group there was talk of Kuwait — why shouldn't the Security Council likewise take Timor in hand and pursue a collective war?

In comparison to the grand opening speeches and the furious moves to engage that typified the working groups, the Platform constitution group did seem self-absorbed, the last refuge of the lawyer's lawyer, the nerd's nerd. Pedro's drafters seemed stuck in a moment before the conference, when it was still necessary to bring us together. But now we were here, talking, *already* doing the work the Platform was meant to support. It was as if Pedro had become too occupied with organizational detail to see the importance of getting on with the substantive work at hand—his enchantment with means blocking his movement to ends.

And yet, fantasizing ourselves already constituted for action—already acting—we also knew that the real work of establishment had not yet begun. Establishing a platform would require more than speeches and shared action fantasies of action. Those speeches were themselves enchanted—while Pedro had gotten on with the actual task at hand. And as we joined him in action, the petty routines and internal relations of our conference world would take over. The media world would fade, and so, for that matter, would Timor. Our earnestness, more public gesture than commitment from the start, would give way to the sharing of private doubts. We would get to know one another, less in the rarified world of the "international community" than in the prosaic world of our Lisbon kindergarten.

But even such a physical place, like the gritty work of constitution drafting, can enchant. Circulating among the working-group rooms which surrounded the plenary session were tables heaped with stray literature. Many participants had apparently brought their reprints, notices of other conferences, Cultural Survival T-shirts, human rights studies, bibliographies, recent publications of the professional press, concert announcements, maps of Lisbon, tourist brochures on the southern beaches. Nothing much was for sale, but the milling crowd gave the plenary an almost mercantile feel. By midafternoon, we knew one another, knew our way around—the place had come to seem like home in its way. And as we came to live ever more in the conference, we would live somewhat less for Timor. By the end, a coincidentally simultaneous massacre in Dili on Timor would barely break into our everyday.

THE PLATFORM TAKES OFF

The social relations that would emerge as by-products of our earnest work for Timor began in unimportant ways—a sharing of pasts, tiny fragments of a shared present, the ride in, the bad coffee, the discovery that my ex-student was the former wife of your government's UN representative, and so forth. We recognized one another in a mutual remove from the client, situating ourselves in a common tactical terrain. We shared a common project, a method, a fantasy of institution building, a process by which to constitute ourselves as a membership with a leadership. Indeed, from our own diverse institutions, nationalities, and professions, we shared Pedro's idea: a council, a secretary-general, a resolution, a preamble, a resolution, points of order, plenaries, working groups, drafting sessions — all the modern technologies.

Was there any conflict not subject to reconciliation in such a pragmatic machine? Our division of labor was expansive, some of us formalists, some administrators, some political tacticians, experts in local or international knowledges, some doctrinal, others more practical. In plenary, one fashionable Latin American woman from New York stood up, feet together in rather high pumps, held her copy of our draft resolution before her and asked if she might make a few suggestions from her experience in the United Nations. Shouldn't our preamble rather say "taking note that," where we had written "deeply deploring that," and shouldn't the operative paragraphs of our resolution be clearly numbered?

As to the second, she was clearly correct. We all knew we should distinguish the perambulatory recitation of norms and facts from the operational engagement with the everyday. Numbering would do the trick, indentation would help. The differences that had separated us — between law and activism, norms and facts — had migrated to a common text where they might, indeed should, be expressed with increased clarity. As to the preambulatory point, we would need to vote. We quickly agreed, voted, to delegate the "taking note"/ "deeply deploring" issue back to the drafting committee for resolution, and having found consensus, we moved on.

What, in our little metropolitan world, had become of Timor, the collective fantasy with which we had kicked off the exercise? At first we heard the Timorese participants speak with the authority of authenticity. For me the moment of transition occurred when I shared a taxi with one Timorese fellow, a young lawyer from Macau on the make, who announced his hope to meet an American lawyer or law professor who might know how one of his clients could purchase a small U.S. bank. Could I help him in this venture, locate such a bank for him, for Timor, for his client whose identity could not be disclosed? My native had abruptly disappeared into professional courtesies and confidentiality. In our little conference spaceship, Timor became a screen on which we could project all manner of common fantasies and anxieties about the real.

To many in the metropolis, of course, this comes as no surprise. When I shared my taxi-ride encounter with a young Canadian friend, he smiled and nodded and we began a friendship. Isn't the client — in a way like the earnest activist, the technical lawyer, indeed, the entire public zone — always a disappointment, an immaturity? We bonded as in-the-know professionals who had come to see the actors in our public spaces and national realities as more or less shrewd manipulations, constructions. In large part, that is what it means to be cosmopolitan, to have transcended the pull of unreasonable local specificities and passions — including the local pieties of global humanitarian action.

Of course this stance can bring cynicism, a corrosive split between private commitment and public realism, public polemics and private doubts. Participants in the international activist milieu often bond around this sort of split, as I did with my Canadian friend. Activists routinely also affiliate with one another by hiding their private sincerity behind a screen of just-you-and-me eye-rolling about the piety of other people's rhetoric. As narrator here, I am also tempted by such multiply split moments. I hope to arrange them, present them, mobilize them, to the right effect. Perhaps readers will share the distance of my observation, feel the plausibility of my account, connect with the author-me in the bemused way one might with a newscaster at a political convention ("Well at this point, Jed, he needs to make a strong appeal to women between thirty-five and fifty-five, yes and here it is, we go now live to the appeal"). Perhaps, when you have finished reading, we will laugh together about the fragility of institutional forms and routines of activist work.

In the metropolis, although we are moved by invocations of the real and the client, and are careful to orient ourselves toward the practical or the redemptive, as representation displaces the represented we find ourselves ambivalent—has our everyday displaced their culture, or has our law finally achieved its relevance for their project? Sometimes the ambivalence seems more than a routinized cynicism, the bonding more than complicit passivity.

This ambivalence was embodied in Portugal for me by a quite urbane and sexy lawyer from an international nonprofit that had styled itself the Unrepresented Nations and Peoples Organization. She seemed smart and savvy, and a new Australian friend and I determined to recruit her for our evolving affinity group. We asked about her organization. They (a small office in The Hague, a "general secretary," three lawyers, a membership, a board, a newsletter) were present for the absent. They had correspondents in Tartu and San Francisco. Although they had recently lost three clients (Estonia, Latvia, and Lithuania), they hoped for continued Baltic financial support out of solidarity with all the places where boundaries, nations, ethnicities, tribes, or governments had been insufficiently coordinated to perfect the transparency of international representation through statehood.

It was noble work, rendered more palpably significant, if strangely doubled, by the lawyer's assertion that she was herself unrepresented. As I recall her account, she had come from a minority ethnic group in Bangladesh, or perhaps Pakistan, grown up the child of diplomats, become a lawyer, worked for a big Washington law firm, and then moved to Holland, where she had been representing the unrepresented now for almost a year. She told her story with a light ironic touch that made it impossible to respond with either earnest relief that the unrepresented had found their spokeswoman or with doubt about why this form, why here, why her?

I liked her immediately and when we discussed the work of her education group over lunch, I proposed that her organization sponsor a gigantic blimp, like Goodyear, which would travel around the world labeled with one or another unrepresented people, tethered outside the Olympics or the Clarence Thomas hearings, wherever. Others joined in as we developed a comprehensive blimp-based program for human rights protection. She wrote me some months later to ask whether I had encountered any "blimps hanging outside campus," and reported that "I went off to Estonia for a conference on Population Transfer, which was quite an experience. Very interesting place. There was something surrealistic about Tallinn, reminded me a bit of that weird bar we went to in Lisbon. Which was lots of fun." She was a cosmopolitan all right.

Was this cynicism or irony, destructive or delicious? The routinization of enthusiasm, too many hours together in a small building, we looked to one another for hints of private doubt, small islands of relief from earnestness. A Scotsman who seemed in working group to have memorized the procedural details of every ICJ case for his dissertation turned out to be an extremely ironic devotee of British punk culture. He joined our clique and followed up on our acquaintance in Lisbon with a package of trashy British comics.

At lunch, smoking by the tennis court, drinking with age cohorts, national cohorts, private in-groups, we recognized with a wink or a chortle that our public idealism would not be supported by the realism of our common projects. We entered the zone of flirtation. Of course this brought with it a turn away from the public narrative of law engaging the Timorese everyday, a turn from activism to narcissism. True enough. There emerged the tawdriness of all conferences everywhere. If we could bring law to bear on Timor together, wouldn't we also sleep with one another? Indeed, who would sleep with whom, who would befriend whom, who would promote, hire, help whom? Who would reveal their loneliness, exasperation, sexual orientation?

How can laughter in Lisbon be defended when people were being slaughtered in Timor? We could say it's only human, that we should blame the naïve idealism of our common project, that laughter is the best medicine. Perhaps it is efficient — it might be just these social strands, the laughs and worries of the professional everyday, more than our textual productions, which would hold us together after the conference closed. In this, the promise of the social and the sexual functioned itself as an idealism, an aspiration, a promise. And I hoped, if only vaguely, that more might come of our affinity cohort than it seemed possible to expect from the official working groups.

This growing private social sensibility offset the sensible, if sterile, formality of our public debates. As the social verged into cliché, the conference plodded along its familiar route: introductory exhortation, working groups, working-group reports to the plenary, work-

ing groups, plenary to adopt constitution and resolutions, press conference, social event. Every meeting begins with a recollection of past
work and ends with a promise of work to come, two moments that
pull us back from the sexual to the social and render the private
cynical. Indeed, this is the very function of the agenda.

At one point my litigation working group flagged, wandered on
the patio, suspended in the idea of litigation, having been unable to
identify anyone actually working on any actual case. We were left
only with duty to the meeting, remoteness from our own individual
everydays, and goodwill for the ultimate cause. We traded anecdotes,
discussed the weather, and experienced our situation as confusion
about the agenda. We asked one another who had brought the agenda.
We waited for leadership and were quite good-naturedly ready to
follow anyone with a plan.

And along came a young Australian lawyer whom we told about
our lack. She sprang into action, jotted a few notes, urged us to
return to the meeting room, and simply began the meeting, intoning
in the flat locution of all UN debate everywhere that it would be
good to begin with a restatement of where we had been, and sure
enough everything each of us had half-mentioned the day before re-
appeared as a subject discussed, an observation made, a point taken.
In the passive voice of recounting we became alive as a collective.
What, we wondered, would she have for us for today? And she posed
some issues, and we threw them about, and she did it again, and
now we were in a hurry, needed to get our report together for the
plenary, and off we went to hear from the other working groups.

When we got there, there wasn't time for our report, but it hardly
mattered. As a plenary we needed to work on our resolution and our
constitution, prepare for the press conference. We didn't want to
waste time reporting what had, after all, already been accomplished
in the working groups. As it turned out, only the constitutional group
really needed to report.

A CONSTITUTED LIFE

When we look back on the Platform's establishment as an institutional narrative, we focus on the final moments, when the constitu-

tion drafters returned with their document. But inside the conference, focusing on our substantive accomplishments and objectives, the constitution drafters had come to seem quite beside the point, the terms of our constitution almost trivial, the procedural disputes predictable. Every platform must apparently have a council, every conference must pass a resolution — regardless of the terrain upon which law acts, these are its points of access. And so we re-created here in the Platform our own model UN, complete with compulsory geographic distribution — for shouldn't the seats on the Platform's Council be distributed among the continents? As soon as it was proposed, we knew it had to be so. And we had one African, one European, one Latin American, one Asian, and, before someone forgot, one Timorese. Even, we were pleased, or surprised, or bemused, someone from the world's largest democracy.

Nevertheless, we focused our determination increasingly on texts, the most practical suggestion often a textual one, as in the case of our dignified Latin American UN delegate. We revised resolutions, elected a board, published polemics, committed to doctrinal interpretations, rendering our experience more visible, also to our own memories. The leadership had the constitution read out by a jovial legal activist, bringing our international locutions alive in his somewhat ironic English translation. There were a few open questions. Were corporations to become members, for example, would they receive extra votes in the Council? All this seemed secondary, legal, the usual technical details, and the urge in the plenary to delegate these issues back to the committee or to vote quickly (either would do) was irresistible. By Sunday afternoon there were too many issues to deal with, each crowding for the plenary's attention. We would soon need to face the press again, this time mobilized into a platform with a resolution. Time in our little world had sped up.

In a way this acceleration was precisely the point — as we moved through stages of mutual recognition and institution building, each hour had seemed suspended, filled with new people, new institutional developments. In such a small space, by the end of the first day the gossip circle could run a full round in well less than an hour. Each hour would find us days, even centuries, ahead of the last in the evolution of our common everyday. We had been strangers, now we almost had a constitution; we had been normative, now we were almost pragmatic; we had been generalists, now we were almost specialists. The acceleration of centuries had slowed the conference to a snail's pace.

By the end of the weekend, we each thought increasingly of our return home, to what seemed a jumbled fusion of two scenes — the scene of our origin, the workplace realities from which we had come to the conference, and the scene of Timor, the object of our endeavors. The two had become somehow fused, or been confused, in the course of the weekend. Here, we were being productive, enjoying one another, liking our jobs. Somehow, after it was over, we would have been changed, would be Timor activists and members of a platform. That, after all, is the point of an establishment conference, a great collective pleasure in the name of empathy, a culture of representation which held out Timor as aspiration, a promise of pragmatism, where our work would have bite, effect, relevance. Like successful conferences everywhere, we would end with a call for action. The idea that "we" would be carrying on "work," each in our own way, on behalf of Timor had become a collective fantasy, at once insistent and worrisome. Indeed, I suspect that only those already dedicated, enacting the resolutions of some earlier establishment, could think about their own workplace realities and Timor without anxiety.

Late in the conference, these underlying doubts and shared anxieties came to rest on Pedro and the constitution drafters. Looking back on it late Sunday, it seemed I had felt uneasy about them all along: five somewhat somber Portuguese men of indeterminate age, suits right out of the Chicago twenties. I wondered what they were putting together for us. Why had Pedro really brought us here? He seemed so earnest about it all, so insistent, more serious across a year's work than we could maintain even for two days. Why didn't he participate in the tiny flirtations of the weekend. Was he really that busy? If it had been somewhat reassuring on arrival to find someone who so clearly knew what we were supposed to do, now it seemed almost ominous. What if we didn't live up to our platform, couldn't bring law to the everyday, if our everyday could never be as unified with Timor as his had become? Would we still get our travel money?

Pedro and his friends had an experience different from the removed disputations of the working groups on education, litigation, or human rights. Their reality was here, with us, however much Pedro sought to project the moment of establishment into the past, onto our agreement to come, or into the future of our rather open-ended commitments to cooperate. He was not promising to be pragmatic; he was being pragmatic. Our indulgent pleasures were his empathy. Our groups had done less well; some had not even found it necessary to report. The human-rights group had foundered on what seemed a choice between the self-determination and human rights "approaches" to Timor, the education group boldly decided to establish an as-of-yet-unfunded prize for student writing on Timor. At best we projected future action, contented ourselves that the purpose of our being together was fulfilled by the establishment of the Platform by the work of the constitution group. As everywhere, talk is suspicious of action.

And to some extent, we had become cynical. By the final plenary, I found myself in an ad hoc affinity group with my Boston colleague, our Scottish, Canadian, Australian, and unrepresented friends and a few other young law professors. We had become the only mobilized group in the meeting other than the team of would-be founding fathers. Although generally earnest in group, we had become caustic in private and could be off-putting. A young German woman who seemed desperate for an alternative public rhetoric, frustrated by the law's increasing distance from her own fantasy of contact with the Timorese everyday, nonetheless found our alternative corrosive, biting, impolite, unhelpful.

She was right to be worried. To my mind, the most likely direction for our group would be simply to abstain from the main action of the Platform and enjoy the hilarity of voting on one after another detailed amendment or proposal, modern spectator participants in a social contract repeated now as farce. We would then go home, remembering pleasant private times but without more than the old earnestness to link us professionally with Timor. The question for this group seemed whether any sense of personal commitment to the cause could survive the private cynicism of activism in these tired institutional and doctrinal forms. Pedro was also right to be worried.

Pedro balked at the idea that some of us might not wish to "join" the Jurists' Platform. Had we not always already joined, by coming? I began to fear that we were all in Timor for the duration.

I had tried once over lunch to connect with the German woman. Couldn't she see us as a symptom of a frustration she must surely share? I hoped she would teeter between the temptations of the discipline and joining us in recognizing the truth of her own experience. The latter seemed too scary, without direction. What was our little group, where was our commitment, what was our program? As it happened, we seemed in control of the plenary voting and were careening madly from one position to another—table that, adopt that, reject that, allying now with one, now with another faction, with Paula still chairing the meeting, with the Director of the Unrepresented, our friend's boss, and so forth. It was fun.

Somewhat offhandedly, as we debated our final resolution, I made a proposal of my own. In part, I thought it might link us back to the group as a whole. And in part it might disrupt the proceedings sufficiently to throw those who would constitute us off their guard. I stood up and made a little speech, proposing that we delete the carefully numbered operative paragraphs in our resolution, following the concerns of our preamble with the statement "1. express our frustration at the limitations of traditional institutional and doctrinal means of addressing our concerns."

I argued that we might thereby leave a mark in the public space of an experience we had shared, an experience of exhaustion, boredom, frustration. Didn't we all feel worn out by the prospect of yet another resolution from some international institution? Hadn't we all been here before? Rather than allow the parallel narratives of public speech and private pleasure to resume their separate paths after we leave, rather than find our doubts disciplined into fealty to a common program, I proposed acknowledging the social experience of our weekend together and learning to live as international legal activists for Timor without the dream (or the excuse) of a law that might be brought to bear for social change.

It was a quixotic moment. I hadn't done the work necessary to mobilize my constituency nor to lay the groundwork for such a suggestion. And I had formulated the proposal so awkwardly that many heard only an exhortation to renewed earnestness — and found it moving. I don't think anyone thought our formal resolution would "have an effect," or that the institution we constituted would be much beyond a shell within which Pedro would raise money to carry on whatever activism he had already begun. Still, unable to think of anything else to do, it seemed absurd to abandon our standard operating procedure. We unanimously adopted the resolution as originally drafted and opened the meeting to a press conference on our conclusions. When the plenary was over, my Boston colleague and I were vaguely down. Perhaps we had been too seduced by cynicism, or immobilized by jet lag, to render our faction effective as a cultural alternative to the Platform's closing pieties. We resolved to strategize more self-consciously in the future — perhaps we could build a cosmopolitan culture outside the clichés of private irony and public activism.

The weekend ended that evening with a collective excursion to see native Timorese folk dancing: gestural primitivism. I passed it up for dinner with friends. The next day I intended to rent a convertible and ride around the Portuguese hills with an old friend and a bottle of wine. The conference would slowly recede into the background. We would come to take it for granted, see its petty social dimensions, its anxieties and erotics as part of our individual private and professional lives, its institutional achievements part of the broader constellation of human rights machinery grown up around the discipline of international law. This had been one weekend in the world of international humanitarian activism: by turns pragmatic, earnest, and cynical. Whatever possibilities our psychosocial dynamics had opened for a renewal we had not managed to exploit.

I still get the occasional jaunty card from one or the other Platform friend. I didn't think I'd ever hear much more about Timor. For a couple of years, I received notices for solidarity demonstrations and sporadic reports on IPJET Council doings. When Timor lept onto the front pages some years later, I lost track of IPJET. And then, a few months after Timorese independence, I got a message from Pedro. IPJET was moving on — "the People of Western Sahara needs urgently our support" — did I want to join in?

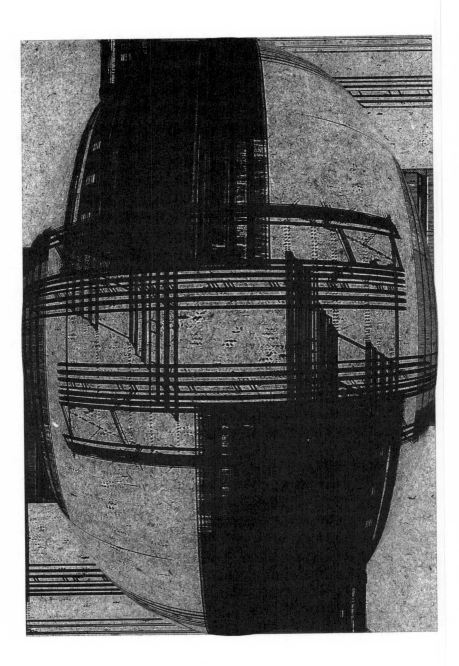

PART II The International Humanitarian as Policy Maker

FOUR

Humanitarian Policy Making: Pragmatism without Politics?

International policy making now affects most every domain in which the contemporary welfare state is active. Indeed, the globalization of policy making may be the most significant change in the structure, site and substance of political culture since the consolidation of the nation state as the primary arena for popular politics a century or more ago. Numerous global policy initiatives have sprung from humanitarian motives, often with compelling results in such areas as arms control, international criminal law, economic development, environmental protection, health and safety, immigration and refugee affairs, labor policy and more.

The outsider posture of critical judgment and denunciation which so often characterizes humanitarian activism is less prevalent when humanitarian policy initiatives are promoted at the international level. In the policy process, humanitarians speak less as representatives of particular clients than as participants in governance who are particularly attuned to humanitarian interests or values. They often speak the pragmatic language of consequences and cost/benefit calculations which can be so difficult to encourage among those accustomed to the more absolutist rhetorics of activism and advocacy.

We should evaluate humanitarian policy making as we would other governance projects — through careful assessment for particular initiatives of the costs and benefits, likely risks, outcomes and distributional consequences for various groups. And humanitarian policy making is prone to the same difficulties as policy making everywhere — underestimating costs, overestimating benefits, over or under estimating the effects of rule changes, overlooking secondary costs, foreshortening time horizons, hyperbole in discussing the pros and cons of proposals, underestimating the plasticity of rules and institutions to appropriation and reinterpretation.

Careful pragmatism about international humanitarian policy initiatives nevertheless remains elusive. For one thing, the water is muddied by very general — and altogether unhelpful — arguments for embracing or rejecting international policy making wholesale; like the idea that internationalization is technically or historically inevitable, or that some problems simply *are* global and therefore require international policy solutions. Or, on the other side, the argument that humanitarianism requires national boundaries and a national welfare state to be successful.

As with humanitarian activism, moreover, it is easy to overstate the humanist potential of international policy making. Many of the difficulties we encountered with human rights activism arise equally in humanitarian policy-making campaigns. Policy makers can also overlook the dark sides of their work and treat initiatives which take a familiar humanitarian form as likely to have a humanitarian effect. It is always tempting to think *some* global humanitarian effort has got to be better than none. Like activists, policy makers can mistake their good intentions for humanitarian results or enchant their tools — using a humanitarian vocabulary can itself seem like a humanitarian strategy. We conclude too easily that international law, say, is a good thing and that more of it addressed to refugee affairs, disarmament, or environmental protection would be humanitarian. It is all too easy to forget that saying "I'm from the United Nations and I've come to help you" may not sound promising at all.

Like the activist initiatives we have considered, policy pragmatism can be thrown off by the blind spots and biases in the professional vocabularies we use to formulate humanitarian initiatives. These distortions can sometimes be brought to light through analysis of the presuppositions common to a policy-making profession — the deformations introduced by the training of an international lawyer, an economist, or a diplomat. More often, people from different professions will come to think about policy in a given field in related ways. Their shared common sense about what does and does not "work" can affect policy making at something like the wholesale level, skewing the approach taken to a range of issues. I am particularly interested in the difficulties which arise when such a policy-making vocabulary comes to dominate the imagination of people working to bring about humanitarian results in a given area.

A policy-making vocabulary can dominate thinking about policy initiatives in a given field for years at a time. For example, during the 1950s and 1960s, policy professionals around the world approached third world economic development in quite similar terms. Development economists provided a template for understanding what "underdevelopment" was and how it could be overcome. Dozens of countries implemented astonishingly similar national policies of import substitution industrialization. Within the vocabulary elaborating and defending these regimes, there were endless technical disputes about how to proceed, as well as political debates about the meaning and content of import substitution industrialization. In the end, there were import substitution regimes of the right, of the left, and of the center. But for thirty years, everyone was playing with the same deck of cards. In the 1970s and 1980s, a new set of economic and political ideas emerged which defined "underdevelopment" quite differently and proposed a completely different mix of policies. This new vocabulary — "neoliberalism" — was taken up in different ways by the center, the right, and the left. Again there were technical disputes — but we also soon found regimes across the globe pursuing policies developed and defended in astonishingly similar terms.

The chapters which follow analyze broad policy-making vocabularies which have been used to pursue humanitarian objectives at particular moments in four areas — economic development, refugee affairs, the extension of market democracy to former socialist states, and the effort to render warfare less frequent and less violent. In each area, I focus on the policy initiatives which captured the imagination of a particular group of professional policy makers for a period of time, and on the common vocabulary they used to formulate, defend and dispute their policy ideas.

In the area of economic development, I examine one prominent vocabulary developed over the last decade or so in the wake of "neo-liberalism." Policy makers interested in economic development have increasingly promoted the "rule of law" as an antidote to under-development. People developing policy initiatives in the rule-of-law vocabulary differ about the technical details—the relative impor-tance of different institutions, the precise laws which need imple-mentation, the sequencing of various components—and rule-of-law projects have been pursued across the political spectrum from left to right. In the next chapter, I explore the blind spots and biases which are common to rule-of-law ideas about development across these technical and political differences. Chapter 6 then looks more deeply at the vocabulary used by policy makers associated with the Euro-pean Union as they sought to extend democracy and the market to Eastern and Central Europe after the fall of the Berlin Wall in 1989, and traces assumptions about the nature of economic and political progress and about the political geography of Europe which skewed their efforts to pursue humanitarian objectives in the former Soviet east.

The policy vocabulary used by international lawyers to define and protect refugees—the subject of the following chapter—has re-mained quite stable since the Second World War. The same period has seen dramatic changes in the nature of refugee flows addressed by the United Nations High Commissioner for Refugees and other international policy makers. Their efforts to respond to widely diver-gent refugee situations has rendered this common professional vo-cabulary increasingly elaborate—but has not changed its basic as-sumptions. If anything, doctrinal hairsplitting has eclipsed efforts to develop more imaginative and pragmatic responses to new refugee flows.

In each of these cases, I am concerned to identify common as-sumptions or terms of reference which blind policy makers to the consequences of their effort, preventing them from viewing their ini-tiatives with cool, pragmatic eyes. But even when humanitarians are able to work pragmatically, disenchanting their tools and entering the instrumental cost/benefit world of modern policy making at its best, problems can remain. The professional vocabulary developed by those seeking to humanize and eliminate warfare over the last century—the discourse of "humanitarian law"—provides the opportunity to explore this sort of difficulty. Policy makers have sought to merge the vocabulary of humanitarian restraint into the strategic calculations of military strategists themselves. In chapter 8, I consider the darker consequences of what must also be counted as a triumph for pragmatic humanitarian policy making at the international level.

In analyzing these specific policy campaigns, a rough list of typical distortions professional vocabularies can bring to policy-making initiatives will be useful. This chapter identifies ideas which hinder a pragmatic assessment of the costs and benefits of global policy making. The list I develop here is not original—each of these difficulties is familiar to policy makers. Indeed, policy makers spend a great deal of time criticizing *other people's* initiatives in just these terms. Nevertheless, it is surprising how often humanitarians embark on policy-making campaigns without a careful assessment of these potential difficulties.

LOOKING FOR POLITICS EVERYWHERE BUT IN THE HUMANITARIAN VERNACULAR

People pursuing humanitarian policy initiatives on the international stage tend not to imagine themselves making political choices or generating consequences which would make a careful pragmatism seem necessary. Like many other policy makers, international humanitarians think of themselves as intervening only exceptionally and technically. They *advise* the prince, they *interpret* or *apply* political decisions taken elsewhere, they *implement* the wisdom of "best practice." These postures encourage all policy makers to underestimate their own political responsibility and potential.

The common idea that intervention is a periodic and exceptional activity encourages neglect of the policy-maker's baseline engagement in the status quo ante and discourages careful assessment of the costs and benefits of doing nothing. These familiar tendencies are sharply heightened at the international level, where it can be easy to think one is not implicated in things happening far away unless and until one has "intervened." More than that, international humanitarians share the perplexing sense that efforts to influence matters in faraway places are not normally legitimate — that international governance, where necessary, *should be* exceptional, temporary, should require a special justification, and, when undertaken, should seek to leave local culture and politics as undisturbed as possible. As a result, humanitarians search for neutral and temporary modes of policy making which mute attention to political consequences and can fail to arouse a sense of responsibility.

When we do think about politics or seek to attribute responsibility for the consequences of our policy making, we tend to look in all the wrong places. When we are unhappy about the outcomes of humanitarian work, we often speak as if hostile forces had somehow captured the policy-making machinery or aborted the implementation of good ideas. This can certainly happen. But a more pragmatic humanitarianism requires a sharper focus on the political effects of the background work done by humanitarian policy professionals themselves — of our own policy vocabulary.

Mistaking Structures for Outcomes

Pragmatic assessment of international policy making gets off the track when it focuses on the structure for, rather than the outcomes of, global governance. Getting governance right — the right mix of centralization and decentralization, appropriate schemes for representation, decision making, transparency, dispute settlement — can certainly be important. Too often, however, humanitarians gets sidetracked in debate over these structural issues — and treat structural outcomes as guarantors and substitutes for humanitarian results.

The clearest example is also the most common — the humanitarian preference for multilateralism. As the military effort against Al Qaida began, international lawyers were adamant that captured prisoners be tried before international tribunals — without feeling the need to articulate an assessment of the consequences of doing so. Would this increase or decrease terrorist activity, strengthen or weaken the military effort, produce faster or slower trials, more or less respect for a defendant's rights? Would this strengthen or weaken humanitarian institutions? Promote or discourage respect for humanitarian values? Thereafter, humanitarians concerned about U.S. policy toward Iraq repeatedly called for multilateral decision making — without saying much about the likely outcomes, beyond the common presumptions that multilateralism makes war less likely or that multilateral intervention means *less* intervention. But these are only presumptions — unexplored commitments which function as substitutes for pragmatic analysis. We know now what happened — but it was striking before the fact how readily opponents sought to substitute debate over the forum for debate over the war itself. Seen a priori, there was no reason to assume multilateral policy making would be more or less interventionist — let alone more or less humanitarian.

Humanitarians often treat a structural preference as a stand-in for a preferred outcome. Arguing that an issue *can only* be handled internationally often substitutes for the idea that a particular humanitarian solution seems possible only at the international level. It is common, for example, to assert that "the environment" requires international policy making. Yet a policy of unrestrained local environmental exploitation could be pursued perfectly adequately without resort to overt international policy making. Environmentalists insist on international policy making when they share the intuition that the policies adopted there will turn out, in fact, to be more environmentally friendly.

Pragmatic thinking requires that these background intuitions be articulated and evaluated. What are the environmental consequences of not intervening? What alternatives are, in fact, available at the local or regional level? Treating the absence of international policy making as if there were no policy at all makes such an assessment extremely difficult to make. At the same time, the false contrast of "international policy" and "no policy" makes it easy to overestimate the humanitarian — or environmentally friendly — nature of international policy making. Yet more international environmental policy may not mean more environmental protection. Collusion with industry to depress environmental standards is also possible when governments act together. Indeed, industry interests may be more disproportionately represented in international forums than domestically.

Sometimes, of course, structural questions do affect outcomes in predictable ways. Take labor policy. The current arrangement of national and international rules, prohibitions, permissions, and enforcements—about sovereignty, about jurisdiction, about trade, about contracting and ownership and labor association—effects a global labor policy, raising some wages and lowering others. When humanitarians argue for an *international* or *multilateral* labor policy, they have in mind more aggressive top-down regulation to raise wages for some workers through stricter enforcement of at least formally universal norms, at some cost to other workers, consumers, or investors. Perhaps such top-down labor regulation can now better be pursued internationally than nationally. It certainly is true that the broad consensus among humanitarians that this is what international labor policy must mean ensures that little else will be attempted.

As a result, however, the fight for international labor policy distracts us from more interesting inquiries into alternative strategies at the national and international levels. Campaigns for international declarations and codifications always threaten to substitute for the more difficult work of implementation and may even make improvement in local labor conditions more difficult to achieve. Focus on building an international labor policy of top-down regulation—giving the WTO a "social charter," drafting conventions on child labor—also distracts us from inquiring into the background rules—of jurisdiction, trade, contract, property—which make national regulation so difficult. For example, we tend not to ask whether U.S. labor protections might be extended extraterritorially on the model of antitrust. Nor do we explore other modes of international labor regulation which might be available. We do not explore the potential for using national and international "fair trade" laws and institutions to challenge labor regimes as subsidies, nontariff barriers, or dumping practices. Focus on structures—international rather than national—and hesitance about intervention quiets the habit of assessing consequences and dissuades humanitarians from developing alternative national and international policy alternatives.

Blaming — or Praising — the Hammer

A related difficulty arises when humanitarians regard particular policy tools — treaties rather than statutes, courts rather than diplomats — as surrogates for humanitarian outcomes. International humanitarians all too often come to think of their tools — multilateral declarations, documents, institutional networks — as having a kind of inherent humanitarian potency. And the commitment to *more* global governance fuels enthusiasm to develop and test drive new techniques. This tendency to enchant our tools should make us wary — it often comes at a cost to analysis of the substantive results of their use.

It is easy to see that in the choice between, say, treaties and statutes, everything will depend on the political context. It is notoriously difficult to enforce a treaty against a state not committed to its enforcement, and we can readily imagine a strong national statute in a leading economy having more international effect than any likely treaty. But we are also familiar with relatively weak treaties being favorably received by local elites and strictly enforced. Vague treaties enforced by humanitarian judges or officials may be preferable to strong statutes passed by legislative bodies with different priorities. And so forth. Advocates of international humanitarianism certainly know this — but they are very prone to forgetting it.

All too often, a default preference for some policy tools over others substitutes for more careful analysis. An international court to try those who commit genocide may well be a good idea, but analysis of the political consequences of its use — either in particular cases or more generally — has been hard to find. Repeatedly, international humanitarians find themselves proposing the *same* tool for a wide range of problems — in the 1950s every global problem needed a specialized UN agency; in the 1990s each attracted its own array of nongovernmental interest groups. The rush to expand visible tools and techniques can encourage us to underestimate opportunities to turn background norms and practices to humanitarian ends. And it stills the pragmatic habit of comparing the tools used at different times or for different problems with one another. Why, for example, do international humanitarians confront human rights abuses with

rules and environmental harms with broader principles and standards? There may well be excellent reasons, but the rush to codify
rights in the one case and to declare principles in the other largely
substituted for a pragmatic—and comparative—assessment of
either.

Most significantly, the focus on the policy-making tools can distract us from the role of ideas in global governance. Global governance is not simply an activity of rules, principles, and the institutions to implement them. It is also importantly an activity of spirit.
More than the sum of public law analogs replicating the functions of
national governments, the international "system" is an activity of
lawyers, economists, political scientists, bureaucrats, civil servants,
street protesters, entrepreneurs, media moguls, and businessmen in
thousands of locations who share a commitment to international
policy making. These people might work for the great international
governmental bureaucracies, but they are equally likely to be found
in national governments, in private enterprises, in nongovernmental
organizations, in the media, in universities or in the streets.

Wherever they are located, these people propose, accept, expect,
hope for, resist, yield to, and interpret the internationalization of social and economic policy, and their shared consciousness is more important in setting the terms and extent of global governance than the
formal powers or presence of the international policy making machinery. Consequently, international policy making is the collective
practice and consciousness of a people—not the people of a nation,
but the people (from central bank presidents to grass-roots campaigners) of the diffuse cosmopolitan and international space. Theirs
is the "consciousness of an establishment," and the politics of global
governance will be their collective politics. When humanitarians focus
on the tools of public regulatory authority, they miss the chance to
contest that shared common sense.

Body Snatchers: The Distracting Politics of Capture

Of course humanitarian policy makers are not altogether blind to
assessment of the political consequences of their ideas—it's not all

structures and tools. But our vocabulary for assessing the politics of humanitarian commitments is far too limited. The shared belief that the tools for humanitarian policy making, like the policy makers themselves, are either benign or humanitarian in their own right makes it all to easy to assume that if there are unexpected or negative consequences, it must be the result of the policy-making apparatus having been distorted, captured, or misused. Sometimes, of course, the global policy-making machinery is influenced by people who do not share humanitarian objectives. Some policy makers are ideologically or politically committed partisans. And the international policy-making machinery often does fail to hear one or another voice or position. When policy making has been captured in this sense, it should be a matter of concern to humanitarians.

The difficulty arises when suggestions of capture crowd out investigation of the consequences of humanitarian policy making itself — of our vocabulary and our activity. Claims that policy making has been captured are always difficult to sustain. Even if the global policy process were not so complex, it would be difficult to link policy alternatives decisively with specific political interests — what *is* in the interests of capital or labor, of the first world or the third? To formulate an answer is to enter the realm of international policy making itself, attuned to perverse effects, reverse interpretations, unexpected costs and benefits. To make policy is precisely to distribute among groups; claims of "capture" are often simply ways of disagreeing with the policies which have been made. But they are also ways of sustaining the humanitarian's own image as in some way outside this sort of distributional politics.

When international humanitarians do reflect on the politics of their ideas, they often do so in a similar vocabulary of capture — worrying that their professional sensibility (or that of their opponents) has been compromised by an a priori commitment to a fashionable doctrine, policy, or method. This does happen, blunting the ability to assess humanitarian initiatives pragmatically. For example, development policy-making experts were bullish for years about import substitution before turning en masse to neoliberal policies of privatization and world prices. While under the grip of each enthusiasm, it would be fair to say that the development-policy profession was not able to embody the breadth of its own expertise. In a similar way, before the Second World War, international policy makers routinely approached ethnic conflict with minority rights and assimilation. After 1945, they switched to self-determination and population transfer, only to reverse again after 1989.

Methodological commitments certainly can skew the ability to assess humanitarian commitments pragmatically. Humanitarian policy makers can become committed to a school of thought — in economics, in law, in political science — and resolve choices among policy alternatives by defaulting to the option which seems to exemplify their methodological commitment — to positivism, naturalism, neoclassicism, institutionalism, formalism or antiformalism. Even in disciplines with vigorous methodological debate, policy choices more often reflect the status of forces among theoretical combatants — the relative strength of theoretical sects — than pragmatic assessments of the appropriate solution to specific practical problems. I think Americans who complain that the international policy-making machinery is too formalist or too "European" in its attitudes about law have something like this in mind. As do national policy makers who claim that the European Central Bank has been captured by economists who overestimate the threat of inflation and underestimate the threats of recession, or third world policy makers who charge that international financial institutions have been captured by neoliberal supply-siders.

In my experience, however, this sort of doctrinal or theoretical capture is less common than it often seems. The practical consequences of one or another methodological commitment are extremely difficult to pin down. Policy alternatives which seem stark turn out to be more nuanced, to have room for more than one methodological commitment. The policy choices against which the discipline is said to have closed its eyes turn out to be present in mainstream thinking. It turns out that within "free market" ideas there lurks an exception for situations of "market failure," which can be interpreted in broad or narrow terms. Making out a case for bias requires saying quite a bit more about how policy makers resolve the various choices internal to such a general policy or methodological choice — how broadly they interpret "market failure," for example. Even then it remains difficult to demonstrate the consequences. A "free market" policy could turn out, if properly structured, to be more friendly to "workers" than its "socialist" alternative.

Nevertheless, there is no question that a priori theoretical commitments can reduce the range of policy tools available. Or that humanitarians, like other policy makers, can become mired in debate between methodological positions which are increasingly divorced from any analysis of outcomes. The difficulty lies here — the effort to root out a priori commitments can push policy makers toward endless methodological debate. Each accuses the other of capture, rendering the opposing position in stark theoretical or methodological terms, and both become detached from analysis of the consequences — and opportunities — for action. Both underestimate the ambivalences and exceptions within the contending schools of thought that open the window for more diverse policy commitments. To suggest that one or another method automatically expresses humanitarian — or anti-humanitarian — interests is less to diagnose methodological capture than to be methodologically captured.

Professions nevertheless do have blind spots — and humanitarians are no exception. It is easy to think of classic examples. Lawyers are said to be too litigious and try to solve things with rules; economists worry only about what's efficient; those in business worry only about the short-term bottom line; military officers always want more hardware and are too prone (or not prone enough) to use it. Nobody seems professionally responsible for ethics or values; everyone over-discounts the future or too sharply privileges the past. When violence breaks out, it makes a difference whether one sends lawyers, doctors, soldiers, priests, therapists, or aid specialists to respond.

If we focus only on lawyers involved in humanitarian initiatives, however, much will depend on which lawyers one has in mind. Public international lawyers do seem to see a world of states, worry about how law can be possible among sovereigns, focus on avoiding the trauma of war, reach out to political science for inspiration, and seek to strengthen global governance. International economic lawyers, by contrast, seem to see a world of would-be buyers and sellers, worry about how the risks to trade can be contained, focus on avoiding economic depression, reach out to economics for inspiration, and seek to strengthen free trade. There is no doubt these disciplines think about an issue like international labor policy very differently. For an international lawyer, the problem will be a lack of governance capacity and a need for norms and institutions to ensure compliance with them. International labor policy will mean a network of international legal rules and standards and enforcement machinery. For an international economic lawyer, the problem will be the transformation of different national conceptions of normal labor practices into arguments for restricting trade. Producing against the background of a different national legal regime can seem like an "unfair" trade advantage. International labor policy will mean a process for adjusting, diffusing, coordinating such claims in ways which will not unduly impede trade flows. The policies which result from thinking about labor in these different ways may well differ dramatically.

As with political or methodological capture, however, it is terribly difficult to link these disciplinary focal points convincingly to outcomes. And it is easy to underestimate the flexibility to be found within each discipline. Are military professionals too prone, or not prone enough, to use force? Economists turn out to have a vocabulary for internalizing factors that noneconomists tend to think of as matters of "value" rather than matters of "efficiency, " just as lawyers have a vocabulary for criticizing and limiting reliance on rules or litigation, broadening exceptions, promoting alternative dispute resolution, structuring administrative discretion and understanding the role of political life in constituting the rule of law. In a similar way, political scientists have a vocabulary for speaking about the influence of rules on the structure and operation of regimes, even if they often preface their stories about multilevel games and predictive stability with denunciations of "idealistic" lawyers who think politics can be tamed by rules or ethics. Just because international economic lawyers focus on trade flows, even have a project of increasing trade, does not mean that they will, for example, be inhospitable to strengthening the international minimum wage, raising health and safety standards, or promoting conditions more conducive to labor organization. Nor is it clear that the trade lawyers' efforts to develop an interface among different-background national legal regimes is biased toward homogenization. In short, to think about professional specializations in these terms is to be oneself captured by them.

There is no doubt that humanitarian people should worry about a capture of international policy making by antihumanitarian ideas, interests, theories. When we sit outside the policy-making process and look at it from afar, we should ask whether policy professions that claim political neutrality or disengagement have in fact been harnessed to antihumanitarian objectives. But we should reject the idea that professional knowledge can or should be politically dispassionate. And we should not ourselves remain outside the fray. International governance distributes, makes some outcomes more likely and some less. Where the results are humanitarian, we should applaud, and where they are not, we should contest them. Doing so places us *in* the policy process, governing, ruling, no longer standing outside lamenting its "capture."

IDEAS WITH CONSEQUENCES: THE POLITICS OF POLICY EXPERTISE

As participants in global governance, humanitarians must come to grips with the politics of our own vernacular, our own underlying consciousness, style, and sensibility. Indeed, only as we better appreciate the limitations of our humanitarian policy-making vocabularies will we be able to shed our hesitance to engage — more pragmatically and more forcefully — in rulership. By professional vocabulary, I have in mind the routine terms used to propose, defend, and criticize humanitarian policy initiatives, as well as the shared assumptions and conceptual boundaries that limit and structure the arguments we make.

The boundary between this underlying vocabulary and the specific commitments we articulate in its terms is a porous one. Aspects of the underlying vernacular can be contested and pop up as a school of thought or a policy fad, just as it can happen that a school of thought so dominates the consciousness of the policy-making establishment that it recedes from view into the underlying vernacular. We are still far from understanding the ways in which a shared policy vocabulary shapes the outcomes of the policy process. I propose here a short list of hypotheses about the consciousness of humanitarian policy makers which might skew pragmatic assessments of their policy initiatives.

Shared Deformations of the Foreign Policy Establishment

Of course, the difficulties are not all those of humanitarians alone. Many of the difficulties burdening humanitarian policy making have their roots in the broader vernacular in which foreign policy is made. To participate actively and pragmatically in global governance, humanitarians will need to understand—and learn to contest—this broader common sense. For example, since the Cold War, internationalists in the United States have come to share a diagnosis of the changed conditions for statecraft. International politics has fragmented, involving more diverse actors in myriad new sites. Nonstate actors have become central to our thinking about economics, statecraft, humanitarian policy making—and security. Military issues have become as much local as international, have become linked to humanitarian objectives and tempered by economic considerations, transforming the meaning of international security. A new politics of ethnicity and nationalism is altering the conditions of both coexistence and cooperation. The threat posed by loose networks using tactics of terror preoccupies the international policy making community.

Interpreting these changes has become a matter of deep ideological and political contestation among intellectuals concerned with international affairs. Unfortunately, common but mistaken ideas—like the idea that international governance is separate from both the global market and from local culture, or is more a matter of public than of private law—sharply narrow the sense among foreign policy professionals of what is possible and appropriate for foreign policy. These mistaken ideas are equally well represented in the thinking of humanitarian policy makers.

Specialists in all fields overestimate the impact of globalization on the capacity for governance because they share a sense that governance means the politics of public order, while a background private order builds itself naturally through the work of the economic market. As a result, they underestimate the possibilities for political contestation within the domain of private and economic law — and overestimate the military's power to intervene successfully while remaining neutral or disengaged from background local political and culture struggles. Policy makers overestimate the technocratic or apolitical nature of economic concerns, including the independence of economic development from background cultural, political, and institutional contexts. A shared sense that cultural background can be disentangled from governance leads specialists to overemphasize the exoticism of ethnic conflict as well as the cosmopolitan character of global governance. The result is a professional tendency to overlook opportunities for an inclusive global politics of identity — for working constructively on the distributional conflicts among groups and individuals that cross borders.

Rather than contesting these ideas, international humanitarians have shared them. Mainstream policy makers have removed global governance from political contestation — and humanitarians have gone along. Careful pragmatism about humanitarian possibilities demands that the consequences of these shared ideas be made visible and opened to contestation.

Over- or Underestimating the Peculiarities of International Policy Making

Humanitarians often misapprehend the peculiarities of policy making at the international level, either over- or underestimating the unity and distinctness of the international system. Doing so can distort judgment about the likely consequences and effectiveness of international policy initiatives, often undercutting the plausibility of claims for their humanitarian potential.

This quite common deformation is also a surprising one. The peculiar dilemmas of international governance are, of course, precisely the focal points of the international policy professional's special expertise, and are widely discussed in the theoretical literature of international law, politics, and economics. International "governance" is more process than institution, depends on law more than force, erects norms on the basis of horizontal consent rather than vertical authority, lacks common fiscal or monetary authority, stretches over numerous heterogenous cultural and political contexts and relies upon decentralized enforcement machinery, or the "mobilization of shame," rather than police. The political culture within which international policy making takes place is structured by the voices and distributional clashes of national identities organized into state and governmental entities rather than by the clashes of class, ideology, religion, or other interests organized as the party, governmental, corporate, individual, or social entities that are more characteristic of national political life.

Each functional branch of the international governance machinery is far more diffuse than its national analog and is enmeshed in various local and national institutions. The international "judiciary" is not a uniform system hierarchically organized around the "World Court," but an ad hoc and shifting set of cooperative and deferential practices among numerous national, local, and international adjudicative bodies; similarly, the "administrative" branch, where the importance of nominally "international" administrative bodies varies considerably in different places, and the implementation structures of private institutions or national and local governments is key.

The claim is that international humanitarians know all this—but forget all this. After promoting international governmental organs as formal or functional imitations of national parliaments, executive, and judiciaries, policy professionals often then make policy in them as if their Potemkin government would operate like the domestic institutions on which they were modeled. They treat the adoption of a norm as the implementation of a policy, mistake the judgments of the World Court for the decisions of a judiciary embedded in a dense and functioning legal culture, mistake treaties and the resolutions of international organizations for statutes, anticipating their implementation. They underestimate the diversity of political, legal, and social contexts within which their policy initiatives will need to be realized, and are drawn to one-size-fits-all policy solutions. The idea here is not only that they fail to respect local cultures, but that they underestimate the specificity of the culture of international governance itself.

When policy makers underestimate the uniqueness of international policy making, they can easily overestimate the humanitarian potential of their initiatives. This happens when they applaud the extradition proceedings for Pinochet in the United Kingdom and the effort to try him in Spain as if there existed a cross-cultural criminal and humanitarian legal fabric that could be strengthened or affirmed by such a sui generis gesture; or propose concluding a treaty to outlaw land mines as if consent to their elimination could have been procured absent recognition of their military uselessness, and as if making them illegal would translate into their elimination; or promote an international criminal court for war crimes, as if the political and military contexts in which war crimes were likely to occur, and the forces which would be brought to bear in prosecution, were somehow analogous to the social forces surrounding other criminal behavior; or when they promote the adoption of human rights norms and codes, without noticing how often doing so substitutes for developing the cultural and political machinery necessary to promote the human dignity they are meant to guarantee.

In each of these cases, the difficulty is not simply that the initiative will be less successful than hoped, or will not succeed until a more complete international government is in place, but that these seemingly progressive and humanitarian initiatives will either make the problems worse or have unintended bad effects. So, a trial about Pinochet in the United Kingdom or Spain, far from being the first step toward a working international criminal law to defend human rights, establishes a random and unpredictable international prosecutorial machinery which undermines the most basic rights of prospective defendants. Or, outlawing land mines and other marginal military techniques, rather than beating the first sword into a ploughshare, reinforces the legitimacy of more violence than it prevents.

It is quite common for international humanitarians to overestimate the integration of the international governance machinery, to fantasize administrative and judicial components subsidiary to a legislature, or think of a distinct commercial sector subject to regulation by public lawmaking. But international policy making can also take too seriously the notion that the international system is a unique world outside culture and politics, a neutral world of expertise, a universal world of sovereign equality, a normative world of respect for sovereign autonomy or the benignly cooperative world invoked by the phrase "international community." It is easy to take the fantasy world of characters policy makers imagine at face value — treating governments as stand-ins for their people, treating the "international community" as something other than a media reference to a particular group of elites, or treating international "civil society" as if it were an embedded part of global cultural and political life, rather than a hodge-podge of advocacy institutions which have managed to gain access to international institutional machinery.

One result has been policy makers who imagine themselves innocent of political commitment or identity, and policy initiatives which present themselves as best practices detached from knowledge of, or responsibility for, distributional choices. The effort to intervene in places like Kosovo or East Timor or Palestine to "keep the peace" or "rebuild the society" or "strengthen the state" or provide "humanitarian assistance" *without* affecting the background distribution of power and wealth betrays this bizarre belief in the possibility of an international governance which does not govern.

Spatial Mistakes and Geographical Misconceptions

International humanitarian policy makers operate with a map of the world in their heads which affects the types of proposals they make, the outcomes they expect, and the consequences of their work. Each profession involved in international policy making has a map of its own: the one foregrounding central banks and currency flows, the other troop movements and supply lines, yet another trade flows and productivity measurement. A broad range of people involved in global governance also share a set of ideas about space and geography. Assessing the humanitarian potential of policy making by these professions requires a sense for the limitations these maps impose on our thinking.

On all these maps, "the international community" is a large and real place. As we might expect, these maps are also marked by the exaggerated size of well-known political and historical hotspots. The perspective is often the foreshortened view from high in the United Nations headquarters building, or from the space one inhabits flying among conferences, summits, or the meetings of commissions, councils, and expert working groups. From this vantage point, the sites of prior international engagement and disengagement loom large — Passchendaele, Somme, Munich, Bretton Woods or, closer to our day, Vietnam, Somalia, Cambodia, Bosnia, Congo, Iraq, or Rwanda. Each offers an opportunity for a range of more and less plausible analogies — humanitarian engagement will work, will fail. Each stands for a "lesson," has added or subtracted from the humanitarian policy maker's toolkit of possible solutions. More importantly, these places, in all their divergent reality, lead policy makers to exaggerate the uniformity of international policy making — their ability, whatever the differences on the ground, to know what a "sanctions regimes" or a "currency bailout" entails and to compare their success here and there. The map encourages policy makers to think of their techniques as having shape, potential, potency abstracted from the context of their application, and precisely to overlook the specificity of context. In a way, navigating on the map becomes a substitute for navigating in the world.

One common consequence of this perspectival remove is the tendency to organize the world in broad cultural families ("East/West") or stages of modernization ("developed/developing"). It is then all too easy to underestimate differences within the "West" or the "South" as well as the extent of contacts, convergence, and cultural influence between these imaginary worlds. The association of the international community with civilization, enlightenment, or liberal virtue can lead policy makers to overestimate the difference between the first and third worlds — "orientalizing" the developing world. This can eliminate opportunities for alliance among people in the first and third worlds who share interests, while encouraging domestic political cultures in the developing world to organize themselves around opposition between domestic "tradition" and foreign "modernization" despite the obvious presence of a third world in the first or a first world in the third.

At the same time, when international policy makers take the first world as the "normal" background condition for policy making and overlook the distinctiveness of the developing world, we get policies that look uniform but that can have dramatically skewed results. We get guarantees of religious freedom which generate religious pluralism in the first world but contribute to the increasing hegemony of modern proselytizing religions in the third, or trade regimes which leave complex social welfare systems intact in the first world, but force the third world to live in a bracing deregulatory wind, unmediated by national or regional regulatory interventions.

International humanitarians are also prone to underestimate the constitutive effect of their own policy work on the world they confront. Take "rogue states" — when global policy makers use the term, they know to what and whom they refer. These places seem similar — their modes of their engagement in the world seem shared, and it seems sensible to work out policy ideas which would work across a range of rogues. And yet, how does a rogue learn his trade, his position, his possibilities? Why do rogue regimes converge in tactic and technique? When we evaluate the humanitarian potential of measures addressed to preexisting difficulties of this type, we are likely to underestimate the coresponsibility of international governance for the world it governs. The same type of argument could be made of "rebel groups," "ethnic minorities," "insurgents," "belligerents," "indigenous peoples," "failed states," and so forth — these are roles in the world, to be sure, but they are also policy categories, and it is easy to forget that the world is also looking at the policy makers, mapping their own possibilities and strategies.

The map by which international humanitarians navigate the policy process customarily depicts political and economic entities quite differently. Political entities usually figure larger than the economic, and are thought to either preexist or to follow the movement of economic forces. Political identities are often associated with places, regions, terrains, while economic entities float more freely, somehow off the map or outside the space of policy altogether. Where institutions are shown at all, they are public institutions — there is a tiny mark for the Federal Reserve and the World Bank, but nothing for General Motors or Shell. Rhode Island might be shown, Luxembourg certainly would be, but Ted Turner, whose private land holdings in the United States alone are larger than Rhode Island and Delaware put together, would not appear. The world's spaces are divided up into political and legal jurisdictions, which don't over-lap—and all of which are at least nominally "countries." Turner is said to own land *in* this and that country—but it is hard to think the sentence "the Mexican authorities govern activities *in* this and that corporation."

People have criticized this professional map in many ways. The most familiar criticism is that it arranges the political world into formally separate public spaces, giving governments more authority than they can responsibly exercise while artificially limiting what the international policy maker can accomplish. As a result, national governments retain the authority to disable international policy making, but not the capacity to resolve problems on their own. There is something to this charge. Humanitarian policy makers sometimes do give exaggerated deference to the formal boundaries of state power. But international policy making has never had a purely formal or territorial conception of political authority. From the first, the humanitarian policy professions have worked with two mental maps—an ideal map of perfect sovereigns holding complete bundles of rights over clear territories, and a map riddled with exceptions, shared jurisdictions, nonsovereign right holders, disputed areas, internationalized territories, and half-sovereigns. To evaluate the humanitarian potential of global governance as a whole, we need to understand a professional practice of at least *two* minds about the centrality of hard political boundaries.

Whether the political boundaries are firm or flexible, the international humanitarian's mental map discourages engagement with things that happen *below the line of sovereignty*. The violence and injustice which attend the creation of states and accompany the ongoing exercise of their authority is less visible to the international humanitarian than what happens *outside and between* these political/legal jurisdictions—in Antartica, in outer space, on the seabed. The international humanitarian is more sensitive to the issues posed by jurisdictional conflicts than jurisdictional exercise, to the space in which a refugee can be found after leaving his country of origin and before settling in his new home than to the places and actions which cause—and might cure—his flight. The international policy maker sees things like smoke or fish when they cross boundaries more clearly than when they stay close to home.

This map identifies potential public intervenors in a space *above* sovereignty, a space in which sovereigns mingle, communicate, have "disputes." For something to get into this space—to be "taken up on the international plane"—it must be a *grave* matter, a *serious* breach, cause *material* damage, result in *irrevocable* harm, *shock* the conscience, or meet any of numerous other substantive tests for reversing the presumption that things below the line of sovereignty are not within the purview of the international policy maker. Sovereigns can do as they like at home—for their actions to be respected *on the international plane* they must meet certain standards. Of the things which cross borders and of the exercises of sovereign power which annoy other sovereigns, international humanitarian policy gives its overt attention only to the most serious and grievous. Its influence on the background conditions in which more and less grievous problems develop is off the screen.

Consequently, international humanitarian policy has an odd shape. The law of the sea divides the world's fish species for regulatory purposes according to their migratory habits, measured by the extent to which they swim across various international boundaries. Or take environmental policy—it covers the oceans, but with decreasing density as one moves closer to shore or onboard a ship, it covers outer space, it covers those pollution flows which cross boundaries, it applies more densely to smoke than to sewage. Of course, with clever and expansive interpretation, international policy makers *could* stretch the reach of their engagement until very little escaped their purview. International policy makers know *how* to blur the boundaries which restrict their ambit, but their default conception is, from this point of view, unnecessarily self-limiting.

Although we might well think "the environment" simply *is* a global phenomenon when we argue for international environmental policy making in the environmental field—when we then *do* international policy making, the environment has become something else altogether. There is the local terrain of physical activity, private activity, economic activity, of snail darters, financiers, and property owners. Above that are public rights to intervene, regulate, distort, reorganize. These are mostly, usually, normally, allocated to national sovereigns and their subentities. The question for international policy makers is when this presumption should be reversed. International environmental issues occur, and international policy making begins, when the activities of fish and air and capital somehow escape those boundaries, cross them, when one or another sovereign has become annoyed at a *particularly grievous* environmental act of another. In this sense, international humanitarian policy making is about the tips of icebergs, ignoring the influence of international governance on what lies beneath the sovereign waterline.

At the same time, this map makes it more plausible to treat economic "forces" as naturally global and political opportunities to regulate them as naturally channeled through the jurisdictional capillaries of government. This reinforces a rather limited conception of what international governance itself can be — international policy making is, and can be, about the bundling and unbundling of sovereign rights. Governance on this map becomes a public matter of exceptional intervention from "above," an oscillation between respecting and reallocating public rights; policy becomes the extension of a public regulatory order *into* or *onto* a preexisting natural private order. The legal structures and political institutions which structure routine economic transactions are easy to overlook.

Making Policy as "Intervention"

Humanitarian participants in global governance imagine their work as intervention, sharing with other international policy makers both the idea that there is no international policy before intervention and a preoccupation with debate about *whether or not* to intervene. Viewed this way, intervention is an exception which requires justification and authorization. This familiar idea has a particular resonance in the international context, where policy makers think of themselves as spatially outside or above the vertical authority of sovereigns. Think of the Red Cross inspector going in and out of prisons, the peacekeeper wearing a UN helmet, the UN agricultural or health adviser on the ground in a rural village. We imagine these people wandering about the scenes of local catastrophe in a kind of parallel universe — there and not there.

This idea has a number of unfortunate consequences for international humanitarian policy. Most importantly, it can distract attention and responsibility from the international policy maker's ongoing engagement with local conditions. This is particularly striking where the international policy regime has been self-consciously designed as a mode of nonintervention or neutrality. One can easily imagine taking responsibility for the effects of a military occupation — perhaps less readily for the effects of a quarantine, or for a regime of enforced neutrality and nonintervention.

Indeed, international humanitarians generally do find it easier to take responsibility for engagements than for disengagements, and for successes than failures. And they find it easier to imagine that intervention can itself be accomplished without disturbing local conditions, without taking responsibility for local political and economic conditions, without compromising their neutrality or participating in the allocation of stakes so central to the quotidian projects of governance.

Moreover, the idea that one should not intervene without good reason and good authority erects a conceptual hurdle in front of every humanitarian initiative. What standing do we have? What makes this situation exceptional enough to warrant engagement? This hesitance to "intervene" is not evenly distributed. It is stronger when the "intervention" will have a clearer impact on background norms and institutions — when it will, for example, affect private property rights rather than public regulatory claims, when the situation can be figured as part of the naturally occurring market rather than the natural domain of state authority, or as part of the naturally occurring local culture, rather than as a technical aspect of a global problem.

These ideas cabin and channel humanitarian policy making. Regardless of the nature of the problem, it will be easier to make policy through public law than private law, when framed as a political rather than an economic matter, or as a technical rather than a cultural matter. In each case, it will be understood to be less aggressive an "intervention," and will require a lower threshold of justification and authority to act.

Innumerable humanitarian policy initiatives have crashed on the rocks of hesitation to engage in "cultural imperialism." A willingness to intervene to achieve economic development or political peace, but not to affect "culture," often skews international humanitarian policy making. Imagine a national market-based economic regulatory scheme aimed to bring about "development." Such a policy can often be supported by international institutions without seeming like an intervention at all—the scheme is a national one, its policies are passive enablers for the decisions of market actors, property rights are left alone. To blame the international institutions for the results would be unfair—they are designed by local elites to whose call the international institutions have merely responded, and the agent of their implementation is the "force" of "the market." The threshold level of justification and authority necessary for international policy making here is very low—commercial and economic policies, nationally developed, market inspired.

Of course this sort of scheme can have dramatic effects on the fabric of social life, moving people from rural to urban settings, transforming educational opportunities, making workers of peasants, changing the distribution of religious belief and the authority of traditional communal leaders, changing the opportunities for young people and for women. The collection of such changes we know as "modernization" is what we mean by development, and is the objective of all sorts of economic policy making, both nationally and internationally.

But now let us imagine an international policy initiative which would bring about directly what these economic reforms have brought about indirectly—transferring ownership of assets to and among private parties, restructuring local production, transforming the social and educational opportunities available for rural and urban workers and for women, secularizing the economy, destroying traditional cultural sites of resistance to economic modernization—suddenly the hurdle of justification and authorization jumps up. Lots of people oppose the intervention, including many humanitarians. Those who favored it begin to lose confidence. Imagine further that an international institution or foreign nongovernmental organization responded to requests by local feminists with a policy initiative to reduce the incidence of a traditional practice like clitorodectomy in the countryside. The bar is much higher — now we are in the core of culture, religion, the family, personal autonomy. Even the most progressive internationalist gets uncomfortable — gets uncomfortable even if it turns out that the original national market-based development policy will have a far more profound effect on the actual level of female genital mutilation in the countryside, or may even eliminate country life altogether.

It is no wonder good-hearted internationalists have a hard time evaluating global governance initiatives in pragmatic terms, or remaining focused on distributional consequences. International humanitarians all too often focus on who makes policy rather than the policy they will make, and on the appropriate form for policy rather than the resulting outcomes of policy making. Their policy-making vernacular shifts their attention to a set of conceptual worries — what is culture and what is economy? what is local and what is global? what is public and what is private? Above all, when will we be said to have "intervened?" And what then was our exceptional justification and authority? By what *right* did we go so far? Discussions about what policy to make are transformed into discussions about how much and whether to intervene, with conceptual boundaries between public and private operating as vague proxies for outcomes.

One particularly unfortunate consequence is the temptation to worry more about the defensibility of international humanitarian action than about the potential for humanitarian results. Preoccupied with justifications, and precedents, for intervention, international humanitarians can see their policy proposals first as signs for the possibility of international policy making itself, and only secondarily as opportunities to bring about a humanitarian effect. In a sense, at stake in every policy-making effort is the much larger promise that international policy making is possible at all. We find humanitarian voices arguing that trying Pinochet in Britain might well be bad for Chile, for reconciliation, for justice, for the victims and the defendants — but it was great for the emergence of an international criminal law of individual responsibility whose humanitarian potential will surely be felt at some future moment. In this way, the idea that international humanitarian work is an exceptional intervention encourages enchantment of our tools and discourages pragmatic assessment of the consequences of our work.

Settled Expectations about the Background and the Foreground

Humanitarian policy makers routinely think of themselves as active interveners into a more passive background. What is the foreground for active policy and what seems the background terrain for intervention will differ — for some, politics will seem the natural background for legal intervention, for others the economy will seem the background for political interventions, for still others, private law and private arrangements will be the background to the interventions of public law and the state. Humanitarian lawyers, for example, are quick to think of ways to rearrange and rebundle legal entitlements, and more likely to see politics or economics as natural processes to which they can only react or into which they can intervene only through law.

In each case, across a range of initiatives, humanitarians are prone to overestimate the benevolence, plasticity, and instrumental potency of the foreground they seek to mobilize for policy making. At the same time, opportunities to mobilize forces in the background are overlooked. Policy makers routinely underestimate their ongoing influence on and responsibility for what seem to be background conditions for their active work, along with the agency of background forces to participate in, resist, and reshape their initiatives. Lawyers often overestimate the impact of legal changes and underestimate the influence of political and economic forces on legal initiatives as well as their own ongoing engagement with economic and political life.

When restructuring the economies of postsocialist societies, international policy makers consistently overlooked opportunities to link their initiatives to preexisting economic, social, and legal relations and underestimated the range of redevelopment strategies which would have been possible by encouraging different background normative configurations. Similarly, those seeking an international humanitarian law to restrict the use of force have repeatedly focused on developing public international law norms articulating how force may and may not be used. They all but ignored what have been the private law rules concerning the production, sale, and transport of arms, the norms and institutional structures facilitating logistical supply, or the norms affecting incentives for people to become soldiers, all of which may well have more effect on the incidence of military force in the world. Some of these rules would be national, some international, some public, some private. Many would have been affected by international policy making. International humanitarians are notoriously inattentive to the ways in which the public law norms they espouse are used to legitimate the use of force — a use (or "misuse") which seems to happen somewhere else, outside the domain of international humanitarian responsibility.

This sort of assumption about foreground and background can skew humanitarian policy making which otherwise seeks to be scrupulously evenhanded. Imagine that different national economies achieve distributive aims by relying on different combinations of public and private law norms. An international arbitration regime which treats public and private norms differently will have quite different effects in the two economies even if its procedural structure and substantive norms are completely neutral. Similarly, an international mediation effort which treats "states" as preexisting political entities and other international "entities" or "institutions" as the artificial constructions of law and policy may be unable to avoid a bias in favor, say, of the Israeli "state" and against the Palestinian "entity."

Moreover, when humanitarians share a broad sense for their work as the arrival of reason, civilization, or modernity into a domain of passion and tradition, it is easy to see how this might rub people there the wrong way, stiffening their resistance. We can easily imagine international humanitarians forgoing possible alliances with what seem background institutions of local life. Identifying local conditions as "traditional" may well reinforce the authority of precisely the institutions humanitarians seek to change. At the same time it can encourage international policy makers to overestimate the novelty of their initiatives, and to miss opportunities for weaving their efforts into the existing local context.

The idea that politics preexists an artificial legal intervention also encourages international policy makers to think of their own policy work as weak, against the powerful forces of nature unleashed through the political activities of others. Although it seems natural to think of Macedonia or Mexico as more "real" than the United Nations High Commissioner for Refugees, it is unclear why we should. And doing so can dramatically affect the range of policy engagements which seem legitimate. It can also make it seem as if one can never get enough international law — but that one always already has an excess of international politics. Humanitarians should be concerned about precisely the reverse problem. There is no shortage of international governance mechanisms and regimes, but almost no attention, by international policy makers or anyone else, to constructing a conscious global politics and shared political culture.

Temporal Myths and Progress Narratives

Humanitarian policy makers also share ideas about time and history which channel and limit their work. Their shared mythology presents international policy making as a grand story of the slow and unsteady progress of law against power, policy against politics, reason against ideology, international against national, order against chaos in international affairs over 350 years. In this story, international governance is itself a mark of civilization's progress: law brought to politics, civilization brought to primitive societies, reason brought to passion, the universal brought to the particular. Through setbacks and breakthroughs, international policy making has always been or aspired to be the same thing: a humanitarian, rational, and civilized alternative to the messy worlds of national politics.

That this story is largely a myth is not surprising — policy makers are as likely to turn their own achievements into the stuff of legend as anyone else. But it can be more than that. Progress narratives of this sort can become policy programs, both by solidifying a professional consensus about what has worked and by defining what counts as progress for the international governance system as a whole. This can redirect policy makers from solving problems to completing the work of a mythological history, orienting or shaping their efforts to build the international system.

These progress myths distinguish the up-to-date from the old fashioned. The idea that postsocialist or third world societies are "behind" and need to "catch up" before it is sensible to think of them as full participants in the international arrangements common to wealthy industrial societies makes it seem more natural to think of these societies being shocked by the market in ways which would be unthinkable within the industrialized West. We need only compare the idea that Portugal or Greece needed to be jump-started on democracy by immediate entry into the European Communities with the treatment accorded Eastern European applicants who need to "catch up" before membership can be contemplated to see the effects of progress narratives of this type.

In today's policy community, those who speak the language of transnationalism, functionalism, and civil society seem up to date. Those who insist upon their sovereign entitlements — however justified — sound like more primitive players. Sometimes this favors humanitarian objectives — when claims of universal humanism overcome the sovereignty claims of evil regimes. But it can also work the other way — justifying interventions by powerful players and transforming the prerogatives of the great powers into the voice of the international community itself.

These historical stories solidify the sense that something called an "international community" exists; indeed, the "international community" seems to exist more firmly in time than in space. Through time it can be said to have acted, to have "agreed" to some things and forgone agreement on others. These progress narratives reinforce the collective identity of participants in global governance — we are those who have stood against politics, against religion, in favor of peace and humanitarianism, and not those who fail to share our secular, cosmopolitan, and pragmatic history. Ours is not the history of a culture or a people or a place, but of an idea, an abstraction, a commitment, an orientation. These stories establish a tradition against which new humanitarian initiatives can be judged. The formal past of sovereignty out of which the international community developed by rearranging sovereign rights makes the rearrangement of sovereign rights itself a sign for progress.

One unfortunate result is the confusion of humanitarian ambitions for society with the progress of the humanitarian professions themselves. It is surprising how many international policy arguments read as arguments for international policy, how often *more global governance* substitutes for strategies addressing particular conflicts and social problems. Although international humanitarians certainly care about human rights, alleviating AIDS, or reducing the violence of warfare, professional progress myths make it easy to conclude that reforms of the human rights machinery to be less formal, or purging the World Health Organization of its attachment to sovereign forms, or relativizing the law of war to erase its formal commitments to distinctions between war and peace, neutral and belligerent, combatant and noncombatant *is* progress—a more important, more general, more historically enduring and reliable progress than the quotidian matter of actually helping any particular person avoid AIDS or land mines or torture.

The idea that humanitarian policy making is already and automatically part of the solution rather than the problem can blind international humanitarians to the regressive consequences of their own activities. We speak of international environmental law as synonymous with the effort to generate environmentally protective norms. And yet a catalog of international norms affecting the incidence of environmental damage would include many norms encouraging or enabling despoilation—perhaps more than the number encouraging protection. International law and policy offer the environmental despoiler, like the war criminal or the human rights abuser, a great deal of comfort and protection. That the effort to address these problems through international policy making retains an automatic humanitarian feel makes these supports for antihumanitarian outcomes particularly difficult to root out.

A strong myth of professional progress also hinders the pragmatic assessment of specific humanitarian initiatives. All too often, the failures of particular humanitarian initiatives are interpreted as warnings to do more, to intensify our effort, along precisely the same lines. International humanitarians can come to see themselves as continuously *becoming*, polishing their tools, embroidering their technique, strengthening themselves, that they might one day tackle humanitarian problems. In the meantime, failures reflect the primitive state of the work, the strength of their enemies, the long road still to travel. So long as the progress myth remains the map for that travel, however, it will be difficult to develop practical policy responses to humanitarian problems in the here and now. It would perhaps be more accurate to say that solutions to particular humanitarian problems emerge as by-products of this system-building agenda, as almost accidental consequences of professional practices of self-effacement, marginalization, and a need not to know that one is governing.

HUMANITARIANS AND THE EXERCISE OF POWER

Humanitarian policy making, when it works, brings about more humanitarian distributions of resources, status, authority, and wealth. International policy making is rulership. Rulers make policy to distribute. But rare is the humanitarian who embraces a will to power this overt. It is not surprising that clear-eyed analysis of consequences would be in short supply among those who seem so allergic to the mantle of rulership. For advocates and activists, this may well be expected — they style themselves outside power, speaking the language of truth and virtue. For would-be policy makers, the tendency to think of themselves as advisers and technocrats rather than rulers is more troubling.

Nevertheless, our policy-making vocabularies encourage this disengagement from governmental authority. A more overt humanitarian politics would require a completely different sort of mental map, a more skeptical approach to the tools we use to engage the world and to the historical myths which provide so many default programs for action. We would need to develop habits for contesting the professional vocabularies we use to imagine, propose, defend, and implement humanitarian policies — for contesting them in terms we associate more readily with politics and rulership.

One starting point would be an effort to unthink habits of mind which occlude the political consequences of our professional vernacular. For this we will need mental exercises and heuristics. We might, for example, try to think about a policy-making initiative without focusing on constitutional questions. As an exercise, we might develop a zenlike agnosticism about *whether or not to intervene*, about the appropriate mix of centralization and decentralization, or about the appropriate level at which policy should be made. By setting these issues aside, we might learn to speak about whether a policy is or is not a good idea by focusing on its humanitarian consequences. If we set aside our preoccupation with the suitability of formal or informal legal structures, substantive or procedural legal rules, or how much discretion is optimal, we might find our way to asking how we wish to transform the distribution of power, status, and authority in society to humanitarian ends.

A related exercise might suppress the presumption that making policy internationally — or in any other of our customary institutional sites — will *itself* be a humanitarian gesture. It is very difficult for international lawyers to remember that more international law may not always be a good idea. But doing so might help us remember and acknowledge the dark sides of our policy making vocabulary more consistently. It may also help us remember the role of international humanitarian policy itself in legitimating the powers and political cultures which present obstacles to our humanitarian ambitions. We might try to release our hold on the conviction that humanitarian policy making is weak, partial, fragile, and in need of our fealty. Rather than marginal players throwing a frail network of norms and institutions over an unruly world, we might come to see ourselves as participants in that world, with our own culture, power, and authority, pursuing projects with consequences for ourselves and others.

All this may lead to conflict and disagreement among humanitarians about the directions and outcomes of our rulership. We have always had disagreements, of course, about the meaning and implications of our shared policy vernacular. By removing the politics of these vocabularies from debate — and by removing ourselves from rulership to the more modest posture of humanitarian professional, expert, adviser — we could imagine our disagreements yielding to better knowledge about the entailments of our commitments. We could more easily remain confident that appropriate solutions would emerge from the further development of our humanitarian expertise.

Having brought a skeptical eye to bear on our expertise, we find that this confidence is no longer well placed. Our professional policy vocabularies do not give clear guidance once we have set aside the conventional wisdoms which have obscured careful assessment of our humanitarian work. For all its nuance and sophistication, our policy vernacular stops surprisingly short of the difficult political and distributional questions we must answer to make humanitarian policy with confidence. Doing so requires debate about the meaning of humanitarianism in the world — and encourages a more engaged politics than is possible in the world of expertise and policy management. The next chapters trace the limits of humanitarian policy vernaculars in the fields of economic development, refugee affairs, and the law of war. My hope is that humanitarians will respond to awareness of the limits of expertise with affirmation, engagement, and vigorous contestation of the routine practices of international policy making.

FIVE

The Rule of Law as
a Strategy for Economic
Development

Over the past ten years, policy makers interested in promoting economic development in the third world have increasingly turned their attention to law and law reform. As a result, "law and development" — the study of law as a policy making instrument for economic development — is back, taught again in law faculties, the focus of policy initiatives at the leading development institutions, the subject of numerous books and conferences.

It is hard to imagine an economic development strategy which would *not* rely in one or another way on law. The set of national development policies which came to be known as "import substitution" in the years after the Second World War required numerous public law schemes to support and protect domestic industries and promote industrialization. Exchange controls, credit licensing schemes, tariffs, subsidy programs, tax incentives, price controls, national commodity monopolies — all were legal institutions, established by statute and implemented by public law bureaucracies. The same could be said of policies designed to promote export led growth in Southeast Asia and elsewhere from the 1960s onward. The neoliberal development policies increasingly favored by international institutions and national governments, beginning with Chile in the late seventies, also required elaborate legal regimes — of both public and private law — to support policies of free trade and private investment, much like the development efforts which were part of the transition to capitalism in former socialist economies after 1989. Schemes to promote and protect private property and commercial exchange, programs for privatization of national firms, governmental firms and public assets, for the establishment of financial institutions and exchange markets—all required legal institutions, and all were promoted as programs of legal reform.

Each of these development strategies arose from an analysis of what development is and how it can best be brought about. Although there were endless technical and political disputes about precisely how each strategy should be implemented, policy makers in each period shared a broad vocabulary for discussing these choices. Within these vernaculars, they developed policies which allocated resources, taking from some and giving to others, to maximize the potential for the broad social and economic transformations evoked by the word *development* as they understood it. The broad development strategies—import substitution, export led growth, neoliberal market development—expressed quite different background ideas about how and to whom resources should be distributed to maximize development. These distributive commitments—to take from agriculture and give to industry, to transfer from public to private management, to favor foreign over domestic investors or vice versa—were then written as law. Each strategy required numerous further allocative decisions—to encourage one investment and discourage another, subsidize one industry at a cost to another.

That distributive policies of this sort characterized development in the decades of government planning after World War II is easy to see. Import substitution and export-led growth strategies depended upon discretionary decisions taken by vast planning bureaucracies interpreting all manner of complex regulations. But the market-based development strategies more common since the emergence of neoliberalism after 1980 or 1989 also require numerous distributive choices. The price mechanism may do much of the allocating, but markets come in many varieties, and prices are negotiated against the background of quite different legal regimes. Renewed interest in law as an instrument for development could offer the opportunity to view and contest these distributive choices and alternative market arrangements.

Unfortunately, too often this has been an opportunity missed. Rather than supplementing the earlier policy vocabularies of import substitution, export-led growth, or neoliberalism, the rule of law has become a development policy vernacular of its own. The idea that building "the rule of law" might *itself* be a development strategy encourages the hope that choosing law *in general* could substitute for all the perplexing political and economic choices which have been at the center of development policy making for half a century. Although a legal regime offers an arena to contest those choices, it cannot substitute for them. The campaign to promote the rule of law as a development path has encouraged policy makers to forgo pragmatic analysis of the choices they make in building a legal regime — or to think that the choices embedded in the particular regime they graft onto a developing society represent the only possible alternative.

The ideas about development which fuel contemporary interest in the law also encourage the hope that law could simplify development policy, toning down its engagement with political and economic controversy. I encounter these ideas first in the classroom. In the first world settings where I have recently taught law and development, the field now draws numerous students from the broad center and center-left of the political spectrum. The more technocratic specialists of the center-right who flocked to the field in the eighties and early nineties and saw law as a technical vehicle for neoliberal market reform seem to have retreated, or have come to express themselves in more restrained terms. But gone also are the social-democratic internationalists of the fifties and sixties who inaugurated the field after the Second World War and who saw law as an instrument for state-led development planning through the implementation of import substitution or export-led growth policies.

These contemporary students of law and development are a genial group, well meaning and liberal in outlook. They share a broadly humanitarian, cosmopolitan, and internationalist sensibility. They also seem to share a midlevel conception of "development policy" — neither a narrow matter of technical economic detail nor a broad vocabulary for political struggle, but something in between. Fifteen years ago, students of development policy in first world institutions were split — between confident, largely right-wing first worlders for whom "development" was a project of technical adjustment or economic management and equally confident, if often angrier, left-wing students from developing societies for whom the term "development" brought to mind the entire field of national — and international — political struggle. For both groups in those days, "development" was a universal phenomenon. For the technocrats of the north, it meant the adjustment of developing societies to economic axioms of universal validity — growth is growth. For students from the south, development meant broad questions of political economy and social theory which must be confronted by all societies, regardless of their place in the world system — politics is politics.

The last decade has chastened both groups. Today's first worlders, in retreat from one-size-fits-all neoliberalism, share an intuition that "development" must mean something particular — to the specific market conditions of transitional or developing societies, and to the cultural setting of each national economy. They are often drawn to technical accounts of what makes underdeveloped economic settings unique — characteristic market failures in particular: demand curves which don't slope gently off to the right, oligopolies, thin markets, peculiar information problems, transaction costs, sometimes even disparities in bargaining power. They are also eager to replace economics with the softer — and often legal — vocabularies of ethics or human rights. Third world students meet this intuition from the other direction — in flight from political generalities, they hope for a more technocratic development science. They aspire to participate in "governance" rather than government, and are also often drawn both to human rights and to more universal ethical expressions of their political aspirations.

For both groups, the economies and political systems of developing societies again seem to differ from those of the north and west — and to differ in ways which encourage attention to particular legal arrangements rather than universal economic or political theories. In this new vernacular, development policy must be attuned to specific political, social, and cultural conditions. Institutional issues are central. As politics and economics have become local, they seem to merge with the professional world of informed, empathetic, and humble expertise. On the economic side, institutional economics, transaction-cost problems, and market failures are back. On the political side, attention to human rights, to cultural and social costs, to policy sequencing, planning, and the institutional mechanics of policy making is in. All this places law, legal institutional building, the techniques of legal policy making and implementation — the "rule of law" broadly conceived — front and center. Unfortunately, however, this new interest in *"law and* development" is often accompanied by an ambition to leach the politics from the development process and to muddle the economic analysis. Students — like policy professionals — often turn to law in flight from economic analysis and political choice.

But development policy requires sharp economic analysis and forces political choices — for neither of which is "law" a substitute. The tools for development policy making — including the legal tools — are distributional. Whether rules of private law or acts of bureaucratic discretion, they allocate resources and authority toward some and away from others. For development to occur, these distributions must put things into the hands of those whose return on their use will cause whatever we mean by "development." If we mean a transformation of the economy through industrialization, for example, resources must be allocated to those whose use of them will have the greatest multiplier effect in that direction.

There are lots of different theories about how to do this — and they are economic theories. If development means more than a one-time growth spurt — means some sort of sustained, upward spiral, or some kind of socioeconomic transformation — then one needs an idea about how a particular set of distributional choices will generate such a change. Development policy making also requires political choices — about whose ox should be gored in the name of which development path. Where there turn out to be more than one equally efficient way to the same upward spiral, political choices among possible strategies become even more salient. There is politics, in other words, right at the start — in the distributive choices which underlie the aspiration for growth and development.

Although often quite sophisticated about the broad choices facing developing societies, contemporary students of development policy tend not to think these choices implicated in efforts to build the rule of law. Some self-consciously refuse the hard choices of economic policy making, advocating instead broad and aspirational commitments to human rights, "freedom," "social welfare," "democracy," "health," or "human flourishing." For others, the tough distributional choices seem far downstream—after development gets underway, they imagine, we will face choices about what to do with our new wealth. For these young policy makers, development means "economic growth *plus* . . ." Growth can be assured, they suggest, by implementing a technical rule of law, following the "best practices" of efficient market economies. Any later *re*-distribution for social equality, educational, or health will involve a completely separate policy commitment. These secondary objectives could then form the basis for all sorts of humanitarian policy campaigns—for human rights, for labor protections, for universal primary education, and so forth. In development planning, their general invocation will suffice—for now, we must focus on the less contentious matter of getting *growth* going. The deferral of these political choices and of any pragmatic assessment of strategies for their attainment makes the development policy which remains seem a matter of relative consensus.

Take proposals to increase women's educational opportunities. From a development perspective, we might do so to harness women's productive capacity—invest in their human capital—on the theory that doing so will be more effective in generating development than other investments. Or we might think doing so removes the distorting effects of prejudice and discrimination, allowing a more efficient market in women's skills and labor. Students of development today are uncomfortable with this type of talk. They prefer to affirm the ethical importance of women's education—women's right to education—and leave vague how this relates to development. Perhaps development simply *means* women's education rather than growth, perhaps we should *assume* women's education will spur economic growth, perhaps we should think of women's education as a redistributive necessity, even at significant cost to growth. The point is not to be forced to choose among these possibilities, and not to focus on the *costs*, to others, to society, to growth, even to some women, of investment in women's education rather than in something else.

Focus on the rule of law as a development strategy fits well with a resistance among today's center and center-left students to think of themselves as rulers, making contestable distributive choices with real consequences. Partly this represents a retreat from the cold realization that policy making breaks eggs, imposes costs, *intervenes* in foreign places with a view to changing them. One encounters instead the vague sentiment that getting governance right, injecting the rule of law, enforcing human rights will somehow bring a softer, gentler development graciously in its wake. Partly the resistance to rulership arises from the intuition that political and economic debates about what development is and how to make it happen have not generated a technical consensus on how to bring about development. As a result, focus on politics or economics places the ruler in the awkward position of having to *choose* in a way which will have consequences that cannot be accurately predicted or guaranteed — but will undoubtedly make some people worse off. This makes people who aspire to act from expertise uncomfortable.

The "rule of law" promises an alternative — a domain of expertise, a program for action — which obscures the need for distributional choices or for clarity about how distributing things one way rather than another will, in fact, lead to development. Unfortunately, this turns out to be a false promise. The focus on rights, on constitutions, on government capacity or judicial independence may all be to the good — but without a sharp sense for how one is intending to affect the economy, it is hard to compare building the rule of law with leaving the economy to operate more informally, and hard to compare building the rule of law one way with building it another.

In this, the focus on law as a development policy shares a great deal with other efforts to replace political and economic thinking with a general appeal to technical expertise and ideas about best practice. The result, by default or design, is a narrowing of the ideological range. Political choices fade from view — as do choices among different economic ideas about how development happens or what it implies for social, political, and economic life. Where once there might have been ideological and theoretical contestation, there is a somewhat muddy consensus.

It need not be this way. One could focus on law in ways that sharpen attention to distributional choices and render more precise the consequences of different economic theories of development. The choices between import substitution and export-led growth, or between neoliberal market-based development and strategies of either import or export promotion, offer the opportunity for sharp debate about economic theory and political preferences. Even during periods of broad consensus — on import substitution or neoliberalism — there are numerous implementation decisions to be made which require both economic theory and political commitment. The choices within and between regimes are made and implemented in legal terms.

A working legal regime is necessary not only to implement development policies, but to collect tariffs, to manage monetary policy, to administer the state, and so forth. Markets are also built on the back of legal norms which remain, for the most part, in the background. Law defines what it means to "own" something and how one can successfully contract to buy or sell. Legal norms and institutions define every significant entity and relationship in an economy — money, security, risk, corporate form, employment, insurance. In this sense, both "capital" and "labor" are themselves legal institutions. Each of these many institutions and relationships can be defined in different ways — empowering different people and interests. Legal rules and institutions defining what it means to "contract" for the "sale" of "property" might be built to express quite different distributional choices and ideological commitments. One might, for example, give those in possession of land more rights — or one might treat those who would use land productively more favorably.

Although some minimum level of national institutional functionality seems necessary for economic activity of any sort, this tells us very little. For development we need to strategize about the choices which go into making one "rule of law" rather than another. Attention to the rule of law offers an opportunity to focus on the political choices and economic assumptions embedded in development policy making. Unfortunately, however, those most enthusiastic about the rule of law as a development strategy treat it as a recipe or ready-made rather than as a terrain for contestation and strategy.

There are two broad themes in the rule of law literature which sustain this sleight of hand, positioning the rule of law as a substitute for politics and economics. Those themes are formalization and corruption—the notion that development requires a formalization of law and the elimination of corruption. Each of these ideas has a long history in the rule of law literature, each suggests a set of tactics for policy making. Each theme heightens the sense both that the rule of law can be injected without political choice, and that its implementation is a precondition to economic growth rather than a choice among alternative theories of development.

Each idea offers a rather simple vision of "law," which forgets much of what has become commonplace within the domain of legal theory for more than a century. It turns out that all the leading economic theories of development have implicit notions of what law is and what it can do. So do all the leading political ideas about how development should be defined and brought about. From a lawyer's point of view, these ideas about law expect the legal order to perform feats we know it rarely can accomplish and expect law to remain neutral in ways we know it cannot. From inside the legal field, merging the "rule of law" with formality and opposition to corruption seems a typical lay misunderstanding. Nonlawyers often think of law as a matter of neutral forms, or think of corruption as something easily defined and outlawed. Insiders to legal culture generally appreciate more readily the limits and alternatives of form, and the difficulty of sharply defining or resisting corruption.

The surprising thing about "law and development" today is the emergence of these simpler images within the legal field. Their presence suggests that some forgetting is going on. Part of what is forgotten is the range of possible legal arrangements, their association with alternative political and legal ideas, and their contestability. It is by unraveling these simplifying assumptions about the "law" in "law and development" that I hope we can return political and economic contestation to development policy making.

LEGAL FORMALIZATION

Since at least Weber, people have asserted that "formalization" of legal entitlements, in one or another sense, is necessary for development — necessary for transparency, for information and price signaling, to facilitate alienation of property, to reduce transaction costs, to assure security of title and economic return, or to inspire the confidence and trust needed for investment. From the start, legal formalization has meant a wide variety of different things — a scheme of clear and registered titles, of contractual simplicity and reliable enforcement, a legal system of clear rules rather than vague standards, a scheme of legal doctrine whose internal structure was logical and whose interpretation could be mechanical, a system of institutions and courts whose internal hierarchy was mechanically enforced, in which the discretion of judges and administrators was reduced to a minimum, a public order of passive rule following, a priority for private over public law, and more. These ideas are all associated with the reduction of discretion and political choice in the legal system, and are defended as instantiations of the old maxim "not under the rule of man but of god and the law."

It is easy to imagine, from the point of view of a particular economic actor, that legal formalization in any of these ways might well enhance the chances for successful economic activity. A clear title may make it easier for me to sell my land, and cheaper for my neighbor to buy it. A clear set of nondiscretionary rules about property, credit, or contract might make a foreign legal culture more transparent to me as a potential foreign investor. The reliable enforcement of contracts might make me more likely to trust someone enough to enter into a contract. Indeed, it seems hard to imagine "capital" except as a set of enforceable legal entitlements — a first lesson of law school is that property is less a relation between a person and an object than a relation between people with differing entitlements to use, sell, possess, or enjoy an object. The developing world is full of potential assets — but they have not been harnessed to productive use. Why? Because no one has clear title to them, nor are there pre-

dictable rules enforcing expectations about the return on their productive use.

The association of legal formalization with development, however,
has always seemed more problematic than this, also since at least
Weber. For starters, it has also been easy to imagine, from the point
of view of *other* economic actors, that formalization in each of these
ways might well eliminate the chance for productive economic activity. A clear title may help me to sell or defend my claims to land —
but it may impede the productive opportunities for squatters now
living there or neighbors whose uses would interfere with my quiet
enjoyment. A great deal will depend on what we *mean* by clear
title — which of the numerous possible entitlements that might go with
"title to property" we chose to enforce. Clear rules about investment
may make it easy for foreign investors — but by reducing the wealth
now in the hands of those with local knowledge about how credit is
allocated or how the government will behave. An enforceable contract will be great for the person who wants the promise enforced,
but not so for the person who has to pay up. As every first-year
contracts student learns, it is one thing to say stable expectations
need to be respected, and quite another to say whose expectations
need to be respected and what those expectations should legitimately
or reasonably be. To say anything about the relationship between
legal formalization and *development* we would need a theory about
how assets in the hands of the title holder *rather than* the squatter,
the foreign *rather than* the local investor will lead to growth, and
then to the sort of growth we associate with "development."

The urge to "formalize" law downplays the role of standards and
discretion in the legal orders of developed economies. We might
think here of the American effort to codify a "uniform commercial
code" to reflect the needs of the business community — an effort
which returned again and again to the standard of "reasonableness"
as a measure for understanding and enforcing contractual terms. We
might remember Weber's account of the "English exception" — the
puzzle that industrial development seemed to come first to the nation
with the most confusing and least formal system of property law and
judicial procedure. Or we might think of Polyani's famous argument

that rapid industrialization was rendered sustainable—politically, socially, and ultimately economically—in Britain precisely because law slowed the process down.

The focus on legal formalization downplays the role of the informal sector in economic life—the sector governed by norms *other* than those enforced by the state or which emerge in the gaps among official institutions. It is not only in the posttransition economies of Eastern or Central Europe that the informal sector provided a vibrant source of entrepeneurial energy. The same could be said for many developing and developed economies. Think of the mafia, or of the economic life of diasporic and ethnic communities. But think also of the "old boys network," the striking demonstrations in early law-and-society literature about the disregard businessmen in developed economies often have for the requirements of form or the enforceability of contracts. Think of routine debates within conventional schemes of contract about efficient breach, or within property about adverse possession. Or about the incompleteness of so many contracts—the room for maneuver left by unstated, unclear, or ambiguous terms. The informal sector is often an economically productive one. And there is also often security, transparency, and reliability in these informal or extralegal sectors—the question is rather security for whom, transparency to whom?

The story of development-through-formalization downplays the range of possible legal formalizations, each with its own winners and losers. In a world with multiple potential stable and efficient equilibriums, a great deal will depend upon the path one takes, and much of this will be determined by the choices one makes in constructing the system of background legal norms. Does "being" a corporation mean having an institutional, administrative, or contractual relationship with one's employees? With their children's day care provider? And so forth. Looking at the legal regime from the inside, we encounter a series of choices, between formality and informality, between different legal formalizations—each of which will make resources available to different people. What is missing from enthusiasm for the rule of law is both an awareness of the range of choices available *and* an economic theory about the developmental consequences of taking one rather than another path.

In a particular developing society, for example, it might be that the existing — discretionary, political, informal, or extralegal — system for allocating licenses or credit is entirely predictable and reliable for some local players even where it is not done in accordance with published legal rules. At the same time it might not be transparent to or reliable for foreign investors. This might encourage local and discourage foreign participation in this economic sector. We might well have a political theory of development which suggests that one simply cannot have access to a range of *other* resources necessary to develop without pleasing foreign direct investors. Or we might have an economic theory suggesting that equal access to knowledge favors investment by the most efficient user *and* that this user will in turn use the profits from that investment in ways more likely to bring about "development," perhaps based on a projection of how foreign, as opposed to local, investors will invest their returns. But the need for such theories — which would themselves be quite open to contestation — is obscured by the simpler idea that development requires a "formal" rule of law.

Interest in the "rule of law" as a development strategy gets in trouble when it replaces more conventional questions of development policy and planning which demand decisions about distribution — traditional questions about who will do what with the returns they receive from work or investment, how gains might best be captured and reinvested or capital flight eliminated. Or about how one might best take spillover effects into account and exploit forward or backward linkages. Or questions about the politics of tolerable growth and social change, about the social face of development itself, about the relative fate of men and women, rural and urban, in different stable equilibriums, along different policy paths.

Disinterest in the distributional choices one must make in designing a rule of law suitable for a policy of legal "formalization" is common in literature promoting the rule of law as a development strategy. Hernando de Soto's famous discussion of the benefits of legal formalization provides a good illustration. In discussing land reform, he is adamant that squatters be given formal title to the land on which they have settled. Doing so, he claims, will create useful capital by permitting them to eject trespassers, have the confidence to improve the land, or offer it for sale to more productive users. Of course, it will also destroy the capital of the current land owners — and, if the squatter's new rights are enforced, reduce economic opportunities for trespassers and future squatters. Formalization of title will also distribute authority *among* squatters — where families squat together, for example, formalization may well move economic discretion from women to men. The implicit assumption that squatters will make more productive use of the land than the current nominal owners may well often be correct. But de Soto provides no reason for supposing that the squatters will be more productive than the trespassers, nor for concluding that exclusive use by one or the other group is preferable to some customary arrangement of mixed use by squatters and trespassers in the shadow of an ambiguous law.

None of these observations is new. Development planners and practitioners have long struggled with precisely these problems. The puzzle is how easily one loses sight of these traditional issues of political and economic theory when the words "rule of law" come into play. There is something mesmerizing about the idea that a formal rule of law could somehow substitute for struggle over these issues and choices — could replace contestable arguments about the consequences of different distributions with the apparent neutrality of legal best practice.

CORRUPTION

A second theme running through enthusiasm for treating the "rule of law" *as* a development strategy is the desire to eliminate corruption. Like legal formalization, the elimination of corruption is linked to development in a variety of ways. Eliminating corruption is promoted to avoid squandered resources, to promote security and predictability, to inspire confidence, eliminate price distortions and promote an efficient distribution of resources. These things will lead, in some way, to development. Many of the advantages of eliminating corruption run parallel to those of legal formalization — eliminating corruption can seem much like eliminating judicial and administrative discretion. Indeed, sometimes "corruption" is simply a code word for public discretion—the state acts corruptly when it acts by discretion rather than mechanically, by rule.

Eliminating corruption may well enhance the chances for some economic actors to make productive use of their entitlements. The state's discretion, including the discretion to tax, and even the discretion to levy taxes higher than those authorized by formal law, may spur some and retard other economic activity. As with legal formalization more generally, however, it is also not difficult to imagine that other actors—including those who are collecting "corrupt" payments—will in turn be less productive once corruption is eliminated. As with the replacement of discretion by legal form, one must link the elimination of corruption to an idea about the likely developmental consequences of one rather than another set of economic incentives. A simple example would be—who is more likely to reinvest profits productively, the marginal foreign investor brought in as corruption declines or the marginal administrator whose take on transactions is eliminated? In my experience, such questions are rarely asked, and yet their answer is not at all obvious. We are back to the need for a political and economic theory about which allocation will best spur development.

Enthusiasm for eliminating corruption as a development strategy arises from the broader idea that corruption somehow drains resources from the system as a whole—its costs are costs of transactions, not costs of the product or service purchased. Elimination of such costs lifts all boats. And such costs might as easily be quite formal and predictable as variable and discretionary. Here the desire to eliminate corruption goes beyond the desire for legal form—embracing the desire to eliminate all costs *imposed* on transactions which are not properly costs *of* the transaction. There are at least two difficulties here. First, the connection between eliminating corruption and "development" remains obscure. Even if the move from a "corrupt" legal regime to a "not corrupt" regime produces a one-time efficiency gain, there is no good economic theory predicting that this will lead to growth or development, rather than simply another stable low level equilibrium. More troubling is the difficulty of distinguishing clearly between the "normal" or "undistorted" price of a commodity and the "costs" associated with a "corrupt" or distortive process for purchasing the commodity or service.

Economic transactions rely on various institutions for support, institutions which lend a hand sometimes by form and sometimes by discretion. But the tools these institutions, including the state, use to support transactions are difficult to separate from those which seem to impose costs on the transaction. The difference is often simply one of perspective — if the cost is imposed on you it seems like a cost, if it is imposed on someone else for your benefit it seems like support for your productive transaction. Here the desire to eliminate corruption bleeds off in a variety of directions. But the boundary between "normal" and "distorted" regulation is the stuff of political contestation and intensely disputed economic theory. When the anticorruption project suggests that the "rule of law" always already knows how to draw this line, it fades into a stigmatizing moralism, akin to the presentiment against the informal sector.

Hernando de Soto again provides a good illustration. He repeatedly asserts that the numerous bureaucratic steps now involved in formalizing legal entitlements are mud in the gears of capital formation and commerce, retarding development. He has been a central voice urging simplification of bureaucratic procedures as a development strategy — every minute and every dollar spent going to the state to pay a fee or get a stamp is a resource lost to development. This seems intuitively plausible. But there is a difficulty — when is the state supporting a transaction by formalizing it and when is the state burdening the transaction by adding unnecessary steps or costs? The aspiration seems to be an economic life without friction, each economic act mechanically supported without costs. But legal forms, like acts of discretion, are not simply friction — they are choices, defenses of some entitlements against others. Each bureaucratic step necessary to enforce a formal title is a subsidy for the economic activity of informal users. Indeed, everything which seems friction to one economic actor will seem like an entitlement, an advantage, an opportunity to another. The point is to develop a theory for choosing among them.

Let us say we begin by defining corruption as the economic crimes of public figures who steal tax revenues or accept bribes for legally mandated services. Even here the connection to development is easier to assume than to demonstrate. Are these figures more or less likely to place their gains unproductively in foreign bank accounts than, say, foreign investors? Even if we define the problem narrowly as one of theft or conversion it is still difficult to be confident that the result will be slower growth. Sometimes, as every first-year property instructor is at pains to explain, it is a good idea to rearrange entitlements in this way, the doctrine of "adverse possession" being the most dramatic example. Practices one could label as "corrupt" may sometimes be more efficient means of capital accumulation, mobilizing savings for local investment. Moreover, rather few economic transactions are best understood as arm's length bargains — it turns out, for example, that the lion's share of international trade is conducted through barter, internal administratively priced transactions, or relational contracts between repeat players. The line between tolerable and intolerable differences in bargaining power, between consent and duress, is famously a site for political contestation. And, just as sometimes what look like market-distorting interventions can also be seen to compensate for one or another market failure, so what look like corrupt local preferences can turn out to be efficient forms of price discrimination.

But those promoting anticorruption as a development strategy generally have something more in mind — a pattern of economic crimes which erodes faith in a government of laws in general or actions by public (or private) actors which artificially distort prices, such as unreasonable finder's fees, patterns of police enforcement which protect mafia monopolies, things of that sort. Here, the focus moves from the image of public officials taking bribes outward to actions which distort free-market prices or are not equally transparent to local and foreign, private and public interests. Corruption becomes a code word for "rent-seeking" — for using power to extract a higher price than what would be possible in an arm's length or freely competitive bargain — and for practices which privilege locals. At this point, the anticorruption campaign gets all mixed up with a broader program of privatization, deregulation, and free trade (dismantling government subsidies and trade barriers, requiring national treatment for foreign products and enterprises) — and with background assumptions about the distortive nature of costs exacted by public as opposed to private actors.

Here the anticorruption project enters arenas of deep contestation. It has been famously difficult to distinguish administrative discretion, which prejudices the "rule of law," from judicial and administrative discretion which characterizes the routine practice of the "rule of law." It has been equally difficult to distinguish legal rules and government practices which "distort" a price from the background rules in whose shadow parties are thought to bargain. And there is no a priori reason for identifying public impositions on the transaction as distortions — costs of the transaction — and private impositions as costs of the good or service acquired. These matters might be disputed in political or economic terms. But the effort to treat corruption reduction as a development strategy substitutes a vague sense of the technical necessity and moral imperative for a "normal" arrangement of entitlements.

It is easy to interpret the arrangement of entitlements normalized in this way in ideological terms. When the government official uses his discretionary authority to ask a foreign investor to contribute to this or that fund before approving a license to invest, that is corruption. When the investor uses his discretionary authority to authorize investment to force a government to dismantle this or that regulation, that is not corruption. When the government distributes import licenses to allocate scarce foreign exchange — an opportunity for unproductive rent-seeking by those waiting in line for the license. When property rights allocate scarce national resources to unproductive users, waiting in line for estates to pass by succession is not rent-seeking. When pharmaceutical companies exploit their intellectual property rights to make AIDS drugs largely unavailable in Africa while using the profits to buy sports teams, that is not corruption; when governments tax imports to build palaces, that is corruption.

Perhaps the most telling problem is the difficulty of differentiating some prices and transactions as "normal" and others as "distorted" by improper exercises of power when every transaction is bargained in the shadow of rules and discretionary decisions, both legal and nonlegal, imposed by private and public actors, which could be changed by political contestation. This old American legal realist observation renders incoherent the idea that transactions, national or international, should be allowed to proceed undistorted by "intervention" or "rent-seeking." There is simply no substitute for asking whether the particular intervention is a desirable one—politically and economically. In this sense, seeking to promote development by eliminating "corruption" replaces economic and political choice with a stigmatizing ideology.

In short, development strategy requires a detailed examination of the distributional choices effected by various legal rules and regimes to determine, as best one can, their likely impact on growth and development. It requires that we identify the choices which might lead to different development paths and compare them in social, political, and economic terms—even if we lack a strong consensus or decisive expertise about how to make them. One makes policy to distribute—by price, by administrative action—hoping to allocate resources to their most productive, most developmentally promising use. It is unfortunate that there is no distributional recipe for development, but that is our situation. There are contending ideas, contending interests, contested theories, complex unknowables. Not knowing, we must decide. We might even experiment.

The law should be a terrain for these inquiries and a site for this experimentation—not a substitution for them. Building a legal regime involves choices which distribute differently and contribute to development in different ways. Sometimes, no doubt, increasingly formal legal rules would be a good idea. Sometimes less governmental discretion, sometimes more vigorous criminal enforcement, broader distribution of supply relationships, less local preference in contracting all might be very helpful. But sometimes we would also expect the opposite. The emergence of the rule of law as a development strategy has become an unfortunate substitute for engagement with the politics and economics of development policy making.

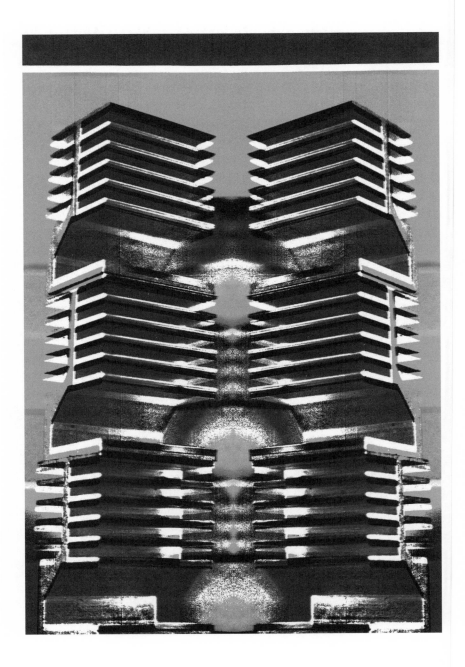

SIX

Bringing Market Democracy
to Eastern and Central Europe

In the years immediately following the fall of the Berlin Wall, many foreign policy specialists were filled with enthusiasm. The entire international system seemed open to renewal, with Europe the epicenter of transformation. More than four decades of East-West stalemate ended more abruptly and completely than had seemed imaginable. The European Union was poised to complete an ambitious legislative program to create a "single internal market" in 1992. For a time, these dramatic changes seemed to place Europe at the vanguard of an exciting rebirth of international humanitarian possibility. The European market program was to be more than a collection of commercial legislation — alongside the introduction of the Euro, it was to be a further step on the road to a durable Western European peace, common citizenship, and shared values. More than an alteration in the geopolitical balance, the fall of the Wall offered the opportunity to extend freedom, democracy and the benefits of a commercial market Eastward, and to return the lost nations of Central and Eastern Europe to a common European home.

It is hard now to recapture the extent to which the end of the Cold War and the simultaneous completion and expansion of the Western market seemed to signal the triumph of humanitarianism as the new language for international affairs. The vocabulary of human rights was central to both efforts. Henceforth — and beginning with the new governments of Central and Eastern Europe — governments would be recognized and states admitted to the international community only when they complied with the norms of international human rights. Their legitimacy was no longer to be measured by the fact of their control over territory, but by their compliance with international norms. Indeed, the word *legitimacy* itself became central to foreign policy thinking—actors were to be understood in a multi-faceted conversation with one another in which their actions contributed to or drew upon a metaphoric stockpile of "legitimacy." Nothing contributed more to that stockpile than humanitarian commitment—nothing withdrew legitimacy more decisively than violations of humanitarian norms and expectations.

In this new atmosphere, European trade experts routinely spoke of commercial freedom in the language of rights. International trade was increasingly linked to human rights protection. The new European Union would be rethought less as a technical regime to facilitate the cross-border movement of various factors of production than as a social and political project to vindicate the "four freedoms" and create a "Europe of the citizen." Multilateralism, with the United Nations in pride of place, would finally take on the significance and centrality denied it during the bipolar standoff of the Cold War. The international community was given a new and central project as the enforcer of last resort for human rights norms. The simultaneous emergence of South Africa from apartheid seemed a triumph for persistent pressure by the international human rights community. If apartheid could be defeated, what injustice could stand? Even the 1990–91 Gulf War seemed a triumph of multilateral cooperation, harnessing military power to the enforcement of international obligations enunciated by the United Nations. Although the predominance of the American military was starkly on view, that power had been exercised with a "New World Order" articulated and partly paid for by Europeans.

For a time after 1989, Europe seemed—at least in the eyes of its own humanitarian internationalists—to stand for human rights, for multilateralism, for the soft peace of open markets, and for a foreign policy of benign humanitarianism. It was common in the years after 1989 for American center-left internationalists to look to Europe as a model, not only for health insurance or social security, but for a committed and forceful multilateralism, dedicated to democracy and free trade, and exercised in the vocabulary of humanitarianism. Indeed, these ideas would guide thinking among humanitarian foreign policy elites of the center left at least until the emergence of terrorism as a central international preoccupation changed the focal point for international humanitarian policy making.

Many of the hopes of those early years would, of course, be dashed in the ensuing decade. It was not all September 11, 2001; humanitarian intervention would seem a far more complicated thing after Somalia, Rwanda, and Haiti. Europe would seem a far more complicated place after the disintegration of Yugoslavia. Human rights would seem a less reliable vocabulary for foreign policy after a decade of seeking to apply a consistent normative standard to places as diverse as China, Chechnya, and the Chile of Pinochet. The American-European alliance would seem far less stable and far less uniformly committed to the politics of multilateralism after the 2000 election. But in 1990, all this lay in the future. In 1989 and 1990, I was living in Brussels, working as a commercial lawyer, largely lobbying the European Union on behalf of American business clients in the context of the 1992 program. In the fall of 1989, two months before the Velvet revolution in Czechoslovakia, I traveled to Prague representing an American human rights organization to observe the trial of a young dissident and rock-and-roll enthusiast. Six months later, the Harvard Law School held a triumphant reunion of its European alumni in Prague, and I found my dissident working in the office of President Havel. It was a dramatic time — and the most exciting challenge facing the foreign policy experts of the European Union was how to respond to the sudden opening in the East. For these specialists, the dramatic story of German reunification, the complex realpolitik decisions of Bush, Gorbachev, and Kohl were all part of the background. Their struggle was to connect the internal legislative transformation of West Europe to the new developments East of the old Wall. From Brussels this seemed the model and test case for the new foreign policy of enlightened multilateral humanitarianism.

The strategies they adopted remain significant not only because they continue to influence relations between the European Union and its neighbors, but because they provide a window into the deformations introduced into the work of policy makers grappling with such dramatic challenges by their professional vocabulary — by what come to be shared assumptions about timing, about geography, and about the meaning and potential for international humanitarianism. The most significant shared assumption was precisely the idea that 1989 represented a sharp break in international affairs, an opportunity for renewal. For international relations experts, this placed 1989 in a series — with 1648, 1815, 1918 and 1945 — of moments at which dramatic changes wrought by war opened the field to legal reimagination.

At the same time, the European Communities 1992 program was seen as the almost-but-never-quite-completed continuation of a project set in motion after the Second World War to build a European political entity by strengthening its common economic life. This simple contrast — 1989 as break, 1992 as continuity — made the European Union program seem in some way "ahead" of the "emerging" East. This interpretive frame was not inevitable. The end of the iron curtain might well have been seen as the return of a continuous European political fabric, as a moment in a long march from feudal centralism to economic democracy. The fall of dictatorships in Spain, Portugal, and Greece only a few years before had been interpreted in precisely this way. Moreover, it would have been possible to see the new European Union after 1992 as the beginning of a new international form of governance, detached from the nation-state system, in which technocratic imperatives and market administration would displace enlightenment ideals of national mass democracy. As anxiety about "globalization" grew in the years after 1992, it seemed ever more plausible to see the beginning of the European Union as the end of the political nation-state.

Nevertheless, after 1989 the boundary between the internal market in the West and the trade regime being extended to East and Central Europe came to mark a chronology of development with distinct policy implications: the East should prepare for admission to the West through the shock of catching up. A recurring motif was the idea that a new Europe could only be built if premodern tendencies and conflicts could be restrained. The possibility of conflict was located both outside and before the Western European status quo. And that primitive other would need to remain outside until it was no longer behind. Bringing "them" into Europe too soon might jeopardize the European project, might set the West back centuries in its development or might signal lack of understanding for the progress Europe thought itself to have made. It was in this sense that European foreign policy elites, however humanitarian in sensibility, resisted expressions like Gorbachev's "common European house" which stressed one geography and one history. History had been broken along the boundary of the iron curtain. The humanitarian project would require an intense effort to speed the East forward without slowing progress in the West.

But after 1989, Eastern and Western Europe lived less in two historical moments than in two legal regimes: the regime of the European Union's internal market and the international trade system. The contrast between the two regimes is this: inside the European Union, Brussels manages a political structure and industrial policy to build an internal market by careful government planning and regulation. The international trade regime is an altogether different scheme, oriented to building down governmental distortions of free-market prices and strengthening the potential for private ordering. Unlike the European Union, the trade system has no managed public policy and no regulatory powers. For the European Union metropolis, these two regimes complement one another in numerous ways — public policy at home, private freedom abroad. At the periphery, the contrast is less harmonious. To be outside is to be subject to the ups and downs of free trade. To be inside is to participate in a highly structured system of planning, wealth stabilization, and transfer payments. For wealthy outsiders, with their own well-developed internal markets and established public politics, the combination may also be advantageous. Switzerland has long since learned to turn the legislative freedom of an outsider in a decentralized trade regime to its own advantage. For the less wealthy, the choice is a less happy one.

In the years immediately following 1989, both Brussels and the East rushed to integrate the Eastern nations into the international free trade regime rather than into the Western internal market. The "internal market" was uniformly thought to be a regime of such singular sophistication as to be beyond the grasp, as well as the needs, of the new Eastern countries. It also seemed too fragile to accommodate partial assimilation — any "broadening" seemed a threat to the project of ever "deeper" economic coordination. The West extended familiar initiatives of trade and foreign aid, modest programs, detached from the internal Union industrial policy. Most of these programs were intensified versions of projects already underway with the Soviet bloc before the rupture of 1989. The new governments in the East promulgated dramatic legal reform exercises to launch their planned economies on a deregulatory free fall toward private ownership and hard currency investment. In the East, the difference between a Western market and the international trade system — between the European Union and the GATT — was simply not perceptible. The goal, in the East and West, was to stabilize the Eastern European regimes in the international trade regime.

As the policy developed, a series of "association" agreements with each of the former Comecon economies aimed to smooth relations between the internal market and the newly privatized and "open" markets of the East. They encouraged further rounds of legal reform in the East to bring their legislative framework into line with that familiar to investors and consumers in the European Union. Relations between East and West were increasingly described in chronological terms, and Eastern Europe was routinely compared to underdeveloped societies of the third world. For national economic planners in the East, negotiations with international bankers, investors, and development institutions began to displace discussions with the European Union. The international trade regime was increasingly presented as a reasonable "first step" toward coordination with the internal market, and perhaps eventually, membership in the European Union itself. It became obvious that Eastern and Central Europe would need to follow the path of development — bypassing the third world, accomplishing what almost no nation in the third world had managed — *before* it could expect meaningful coordination with Brussels, let alone membership. What *sense* does it make, I was often asked, to give these people the regulatory equivalent of a Mercedes when they have not yet developed the capacity to drive a Fiat?

This frame has continued to govern thinking about relations between the European Union and nations to its East through negotiations toward their eventual accession. As currently conceived, even after membership, Eastern nations will remain in a halfway house of transitional measures for years. The idea of a smoothly managed — if lengthy — progress from one regime to another had obvious advantages for policy makers seeking to clarify the way forward. That it seemed a *natural* progression from primitive to modern made it all the more politically plausible. At the same time, this frame helped make immediate membership in the European Union unthinkable for the new states of the East, even as the German Democratic Republic was swiftly reunited with the Federal Republic. And there seemed no plausible analogy between the former Comecon nations and Spain, Portugal, and Greece, for whom early membership had seemed a political imperative as they emerged from dictatorship in the 1970s.

Still, we can only speculate whether the articulation of a clear path through the international trade regime did more to retard than to speed eventual membership. What does seem clear is that this set of ideas sharply constricted the range of policies humanitarian policy makers in Brussels — and in the East — considered in structuring both membership and nonmembership.

In fact, both the European Union's internal market and the international trade regime are heterogenous combinations of legal and institutional arrangements that have been the subject of intense struggle. These elements could well be combined in a wide variety of ways, with quite different distributional consequences. Although different in overall sensibility, the two regimes overlap in numerous details. It would have been possible to design an international trade regime more or less like the managed markets of the Union — just as it would have been possible to build the internal market with a variety of different regulatory components favoring similar or different groups to those whose interests flourished in the international trade regime.

In short, there was no *one* path of law reform for Eastern Europe.

But in the years after 1989 it certainly seemed that there was. Both the trade regime into which the East Europeans were initiated and the internal market regime of the European Union were understood as coherent embodiments of an idea: free trade for the East, industrial policy for the West. The difference between these ideas was sharpened by the sense that they lay along a natural evolutionary path and could be understood to be appropriate for entire countries in different geographical areas. Humanitarian foreign policy experts concerned about the social consequences which accompanied the end of communism in the East found themselves urging governments, in the East and the West, to move *more quickly* along the same path from one regime to the other as was being proposed by other analysts. Pragmatically assessing and contesting the detailed components of each regime and the distributional consequences of various possible relationships between them did not seem possible.

INTERNATIONAL TRADE: NORMALCY AND DEVIATION

Broadly conceived, the international trade regime distinguishes normal from deviant traders and trade relations. The distinction is at once spatial and temporal. As seen from the trade regime, normal trade is open, structured solely by comparative costs, and pursued by private actors without governmental intervention. Normal traders are diversified, developed economies with stable currencies that free private enterprises to participate in trade without abnormal state support or regulation. Everything else — subsidies, dumping, cartels, dependence, instability, state trading, underdevelopment, undue vulnerability to imports, exchange rate instability, and international price supports — is abnormal.

In normal situations, governments adopt a passive laissez-faire attitude. The regime of "private international law" sustaining normal trade contains rules about property and contract, mechanisms to stabilize jurisdictional conflicts and liberate private actors to choose forums, as well as ad hoc mechanisms of dispute resolution. The dominant players are private traders, and to a far greater extent than in even the most laissez-faire national system, they legislate the rules that govern their trade through contract. When governments do participate, they operate "commercially," as private actors.

The public law international trade regime is supplemental to this private structure, concerned either with reducing or punishing interventionist abnormalities. The basic GATT principle of "nondiscrimination" prevents national governments from treating traded goods less well than domestic goods. Successive rounds of GATT-sponsored negotiations to reduce or eliminate tariffs and quotas encourage governments to dismantle measures which distort prices. The "most favored nation" principle multilateralizes the results of these bilateral negotiations. An expanding effort to eliminate "subsidies" and "nontariff barriers" to trade targets other price-distorting governmental action. At the same time, a variety of exceptional curative or protective measures are permitted or encouraged in deviant situations, such as those involving state traders or developing countries. Thus, the international financial system aims only to liberate financial flows and trade in currency. It treats stable currency convertibility as normal and intervenes only to prevent *abnormal* exchange-rate swings. The International Monetary Fund is mandated to provide temporary technical assistance and austerity-directed intervention in abnormal situations to encourage "structural adjustment" back to normality.

The trade policy of the United States and the external commercial policy of the European Union share this broad vision. In normal situations with normal trading partners, tariffs and quantitative restrictions are to be reduced to a minimum. If a trader acts abnormally, its imports may be restricted or subjected to special duties. The most well known examples concern dumping and foreign governmental subsidies. Consistently deviant traders—the underdeveloped or former state trader—are urged and aided to undertake the internal reform necessary to come up to speed with the requirements of a "modern" market.

This general vision remains largely a myth. The international trade regime is mostly composed of exceptional measures designed to overcome perceived abnormalities. For developed societies this means defense against "predatory" foreign deviations from normal trade practice as well as international arrangements to "normalize" or "stabilize" certain markets. After numerous general reductions, there remain modest tariffs on manufactured goods produced by OECD countries. Stable agricultural prices and trading conditions are broadly supported, at least for the products of developed nations. Most developed economies maintain elaborate regimes permitting outright quotas or exclusions in situations deemed likely to harm domestic production. For products — like textiles — whose import poses particular dangers to producers in the developed world, elaborate multilateral regimes of quotas and "voluntary" export restrictions have supplanted the open aspirations of the GATT system. Meanwhile, a wide range of insistently "deviant" actors — starting with the state traders of the Soviet bloc and the import substitution regimes of the postwar developing world and continuing to the China of today — have been accommodated by the GATT through negotiations which leave intact all sorts of long-term "distortive" policies on both sides.

More significantly, inside the West, the idea of a "normal" framework for private commerce is widely understood to be incoherent. Advanced industrial societies have quite different conceptions of the "normal" level of environmental, labor, and other regulation. For almost a century, it has been a commonplace of legal thought that all prices are bargained in the shadow of *some* regulatory structure. The effort to distinguish "price distortive" from "market supportive" regulations dissolves readily into a political choice among alternative markets. Moreover, all advanced industrial economies have embraced a wide range of different forms of property ownership, corporate finance and control, public-private partnerships, and privately regulated markets — all of which have emptied the central opposed categories of private property and public policy of much of their iconic meaning. Modern economies, as everyone who participates in running them knows, resemble the crude ideological image of undistorted exchange among private actors no more than complex modern administrative states resemble the charming Enlightenment models of representative democracy familiar from high school civics classes.

But none of this has led to a questioning of the international trade regime's archaic background commitment to a distinction between the normal and the abnormal trader. On the contrary, the sense that modern industrial legal regimes are "sophisticated" simply confirms the relative primitivism of traders and trade relations "outside" the internal market. As a result, regulatory minimalism — like many myths of origin and identity — dominates initiation rituals for newcomers to the international trade system long after it has been sidelined by long-term participants. Newcomers must open their markets to investment and export from the first world. They must reform their internal legal order to create what are imagined as the "normal" domestic preconditions for trade: stable convertible currency and the absence of government subsidies, price supports, or other abnormal interventions which might distort prices.

For developed normal traders, the link between domestic and trade policy is severed. The internal market is a sophisticated operation, appropriate for an advanced economy. Trade remains a realm of arm's length exchange undistorted by public policy, conducted among traders who have forsworn the benefits of governmental intervention on their behalf. For newcomers, however, the international trade regime lays out a program for internal regulatory reform. Deviant traders live far more directly in the international economic order than do developed market societies. The trade regime is structured as a relationship between those who have transcended its limitations in their internal economic policies and those who must first submit to its primitive logic.

INSIDE THE EUROPEAN UNION:
REGULATING THE INTERNAL MARKET

From the start, the European Communities were structured by the interaction between an economic and a political idea. These two ideas came together most dramatically in the institutional and legislative program to complete the internal market by 1992. But because much of the novelty of the regime lies in the relative invisibility of its politics, the European Union can seem to epitomize the mature laissez-faire normal trader.

The economic idea combines deregulation and technocratic expertise, and at first appears quite similar to the international trade regime. Indeed, it has at times seemed, to Member States with comfortably corporatist market regulatory histories and business-government relations, to require the same sort of internal reform now required of non-Members seeking to participate in the trade system. The European internal market was to be built primarily by liberating private forces over a larger geographical terrain through the dismantling of national-government regulatory differences and tariffs, which seemed to splinter the European market into national components. Eliminating these differences would sneak up on national sovereignty precisely in the style of the international trade regime.

At the same time, however, the mechanisms of that integration, the tools to build the internal market, would be large-scale legislative and administrative interventions. Eliminating national boundaries to market flows did not mean eliminating price distortions. It meant harmonizing them, coordinating them, negotiating an acceptable relationship between them. The regime did not aim to replace national public authority with an international liberated private authority — quite the opposite. The economic regime required a harmonization of regulation, an aggressive antitrust regime, and a continual bargaining among public authorities about their regulatory efforts.

The political idea combines centralization with sectoral functionalism. Although the European Union is committed to a project of government building — through the coordination, harmonization, and unification of legislation — it has from the start claimed not to be building a European federal state. The European regime was to be the technical implementation of legally delegated sectoral competences rather than the juridical concentration of power thought characteristic of an incipient sovereign state.

The European Union pursued its economic idea, after the initial elimination of internal customs duties and the establishment of a common external tariff, through the progressive elaboration of a series of market freedoms and common policies. Implementation of the internal market freedoms (free movement of workers, goods, and capital, freedom of establishment, freedom to provide cross-border services) has repeatedly moved from liberalization to regulatory har-monization. Sometimes Brussels has set minimum standards and re-quired "mutual recognition" of each state's regulatory standard by its neighbors. In other fields, they have developed a unified European Union–wide regulatory regime. In every case, the result has been a highly regulated market—before and after. For example, the "free movement of workers" means the harmonization of social security and vocational training regulations. The "free movement of goods" means common environmental regulation; the freedom to provide cross-border services means a European Union–wide regime for in-surance brokers and agents; and the free movement of capital means common banking and securities legislation, tax harmonization, and monetary union.

The European Union conducts independent economic policy in three main areas: agriculture, competition, and social policy/transfer payments. Agricultural policy began as a postwar effort to stabilize markets, increase food productivity, increase the income received by farmers, ensure supply, and regulate prices. It remains the largest budgetary item. Competition policy—regulating the activity of firms to ensure fair and continuing competition—has become the most significant arena for the Union to pursue an active industrial policy regarding such general issues as the desirability of corporate mergers or the structure of the air transport and telecommunications indus-tries. Beyond agriculture and competition policy, the European Union pursues an aggressive environmental and social policy and oversees large transfer payments from wealthier to less-developed re-gions of the Community.

Taken together, these economic freedoms and industrial policies have made government a power throughout the market. They have transformed the deregulatory ambition of the trade regime into the aspiration for ever-more-sophisticated technical regulation. Opposi-tion to national regulatory distortions has animated a new techno-cratic regulatory process of mutual accommodation among national regulatory authorities.

The political center for this market governance is less visible than it is in a more conventional national liberal-market democracy. The commitment to sectoral functionalism submerges the regulatory process in a welter of technical committees managed by the technical experts and career civil servants of the European Commission. Because the political apparatus in Brussels is structured to supplement sovereign states, rather than displace them, the politics of industrial policy and market intervention remain oddly difficult to locate. Rather than political contestation, one finds only technical administrative action — itself dispersed among myriad national and international institutions.

As a result, Henry Kissinger's famous quip that Europe had no telephone number to call remains correct — but that does not mean there is no governance going on. The political arguments which move the regulatory establishment in Brussels are not rooted in the implementation of a party's political program. Brussels responds to small-scale and technical arguments about the efficient or most appropriate form for regulation, or to arguments about the impact of a given regulatory initiative on the *general* ambition to strengthen the European Union regime or advance the common market idea.

Of course, the Brussels government is more than a bureaucracy exercising formally delegated competences. All of the avatars of classic parliamentary democracy are there: judiciary, parliament, executive, the rule of law. Just as modern economies have left the crude ideological certainties of property and contract or the simple distinctions between public and private far behind, this regime has transcended earlier, more primitive visions of democratic participation or the separation of powers.

Familiar forms of political life have been transformed as they have migrated to Brussels. The European Union decision-making process has shifted legislative competence from parliaments to the executive as it has moved authority from the regions to the center. The administration has become a more transient and flexible participant in the legislative process. The judiciary has transcended its classic role to become the only institution empowered to control the executive organs and an active participant in the effort to build the Union and promote the internal market. Perhaps most dramatically, the Union has institutionalized the Parliament as a promise, place holder for the democratic aspiration through a complex practice of advisory "codecision" in which the administration and judiciary are the parliament's closest allies, rather than competitive adversaries.

The result is a political culture with a technocratic and legal face, in which politics is treated as having somehow already happened elsewhere — in the Treaty, or the European Summit, or in the Member States, or in the Council. The Member States, by contrast, are either implementing Union legislation or adjusting the imperatives of an internal market to their own, largely executive, sovereignty. The result is a political instance freed from the institutions and pressure points of a national mass politics and responsive only to the bureaucratic imperatives of managing an industrial policy and the wishes of national governments. Politics is either an aspiration for institutional designers or has been transformed into a management problem for updated institutional players.

Although aspects of the old politics are remembered with nostalgia — European Union elites have been engaged for more than a decade in a discussion about the perceived "democracy deficit" — waves of institutional reform aimed to cure the problem have only confirmed the transformation of political struggle into a process of technocratic management. Democracy is a policy orientation, a management spirit, a function of information sharing more than power sharing. In a market-driven governmental structure of delegated powers, institutional reforms will always lag behind increasing regulatory competences. At the same time, popular demands for governmental legitimacy can drag on the system's ability to respond flexibly to a changing market. The result is a long-term structural deficit — between the forward march of regulatory capacity and its democratic legitimacy — which must simply be managed by policies appearing to engage the "European citizen" directly (signage changes, education about European rights and culture, expanded competence to crack down on immigration or crime) and a continual process of institutional reform, in which the technical levers of macroeconomic policy and economic regulation are placed safely forward of the temptation to political backsliding from the internal market project.

In one sense, the European Union's vision tracks the mature normal democratic market trader of the international trade regime: politics displaced by economics, public by private. By continually aspiring to the democratic, the European Union shares something with its less-advanced neighbors. Just as the economic model of the internal market, with its deep public-private partnerships, contrasted with the austerity shocks and regulatory abstinence demanded of outsiders, however, so also this vision of a technical industrial policy unmoored from more traditional forms of democratic participation contrasts sharply with the institutional reforms urged on the East. Deviant neighbors, who must "democratize" before being considered for participation, face a European Union which has transcended the necessity for democratic self-organization, replacing democratic institutions with the rhetoric of continuing democratization.

AFTER THE FALL: BRUSSELS ENGAGES THE EAST

In the years after 1989, European Union policy makers struggled to integrate the former Comecon nations into the international trade regime rather than into the internal market. As more comprehensive relations were built through the conclusion of "association" agreements holding out the promise of negotiations toward membership, shared assumptions among policy makers in the East and West organized more than a decade of negotiations on the principle of "return to normalcy" and "catching up" by the East.

The 1989 rupture seemed to release the East from primitivism, from ideology, from the priority of politics over economics, public over private, belief over reason. Enlightened thought in Brussels sought to treat the East as "normally" as possible—given how primitive and unprepared they were. Special treatment—beyond rather modest "transitional" assistance—was thought unnecessary, and probably unwise. Subsidies, unique technical standards, multiple currency rates, wage protection, incomplete privatization—all seemed unfortunate deviations, echoes of a prior addiction, the sooner given up the better. Any effort to negotiate an accommodation *between* regulatory regimes and economic interests in the East and the West seemed altogether inappropriate. The point was to encourage the East to transform *itself* as quickly as possible.

Eastern countries were expected to return to normalcy one by one, in accordance with their own abilities to throw off residual deviationist practices and carry on normal relations with normal traders. Moreover, returning to normal was thought to be a matter of fact rather than policy, rather easily measured by the confidence of foreign private actors. Reform programs were thought to have been successful when they attracted foreign capital and trade. Foreign investors were not seen as people with interests, but as the most neutral and objective assessors of whether an economy was or was not normal. The European Union, faced with what it saw to be the greatest geopolitical transformation and regulatory challenge in fifty years, concluded that, ultimately, there was little they or any normal government could or should do. Emerging traders must take their cues from private rather than public actors. Much as we would like to help, governmental accommodation in the West will only weaken and delay the reform process in the East. As for the governments of the East, they should be helped to see that private actors will respond best to public gestures of self-restraint and aggressive internal reform oriented to the shared image of what a normal trader does, or once did, or should do, to develop.

The internal policies of the normal trader were not themselves thought to be implicated in the transition. The transition happened to *them* — they needed to catch up, to develop. Transition was a matter between the international trade regime and the internal regimes in the East, and seemed to have no implications for the ongoing internal market project. The European Union might need to protect its borders more assiduously from the spillover effects of abnormality and transition — from unwarranted immigration, worker, and capital flows — but it did not need to adjust its own internal market. After the fall of the Wall, a first priority was to ensure firm controls on the Western side of the border. Meanwhile, in the East, patterns of production and trade, forms of economic organization, and above all the prices at which things were traded would all need to be changed — shocked to world levels.

In thinking about development policy for the Eastern economies, experts in both East and West shared a preference for export-led growth stimulated by foreign investment with a trade orientation toward the Western metropolis. These were the days of neoliberal ascendancy in development policy circles. Export promotion did not mean the careful government managed export regimes which had brought development to the Southeast Asian tigers. It meant privatization of ownership and decision making, opening the market to foreign trade at world prices, and seeing who bought what. Because East European countries should naturally prefer normal to abnormal trade, they should — and largely did — favor development strategies based on hard-currency investment and Western-oriented export-led growth rather than continued trade with other ex-deviants. Government efforts to restructure domestic economies toward general currency convertibility, to discourage trade with the Soviet Union and to encourage hard currency investment are "deregulatory," "normalizing," or "transitional," rather than "interventionist." The Eastern countries were to be opened to normal world trade while the European Union continued to resist the import of Eastern products which were "abnormally" produced or marketed. Outward investment from the East was seen to be inhibited primarily by abnormally soft currency rather than policy, so that hard currency earnings were only thought possible through export until normal convertibility was achieved.

It is now difficult to reconstruct precisely how humanitarian policy makers in the West and East came to such a clear common understanding of what was necessary for Eastern and Central European nations after 1989. Third world societies have developed a far wider range of different relationships with both the international trade regime and the individual economies of developed metropolis trading partners. The international trade regime itself had already built long-term relationships with deviant traders both large and small, from the Soviet Republics to China. These relationships were built precisely through negotiation between economic interests on both sides in an effort to accommodate differing regulatory regimes — in an odd way the sort of bargaining which was also pursued within the European Union through its technical regulatory procedures. It had something to do with the time — with the dominance of neoliberal ideas about development after the Thatcher and Reagan years — and something to do with the place, the idea that these were *European* societies for which it was normal to expect normalcy, and whose various existing economic interests were all the results of intense ideological deviance and a historic rupture from progress toward advanced industrial democracy.

We should remember, however, that prior to 1989 the legal arrangements for trade relations with the Comecon countries were not substantially different from those governing trade with other nations. Tariff treatment of goods from the East was not substantially different from that accorded other nations, primarily as a result of substantial progress in general tariff reduction. Of course, some Comecon members remained outside of GATT and some special restrictions applied, particularly to the Eastern-bound export of products with military or security implications, and the atmosphere for settlement of trade disputes could be cold. As to quotas, although the European Union had distinguished between state- and market-trading partners, it subjected both to a similar institutional regime. Although quantitative restrictions had mostly been eliminated for market economies — and were largely eliminated by GATT — they remained in place despite GATT membership for Czechoslovakia, Hungary, Poland, and Romania.

Indeed, Brussels was well on its way toward regularizing trade with the East prior to 1989 — it had been negotiating trade agreements with individual Comecon countries since 1980. This process was hastened by the governmental changes of 1989, but not substantially changed. These trade agreements generally committed Brussels to end most remaining quantitative restrictions (often excluding sensitive products such as textiles, coal, and steel), bringing former Comecon nations up to normal GATT treatment, to "cooperate" in easing trade relations, and to provide a framework for discussion of other outstanding issues, including agricultural trade.

These trade agreements were designed to bring the socialist countries into the normal framework of international trade — without any aspiration to alter their internal regime. Much was made in the West of the fact that the trade agreements did not address many blocks to Eastern-bound export (export licensing schemes, remaining tariffs, governmental regulations, currency convertibility, etc.). The list differed in detail, but was similar to the list of issues to be taken up in trade negotiations by Brussels with any number of governments around the world. This was the normal work of trade policy, and required ongoing bilateral accommodation. After 1989, this became the work of the IMF, the development banks, and the private investors, exerting *unilateral* pressure on the Eastern countries to protect the West from deviant traders and the price distortions of subsidy and dumping regimes.

THE TRANSITION: POLICY IN BRUSSELS

The special programs and initiatives begun in Brussels in 1989 aimed to speed and complete the normalization already under way through trade normalization, emergency aid, and transitional assistance to attract Western capital. In the trade area, they sped elimination of quantitative restrictions (putting involved countries such as Hungary on an equal footing with GATT members), suspended some national quantitative restrictions for one year (an improvement over GATT treatment for products such as shoes, toys, and automobiles), and gave the Eastern countries benefit of the "Generalized System of Preferences" extended to developing countries under GATT. The result: trade normalization plus the sort of special treatment afforded "less developed countries" elsewhere in the world.

On aid, Brussels initially budgeted 300 million ECU annually under the so-called PHARE program for Poland and Hungary. Although this figure was increased several times over the next years — primarily as other recipients were added — the goal and structure of the program did not change. Most of the funds were earmarked for food aid. Food aid funds were to be spent in the European Union to purchase food at market prices for shipment to the East, where it could be sold at local prices to create a local currency fund for infrastructural assistance. Much of the rest was set for training and technical assistance projects either in an established university or vocational exchange program or in a local project identified by the recipient government, often retraining for manufacturing in joint ventures newly established with Western investors.

Access to Western capital was to be facilitated through loans made or guaranteed by the East European Development Bank, through extension of existing government insurance schemes for overseas private investment, through local government guarantees of foreign investment, and through local government law reform to attract Western private investment. These initiatives were all structured to encourage private ownership and control, convertibility of profits, and governmental deregulation. All were aimed to stimulate a Westward export orientation for the former Comecon economies.

Taken together, the Union's trade, aid, and investment policies with ex-Comecon nations resembled those in place with a large number of developing countries and designed to connect their economies with Brussels through the international trade regime. Indeed, the preferential trade regime established for participants in the Lome Convention more than a decade earlier and extended to more than sixty developing nations provided the most accurate parallel. In it we find preferential trade terms for LDC exports and minimum financial and technical aid, usually in the export sector for products not manufactured in the European Union itself. These programs—like the entire commercial policy of the European Union—are managed by Brussels, rather than the Member States, precisely to support the Union's internal market integration. It was immediately clear in 1989 that any discussion about expanding the Common Market would have to wait at least until the Internal Market had been "completed" in 1992. That the Eastern countries would need at least that much time to "catch up" made phasing things this way seem fortuitous. More recent discussions about membership for countries from the East have continued to focus on preserving the Union's regulatory process while continuing the progressive normalization of new members after their accession.

THE TRANSITION: POLICY IN THE EAST

Policy making in Eastern Europe focused throughout the transition period on internal legal, political, and economic reform. Broad changes in both public law (often including new administrative and election laws, constitutional court structures, and penal codes) and in private or commercial law (usually including at least company law, banking law, labor law, property law, and exchange regulations) aimed to provide what are thought to be the preconditions to for a country to participate as a "normal" trader in the international trade regime. Some of these efforts, such as early and insistent development of a stock exchange, seemed vaguely beside the point. The most significant were the privatization programs and the legal incentives aimed at attracting foreign investment.

Policy makers in the East focused on establishing a Westward oriented export economy attractive to Western financial investors. Pre-existing legal and institutional structures were swept aside, economic ties with the East largely ignored. This Westward focus could be read in the choice of deals governments agreed to guarantee or subsidize, in the incentives for profit repatriation, and in the choice and scale of entities first slated for privatization by sale or investment. Programs of privatization and other legal reform were structured with the aim to demonstrate a commitment to deregulation and private commercial activity. Although the impetus for privatization and incentive for foreign investment often came from the government, and these immense law reform projects had broad-reaching political effects, they were not understood as opportunities for political contestation or negotiation, even by progressive policy makers. Prices for government assets were to be determined by auction, rather than negotiation or regulation. Private Western assessments of asset value were rarely questioned, and preexisting industries were restructured into units attractive for investment rather than production.

Eastern European reformers drafting privatization legislation were quite rightly preoccupied with the practical difficulty of devising workable programs to attract foreign investment and establish the basis for a market economy. Their efforts were encouraged by a variety of international advisers, financiers, investors, and bureaucrats urging rapid transfer of ownership and control over economic resources to private hands. Opportunities for the sorts of regulatory compromise among existing economic interests typical of industrial policy making in Brussels were forgone.

Reformers in the East, supported by Western advisers, repeatedly adopted a familiar, if extreme, version of the classic laissez-faire economics more common to Western fantasy than practice. The privatization schemes suggest the strength of ideas associated with this vision of the market. The idea of the "transaction" as a politically neutral arrangement: privatization was organized as a sale or contract which, although negotiated, shaped, and often guaranteed by government forces and existing managerial interests, would be made to seem to respond to price and profit rather than plan. Or the idea that corporate (private) and administrative (public) forms are and should be distinct: privatization meant changes in the legal form of property ownership rather than, or in addition to and prior to, changes in actual control or economic structure. The focus on ownership led to an apparently natural priority for financial over industrial policy, Eastern governments repeatedly opting to organize and insure capital rather than labor.

Or take the idea that there is a natural progression from private to public law, in which securing and enforcing the private legal arrangements of the market forms a basic apolitical work of government, on top of which public law can be used for exceptional or transitional "interventions." Privatization programs in the East began by transferring assets and control to new forms of ownership, on the theory that private owners would know better than government planners what to do with them. Once normalization had been achieved, it was thought that regulation could then be designed to correct for difficulties which had emerged from the natural movements of the private market. The sense that this sequence is simply natural substituted for any attention to phasing in the transition process. The privatization schemes became deregulatory free falls in which the governments forswore the sort of industrial policy associated with the European Union's 1992 internal market — or with contemporary privatization experiences in Britain and elsewhere. Pressure for more "social democracy" in the transition was channeled to issues such as worker participation in corporate ownership, often on the "normal" German model, rather than to extensions of wage protection or social security — particularly in cases in which worker ownership could be the basis for transfer of control to management without foreign capital.

Transition policy in the East was not designed to maximize bargaining power in discussions with the European Union about coordinating regulations or accommodating diverging economic interests. Rather, the goal was internal reform to permit world prices and foreign investors to determine the value of human and other capital in the East. Policy makers differed in the stress they put on "shock" therapy for Eastern European transition. But the shock being considered was the same — the shock of rapid deregulation until the country "finds its level" in the international division of labor, a shock to primitivism, from which a modern market economy might or might not develop.

ALTERNATIVES: IMPROVING THE TERMS OF ENGAGEMENT

Policy makers with humanitarian and progressive sentiments — whether in Brussels or the East — might well have imagined a different sort of shock: the shock of moving immediately to the structured public-private partnerships and mixed economic forms familiar in all modern developed market economies, from which movement to a place in the international division of labor might slowly be accommodated. That they did not suggests that the humanitarian enthusiasm in policy making circles after 1989 was simply swamped by background assumptions about the nature of markets, the meaning of progress, and the apparently natural relationship between Eastern European transition and Western European continuity.

The astonishing thing is that there were other models readily at hand. The most accessible were probably those provided by nations which had become members of the European Communities before 1989 — Spain, Portugal, Greece — or the model of relations with members of the European Free Trade Association with whom Brussels had negotiated an elaborate regime of shared regulatory initiative and mutual accommodation. Even the association agreements with other countries thought unlikely candidates for membership —

such as Turkey or Israel—were drawn with a more permeable sense for the boundary between the internal and external markets of the European Community system.

Membership had been used to integrate neighbors of varying levels of economic development, from Britain and Denmark through Ireland to Spain, Portugal, and Greece. Sweden, Finland, and Austria would soon follow. For Spain, Greece, and Portugal, membership was seen as a tool to strengthen democratic and free-market commitments and to bring about economic development. The accession process had also proven extremely flexible, accommodating long and complex transitional arrangements, currency conversion restrictions, local aid arrangements, insulation from free-market forces, and specific sectoral weaknesses. Even after the expiration of the transitional arrangements, members did not find themselves in a unified legislative or political field. The 1992 program was largely premised on accepting a great deal of internal regulatory "variable geometry"— mutual recognition of differing standards, divergent policy objectives, and integration velocities.

Membership would not have foregrounded trade and aid. Inclusion in the internal market has been understood as an *alternative* to a free-trade zone, involving a far wider range of regulatory accommodations. Members have received enormous transfer payments to spur economic development, either as part of normal European Union programs, or as part of special "cohesion" initiatives for underdeveloped regions. These funds dwarf the modest aid packages extended to the East after 1989. Significantly, if unsurprisingly, the last sticking point in recent negotiations setting a date for accession to the Union was a scheme to delay and diminish the accessibility of existing Brussels funding to the new entrants from the East.

Membership was not the only longer-term option. The closer neighbors come to membership, the more wary they might rightly become about accession to the political and legal culture of Brussels. Membership means submersion in the technocratic and largely undemocratic decision making of Brussels, the assertive judicial processes of the Brussels legal regime and an acceptance of a country-by-country economic integration into the Western market. Membership means a large-scale and largely irreversible transformation of a nation's substantive law, governmental structure, and international status, as well as accession to a sophisticated environment of market intervention and regulation.

At the same time that Brussels was pursuing country-by-country trade negotiations with the former Comecon nations, it was also encouraging the members of its largest trading partner, the European Free Trade Association, to pursue a different tack. Industrial products already circulated among the eighteen members of the European Communities and EFTA largely without tariffs or quantitative restrictions. The EFTA countries seemed the economic and political peers of the Member States. They had not been admitted to membership as a result either of hesitation on their part (Norway had already turned down a membership offer, and would again), reluctance on the part of Brussels, or bad timing.

The negotiations with EFTA to establish a European Economic Space linking EFTA and the European Communities were conducted on behalf of all members of the two organizations, as if each aggregated a set of economic interests which could be bargained about bilaterally, adjusted, accommodated. Negotiations with the East could hardly have been more different. In the first place, there seemed little to negotiate — first the East needed to catch up. Brussels would wait, benignly, monitoring and assessing progress, and granting access as Eastern reform progressed, country by country. A common Central European strategy seemed neither possible nor desirable. Brussels preferred to deal with EFTA members together — partly to stave off individual membership applications which would require complex institutional negotiations, at least until the completion of the 1992 internal market program, while simultaneously building a larger and more uniform internal market by accommodating their economic interests in internal market regulation along the way.

Accommodation and negotiation of economic interests between EFTA and Brussels was to be an ongoing part of relations *within* the European Economic Space. The EES negotiations contemplated participation by the EFTA countries in the internal regulatory and legislative procedures of the European Communities. The EFTA countries

would accept the European Union's internal market regulatory structure — but they would participate in its development. The EC and
EFTA countries would develop common policies in such areas as
competition law, environmental protection, and worker safety. In the
end, the EES proved insufficient for Austria, Sweden, and Finland,
who successfully pursued membership. For Iceland, Norway, and
Switzerland, it has remained an alternative. Meanwhile, the Eastern
European countries were encouraged to pursue their own deregulatory reforms, outside the internal market, and to progressively accept existing internal market regulation over which they had not had
input, until deemed ready for accession on terms which would delay
their participation in agricultural subsidies and cohesion funding
even after membership.

It is difficult, from the outside, to perceive the European Union as
a complex regulatory regime with an active industrial policy. To
many outsiders in the third world it seems a free-trade association —
and the demand that they normalize as deregulatory free traders before participating makes a kind of sense. But the international trade
regime is not the same as the internal market of the advanced industrial world. The differences between these regimes are made to seem
normal by common ideas about natural evolution from an idealized
system of private property and representative democracy to a more
modern technocratic scheme of public-private policy management.
Humanitarian policy makers share these common ideas — and consequently fail to assess the full range of options available to developing
economies. Instead of pragmatic policy making, we find the repetition of broad ideological narratives about the relations between the
normal and the deviant, the advanced and the primitive.

As a result, policy makers built a rather unhappy path forward for
the former socialist states of Eastern Europe. They would begin in
the international trade regime as a new third world, experiencing
massive internal economic and social dislocations in the name of a
"market" which was understood to preclude humanitarian and progressive policy making. After a period, if successful, they would be
admitted to the regulatory — if not yet the full funding — machinery
of an internal market designed to accommodate a range of national

economic interests other than their own, which had been bargained in a technical legislative process from which they had been excluded. The restructuring of East European society was severed from the construction of the Western internal market.

A more pragmatic international humanitarianism might have captured other possibilities. Policy makers might have imagined an association strategy of engagement with the internal market rather than acquiescence in the international trade regime. Such a strategy might have been built on the basis of existing patterns of economic life in the East — treating them as interests to be accommodated rather than relics to be cast aside. Rather than pursuing negotiations on two tracks — a modern regulatory regime for industrial policy in the West, a regime of free trade and aid for the East (or the South) — the two tracks could have been brought together. Placing policy choices on a single table might have encouraged pragmatic assessment of their distributive costs and benefits for different economic and social interests — rather than their association with stereotyped narratives of evolution or natural progress.

Throughout this period, I participated in innumerable conversations with policy makers in Brussels about the transition. I was repeatedly struck by the difficulty of making any such alternative seem even remotely plausible. The people I spoke with were very well meaning and truly interested in achieving the most humanitarian result possible. They were not, by and large, neoliberals. Indeed, they had very little experience in the field of development policy where neoliberal ideas had begun to catch on. In their prior policy work *within* the Union, they were nothing but skeptical of the neoliberal winds blowing from Thatcher's Britain or Reagan's America. Their ideological sympathies lay far more comfortably with Western European corporatist models of ongoing government cooperation with "social partners" of business and labor.

Nevertheless, suggesting any ongoing negotiation with Eastern European social partners, or any effort to link the structure of the internal market to the existing economic needs and opportunities East of the Berlin Wall, was an absolute conversation stopper. It violated the first, obvious, taken-for-granted fact about the situation. They were behind. We were ahead. They had to catch up first. Harsh as it seemed, this was accepted as simply incontrovertible — as were the transition policies I have described here. Without a vigorous habit of skepticism about these unstated temporal and geographic assumptions, no pragmatic analysis of the many possible policy alternatives was possible.

SEVEN

The International Protection of Refugees

Much humanitarian work involves persuading other actors to address humanitarian concerns. Individual activists do this through their advocacy, just as international organizations lobby national governments to take action. Alongside this work, humanitarian professionals elaborate vocabularies to justify and empower their advocacy, design strategies for persuasion, and struggle to strengthen their advocacy institutions. These activities are also a form of policy making. International humanitarians argue with one another about how their tools should develop, about which rights to promote, which violations to stress, and about which procedures work best or how international institutions might best be restructured.

Humanitarian policy making often means *strategizing* about the law — about how it should be developed and deployed to best effect. When should rules be interpreted strictly and when is flexibility required? When should we stress the autonomy or neutrality of international legal norms — and when should we focus rather on their pragmatic link to political realities of one or another sort? These second-order policy debates can have an enormous effect, influencing the development of international law and the agenda for institutions advocating for humanitarian objectives.

But work on the tools can also get in the way of work on the problem. Debates about the development of humanitarian law can supplant work on its enforcement. More significantly, strategic debates can take on a life and shape of their own, influencing the development of doctrine in ways which turn out to hinder the achievement of humanitarian objectives. I saw this up close for the first time in 1984, while working in the legal offices of the United Nations High Commissioner for Refugees in Geneva.

The United Nations High Commissioner for Refugees, or UNHCR, has been the leading international organization in the field of refugee affairs for more than fifty years. International refugee lawyers — termed "protection officers" in UNHCR argot — form a small and relatively homogenous professional group. They account for much of the writing in the fields of refugee and asylum law, and have been responsible for developing most of the international instruments of refugee protection. They both manage the law — developing it, strategizing about it — and use it in their advocacy.

While I was there, the UNHCR was reevaluating its relationship to the asylum laws and procedures of national states. Particularly in Western Europe, asylum law was politically visible and in the process of being significantly tightened in one after another state. Seeing a potential for humanitarian abuse, the UNHCR was looking for ways to become involved. The debates which ensued provide an excellent window on the process by which this sort of very well intended effort to reform the vocabulary for advocacy can become stuck. Indeed, twenty years after I left Geneva, these debates continue to shape refugee policy in almost the same way as when I left them.

I should say that the lawyers at the UNHCR were extremely dedicated and well informed about refugee law. There were constantly working to assess its strengths and weaknesses, commissioning studies and seeking advice about its possible improvement. They were self-consciously pursuing not only the enforcement and implementation of refugee law in specific cases, but also the long-term strengthening of the legal protections available. The problem was *not* that they were rigid or formalist about their doctrinal categories. Sometimes they were, sometimes they were not. Often they were extremely flexible and imaginative.

The problem was rather that their debates about what to do became increasingly preoccupied with worries about the right relationship between rule following and political flexibility or between fealty to law and savvy political strategy — to the exclusion of concern about what would work to resolve the humanitarian issue at hand. They were right to think about long- as well as short-term effects — humanitarian policy makers all too often ignore the long run or substitute vague hopes about the future for careful analysis. The difficulty was that their careful analysis focused on everything but the causes and consequences of refugee flows and treated strengthening the UNHCR itself as the only significant long run effect worth consideration. They lavished attention instead on debates about how one might link the imaginary worlds of international law and politics or national and international authority and how one might consolidate the High Commissioner's authority. These debates shaped the proposals they made and transformed the terms used to define their authority, but remained strangely detached from what happened to refugees themselves. To understand precisely how this happened, some background on the UNHCR and its refugee protection work is required.

THE UNHCR: NEITHER RESETTLEMENT
NOR REPATRIATION

The UNHCR was formed five years after the Second World War as a compromise. Immediately after the war, international public and private agencies sprang up to provide assistance to the millions of displaced persons in Europe. The United Nations Relief and Rehabilitation Administration (UNRRA) administered refugee camps and repatriated displaced persons to their countries of origin. The United Nations established the International Refugee Organization (IRO) to aid in the large-scale resettlement of refugees who were unwilling to return home. When the original three-year mandate of the IRO came to an end, the international community was unwilling to continue financial assistance for displaced persons. Yet, amid rising East-West tensions, it was evident that the postwar refugee problem had not been resolved. People continued to flee westward and war-torn states which had first welcomed the new arrivals claimed that their economies could handle no more. Enter the UNHCR.

The UNHCR would not carry on the assistance work of the IRO. By and large, that burden would be turned over to voluntary assistance organizations and the front-line European states receiving the refugees. Nor would the UNHCR promote repatriation, which no longer seemed appropriate for people fleeing the East. Disengaged from both repatriation and resettlement, the High Commissioner would also lack the financial resources to provide food, shelter, or other forms of assistance to refugees. The role the international community marked out for itself was to be quite specific — providing international legal "protection" to those who could be certified as bona fide "refugees." Other displaced persons — and refugees seeking other forms of assistance — would need to turn to voluntary agencies and national states.

The UNHCR's role would be to provide international legal protection and advocacy for those among the displaced who were refugees. This gave new and quite specific meanings to the terms "refugee" and "protection" — as well, by contrast, to "displaced person" and "assistance." The relations among these terms — and their relationship to the institutional identity of the UNHCR itself — continue to shape debate about refugee policy. International legal documents — the Statute of the United Nations High Commissioner for Refugees and the 1951 Convention on the Status of Refugees — were drawn up to distinguish "refugees" from other displaced persons. Refugees were individuals outside their country of nationality "owing to a well founded fear of being persecuted for reasons of race, religion, nationality or political opinion" in the words of the 1951 Statute. The UNHCR would "protect" people whose eligibility as refugees had been certified.

In this sense, the UNHCR was established in part by creating a classification for it to administer, setting in motion years of legal work to define the UNHCR's "mandate" by applying the Statute's definition of a refugee to people whose status was ambiguous or uncertain. People who were not "refugees" but were outside their country of nationality were displaced persons — a default category. In the context of the Cold War, of course, certification of Eastern Europeans in flight to the West did not seem difficult. For later refugee flows, applying this definition to individual displaced persons became far more complex.

The UNHCR would offer "protection" to people certified to be refugees. Although the origins of this term are obscure, it suggested the diplomatic protection normally accorded a national by his sovereign under international law. The UNHCR would step in to offer refugees a legal bridge from the time they lost the protection of their country of origin until they were legally normalized elsewhere. Granting the status of "refugee" to such persons was itself a form of protection — giving them a clear legal status at international law.

The early work of the UNHCR was primarily legal and technical — identifying people as bona fide "refugees," issuing travel documents, assisting in obtaining recognition of their various legal statuses (marriage, property, etc.), and advocating ever more precise guidelines for handling recognized refugees. Protection seemed largely nonpolitical to those undertaking it. The UNHCR's work seemed "humanitarian" both in the sense both that it helped people in difficult circumstances and that it was separated from national political and ideological controversies.

The analogy to diplomatic protection was not helpful in understanding the legal consequences of being certified as a refugee. Diplomatic protection occurs when one sovereign feels that its sovereign rights have been violated by the treatment accorded one of its nationals by another sovereign. It then represents that national on the international plane. At issue are the reciprocal rights of sovereigns — that the injury has been done a national, or that a national gets "protected" is, strictly speaking, a secondary matter at international law. Perhaps more significantly, the substantive sovereign rights which might be violated by one sovereign in its dealings with nationals of another are numerous.

It was clear that the minimum treatment required for refugees would be far less. They could not be turned back to the nation from which they fled — the principle of "nonrefoulement." Their existing private rights, property, and civil status should be recognized once they were settled — like those of any other foreign citizens. In the early years, once "certified" or "recognized" as refugees, people received relatively predictable treatment in their country of settlement. When the UNHCR advocated "recognition" of a person's "refugee status" it seemed to mean something like legal assimilation. Nevertheless, what it meant to "recognize" refugee status remained legally vague and differed from place to place. When protection officers wanted to advocate specific forms of treatment, they did so by calling upon states to recognize such a treatment as a "right" flowing from refugee status.

By associating the word "refugee" with the particular class of people fleeing political persecution, the UNHCR was protecting more or less the same group of people for which the institution of political asylum had long been used. Asylum had been seen as a sovereign response to an individual's loss of nationality or sovereign protection—it would not have been surprising to see "asylum" as the appropriate "recognition" for a person's "refugee status." Indeed, asylum has an elaborate history in public international law and is, in every national jurisdiction, a legal as well as a political institution. Many refugees today do, in fact, seek asylum and many countries limit asylum to legally certified refugees.

From the start, however, international protection work proceeded on a track parallel to national "asylum" law and policy. UNHCR policy makers associated *international* protection of refugees with the provision of an international legal status giving these people access to the UNHCR's advocacy. Refugee law became a component of international human rights and humanitarian law generally. Refugee law restrains sovereignty discretion—the status must be "respected." As early refugees in Europe resettled to the West, they were legally assimilated as residents—but they were generally not processed formally for political asylum. Asylum was a matter of national law and sovereign discretion, and seemed more appropriate for individuals with a distinct political profile. These two terms—refugee and asylum—came to describe a division of labor between national sovereigns and the international community. Refugee status focused on the period after flight and before resettlement, and was legally presided over by an international institution. Asylum focused on the treatment provided individuals—at least some individuals—resettling in a given state. As a result, protection officers increasingly became convinced that asylum was something about which they would *normally* have nothing to say.

In the intervening decades, the westward flow of Eastern Europeans was eclipsed by sudden, large-scale transboundary migrations in the third world — so called South-South refugee flows — and by the movement of many individuals to the North from areas of the third world where postcolonial political and economic conditions had deteriorated. This shift drew into question almost every assumption about international refugee work. Refugees today are less often middle-class people who need legal assimilation in a second European culture than destitute people with a wide variety of special needs. Making individual determinations of "refugee status" has become increasingly beside the point. People moving from South to North typically encounter national immigration authorities — and enter national asylum procedures — before they have been certified as refugees by the UNHCR. South-South refugee flows are often far too massive or chaotic to make individual determinations practical. Refugees are in immediate need of humanitarian assistance — food, shelter, medical care — not documentation. International documentation no longer translates effectively into any particular solution — indeed, it can complicate both repatriation and resettlement. National immigration policies — including asylum procedures — have become the central legal arena for determining the treatment of displaced persons, regardless of the motives for their flight. Overall, the UNHCR has had to confront a much wider range of difficult decisions about what refugees need, what they want, and what solutions it is appropriate for an international agency to pursue.

In many ways, the UNHCR's response to this changing context has been a model of successful institutional adaptation. An "assistance" division was added to the UNHCR, and assistance — the provision of shelter, water, food, or medical care — has come to comprise a far greater portion of the High Commissioner's work. The UNHCR has continually reinterpreted its mandate to legitimate participation in new humanitarian challenges affecting refugees — most recently asserting an entitlement to protect those fleeing persecution based on "gender." Formal legal determination of refugee status, once an end in itself, now often seems to be merely a bureaucratic prerequisite to assistance. Advocating signature and ratification of the instruments of international refugee law has become a part of a larger propaganda effort. For the protection of refugees, the UNHCR relies far more heavily upon sophisticated political negotiation and the provision of financial or technical assistance in specific cases than upon assertion of uniform legal standards.

Protection officers now readily acknowledge the political nature of their work and are willing to negotiate a wide range of solutions beyond those expressly mandated by the instruments whose ratification they publicly urge. Moreover, they continually exhort one another to pay more attention to the politics of context, cause, and solution. Protection officers are quite forthcoming in admitting that their work is and must be context specific and political. For more than thirty years, they have sought to align their work more closely with national asylum policies, expanding their mandate to protect "asylum seekers" and developing recommendations for fair and efficient asylum procedures. In 1999, the UNHCR Executive Committee adopted a proposal on "recommended practices" for the detention of asylum seekers, and in May 2001, they pursued global consultations on "fair and efficient" asylum processes.

In other ways, however, the protection business at the UNHCR has not changed since 1951. Although willing to think flexibly and politically about their work, protection officers cling to the idea that their work has a coherent and consistent grounding in a formal international legal consensus. The distinctions between international and national levels of authority and between legal and political types of work, which gave the UNHCR its distinctive postwar identity, as an international and legal humanitarian agency, continue to affect the UNHCR's work. Lawyers continue to dominate protection work and to think in the legal terms developed in the immediate postwar era. The work of protection continues to focus on determination of refugee status, if only for the purpose of ascertaining entitlement to UNHCR assistance. Refugee law—rooted in postwar international legal instruments—continues to be distinguished from the law of asylum, considered a matter of national law and sovereign discretion. Protection officers feel their footing is most secure when working with terms—such as "refugee" or "non-refoulement"—which have clear international legal definitions.

When they move out from this core activity—to advocate particular solutions in particular contexts, for example—they associate their activity with flexibility, informality, strategic thinking, and an emphasis on results rather than concepts. Protection officers advocate national adherence to international legal instruments concerning refugees—but these oblige states to very little. At the same time, they acknowledge that a diversity of national solutions, including asylum, may be politically appropriate in particular contexts. Their humanitarian advocacy has become an endless struggle to find a normative link between an international legal status and a national political solution. Debates about how this might be possible have preoccupied protection officers for decades. All the while, they have continued to treat the politics of refugee flows—their causes and cures—as outside the bounds of normal professional debate about protection.

Modern protection officers must reconcile this antiquated image of protection as a matter of formal rules and legal status with their willingness to engage in a wide variety of political or humanitarian compromises. Sometimes they do this by separating their formal public role from their private and informal willingness to wheel and deal. What they will say in meetings of the Executive Committee is not at all what they will say at lunch. They often simply allocate legal niceties and political deal-making to different parts of their job. They might say, for example, that while determining refugee status remains a technical legal task, advocating solutions is appropriately a matter of political negotiation. Or they might associate these different activities with different areas of law. It is quite common to hear international refugee lawyers speak of refugee law as a matter of formal and internationally consistent rights, while seeing asylum law as a matter of national political discretion. When working within the former, they live up to their legal self-image. When working within the latter, they do what is necessary, given the regrettable immaturity of the international legal system. And it is no surprise to find that lawyers administering national asylum procedures will see things precisely the other way around.

When protection officers want to think more flexibly about solutions, they call this work "humanitarian" or "reality" or "in the field." When they want to emphasize their distance from this more flexible work, they call it "politics" and stress their deference to national sovereign discretion. Engaging with asylum can be a way of expressing flexibility. Thus, where refugee law seems too formal to respond effectively to a given refugee flow, protection officers might stress their interest in "humanitarian assistance" and offer to extend their "good offices" to asylum seekers *as well as* refugees. Their point is not that all these refugees should necessarily get asylum — that remains an act of sovereign discretion. Rather, they mean to bracket for the moment the question of the UNHCR's status or entitlement to become involved in or insist on a particular outcome. They come simply to advocate on humanitarian grounds for people who seek asylum in a given national context. *Real* refugee protection, by contrast, gives the UNHCR a formal entitlement to engage and an international legal basis which lends legitimacy to the "good offices" they offer. Strategic engagement with the issue depends *both* upon retaining the distinction and being perceived to relax it.

These conceptual divisions, however helpful to UNHCR lawyers in maintaining a professional self-image as simultaneously neutral and engaged, legally precise, and politically savvy, have plagued efforts to develop a pragmatic humanitarian strategy for dealing with refugee crises. They have parceled the legal work of the UNHCR into distinct discourses, rendering humanitarian policy making the prisoner of these distinct professional conversations. Humanitarian advocates have found themselves struggling more to link and defeat the resulting scheme of categories than to confront refugee crises in a spirit of open-minded pragmatism. Despite decades of trying, the UNHCR has remained strangely cut off from discussion of the national causes for and solutions to refugee flows.

The UNHCR's approach to the law of asylum offers a window on these difficulties. As refugee law became internationalized, protection officers emphasized its relationship to asylum law — but also asylum's national, political, and "discretionary" character. Asylum — which had been an international and national institution, at once legal and political in character — was now treated and lamented as a matter of national political discretion. International refugee lawyers have tended to overemphasize both the need to tie national asylum to international refugee status and the difficulty of doing so. As a consequence, those involved in refugee protection work have actually contributed to the gap between international law and national politics. In seeking to respond, the protection profession has repeatedly became mired in frustrating legal debates about the normative link between refugee status and asylum. The most obvious, if also the most frustrating, of these has been debate about an international legal "right" to asylum for refugees.

A more pragmatic approach to humanitarian advocacy might have rejuvenated asylum as an international legal concept and treated "refugee" as a term with national political bite. Some international refugee lawyers, at both the national and international level, have sought to break free from the constraints of their shared professional vocabulary. But the constrictions of an artificially narrow professional vocabulary continue to shape what seems possible for most humanitarian policy makers concerned about refugee affairs. Debates about the UNHCR's jurisdiction, protection strategies, and proposed solutions to refugee crises offer object lessons in humanitarian advocacy turned in upon itself.

MANAGING THE UNHCR'S JURISDICTION

Protection officers have poured energy into delimiting the boundaries of the UNHCR's institutional mandate. In the UNHCR's vernacular, the High Commissioner's "mandate" is his legal authority. His "competence" is the range of activities permitted by the mandate, and the term "jurisdiction" refers to the legal discourse which frames and analyzes the scope of both. The protection division distinguishes the High Commissioner's mandate and competence both from that of other international institutions and from national governments. The key to the mandate is the international legal definition of "refugee." Jurisdictional debates contain arguments about both expanding the definition of "refugee" and extending the High Commissioner's protection work beyond those who are, strictly speaking, refugees.

These arguments are legal—interpretations of the documents that established the High Commissioner's office and defined the status of "refugees." The more stable the international legal status of refugees, the more stable the High Commissioner's competence and authority. The larger the "refugee" category, the larger the mandate. It is not surprising that the High Commissioner's office has worked to promote recognition of "refugee" as an international legal status. The UNHCR is proud to have contributed in this way to the progressive development of refugee law. When protection officers strategize about how best to strengthen refugee law, they debate the merits of operating on the basis of a strong but narrowly defined legal status—versus expanding the range of those whom they seek to protect on the basis of a weaker and more vaguely defined mandate.

The UNHCR's mandate is most sharply defined when refugee status seems most formal, most legal, most international. One way to sharpen the UNHCR mandate is to contrast refugee status with something else—often "asylum." The more asylum seems a matter of national political discretion, the sharper the UNHCR's distinctive competence—and the more urgent the need for international protection. On the other hand, the mandate is *broadest* when refugee status is flexible or when the office can find an exceptional pretext to work on behalf of displaced persons who do not fit precisely within the narrow confines of the refugee definition. People seeking asylum may well think of themselves, at least in lay parlance, as refugees. They may be able to meet the formal legal criteria for certification as a refugee—but they also may not. One way to broaden the Commissioner's mandate is to become involved—at least exceptionally, on humanitarian grounds—with people seeking asylum even where they have not been formally certified as refugees within the terms of the UNHCR Statute.

It is often said that the sharp break between national political discretion over asylum and international institutional responsibility for refugees dates from the late-nineteenth-century period of high positivism, and is an unfortunate legacy of international law's *earlier* respect for an absolute sovereignty. With the rise of international institutions over the last century, the argument goes, these distinctions have softened. But this is not the case. Quite the contrary — the distinction between an international legal refugee status and an asylum practice of national political discretion was sharpest in the 1960s, precisely as the UNHCR asserted its identity and authority as an international institution most strongly.

Prior to the period of high positivism, individuals were thought to live in a relatively uniform legal system, bound by natural law wherever they found themselves. The idea of an individual losing protection or having to apply for new protection did not arise — nor were asylum and refugee status legally distinguished. During the high positivist period, the sovereign was at the center of the story — but there was no alternate international competence responsible for "refugees" and no international law specifically relating to refugees. Asylum remained an international legal institution, used in a wide variety of different ways. Efforts to secure boundaries and regularize the flow of aliens across them were surprisingly diverse, and grants of asylum were not conceived as discretionary privileges. There could be no temporal "gap" between national jurisdictions — one was always subject to one or another sovereign. A person without citizenship might be "stateless," but no institutional intervenor had responsibility for people in this situation.

The development of a refugee status in international law, on the "international plane" so to speak, lifted refugee law above the water line of sovereignty. How one got to be a refugee, and what happened to you after you were resettled remained below the line, outside the purview of the international institution. As refugee law developed, asylum also came more and more to be seen as a status to be granted rather than a condition to be enjoyed — the difference between the two statuses was the grantor. Once these statuses were conceptualized on distinctly different levels, it became more difficult to imagine bridging the gap between them. One could call upon states to respect the status of refugees — but this implied nothing about how they should arrange their asylum practices. Of course, there were many complex causes for the hardening of national hearts toward refugees and other migrants. The elaboration of a sharp distinction between international humanitarianism and national sovereignty may well have given comfort to those whose hearts grew cold. At the least, it undercut the authority of the agency given the international mandate to respond, precisely as it established an international legal basis for the UNHCR's legitimate jurisdiction. The space for international institutional action was created not only by contrast to national competence, but also by excluding concern with the causes and solutions to refugee flows.

Nevertheless, protection officers have engaged in nonstop debate about precisely these issues. In the immediate postwar period, jurisdictional debates focused on establishing and interpreting the term "refugee." The General Assembly blurred the "problem of refugees and stateless persons" and instructed the UNHCR to provide for the "protection of refugees and displaced persons." Asylum was not mentioned. By the 1960s, with growing institutional self-confidence, the protection office sharpened the distinction between international refugee law and national asylum practices. The legal documents of the time distinguished between "seeking a permanent solution" (an international legal matter) and "integration in countries of asylum" (a national political matter.)[1] The UNHCR was routinely exhorted to "promote permanent solutions . . . by facilitating the voluntary and rapid settlement of these refugees in countries of asylum . . . taking into account the specific requirements existing in each country of asylum."[2] As the mandate was extended formally, reference was increasingly made to the solution of *national* asylum. Where a single paragraph had previously sufficed, encouraging the UNHCR and national governments to become involved in and solve a particular refugee problem, there were now customarily two paragraphs: one addressed to the UNHCR expanding its mandate or asking for the use of its "good offices," and one addressed to states requesting that they assist UNHCR and provide "asylum or solution."

Once sharpened in this way, these distinctions began to blur. By the 1970s, the international legal community was routinely using the phrase "refugees and asylum seekers" when speaking of those on

---

[1] See, e.g., G.A. Res. 1673, 16 U.N. GAOR Supp. (No. 17) at 63, U.N. Doc. A/5100 (1961); G.A. Res. 1959, 18 U.N. GAOR Supp. (No. 15) at 42, U.N. Doc. A/5515 (1963).

[2] G.A. Res. 2197, 21 U.N. GAOR Supp. (No. 16) at 48, U.N. Doc A/6316 (1966).

whose behalf UNHCR would work. In the case of boat people from Southeast Asia, the use of the term "asylum seeker" was chosen to avoid commentary on the legal validity of claims by boat people to be refugees. Once asylum had been split from refugee law, however, there seemed no logical limit to those within the UNHCR's mandate if "asylum seekers" were included. To many protection officers, embracing asylum seekers seemed to erode the status of "refugees." This would both downgrade an important UNHCR function — certifying refugee status — and soften the basis for UNHCR's broader mandate. Were refugee status to lose its unique international legal connotation, the UNHCR would become the servant of national governments, who might grant or withhold asylum as they liked. To expand the mandate in this way, they argued, would weaken the UNHCR's long-term ability to respond effectively to the humanitarian needs of "real" refugees.

Similar fears accompanied the UNHCR's subsequent effort to develop new approaches to asylum law that could overcome its segregation in national discretion. So long as asylum is neither legalized nor internationalized, the UNHCR is now thought competent to work in partnership with states to develop common guidelines for asylum procedures. The ambivalence of the international refugee law establishment about this development is palpable in the UNHCR Executive Committee's embrace of flexible negotiations with national governments over European asylum laws in 1980: "while there was a need to develop legal concepts relating to international protection in the light of the special conditions prevailing in different regions, this should not detract from the absolute character of the fundamental principles already established in the field."[3]

Debates about this ambivalence have preoccupied refugee law professionals worried about the UNHCR's jurisdiction. Protection officers remain focused on managing the relationship between a sharply defined legal basis for the UNHCR's legitimacy and the legitimacy which comes with broad flexibility. Whether either — or any blend of the two — was an appropriate humanitarian response to a given refu-

[3] Report of the Executive Committee of the UN High Commissioner for Refugees, at (d), U.N. Doc. 12A/A35/12/Add.1 (1980).

gee crisis has often disappeared from view beneath concern over how their relationship would affect the UNHCR's own international status and authority.

SEEKING SOLUTIONS FOR REFUGEES

Inventing solutions for refugee flows often seems beyond the legal portfolio of the protection office — a matter either for assistance professionals or for national authorities. The split between the UNHCR's international legal mandate and the national political terrain on which solutions must ultimately be achieved has diminished the UNHCR's capacity to address solutions. But when solutions have legal implications, protection officers do become involved. If the General Assembly calls on states to provide "durable solutions," protection officers will draw up general recommendations about the minimum standard of treatment which should legally count as a durable solution. Over the years, the UNHCR has developed recommended minimum standards in numerous areas — including detention conditions and national asylum procedures. This work channels the UNHCR's interest in solutions toward treatment which can be articulated in procedural, legal, and universal terms.

As a result, the rights and duties triggered by refugee status and the content of asylum have been elaborated separately. Discussion of the protection due refugees sounds legal and international: one speaks of "rights" and "duties" resulting from a status determination. The perquisites of asylum, by contrast, are diverse and depend upon the particular constellation of national prerogatives which conspired to grant asylum.

More often, protection officers seeking solutions will engage in ad hoc negotiations with governments about treatment, access to legal and other international assistance, and resettlement or repatriation. In this work, the protection officer may well use legal arguments — insisting that minimum standards of one or another sort be met — but he or she is likely to think far more flexibly about what to insist upon than in work elaborating the mandate. In thinking about the UNHCR's jurisdiction, protection officers default to formal legal interpretation. In thinking about solutions, they default to strategic flexibility. It seems easier for a protection officer, when asked what he seeks, to say "all I can get" than when asked whom he protects, to say "anyone I can find." Divergent regional or national solutions to different refugee flows seem acceptable — a floating and unstable jurisdiction for the UNHCR does not.

Jurisdiction discourse treats refugee and asylum as statuses granted by different authorities — in the world of solutions, refugee remains a status, but asylum is more of a condition. By downplaying the legal aspects of asylum, protection officers can treat their involvement as an ad hoc and compassionate exception to their normal work. In an odd way, the apparently political and national character of asylum helps the protection officer differentiate between his strategic work on solutions and the legal nature of UNHCR's justification to be involved. Negotiating about national asylum procedures, reviewing national standards of treatment, makes work on solutions seem flexible and pragmatic — regardless of whether it actually delivers more or less humanitarian outcomes for particular refugees. To connect with national governments, speak their own language, leave behind the tidy legal world of Geneva with its preoccupations about the mandate *is to be* pragmatic. And being pragmatic, feeling strong enough to go behind enemy lines, out in the field, down to the level of national politics, requires the self-confidence of a strong, autonomous international legal personality and status — precisely the result of a more legal jurisdictional practice.

The protection officer thinking about solutions confronts a choice — between the high road of international normative treatment and the low road of ad hoc political agitation for more favorable conditions at the national level. Sometimes one can follow both; sometimes they reinforce one another. But protection officers also seem to sense that each can undercut the legitimacy of the other. The authority to intervene depends on an international, legal, neutral reputation which would be put at risk by too overt a political engagement, just as the formal and general world of international norms seems insufficiently flexible to permit the wheeling and dealing necessary to achieve real solutions. In general, the UNHCR has erred on the side of preserving its reputation for legal neutrality, and kept its distance from participation in solutions — as from asylum.

The high road to solutions begins by treating the procedural activities of the UNHCR as legal attributes of refugee status. For example, because the UNHCR is entitled to issue travel documents or provide consular services, a person with refugee status might be thought to have a "right" to travel documents and a right to have them respected. In this sense, solutions are deduced from jurisdiction. When the UNHCR's jurisdiction ends, so does the refugee's entitlement to solution. If the UNHCR's mandate lapses with legal assimilation to a new country—the refugee problem is thereby "solved." By reverse engineering solutions from the limits of refugee status, the high road to solutions focuses on ending the conditions for international protection—solving the UNHCR's problem—rather than solving the refugee's problem. The conditions for asylum are out of the picture. The limitations of this approach have become ever more apparent as refugee flows have shifted to the south and legal reassimilation seems less central to the refugee's immediate needs.

The low road of a purely pragmatic, case-by-case approach also has limitations. It is understood to occur outside the realm of international legal standards, and the protection officer finds it difficult to say anything more than that an asylee gets whatever a state decides to grant. Leaving asylum on the low road means international law has little to say about its content—and the UNHCR little basis for pragmatic engagement. The International Law Commission's 1950 definition of asylum suggests the unhelpful role international law has taken in this field: "the term 'asylum' designates the protection which a state grants on its territory to a person who comes to seek it."[4] One UNHCR protection officer defined asylum as "the protection accorded a person seeking protection."[5]

This low road is a recent doctrinal invention. For hundreds of years, the international legal hospitality and protections granted foreign citizens by sovereigns came in all shapes and sizes. Asylum grew up as a right against the former state of nationality, and was under-

[4] Resolution on Asylum, A.I, Institute of International Law, Bath Session 1950, 43(1) AIDI 157, 45 *American Journal of International Law* 45, suppl. 15(1951).

[5] Coles, "Temporary Refuge and the Large-Scale Influx of Refugees," Australian Yearbook of International Law (1983):190 at page 200.

stood not as a status to be granted by discretion, but as protection which flowed automatically from the territorial jurisdiction of the receiving state. Oppenheim, writing early in the past century, treats asylum as the automatic consequence of crossing a jurisdictional boundary—not as a status to be granted by national governments:

> The fact that every State exercises territorial supremacy over all persons on its territory, whether they are its subjects or aliens, excludes the prosecution of aliens thereon by foreign States. Thus, a foreign State is, provisionally at least, an asylum for every individual who, being prosecuted at home, crossed its frontier.[6]

This view of asylum is hardly more humanitarian in outlook than that of protection officers. It was reverse engineered from the nature of international sovereignty, rather than from the needs of refugees. Nevertheless, it is not clear matters have advanced now that the entitlements of the UNHCR's jurisdiction have replaced sovereignty as the engine for refugee protection. International lawyers have transformed an institution derived from sovereign rights into a sovereign license by overemphasizing the political and discretionary character of asylum determinations. The sovereign right to grant asylum began as a protection for asylum status against the claims of the sovereign from which the asylee fled—it has been turned into a threat to the legal nature of asylum.

It has now become difficult to imagine an asylum doctrine which is not a matter of national discretion. And it seems equally difficult to imagine placing asylum on the high road by transforming it into an international legal right. All efforts to do so in the postwar period have failed. But that need not have been the end of the matter. Protection officers *might* have developed a vision of asylum as an international response to misfortune and dislocation. They might have interpreted international human rights norms to strengthen the content of asylum guarantees. For example, the language of Article 14 of the Universal Declaration of Human Rights paragraph (1) provides that: "Everyone has the right to seek and to enjoy in other countries asylum from persecution."[7] Contemporary international

---

[6] L. Oppenheim, *International* Law 551 (McNair ed. 4th ed., 1928).

[7] G.A. Res. 217A, U.N.Doc. A/810 at 74 (1948).

lawyers tend to read this article as if the words "if granted" were placed before the words "to enjoy." If we suspend the sense that the only important question is the legal obligation of the "granting" sovereign and instead view the asylum to be sought and enjoyed as an international institution, we might read Article 14 so as to give asylum international content without interfering with its sovereign roots.

It is not at all clear, for example, that asylum must be granted to be enjoyed. As Oppenheim noted, to be abroad under a system of territorial jurisdiction is to enjoy an asylum. In this sense, Article 14 merely restates the limits on extraterritorial sovereign jurisdiction. This protection need not be granted and may, under normal circumstances, not be withdrawn except in accordance with rules governing expulsion, including nonrefoulement. If the right to seek asylum is to mean more than the right to depart one's country, it must mean that this preliminary protection continues while any procedure for reviewing the permanence of asylum is conducted. One could characterize this notion of asylum as an obligatory grant of temporary protection, but to do so would return to an emphasis on sovereign discretion and obligation. The point would be to elaborate asylum from the international system of jurisdiction which constitutes it. By doing so, the overwhelming modern emphasis upon asylum as discretion might be diminished.

Moreover, it is not at all clear that an asylum granted on any terms would be "enjoyed." From the individual asylee's point of view, an asylum which did not respond to his needs for protection would not be an asylum. Moreover, from an international perspective, the words "to enjoy" signal the respect which an individual can expect to be shown in his asylum by other states, including his home state: the asylee has a right to enjoy his asylum in one state without interference from other states. This view is also merely a restatement of the sovereign obligation to respect territorial sovereignty. Yet such respect need not be accorded an asylum on any terms. An asylum which was not voluntary, for example, need not be respected, for no state can imprison or detain the citizens of another without cause and maintain friendly relations. By voluntary, we must also comprehend reversible, for no sovereign need respect attempts by another forcibly to enslave, conscript, or refuse exit to its nationals. To be respected, asylum, as an institution expressing territorial jurisdiction, must be enjoyed in the territory of the host state. Moreover, if we think of asylum as the expression of territorial jurisdiction, it must be conditioned as territorial jurisdiction is itself conditioned, upon respect for fundamental human rights and upon reciprocal respect for sovereign integrity. Thus, if the asylee is permitted to use the host territory for commission of international crimes or violations of another state's territorial jurisdiction, the asylum would not need to be respected and could no longer be enjoyed.

If we think of asylum as the safety of integration into a territorial jurisdiction, however, it may not be too much to think of a substantive integration. After all, the asylee can be protected from his home state only to the extent of his actual assimilation to new jurisdictions. Thus, if he is to be subject to host state jurisdiction, it might seem that the host state must replace such normal functions of the territorial sovereign as registration of births, deaths, marriages or property transactions. If asylum is the product of territorial jurisdiction, it must take on the attributes of territorial jurisdiction.

It also seems clear that asylum, if it is to be respected as a "not unfriendly" act, must be not only a genuine extension of territorial sovereignty, but a justified one. It would clearly be not only unfriendly but illegal to grant asylum extraterritorially to foreign citizens resident in their home states or to grant asylum to all travelers from a foreign state, particularly if they constituted a significant proportion of a foreign sovereign's subjects or did not desire asylum. Thus, one might infer from the obligation to respect asylum granted, the reciprocal duty to grant asylum only in deserving or exceptional cases: to refugees or for political reasons.

In short, by seeing asylum as an institution developed in response to changing notions of sovereignty, it would be possible to give asylum an international meaning which reconnects it to the protection required by an asylee and the conditions under which that protection must be respected by other states and will therefore be effective. Such an institution of asylum would permit protection officers to ask when territorial sovereignty deserves respect, when hospitality is just, and what solutions are appropriate for the widest variety of refugees. In discussing asylum, the protection officer might think of himself sitting with host governments facing a refugee in need of a solution, not sitting face to face debating the granting of an international legal status.

Some tentative steps have been taken along these lines. For example, international refugee lawyers have begun to develop common standards for recognizing "asylum elsewhere" as a grounds for refusing to consider an asylum application. At the regional level, among European states — as over many years among Latin American states — common criteria for recognizing asylum have been proposed. As efforts along these lines develop, we might hope that asylum could become an international solution which responds appropriately to a given refugee's situation. One might think of a request for asylum as a request for the government concerned to work in the tradition of territorial sovereignty, with the UNHCR acting as the refugee's advocate, to identify and provide appropriate protection. Advocacy of specific asylum terms would be grounded in the particular needs of a given refugee or refugee group rather than in the doctrinal elaboration of some imaginary legal status.

Perhaps. But this has not been the focus for work by international refugee lawyers concerned about solutions. By embracing asylum in a way which reinforces the distinction between asylum and refugee status, the protection officer limits his ability to pursue solutions. Protection activity becomes separated from the conditions of solution by a veil of legality. The protection officer is forced to choose between what are imagined to be two distinct paths to solution: the one legal and legitimate, if somewhat constraining; the other political and somewhat suspect, if seemingly more responsive to diverse conditions. But if protection officers have not focused on solutions, we might ask what they have been doing *instead*. The answer is pursuing a series of policy debates about how to link the legal status of protection with durable political outcomes.

PROTECTION DEBATES: NEITHER JURISDICTION
   NOR SOLUTIONS

The primary work of protection officers has been to develop arguments about the relative merits of political and legal approaches to refugee problems and strategies for linking the UNHCR's international legal status with national political solutions. These debates are both more pragmatic than debates about jurisdiction and more legal than those about solutions. In this middle ground, debates about asylum are often central — but not asylum as it was seen in discussions of the UNHCR's mandate, as a legal status granted by national states. And not asylum as seen in more ad hoc negotiations about solution — as a matter of political discretion. Each of these debates begins with a disjuncture between the legal refugee status over which the UNHCR has jurisdiction and the political solutions which only a nation state can provide — and then proceeds to argue about how they can be normatively linked. But the goal is not only a link. At the same time, it is important to confirm the distinctiveness of the UNHCR's legal and international status — and the flexible political nature of solution. These domains must not only be linked — they must be kept separate.

It turns out to be quite difficult to write about protection in such a way as to sustain such different images of the UNHCR and the national sovereign. What doing so has to do with protecting refugees remains obscure. Most protection discourse about asylum, oddly enough, is about neither who gets it nor what they get, but about doctrinally accommodating sovereign discretion over the grant of asylum with international and individual interest in its content. The resulting debates return repeatedly to the distinctiveness of international law and politics — and to their engagement. To get a sense for the nature of protection work elaborating refugee policy, it is worthwhile to revisit three classic debates which have preoccupied international refugee lawyers: debates about "the right to asylum," about "admission and nonrefoulement," and about "temporary refuge." It is difficult to comprehend the enormous amount of energy which has been devoted to these debates. They have come to represent a legitimate domain of work in their own right: contribution to the progressive development of refugee law.

Debate about the "Right to Asylum"

Most contemporary treatments of asylum begin with, and many are devoted exclusively to, consideration of a right to asylum. These works carefully distinguish the right of asylum (or the "right to grant asylum"), which is acknowledged to be the sine qua non of the institution of asylum, from a right *to* asylum (or the "right to be granted asylum") which, all acknowledge, is more controversial. Because one is seen to be a right of one sovereign against another sovereign and the other is seen to be an individual's right against a sovereign, they do not seem inconsistent. Moreover, were the legal system "complete," we would have both. A properly articulated legal regime could fulfill *both* the aspiration to protect sovereign autonomy (the right of asylum) and an international scheme of refugee protection (right to asylum).

But, of course, as policy makers have recognized, an individual's right to be granted asylum can conflict with a sovereign right to grant asylum if that sovereign right is understood to imply the unfettered discretion to refuse to grant asylum. When these two rights conflict, the right of asylum prevails. Scholars discuss the right to asylum in order to rehabilitate it within a regime dominated by the right of asylum — to strengthen it by advocacy and restatement.

Most commentators have concluded, if reluctantly, that there is no right to asylum, although they recognize that there may be other obligations (such as municipal rights, nonextradition, nonrefoulement, humanitarian duties) protecting asylum seekers. A minority of commentators argue that there is now a right to asylum, although they recognize that the right may be a qualified one — progressively developing, subject to exceptions, or not fully enforceable or accepted. Those of the majority take a harder line with respect to the qualifications acknowledged by the minority, arguing that there can be no right until it has been fully developed and accepted, is associated with a correlative duty, or is enforceable. Those of the minority take a harder line with respect to the exceptions acknowledged by the majority, arguing that international law can be composed of municipal legal principles and that the humanitarian obligations which make up the penumbra of human rights law are developing into valid rights.

The majority views international law as a world of sovereigns and relies upon traditional notions about the consensual and formal sources of international legal obligations, the distinction between law and morality, and the primacy of sovereign autonomy. The minority supports, both historically and doctrinally, the possibility of international legal rights and duties for individuals, and relies upon rehabilitated naturalist notions of sovereign cooperation, the interdependence of law and morality, and a more liberal view of soft, informal, nonconsensual or instant sources of law.

The fascinating aspect of this debate, however, is its inconclusive and repetitive structure. Both sides accept the basic division of asylum into a sovereign capacity and an individual benefit. Both accept the basic structure of international legal obligation and treat the existence of an obligation as the sine qua non of protection. Each develops a position qualified by exceptions designed to meet the objections of the other. Neither can account for the capacity of its acknowledged exceptions to devour its position when confronted by the challenge of the other. Most importantly, neither alone is able to account for sovereign autonomy and cooperation simultaneously.

Taken *together*, however, the well-worn debate accomplishes what the independent discourses of jurisdiction and solution were unable to accomplish: finding a place for both sovereign autonomy and sovereign cooperation. So long as the debate continues, there is room for positivists and naturalists. Each is present in each line of commentary, whether as the dominant voice or as the voice of the exception.

It is not surprising that a debate in such equilibrium should seem both frustratingly irresolvable and an unimportant matter of preference. The importance of this debate lies in the agreement by both the majority and minority that a right to asylum would be a desirable addition to international law. Both sides are assessing the progress of international law toward capturing the institution of asylum by legalizing and internationalizing the one place which in discourses of both jurisdiction and solutions had been reserved for sovereign discretion. The goal of this project is to overwhelm the boundary between international law and national politics; the debaters merely disagree on the appropriate measure of their success. It is not surprising that their debate has stalled, for these commentators all accept both the distinction between international law and national politics and the characterization of asylum as a matter of sovereign discretion. They cannot overwhelm a distinction which they are not prepared to reject.

As a result, it seems inevitable that the "no right to asylum" school will remain the ascendant one, just as jurisdiction discourse will remain ascendant over solutions discourse. Moreover, so long as this remains the structure of debate, attempts to storm the high ground of sovereignty by establishing a right to asylum either will fail or will relocate national discretion elsewhere, exactly as the minority school acknowledged the claims of the positivist majority in its exceptions and qualifications of the right it professed to describe. In this light, attempts to create a right which "has no remedy," "lacks enforcement," or "may be a right against the international community as a whole rather than against any particular state" can be seen as continuations of this debate rather than resolutions of it.

Thinking of the debate about a right to asylum as an irresolvable repetition of the conflicts distinguishing solutions and jurisdiction discourse reveals how distracting the debate can be. If the task of protection is to get asylum for people, seeking a "right to asylum" distracts protection lawyers into either wishful thinking or resigned skepticism. Until there is a right, nothing can be done and yet no right seems defensible or achievable which does not confront us with a new manifestation of sovereign discretion. Moreover, and most disturbingly, this debate, by accepting and reinforcing the disjuncture between international law and national discretion, prevents the UNHCR from capitalizing on the new roles thrust upon it by changing conceptions of its mandate for asylum situations and its ability to participate with states in developing flexible solutions for the divergent problems of refugees. To continue this debate places faith in an infinite legal process rather than institutional action.

The Debate about "Nonrefoulement" and "Admission"

In the battle to overcome the disjuncture between jurisdiction and solution, the "right to asylum" debate, with its emphasis on the international legalization of asylum, is the heavy artillery. More successful, if in the final analysis equally distracting, have been more subtle efforts to overcome this disjuncture by relocating it in various doctrinal alternatives whose conflicts can ostensibly be more easily resolved. One such effort has revolved around the concept of "nonrefoulement."

Like the debate about the right to asylum, discussion of the nonreturn of refugees to their country of origin begins with an assumption about the distinctiveness of asylum and refugee law. Like the debate about the right to asylum, the nonrefoulement debate seems directed toward reconnecting these two realms. The connection which is pursued in nonrefoulement, however, is more subtle than the legal takeover pursued by the right-to-asylum debate.

Policy makers discussing nonrefoulement proceed in several stages. The first step is to develop nonrefoulement as an international legal obligation. International lawyers have devoted a great deal of energy to developing and strengthening the international legal principle of "nonrefoulement," not as the source of a right to asylum coterminous with it, nor as the source for asylum's substantive content, but as an independent obligation of refugee law. As a result, the practice of nonrefoulement has, over the last 150 years, been transformed by scholarly attention into the "principle of nonrefoulement," seen as a "fundamental" international legal obligation forming the cornerstone of refugee law. Although there are exceptions and state practice is anything but conclusive, scholars insist that the principle of nonrefoulement has become binding as a matter of both treaty and customary law.

The important point is not whether these scholars are correct in their assertions about the status of the nonrefoulement principle, but the strength of their insistence and its consequences for the structure of further debate. Whether they are correct or not, it is on the basis of these assertions that one thinks of refugee law as law at all on the international plane. If nonrefoulement has an international legal character, refugee law can be a legitimate subspecies of international law even if one eventually concludes that nonrefoulement has not (yet) acquired binding force. Refugee law as a whole takes a leap toward legalization when nonrefoulement is transformed from a practice into a "principle."

In the process, other aspects of refugee treatment are left behind or, more accurately, come to be thought of as matters of national discretion. The various protections beyond nonreturn which add up to asylum now contrast starkly with the internationalized legal principle of nonrefoulement. Indeed, scholars sometimes develop the international legal "principle" of nonrefoulement in express contrast to the "institution" of asylum. This contrast helps preserve the notion that both national discretion and international cooperation can be preserved in the system of refugee protection as a whole. States will be required to do something— not return refugees—as a matter of international law, but their sovereign discretion to refuse asylum will not be disturbed.

The nonrefoulement discussion does not rest once states are thought to be under an international legal obligation not to return refugees. The next step is to formalize the various treatments which might form part of a refugee's reception in a national culture and connect them to nonrefoulement by a process of definition, analogy, deduction, or normative implication. This process has generated a large number of "treatments," the most important of which are recognition as a "refugee," "nonrefoulement," "admission," and "asylum."

Movement between these four terms is not smooth. There is a disjuncture between nonrefoulement and admission which is like the disjuncture between jurisdiction and solution. The first terms—nonrefoulement, jurisdiction—are conceived as matters of international law, the last—admission, solution—as matters of national discretion. We again find two levels of analysis corresponding to two moments in a refugee's journey from home to host country. Efforts to link the nonrefoulement obligation to admission are thus directed to overcoming the same disjuncture which bedeviled discussion about the right to asylum.

But here, the disjuncture does not seem as stark as that between jurisdiction and solution or between the right to and the right of asylum. Recognition of an individual as a refugee is the core of international institutional jurisdiction. Nonrefoulement, while a matter of international law, is an obligation of states. Unlike asylum, nonrefoulement is not a status to be granted, and can be practiced by states without interfering in their discretion to grant asylum. Asylum is both national and discretionary. "Admission," by contrast, implies a formal process of legal entry which, although firmly within the national sphere, might be conducted in accordance with legal norms. Thus, nonrefoulement and admission reach out to one another—seem closer to one another than do "refugee" and "asylum." Nonrefoulement reaches out from the camp of international legal competence, admission from the camp of national discretion. If only nonrefoulement and admission could be joined, the refugee would slide smoothly from the international protection of refugee status to the national protection of asylum.

The two central terms could be joined if they were seen as corollary international legal obligations: if nonrefoulement implied admission. But this connection would threaten the fragile link between admission and asylum. Nonrefoulement and admission could also be joined if both were viewed as matters of national legal practice. But to do so would threaten the connection between nonrefoulement and refugee status. Either of these strategies of connection—legalization or decentralization—would be like the right to asylum. They would overcome the disjuncture between national discretion and international law by transforming one into the other. As in the right-to-asylum debate, moreover, we would expect these approaches to relocate the lost term elsewhere, failing to smooth the passage from one sphere to another.

The debate over nonrefoulement, however, is far more sophisticated. The initial separation of refugee status and nonrefoulement split an international legal obligation from the competence of international institutions. The separation of admission from asylum split the legal treatment of asylum seekers from the sphere of sovereign discretion. These divisions made it easier to imagine admission as the logical complement of nonrefoulement because it could be legalized and yet remain within the national sphere. Such a link would be far more stable than merely suggesting that nonrefoulement, an international legal obligation, should "guide" admission, which remains a matter of national discretion. Once a doctrinal link has been established between admission and nonrefoulement, nonrefoulement becomes the consistent legal face of asylum, and asylum the variable national face of nonrefoulement. The two institutions, which seemed to inhabit different levels and were understood as one another's other, could be made to seem compatible by the link between admission and nonrefoulement — without eliminating either international law or national discretion.

Nevertheless, this link is also unstable. The doctrinal link between nonrefoulement and admission threatens the vision of a differentiated refugee and asylum which the debate inherited from solutions and jurisdiction discourse. Consequently, this debate proceeds by repeatedly splitting terms on either side of the disjuncture, in a search for a more stable link. Sometimes this occurs by introducing a new term between admission and nonrefoulement, such as "nonexpulsion." This makes it seem easier to retain the association between admission and asylum as matters of national discretion. At the same time, nonexpulsion is a standard of national treatment more easily linked to nonrefoulement. Thus, scholars who investigate the meaning of the principle of nonrefoulement have distinguished between "expulsion" and "nonadmittance," or further, between "administrative" and "legal" expulsion or expulsion of the "legally" and the "illegally present." These distinctions constantly re-create the basic disjuncture between the international legal obligation and the sphere of national discretion. If refoulement is thought to mean extrajudicial expulsion, a state is legally obliged to pursue deportation procedures for refugees in their territory but retains the authority both of nonadmission and of setting substantive terms for expulsion. Similarly, scholars split the term "admission," rehabilitating a disjuncture between, for example, "mere presence" and "legal admission" to regain a sphere for national discretion once control over admission has been lost either legally to the international normative sphere of nonrefoulement or as a matter of fact.

It is no wonder, meanwhile, that refugees are piling up in detention centers legally located "at the border." If this debate were to stop at any point, the disjuncture would reappear. By continuing to split the difference and shift among such an array of similar terms, one creates the illusion of a coherent legal fabric linking refugees to asylum, however difficult it may be to pin down. The problem with continuing this debate, however, is that it distracts attention from both the causes of refugee flows and their solution. One focuses instead on an ever finer set of distinctions among terms which share something doctrinally with these issues but do not address them. Choice among these terms comes to be made out of fealty to the coherence of the doctrinal structure rather than out of concern for refugees or asylum conditions. A discussion about the relationship between nonexpulsion and nonadmission is, in a way, a discussion about the balance of power between the international protection of refugees and the terms of their treatment by national authorities. But it is only in an oblique, associative way that this debate grapples with refugees or asylum. It would be more accurate to say that these debates substitute for a more direct approach. Discussing the meaning of nonrefoulement or the implications of admission feels like getting to the bottom of the problem of asylum. On the contrary, however, it avoids confronting asylum, preferring instead to imagine asylum as the constantly receding repository of an untouchable national sovereignty. These debates are more useful as a way to preserve the sense that international and national competences are appropriately "balanced" in refugee law than in finding solutions for refugees. It is not surprising that the terms of the debates remain murky. Clarification might abandon the enterprise of doctrinal mediation altogether.

The Debate about "Temporary Refuge"

If the refoulement debate suffers from a tendency to drift into doctrinal distinctions removed from the sources and solutions to refugee problems, the third major debate within protection discourse about asylum is self-conscious about its return to realism. As such, it typifies a third type of response to the disjuncture between refugee law and asylum. The debate about what has been termed "temporary refuge" frankly acknowledges what it sees as an inevitable disjuncture between the international legal exhortations of international institutions and the practice of national politics. Refugees are one and asylum is the other.

To those who worry about temporary refuge, the better part of valor is to confront this stubborn fact directly. Any attempt to bridge the gap seems likely to drift into wishful speculation or threaten the autonomy of international law and national discretion. People who debate temporary refuge criticize attempts to link nonrefoulement and admission for "diluting" the purity of nonrefoulement or for ignoring the absolute national discretion of asylum. The key, they say, is to turn the vice of this inevitable disjuncture into a virtue. This can be done by developing a middle term — temporary refuge — between nonrefoulement and admission which self-consciously distances them from one another.

In advocating "temporary refuge," international lawyers urge states to provide refuge until alternative arrangements can be made — often by international agencies — for their ultimate protection. Ultimately, they might go home, or be resettled, or get asylum. The "refuge" states are urged to provide in the meantime is deliberately left vague. It is certainly not thought of as an internationally uniform legal status. The suggestion that refuge be "provided" is also typically left ambiguous, implying neither an international legal obligation nor a national political discretion. As a result, this approach represents an institutional adaptation to a more fluid protection environment than either of the distinctively normative protection debates.

Those who advocate "temporary refuge" appear to have given up the attempt to develop a normative link between international competence and national politics. Consequently, this approach leaves the disjuncture between nonrefoulement and admission intact. Nonrefoulement remains an international legal obligation compelling provision of refuge. The temporary nature of this refuge ensures that admission remains a matter of national discretion. Rather than interpreting nonrefoulement broadly, to reach out toward solution, this approach interprets it narrowly, to imply only that the cause of the refugee flow be acknowledged and provision be made for some international response. Similarly, this approach interprets admission and asylum narrowly, as matters of national political will disconnect from mere presence. Temporary refuge is thus neither asylum nor nonrefoulement. It is a middle position disjointed from both international law and national discretion.

The trouble is that this middle position is a hybrid of the two poles against which it distinguishes itself. Thus, to distinguish itself from asylum, and reassure us that its provision would not disturb national discretion, temporary refuge is treated as a temporary national obligation which implies some more permanent international response to the refugee's difficulties. Compliance with the international obligation is made to seem as cost free as possible — eventually the international agency promises to support or relocate refugees given temporary refuge. Likewise, in contrast to refugee status or nonrefoulement, temporary refuge is treated as a matter of national decision to be achieved by negotiation between the international agency and the national authority. It cannot be granted or certified by the UNHCR alone.

The defenders of temporary refuge rightly tout this hybrid quality for linking international solidarity with national solutions. It is even possible, in a variation of this approach, to view temporary refuge as the combination of nonrefoulement and admission, differentiated from refugee status and asylum. Whether seen as a way of avoiding the difficulties of the nonrefoulement/admission debate or as a way of finally combining the two terms, temporary refuge offers the protection officer a way of responding to contemporary refugee problems without abandoning his institutional identity or sense of the international law doctrine of refugee and asylum law.

The distinctive nature of temporary refuge seems at first to protect the purity of both nonrefoulement (as a binding international norm) and asylum (as a sovereign discretion). But this hybrid quality also raises difficulties. Perhaps it is understandable that advocates of temporary refuge have remained somewhat vague about its status, writing sometimes as if provision of temporary refuge were the essence of some legal obligation (like nonrefoulement) and at others as if it were pragmatic good sense when political conditions made fulfillment of more stringent international legal duties unworkable. But precisely because temporary refuge combines obligation and pragmatism, thereby protecting both nonrefoulement and asylum, it also threatens what have become the symbols of international cooperation and sovereign autonomy.

Thus, opponents of temporary refuge have argued that if it is to be pragmatic or grounded in the host state's peculiar capacity to comply, it threatens the absolute obligation of nonrefoulement. Similarly, it has been argued that if temporary refuge is *binding* (perhaps as nonrefoulement through time), it threatens the discretionary character of asylum and admission, especially if the link to international burden sharing cannot be established with equal normative and practical force. These criticisms rely, as did the defenses of temporary refuge, alternatively upon its claim to be different from both refugee law and asylum. As such, the debate about the validity of temporary refuge repeats the debate which seemed interminable in the context of a right to asylum and nonrefoulement.

Various responses, both doctrinal and practical, have been developed by advocates of temporary refuge to overcome this conceptual difficulty. Sometimes they suggest that temporary refuge need not mean assimilation nor respond to the full scope of a refugee's needs, as would asylum, or that it is a binding obligation only in cases of mass influx where there might, for other reasons, be no alternative but to comply. These resolutions, however, conspire to create a status for refugees which responds to an international conceptual problem rather than to the needs of refugees or governments. In the extreme, temporary refuge might seem to be better made as unpleasant as possible to protect the doctrinal link to international burden sharing.

Numerous national governments have done precisely this — establishing "temporary refuge" camps "at the border" which resemble prisons and are designed to discourage further refugee flows. The temporary refuge debate, although billed as bringing a new realism to discourse about refugees, results in refugee conditions which reflect the conceptual disjuncture of refugees and asylum rather than the needs of refugees. The limbo which this new "realism" creates for refugees may be necessary to protect the image which international lawyers share of a national discretionary asylum and their vision of exclusive international legal and institutional competence to deal with refugees, but it is not necessary to respond to the needs of either host sovereigns or refugees.

Each of these debates represents a creative response to a difficult conceptual problem. They are successful in linking international and national or legal and political only because they are interminable, continually deferring the moment of connection. No single position within any of these three debates satisfactorily permits a sustainable international normative involvement in national discretion. In the meantime, these debates distract institutional attention from both causes and solutions. Instead, we have a complex professional rhetoric of legal labels, competing with one another in an imaginary doctrinal world. This distracting practice splits protection work into specialized categories which are the result of conceptual distinctions rather than the divergent functional requirements of refugee situations. Moreover, once specialized, the debate between pragmatists and formalists can be continued indefinitely without becoming a difference about refugee treatment at all.

Indeed, the splits among these voices can become central to the self-image and professional identity of the humanitarian policy maker. A protection officer whose solutions work seems to involve political deal-making wants legal clarity about who is and who is not a refugee so that the mandate will provide the legitimacy he feels his other activities lack. By contrast, the protection officer whose work with asylum occurs in a formal and legalized culture wants a jurisdictional discourse which can be expanded to absorb the pragmatic considerations his solutions context cannot provide.

It would be encouraging if the creative flexibility shown in the development of these policy debates translated into an imaginative pragmatism in response to refugee flows. Sometimes, to be sure, it does. But strategizing about the law, about institutional identity, about the relationship between national sovereignty and international jurisdiction is different from strategizing about the needs of refugees and the consequences of various policy paths for the causes and solutions to refugee flows. So long as policy makers continue to act as if separate realms of international law and national politics exist and imagine the work of humanitarian policy to be their reconciliation, an institution like asylum can come to be seen as the perfect liminal space, available not for refugees, but for the deployment of policy-making expertise.

EIGHT

Humanitarianism and Force

International humanitarians abjure war. Reducing the frequency and violence of war have been central objectives for humanitarian policy making. International law has been an indispensable tool, fashioned, promoted, interpreted, and applied to moderate the use of military force. More than a hundred years of policy making about warfare has yielded a heterogenous regime of legal doctrines, principles, and institutions. These have been progressively absorbed by military cultures around the world and may well have prevented untold suffering. We can only guess at the relief provided countless prisoners and other victims of war by institutions like the International Committee for the Red Cross.

Policy making in this field, however, has not been immune from the dark sides which plague other humanitarian efforts we have seen — human rights, development policy, democratization, or refugee affairs. Those seeking to bring law to bear against warfare have also enchanted their tools, overestimated the significance of legal pronouncements, and mistaken legal warfare for humanitarian warfare. Their efforts have also been skewed by unhelpful ideas about geography and assumptions about progress. They have been inattentive to the political and distributional effects of their interventions into war making. In short, humanitarian engagement with warfare has had its share of blind spots and biases.

Among international legal professionals, the words "international humanitarian law" now refer quite specifically to the body of rules developed over the past century and a half to constrain the use of force during war—the "law in war" or *jus in bello*. I have been using the term "humanitarian" in a far larger sense—to refer very generally to people who aspire to make the world more just, to the projects they have launched over the past century in pursuit of that goal, and to the professional vocabularies which have sprung up to defend and elaborate these projects. The world of war allows us to trace the development of these broad humanitarian aspirations into concrete legal or institutional projects and then into a specific professional vocabulary for policy making.

Over the last century and a half, the aspiration to limit the violence and incidence of war has been expressed in a variety of international legal projects. Rules limiting permissible violence on the battlefield have been one. Large-scale intergovernmental institutions to promote peaceful settlement of disputes or collective deterrence of aggression have been another, as have a variety of more limited doctrinal or institutional innovations. Each of these efforts has had to confront the extreme gap between the peaceful or humanitarian aspirations associated with international law and the political freedom—and violence—associated with war.

For many years, the various strategies and projects humanitarian lawyers developed to confront war diverged considerably. Those codifying rules for the battlefield, for example, treated war as inevitable, and the politics of war making as beyond their jurisdiction. Rather than confronting the incidence of war directly, they worked—often in close cooperation with military professionals—to make rules which might limit the violence of battle. Other international lawyers focused directly on the political decision to make war, building intergovernmental institutions which might constrain sovereign discretion. Still others elaborated the theoretical materials of international law and culled the history of diplomacy for customary practices which might suggest accepted principles to limit war making.

In the last years—starting after the Second World War and culminating in the years since the end of the Cold War—these divergent strategies have come together. Parts of the "humanitarian law" vernacular have spread from the narrow group of experts associated with the International Committee of the Red Cross to politicians, media commentators, human rights activists, and military strategists thinking more broadly about the use of force. At the same time, humanitarian law has been transformed, placed in the context of a broader constitutional idea about the role of warfare in global governance and linked more directly to the law of international human rights. International lawyers have developed an integrated way of thinking about warfare, which combines elements of the human rights tradition, as well as the traditions of humanitarian law and collective security. They term this scheme the "modern law of force," and associate it with the transformation of the United Nations Charter into a modern constitutional scheme for global governance.

The modern law of force represents a triumph for a quite specific modern way of thinking about the relationship between law and politics. In developing it, humanitarians have grasped the nettle of pragmatism, thinking and acting strategically about power, infiltrating the decision making of those they would bend to humanitarian ends. It is here that we can most readily apprehend the advantages — but also the dark sides — of humanitarian pragmatism.

HUMANITARIANISM ABOUT WARFARE: THE EMERGENCE OF PRAGMATISM

Pre-Modern — Humanitarianism before the United Nations

A modern and pragmatic sensibility emerged only slowly among humanitarians concerned to limit warfare. Although it is customary to date modern humanitarian attention to war to the conflicts of the midnineteenth century — the American Civil War, the Crimean War, the European colonial wars and the persisting dynastic and developing nationalist struggles within Europe itself — it would be another hundred years before contemporary pragmatism would consolidate its hold on the field. Only since the 1945 United Nations Charter have we had a conceptually integrated and pragmatic legal vocabulary for speaking about force. The story of that achievement is worth a brief retelling.

Horrified by the brutality of mid-nineteenth-century military conflict, people with humanitarian sensibilities for the first time found a common international voice and organizational base from which to promote international legal and institutional projects to limit the suffering of war by constraining its means. The International Committee of the Red Cross, founded in 1863, encouraged numerous national and local efforts to respond to wartime suffering and the medical needs of the battlefield. The international leadership for these efforts turned quickly from the provision of medical care to the development of international law, working closely with political and military professionals who were themselves beginning to think about elaborating uniform rules to guide conduct on the battlefield.

During the ensuing years, this collaborative legal effort remained largely independent of broader pacifist campaigns which arose from diverse humanist sources—church leaders, proponents of woman's suffrage, heirs to the abolition movement, as well as political activists of all types—anarchist, socialist, populist, progressive, Catholic. Many from these groups also sought to ameliorate suffering during war, to promote better medical care on the battlefield and improve treatment for the wounded and other victims of war. Others responded to particular national war movements in the broad language of pacifism and humanitarianism. Over the next century and a half, these diverse movements would repeatedly break into the world of international legal and institutional responses to warfare—but their contribution would often rather quickly be forgotten among international lawyers and other professionals in the field.

The origins of modern humanitarian law lie more directly in the work of the various nineteenth-century statesmen and diplomats who promoted the codification of rules relating to particular weaponry and types of warfare—often at the behest of their military staffs. As they prepared for war in the Crimea, France and Great Britain thought it would be useful to codify limitations on maritime conflict, in part to reassure Scandinavian states they hoped would remain neutral. The result was the 1856 Paris Declaration Respecting Maritime Law. The Russian war minister encouraged Tsar Alexander II to sponsor an effort to outlaw exploding bullets, resulting in an intergovernmental conference and the 1868 St. Petersburg Declaration renouncing the use of specified explosive projectiles. In 1863, the U.S. government published a manual of instructions for union

troops during the civil war written by Francis Lieber, a professor at
Columbia University, which became a model for national codes developed for national armies in various European states in the ensuing
decades. Statesmen gathered in Brussels in 1874 to consider a comprehensive restatement of the rules of war drawn up by Alexander
II—a document which formed to basis for the 1899 and 1907
Hague Conventions on land warfare.

These codifications were not well integrated into the broader international legal thought of the period. The most important texts were
products of diplomacy, rather than legal elaboration. Some did contain broad principles about war, but the legal status of these principles was not obvious. For example, the preamble to the St. Petersburg Declaration noted "that the only legitimate object which States
should endeavour to accomplish during war is to weaken the military forces of the enemy." This was a military idea, a political idea, a
diplomatic formulation—it was not something already established in
international law to which the text need only refer. Over the next
years, these texts entered international law through compendiums of
diplomatic practice and expression, and were only slowly integrated
conceptually with broader international legal ideas.

In 1899, The Hague Convention on land warfare included a provision—the Martens Clause—to clarify matters by treating its new
codifications as supplemental to an existing body of law.

> Until a more complete code of the laws of war is issued, the high
> contracting Parties think it right to declare that in cases not in-
> cluded in the Regulations adopted by them, populations and bel-
> ligerents remain under the protection and empire of the principles
> of international law, as they result from the usages established
> between civilized nations, from the laws of humanity, and the re-
> quirements of the public conscience.[1]

The Martens Clause referred outward in this extremely expansive
way—to diplomatic usages, legal principles, public conscience—in
part because there simply was no clear "law of law" to which reference could be made in 1899. During the nineteenth century, inter-

---

[1] J. B. Scott, ed., *The Hague Conventions and Declarations of 1899 and 1907*, 3rd ed.
(New York: Oxford University Press, 1918), pp. 101–2.

national law's own attitude toward war had become increasingly muddled.

A hundred or more years before, it had been clear to legal scholars and statesmen alike that sovereigns — like individuals — existed in a world of natural law governing their behavior toward one another, as much in war as in peace. From at least the mid-seventeenth century, doctrines of "just war" were thought to limit both the cause and the conduct of war. The seventeenth-century scholars to whom nineteenth-century scholars attributed the first systematic intellectual work on international law — Grotius, Vitoria, Suarez — had all thought in "just war" terms. In the nineteenth century, however, the distinction between just and unjust war faded, a casualty of a loss of faith among policy elites in the plausibility of natural law limits on statecraft.

Looking back, it is hard to say whether the idea of "unjust" wars in fact limited the use of military force. Already in the seventeenth century it was apparent to international lawyers that princes would think their own struggles just and those of their opponents unjust. They advised princes to seek legal and religious counsel before combat, but often also concluded that all wars had reasonably been thought just by those who fought them. We can easily imagine just war doctrine having done less to restrain than to encourage war by delegitimating the enemy and justifying the cause. Whatever its humanitarian merit, the natural law of warfare gave way in the face of nineteenth-century "positive" conceptions of international law and an increasingly autonomous national state.

As international law's attitude toward war lost focus, the decision to go to war lost its legal moorings. In the course of the century, international law itself emerged as a distinct subject — sharply different from both domestic law and international private law. It was different because it concerned the legal relations among sovereigns, who were increasingly understood to occupy a separate legal universe from other people and institutions. Sovereigns were at the apex of national public legal orders, and their relations with one another were primarily matters of diplomacy and politics rather than law. The international law governing relations among sovereigns was being dramatically rethought, and would henceforth be rooted in the "positive" consent of sovereign powers rather than broad principles of natural law.

This large transformation left international law with very little to say about the decision to go to war — a silence which seems to have been rooted in the assumption that war was an unrestrained prerogative of sovereign power. Occasionally international legal scholars said as much. In general treatments of international law, however, warfare was also sometimes presented as a plausible way to defend and enforce sovereign rights. As the distinction between international law and politics sharpened, it was often unclear whether war was the pure domain of the political or the continuation of legal rights by other means.

The humanitarian lawyers who came together to codify battlefield rules began to think they were building something new — a distinct body of rules governing military campaigns among the civilized nations which signed on to the conventions they drafted: a law *in* war. International law writers began to separate international law into rules governing conduct in peace and in war. By the end of the century, peace and war were two different legal universes — each allocated a volume by leading treatise writers. Movement between the volumes — the central preoccupation of just war doctrine — remained offscreen.

This confusion in nineteenth-century thinking about the relationship between law and war has not been well understood by contemporary international lawyers looking for a more continuous story of law's progressive development. A leading treatise on international humanitarian law, published by the International Committee for the Red Cross, remembers the nineteenth century this way:

> International Humanitarian Law (IHL) developed at a time when the use of force was a lawful form of international relations, when States were not prohibited to wage war, when they had the right to make war (i.e., when they had the *ius ad bellum*). There was no logical problem for international law to prescribe them the respect of certain rules of behavior in war (the *ius in bello*) if they resorted to that means.[2]

---

[2] Marco Sassoli and Antione Bouvier for the International Committee of the Red Cross, *How Does Law Protect in War? Cases, Documents and Teaching Materials on Contemporary Practice in International Humanitarian Law* (Geneva, 1999), p. 83.

It would be more correct to say that there simply was no *jus ad bellum* — or *jus in bello*. There was law about warfare — primarily composed of newly codified rules limiting weaponry and references to a broad set of principles and rules in which international lawyers were fast losing faith. In 1874, when the Institute for International Law considered the law of war, much was uncertain. How did the new codifications fit with prior principles? How could international legal limits on warfare be squared with sovereign autonomy? What was the status of their scholarly statements?

In the end, law governing the decision to go to war languished for a century after the decline of natural law — until it was revived by the United Nations Charter as the modern "law of force." Although humanitarian voices launched numerous efforts to constrain war in the intervening years, they were political, religious, or diplomatic rather than legal. With few exceptions, even an explicit "right to make war" appeared among the enumerated rights of sovereignty only after the First World War. It would only be in the twentieth century that international lawyers would further subdivide the law about war into two branches — reviving the Latin expressions *jus in bello* and *jus ad bellum* to refer to law governing the conduct of and the legitimate causes for warfare, each addressed to a different audience. The *jus in bello*, with its specific rules and principled focus on military efficiency, was designed for military commanders. The *jus ad bello*, which combined broad justifications for warfare with complex institutional and diplomatic machinery for avoiding it, was oriented to statesmen. In the nineteenth century, humanitarians focused on constraining the military in battle, leaving the political decision to begin war outside the scope of humanitarian law.

But this is not the whole story — several crucial legal doctrines remained, orphaned by the emergence of what would become *jus in bello*, or humanitarian law. The most significant was what would become the doctrine of "self-defense." In the eighteenth-century writings of Vattel and other prominent legal scholars, the idea of "self-protection" had been important in a variety of different doctrinal contexts, and had been one justification for war making.[3] By

---

[3] See, e.g., Emeric de Vattel, *The Law of Nations; or, Principles of the Law of Nature,*

the mid-nineteenth century, the idea of a just war for self protection had gone the way of natural law. But the term "self-defense" continued to find its way into diplomatic and legal intercourse. The most often cited instance of its use was by Daniel Webster, then U.S. Secretary of State, in a famous incident between the United States and Great Britain involving the steamer *Caroline*. A British subject from Canada had led an attack on the American steamer in the Niagara River within New York's waters. The British asserted that the steamer had been destroyed as a public act of force in self-defense. In his diplomatic communications with the British, Webster acknowledged that Britain could trespass on the "inviolate character of the territory of independent states" in self-defense, but only where the "necessity of that self defence is instant, overwhelming, and leaving no choice of means, and no moment of deliberation."[4]

It is difficult to square this very narrow formulation with the idea that sovereigns were politically free to make war when they chose — let alone that they had a legal right to make war as they wished. Nevertheless, international lawyers today often cite the *Caroline* incident correspondence as an early formulation of an inherent international legal right to self defense. If Webster was invoking a principle of international law which restricted the legitimate use of force to threats this immediate, "self-defense" would have been a *jus ad bellum* all on its own. It would have been only a short step further to restrict war to the defense of one's rights — to treat war as a mechanism for enforcing international legal norms regulating sovereign prerogatives, rather than as the free instrument of the sovereign's absolute political authority.

More likely, Webster was using a convenient diplomatic formulation, drawn loosely by analogy from the broader common law. In the natural rights universe of the early common law, "self-defense" was a well-recognized defense to accusations of battery and trespass. The imminence of violence was a well-understood component of

---

Applied to the Conduct and Affairs of Nations and Sovereigns (reprint: Washington, D.C.: Carnegie Institution, 1916), chap. XXIII, par. 283 p. 106; bk. II, par. 49ff.; bk III, chaps. I and III, pp. 235 ff., 243 ff.

[4] The *Caroline*, J Moore, *Digest of International Law* 2 (1906): 412, quoting a communication from Webster to Lord Ashburton of August 6, 1842.

those doctrines. Webster also framed his argument in terms of "necessity" — also a well-understood common law doctrine of justification for acts of public or private authorities which would otherwise give rise to liability or sanction. In an earlier communication about the *Caroline* incident, Webster wrote:

> It will be for [Her Majesty's Government] to show, also, that the local authorities of Canada, even supposing the necessity of the moment authorized them to enter the territories of the United States at all, did nothing unreasonable or excessive; since the act, justified by the necessity of self-defence, must be limited by that necessity, and kept clearly within it.[5]

Diplomats in midcentury continued to feel it plausible to make arguments in the language of well-known common law principles. As these principles were integrated into "classical legal thought" after the Civil War, it became ever less plausible to do so.[6] The distinction between law and politics was sharpened, along with the distinction between public and private law. Sovereigns were understood to be bound only to the extent they had agreed to be bound by treaty — or by customary practice. In 1900, the British could easily have responded to Webster by asking when, precisely, the United Kingdom had accepted this narrow formulation. Analogy from the private law of trespass would have been interesting — but not compelling as a matter of law.

Self-defense was occasionally mentioned in late-nineteenth-century treatises as a justification for war — without any broad conception that war, in fact, needed a justification. "Reprisal," a form of self-help, was another doctrinal orphan from an earlier moment. Repri-

[5] Letter of Mr. Webster to Mr. Fox of April 24, 1841, 29 British and Foreign State Papers 1129, 1138 (1857).

[6] The term "classical legal thought" was coined by Duncan Kennedy to refer to the legal "consciousness" dominant in post–Civil War America. He has since placed this consciousness in a global theory of legal influences. See Duncan Kennedy, *The Rise and Fall of Classical Legal Thought* (Cambridge, MA: Afar, 1975, 1998); Duncan Kennedy, "Toward an Historical Understanding of Legal Consciousness: The Case of Classical Legal Thought in America, 1850–1940," *Research in Law and Sociology* 3 (1980): 3–24; and Duncan Kennedy, "Two Globalizations of Law and Legal Thought, 1850–1968," 3 *Suffolk University Law Review* vol. XXXVI: (2003), 631.

sal was said to permit otherwise illegal acts of retaliation in response to another state's illegal act. The goal of reprisal was to restore a right by forcing the other state back into compliance with law. The "illegal" acts which gave rise to a reprisal right would themselves have been violations of the law of peace. Like self-defense, reprisal *could* have been part of a systematic *jus ad bellum*. Looking back, it is tempting to say that warfare was illegal unless justified — as reprisal, as self-defense, or in some other way. When justified as reprisal, it would be easy to think of force as an instrument of law — a decentralized enforcement machinery for international legal norms.

But these doctrines simply did not function in this way — they drifted around in nineteenth-century treatises, analogies cut free from their roots in private law. The classic statement of the international doctrine of reprisal came only in a 1928 arbitration between Germany and Portugal. By 1928, international lawyers seeking to develop international law very commonly did so by self-conscious analogy to private law, and the Swiss arbitrators articulated the reprisal right as a doctrine of self-help in terms which could have come from any civil code. Sovereigns, it was then said, related to one another in a society of nations parallel to the national society of individuals. Numerous European international lawyers were hard at work combing private law in a systematic search for analogies to the relations between sovereigns in international "society" — in self-conscious opposition to the late-nineteenth century conviction that no such society was possible among public sovereign authorities. Reprisal itself would be revived after the Second World War as the doctrine of "countermeasures" — in the law of state responsibility rather than in the law of force. In the late-nineteenth century, none of this was plausible — the whole reason for having a distinct international legal order was that sovereigns were different, autonomous, public, political.

Indeed, a number of quite precise doctrines regulating the use of force simply disappeared in the nineteenth century — primarily those which authorized the mixed public and private use of force, or otherwise compromised the emerging conception of a unitary public sovereign with a monopoly over the discretionary use of force. Privateering, for example, had been a complex legal arrangement through which "letters of marque" authorized private vessels to carry out belligerent acts. It was eliminated from the legal vocabulary by the 1856 Paris Declaration.

By the First World War, international legal writing related to war contained a range of quite different rules, with different histories. There were general principles about sovereignty developed in the nineteenth century, stray doctrines and principles left over from natural law or borrowed from private law, specific examples of diplomatic practice, codified rules limiting the use of particular weapons — asphyxiating gases, expanding bullets — and the 1907 Hague Convention rules "respecting the laws and customs of war on land."

The codification efforts of the late-nineteenth- and early-twentieth century at The Hague represented one effort to bring order to these diverse ideas. Through codification, diplomatic practices could be made legal, and rules with diverse origins could be made universal. Legal scholars also sought to organize ideas about force, both by restating the rules in ever longer treatises, and by situating them in a single conceptual framework. One way to do this was to tease common "principles" from the materials of state practice. Since states had agreed to numerous specific limitations on their war-making powers, it could be said that they recognized the "principle" that a belligerent's right to injure the enemy is not unlimited. It was a short step from there to the idea that acts of war must be proportional to their legitimate objective, and to the "principle" that warfare must distinguish between military and nonmilitary targets. Already in the late-nineteenth century, treatise writers were precipitating such general principles of "customary law" from the diplomatic record and from the preambulatory wording of nineteenth-century codifications. The ideas were not new — seventeenth-century Spanish international lawyers had discussed the legal treatment of indigenous peoples in terms which called for balancing military objectives with humanitarian concerns and measuring the proportionality of acts of violence in war.

It was novel to attribute these principles to a universal international law rooted in diplomatic practice and the specific history of European nations. In part, the late-nineteenth century pressure to develop principles of this type came from a scholarly desire to pull everything together in a single conceptual system. These new principles also encouraged a new form of dialogue between international lawyers and military men — for whom humanitarianism came to mean professional efficiency in the prosecution of the war.[7]

The late-nineteenth-century intellectual effort to develop a unified international legal order also responded to the aspiration for a legal regime of universal applicability. During the nineteenth century, precisely as faith in natural law declined, the great powers engaged in an extremely wide range of military conflicts across the globe, against all types of opponents. The new codes of conduct had been designed for reciprocal application among the European military powers in warfare among them. They made frequent reference to their roots in the practices of "civilized" nations. A universal regime to limit the use of force could apply also, at least in some form, to war with the uncivilized. Legal scholars and statesmen developed a range of intellectual strategies for extending international law to the colonial world. Indeed, it might be more accurate to say that late-nineteenth-century international law was a product of thinking in the imperial center about relations with colonial subjects.[8]

Early in the century, it seemed plausible to imagine more than one international law governing different parts of the globe. Wheaton, the leading American nineteenth-century treatise writer, put it this way in 1836:

> In often happens, too, that what is the law of nations in one part of the world is not so in another, as we shall show in the proper place in respect to prisoners of war. . . . So also Bynkershoek . . . says that "the law of nations is that which is observed, in accordance with the light of reason, between nations, if not among all, *at least certainly among the greater part, and those the most civilized.*" Montesquieu says, that "the law of nations is naturally founded upon the principle that all nations ought to do to each other in peace as much good, and in war as little injury, as possible, consistently with their true interests. The object of war is vic-

---

[7] See, e.g. the famous letter, dated December 11, 1880, from Count Helmuth von Moltke to the international legal scholar Johann Gaspar Bluntschli, reprinted in Harry Pross, ed. *Die Zerstörung der deutschen Politik: Dokumente 1871–1933* (Frankfurt: Fischer Bücherei, 1959), 29–31.

[8] This idea has been systematically developed by Antony Anghie. See, e.g., Antony Anghie, "Finding the Peripheries: Sovereignty and Colonialism in Nineteenth-Century International Law," *Harvard International Law Journal* 40 (1999): 1.

tory; that of victory is conquest; that of conquest is self preservation. From this and the former principle ought to be derived those laws which form the law of nations." After thus stating the principles on which the law of nations *ought to be founded*, he proceeds to say, that "every nation has a law of nations — even the Iroquois, who eat their prisoners, have one. They send and receive ambassadors; they know the laws of war and peace; the evil is, that their law of nations is not founded upon true principles."[9]

By the end of the century, this no longer seemed satisfactory — the goal was a single universal international legal order. The idea that the world might be divided along a central axis of civilized and uncivilized, and that general principles of law bound both spheres, although in different ways, was a common way to square the desire for a universal law with recognition of extremely diverse conditions. Proportionality and necessity would govern the use of force everywhere — but would mean different things among the civilized, and between the civilized and uncivilized.[10]

As they developed a conceptually integrated international legal order in the decades leading up to the First World War, international legal scholars wrote increasing about war as a *legal status*. War began with a declaration, ended with a treaty of peace. Those in the status were *belligerents*. Belligerents had rights — and duties — particularly vis-à-vis states which were not party to the conflict — who

---

[9] Henry Wheaton, *Elements of International Law: with a Sketch of the History of the Science*, Philadelphia (1836), pp. 43–44 (citations deleted, emphasis in the original).

[10] Here is John Westlake, writing in 1907: "The advance of public opinion has even condemned all action in war the connection of which with the weakening of the enemy's military forces is not proximate. Slaughter of non-combatants or carrying them off as prisoners, and the devastation of territory not necessary for covering the retreat of an army or for any other directly military purpose, but intended to create general terror or distress, may indeed help to break down resistance but are universally condemned. . . . But often the inroads or other outrages committed by savages or half-civilised tribes can only be repressed by punitive expeditions, in which the whole population must suffer for want of a government sufficiently marked off from it. All civilised states which are in contact with the outer world are, to their great regret, familiar with such expeditions in their frontier wars, and the principle that to weaken the enemy is the only legitimate mode of action can have no application to them. But no humane officer will burn a village if he has any means of striking a sufficient blow that will be felt only by the fighting men." John Westlake, *International Law* (Cambridge: Cambridge University Press, 1907), pt. II, pp. 54–55.

might have the status of *neutrals* or *nonbelligerents*. As a status, war was limited — to the belligerents and to the period between declaration and peace. It remained unclear, however, whether a sovereign could go to war on a whim. If war were a legal status, it seemed at least plausible that the conditions for entering the status could also be legally defined. It now seems only a small step to transform doctrines of self-defense or reprisal into exclusive legal justifications for warfare, or to harness warfare to the defense of rights, rendering it an instrument of the peacetime legal order itself.

In the last years before the First World War, international lawyers did begin to elaborate the entailments of war as a legal status. The most significant consequence was to strengthen the inviolability of noncombatants, nonbelligerents, and neutrals. The legal status of "neutrality" acquired more distinctive rights and duties. As far as I have been able to discern, however, no international lawyer prior to 1914 succeeded in pulling these pieces together in a unified legal system itemizing the legitimate legal grounds for war, or harnessing military force exclusively to the defense of right.

And then war came. World War I was a profound shock to those who had hoped to restrain warfare by doctrinal elaboration. Freud's 1915 essay "Thoughts for the Times on War and Death" put it this way:

When I speak of disillusionment, everyone at once knows what I mean. . . . [W]e were prepared to find that wars between the primitive and the civilized peoples, between those races whom a color-line divides, nay, wars with and among the undeveloped nationalities of Europe or those whose culture has perished — that for a considerable period such wars would occupy mankind. But we had permitted ourselves to have other hopes. We had expected the great ruling powers among the white nations upon whom the leadership of the human species has fallen, who were known to have cultivated world-wide interests, to whose creative powers were due our technical advances in the direction of dominating nature, as well as the artistic and scientific acquisitions of the mind — peoples such as these we had expected to succeed in discovering another way of settling misunderstandings and conflicts of interest. . . .

But if such a war indeed must be, what was our imaginary picture of it? We saw it as an opportunity for demonstrating the progress of mankind in communal feeling since the era when the Greek Amphictyonies had proclaimed that no city of the league might be demolished, nor its olive groves hewn down, nor its water cut off. As a chivalrous crusade, which would limit itself to establishing the superiority of one side in the contest, with the least possible infliction of dire sufferings that could contribute nothing to the decision, and with complete immunity for the wounded who must of necessity withdraw from the contest, as well as for the physicians and nurses who devoted themselves to the task of healing. And of course with the utmost precautions for the non-combatant classes of the population — for women who are debarred from war-work, and for the children, who, grown older, should be enemies no longer but friends and cooperators. . . . Then the war in which we had refused to believe broke out, and brought disillusionment. . . . The warring state permits itself every . . . misdeed, every . . . act of violence, as would disgrace the individual man. . . . It absolves itself from the guarantees and contracts it had formed with other states, and makes unabashed confession of its rapacity and lust for power, which the private individual is then called upon to sanction in the name of patriotism. . . .

It cannot be a matter for astonishment, therefore, that this relaxation of all the moral ties between the greater units of mankind should have had a seducing influence on the morality of individuals . . . and men perpetrate deeds of cruelty, fraud, treachery and barbarity so incompatible with their civilization that one would have held them to be impossible. Well may that civilized cosmopolitan, therefore, of whom I spoke, stand helpless in a world grown strange to him.[11]

However disillusioning, the war was also a spur to action for humanitarian policy makers, who regrouped and broadened their con-

---

[11] Sigmund Freud, "Thoughts for the Times on War and Death" (1915) in *Collected Papers* (translated by Joan Riviere) (1915; reprint, New York: Basic Books, 1959), IV: 289–94.

stituency. In the years following the war, they launched a series of projects to prevent a recurrence of 1914. It seemed clear that what would henceforth be termed the "traditional" law of war had utterly failed. Both major pre-war efforts by international humanitarian lawyers — to codify battlefield limitations and to write synthetic elaborations of legal principles — fell into disrepute. War had turned out indeed to be a free act of sovereign power. The new humanitarian task was to restrain that power. The most promising avenue was not law but institutions and diplomacy.

The central problem seemed the decision to go to war, not the regulation of conduct on the battlefield. Humanitarians enthusiastic about the League of Nations were often explicitly opposed to reviving the Hague system. At the League, humanitarians would build a new diplomacy, rooted in the reality of collective security. The League would be a political institution, a standing consultative assembly of nations with a brief to facilitate peaceful settlement and peaceful change in the international political order. War would be reduced by an obligatory "cooling off" period. In Article 16 of the League Covenant, members pledged to treat an attack on any member as an act of war against all, and undertook to subject the attacking state to isolating sanctions. The Council of the League could then recommend military action against aggressors — a power which it was hoped would deter states from exercising their discretion to make war. Self-determination for the peoples of eastern and central Europe would bring new voices to the table, eliminating the frictions which led to war. A mandate system would oversee the orderly dismantling of the Ottoman Empire and offer a stable regime to peoples not yet thought ready for self-government. Alongside the League in Geneva, the International Labor Organization would respond to the newly interdependent economic world with humanizing social regulation. The League system of Mandates would prepare colonial peoples for self-reliance.

The humanitarians in Geneva drew inspiration from the new disciplines of political science and what would become international relations. Law was out. Politics was in. None of these efforts sought to outlaw war. The most famous — if ultimately unsuccessful — interwar effort brought statesmen together to "condemn recourse to war" and "renounce it as an instrument of national policy" in the 1928 Kellogg-Briand Pact. It was, of course, to be a short-lived renunciation. The League promise to prevent war was almost equally short-lived. But these were not the work of idealists or legalists. Their architects were disenchanted with legalism and thought themselves thoroughly modern and realistic in their engagement with policy and politics.

Meanwhile, back at The Hague, international lawyers sought to revitalize the legal tradition. The old international law was to be rejected. It was too abstract, detached from the realities of politics and diplomacy. To control war by elaborating the entailments of a *legal status* suddenly seemed quaintly nineteenth-century — even if this had never, in fact, been part of nineteenth century international law. Indeed, the "traditional" law of war was largely the product of post-1918 efforts to describe what needed to be rejected, reformed, or modernized. After 1918, international lawyers regularly described a "traditional" law alongside the modernizing efforts they proposed to replace it, offering it as a consistent baseline for modernization. The traditional law was said to have defined war as a legal status with distinct rights and obligations. It could be elaborated by scholars through careful study of international custom and state practice. In this scheme, war began with a formal declaration and ended upon surrender or in a treaty of peace. The rights of neutrals, as those of belligerents and nonbelligerents, were sharply defined. Limits to warfare could be deduced from these status boundaries. War could be seen, doctrinally, as a defense of right.

These scholarly elaborations of a traditional law were a sideshow. The focal point for legal renewal between the wars was the development of a new law about warfare which would be codified, specific, rooted in sovereign consent, negotiated among military and political authorities, and confirmed in writing as an expression of sovereign will. In this sense, the Hague codifications of the late-nineteenth century — indeed, all of the law in war from the 1856 Paris Declaration forward — could be seen as forerunners of this new international law. In this spirit, international lawyers forged new agreements to limit weaponry and the means of war — Hague rules for "aerial warfare" in 1923, a Geneva Protocol prohibiting the use of "asphyxiating, poisonous or other gases" in 1925, and the 1930 London Treaty on submarine warfare.

By the time war broke out again in Europe, a diverse array of international legal and institutional efforts to limit war had been developed — the League machinery of collective security and peaceful change, the Kellogg-Briand renunciation of war, detailed rules about military conduct in war, an emerging discourse of general principles for regulating warfare, and an array of doctrines from the traditional law of the nineteenth century. A range of different organizations provided voice to humanitarians supporting and elaborating elements of this scheme. The International Committee of the Red Cross, various professional associations of international lawyers, citizens committees, labor organizations, religious and pacifist groups were all mobilized between the wars to support these international humanitarian schemes to limit and avoid war.

The Modern Law of Force and the United Nations

After the Second World War, many pre-war international legal projects were revived within the context of the United Nations. Although they coexisted uneasily at first, in the ensuing years they were integrated ever more completely into a "modern law of force" rooted in a pragmatic understanding of the UN Charter as a constitutional arrangement for global society.

Although the League scheme had not lived up to its political promise, eventually the Allied Powers had, uniting to defeat an Axis of states bent on aggressive war. This alliance became the model for the UN system of collective security. At the same time, the pre-war law in war was broadened to protect civilians. Individuals, as well as states, were made responsible for violations. A further codification effort culminated in the 1948 Geneva Conventions on the conditions of sick and wounded in war, the treatment of prisoners of war, and the protection of civilians in time of war. The various war crimes trials — most notably at Nuremberg — developed the laws of force and applied them directly to individuals. Postwar efforts to develop an international law of human rights intersected with the law of armed conflict in numerous ways, most notably in the 1948 Genocide Convention. These extensions of the laws in war — to civilians, to individuals, to genocide — brought international humanitarian law ever closer to the broader world of international human rights.

Throughout the postwar years, negotiations over disarmament treaties and agreements to limit the spread and use of weapons became a continuous part of international life — most notably in the area of nuclear nonproliferation and disarmament. New conventions were signed on particularly harmful weapons — lasers, chemical weapons, land mines — as well as on the protection of cultural property and the avoidance of environmental catastrophe in wartime. An institutional regime for nonproliferation was established. Humanitarian policy makers sought to extend the law in war to unconventional warfare, guerrilla wars, civil wars, and wars of decolonization, and to strengthen the international criminal law regime. The International Court of Justice confirmed and elaborated basic principles of the law of force in several leading opinions. Jurisdictional innovations from human rights law, which encouraged adjudication anywhere for egregious violations elsewhere, were applied to alleged war criminals. In the 1990s, ad hoc criminal tribunals were established in loose imitation of the trials at Nuremberg, and in 1999, international humanitarians successfully promoted the establishment of a permanent International Criminal Court.

More importantly, international lawyers, diplomats, and humanitarian policy makers understood these developments within the broader context of a revived law of war. War was no longer the free act of sovereign will. International lawyers no longer treated sovereigns as free political actors — the discipline split sharply from the field of political science on precisely this point. Instead, sovereigns were understood to be part of an international community, their use of force conditioned by membership in that community. The Charter system was more than a political regime of collective security — it was also a new legal order which inaugurated a new law of war. In discussing warfare, international legal treatises no longer gave pride of place to the law in war — many eliminated it altogether or treated it as a technical subspecialty. The International Committee of the Red Cross — international humanitarian law itself — was no longer at the center of the effort to limit war through law. For the first time in more than a century, the decision to go to war could be understood in legal terms.

The United Nations Charter aimed to establish an international monopoly of force and placed responsibility for maintaining the peace with the Security Council. In the words of Article 1.1 of the Charter, the United Nations would

> take collective measures for the prevention and removal of threats to the peace, and for the suppression of acts of aggression or other breaches of the peace, and to bring about by peaceful means, and in conformity with the principles of justice and international law, adjustment or settlement of international disputes or situations which might lead to a breach of peace.

Uses of force outside the Charter framework were prohibited. Members agreed, in Article 2.4, to "refrain in their international relations from the threat or use of force against the territorial integrity or political independence of any state, or in any other manner inconsistent with the Purposes of the United Nations."

As originally conceived, the Charter system made any *first* use of force a "breach" of the peace — suspicious and presumptively illegal. Self-defense was permitted as a *response* to a first attack under Article 51, until the Security Council took up the matter. The Security Council could itself then authorize collective warfare to "maintain or restore international peace and security." No state could legitimately be the first to use force — collective security, alongside the peaceful settlement of disputes, became projects of the Security Council.

Like any complex constitutional order, this scheme would need to be interpreted and kept up to date in a changing political world. As it turned out, the Cold War stalemate among the great powers blocked development of the Security Council's role in collective security. Alternative institutional mechanisms needed to be found — in the Korean War, the United States and its allies relied on the General Assembly for authorization. In the 1960s and 1970s, successive Secretaries-General developed new roles for the United Nations *between* the Cold War antagonists in a variety of third world conflicts. They developed new methods of diplomacy and "good offices," and promoted the insertion of UN "peacekeepers" between adversaries to maintain and monitor cease-fire arrangements. These and many other innovations needed to be imagined and defended within the terms of the Charter — a job which often fell to international lawyers with humanitarian sensibilities.

In developing arguments for these policy innovations, international lawyers articulated the Charter scheme in terms familiar from postwar constitutional interpretation — functional, pragmatic, realistic about power. Numerous governments initiated military action after 1945 — not once, until the 1991 Gulf War, with the Security Council's authorization. International lawyers interpreted these events — supported them, opposed them — in light of the Charter. In the process, they developed its principles. The Charter prohibition on the use of force was not absolute. The "inherent right" to use military force in "individual or collective self-defense" protected by Article 51 could be — and was — interpreted broadly as well as narrowly. A close reading of Article 2.4 revealed other loopholes — force not directed "against a state," not "inconsistent with the Purposes of the United Nations." The Charter began to be read as a constitutional document articulating the legitimate justifications for warfare. Lengthy articles and books were written parsing the meaning of "aggression" and "intervention." We might blame the Cold War — this was not how the scheme was supposed to function. But the new law of force was also a remarkable achievement of legal imagination. If the institutions had not functioned perfectly, the broader legal vocabulary had functioned far better than expected. It became increasingly common to discuss decisions to go to war, and the conduct of war, in the vernacular of the Charter and the laws of force.

The signature theme for this modern vocabulary of force was *realism* — about war, about sovereign power, about politics. The United Nations institutions were designed quite self-consciously to respond to objections raised by realists — particularly in the United States — to the design of the League.[12] The Security Council scheme was not a legal pipe dream. It would harness the wartime alliance of great mili-

---

[12] The classic account remains Leo Gross, "1648–1948: The United Nations Charter and the Lodge Amendments," *American Journal of International Law* 41 (1947): 531.

tary powers to defense of the new world order—and each would be given a veto in the Council, ensuring that it would respond to the realpolitik of possible consensus among them. Indeed, this "politicization" of the Charter led many leading international lawyers to impugn the "legality" of the entire scheme.[13] The professionals at the Red Cross were also standoffish. In their tradition, it was more realistic simply to accept that war would occur, and work to blunt its impact through rules painstakingly wrung from the military itself.

The realism of the scheme was also expressed in its organization along functional lines—with numerous specialized agencies to address specific problems. The constitutional design for each would follow its function—weighted voting and special membership structures proliferated in the postwar institutional system. The Secretary-General's efforts to seize opportunities for political engagement on behalf of universal principles and humanitarian aspirations—famously in the person of Dag Hammarskjöld—epitomized this new realistic legal spirit. Oscar Schachter, a leading international legal scholar and humanitarian spoke of Dag Hammarskjöld's vision in these terms:

> Hammarskjöld made no sharp distinction between law and policy; in this he departed clearly from the prevailing positivist approach. He viewed the body of law not merely as a technical set of rules and procedures, but as the authoritative expression of principles that determine the goals and directions of collective action. . . . Hammarskjöld's reliance on principles and legal concepts may appear to be at variance with the flexibility and adroitness that characterized much of his political activity; yet on reflection it will be seen that these apparently antithetical approaches were both essential aspects of a skilled technique for dealing with the specific problems which he faced. . . . It is also of significance in evaluating Hammarskjöld's flexibility that he characteristically expressed basic principles in terms of opposing ten-

---

[13] The most famous doubter was Hans Kelsen, whose commentary on the Charter repeated many accusations he had leveled at the League Covenant before the war. See Hans Kelsen, *Legal Technique in International Law: A Textual Critique of the League Covenant* (Geneva: Geneva Research Center, 1939); and *The Law of the United Nations: A Critical Analysis of Its Fundamental Problems* (London: Stevens and Sons, 1950).

dencies (applying, one might say, the philosophic concept of polarity or dialectical opposition). He never lost sight of the fact that a principle, such as that of observance of human rights, was balanced by the concept of non-intervention, or that the notion of equality of states had to be considered in a context which included the special responsibilities of the great Powers. The fact that such precepts had contradictory implications meant that they could not provide automatic answers to particular problems, but rather that they served as criteria which had to be weighed and balanced in order to achieve a rational solution of the particular problem. . . . He did not, therefore, attempt to set law against power. He sought rather to find within the limits of power the elements of common interest on the basis of which joint action and agreed standards could be established.[14]

At the same time, this new vocabulary would stand for a broader ethical commitment. To speak of war — or peace — in these terms was to be humanitarian. The United Nations joined hands with nongovernmental institutions to mobilize world public opinion behind humanitarian objectives through inspections, reports, inquiries, and the politics of shame. The United Nations promoted health, refugee resettlement, children's education, economic development, and human rights. And it offered a vocabulary for speaking ethically about making war, and about the humanitarian disasters of war. The laws of war were increasingly expressed in the language of criminal justice — war crimes, war criminals — and in the language of human rights. If states had agreed to treat prisoners of war humanely, we should rather say that each prisoner of war has a *right* to humane treatment. The same can now be said of civilians. Indeed, the effort to expand the law in war from military casualties and prisoners to civilians — and then to environmental damage — followed the progressive merger of the humanitarian law vocabulary into a broader discourse of international humanitarian virtue.[15] To defy the United

---

[14] Oscar Schachter, "Dag Hammarskjöld and the Relation of Law to Politics," *American Journal of International Law* 56 (1962): 1–4, 7.

[15] For a powerful description of the new fusion of human rights and humanitarian law, see Ruti Teitel, "Humanity's Law: Rule of Law for the New Global Politics," *Cornell International Law Journal* 35, no. 2 (2002): 355.

Nations system, not to speak in this language, would be to defy the international community, the world — civilization itself.

In this new regime, at once realistic and ethically broad-minded, rules were kept in their place. Although the law in war continued to be developed through detailed codifications, the rules were not deduced by commentators from abstract ideas about sovereignty or interpretations of historic custom. They were forged through tough bargaining among military experts, diplomats, and professional humanitarians. Of course, the resulting treaties were limited by what national military authorities were prepared to accept — but one could also expect them to be transposed into national legal regimes and observed. In their enthusiasm for this new realism, it was easy to forget that the International Committee of the Red Cross had always worked closely with military and diplomatic authorities, and had not sought to deduce rules from abstract ideas about the international legal order. This had been the tradition for the law in war since the 1860s. It was similarly easy to forget that interwar humanitarians had also not been starry-eyed legalists. The Kellogg-Briand pact, for example, now commonly remembered as a legalistic effort to outlaw war, was designed in precisely the opposite spirit — as a coming together of diplomats to recognize the reality of global interdependence and renounce war as an "instrument of policy."

The new law of force also elevated principles and standards above technical rules. Standards were promoted *both* to render the legal order more realistic in its relationship to power and to blend it more smoothly with the new ethical vocabularies of human rights and broad humanitarianism. Latin phrases were gone. In the new law of "force," even the word "war" was replaced with the more malleable and suggestive terms "threats to the peace, breaches of the peace and acts of aggression" or "intervention" into the "domestic jurisdiction" of a state. The Charter justifications for the use of force were also cast as broad standards — self-defense, restoring or maintaining international peace and security, responding to acts of aggression, or when "consistent with the principles and purposes of the Charter." The use of force for humanitarian purposes — "humanitarian intervention" — appeared for the first time as an explicit legal argument.

In a parallel development, the detailed codifications of The Hague or Geneva were now routinely presented as instantiations of a few general principles. The formal distinction between combatants and noncombatants became a "principle of distinction" between military and nonmilitary objectives. These principles could often be linked loosely to earlier customary law or just-war ideas. Indeed, the vocabulary of "just war" has made something of a comeback among academic commentators, at least in the last decade or so, reflecting the more porous boundary between ethics and law.

The rules developed since the 1860s are now presented as having ripened into customary obligations, if not in their details, at least in their broad outlines. They all boil down to a few broad commitments, humanitarian first principles, ethical baselines for a universal modern civilization — simple ideas which could be printed on a wallet-sized card and taught to soldiers in the field. The means of war are not unlimited. Each specific use of force must be necessary. The military must distinguish civilian and military objectives. The use of force must be proportional to its objective. The military must act humanely, professionally, and with dignity.

It took some time after 1945 for the various strands of this new law of force to come together in a single constitutional vision. In the early decades, different strands of realism vied with one another. The most striking difference was that between the military orientation of *jus in bello* and the political orientation of *jus ad bello*. Some thought the most significant promise in the UN scheme was the construction of a political forum for continuing the wartime alliance, protected by the veto from disconnecting with the wishes of the great powers. For others, the tension between law and politics was more realistically managed by tightly drawn texts, adopted by consensus. For others, the key to realism was standards which could guide military judgment.

For many years, a rivalry persisted among those promoting the *jus in bello* between human rights professionals and those working with the International Committee of the Red Cross. To preserve their public neutrality and maintain the confidence of national military leaders, the ICRC has traditionally reported only to governments, and only on the basis of confidentiality. It has been more comfortable monitoring compliance with precise rules than broad standards. It has thought itself unique in recognizing the need for partnership with the military, for tempering humanitarian commitments for application to the real world of statecraft. Human rights advocates have had a completely different strategy—speaking publicly in international settings, they have sought to shame governments into compliance and have always been more at ease framing arguments in broad standards. Both were realist strategies, both promised a partnership with statecraft, but in different terms.

These differences softened with time. As the Security Council failed to live up to the promise of great-power management, those most invested in its political promise shifted their focus to the political work of the General Assembly—and then to the Secretary-General's peacekeeping efforts. As they did so, they revisited the Charter, and began to defend their political goals in its terms, interpreting and expanding its legal terms. Thirty years after the war, these strands had merged into a more unified constitutional vision—which continued to address different audiences and situations in a diverse vocabulary of rules, standards, procedures, and institutional arrangements.

Since the end of the Cold War a common vocabulary has been forged among these various strands of postwar humanitarianism. The expansion of humanitarian law toward issues of concern to the human rights community—most dramatically in new rules for the treatment of civilian populations—is part of the explanation. The transformation of humanitarian rules into standards aided the rapprochement. The human rights community has embraced humanitarian law, transforming its standards for evaluating treatment into rights. Civilians are now said to have a "right" to be distinguished from combatants, just as prisoners of war have "rights."

Differences remain, of course—repeated throughout the international humanitarian world as differences in perspective, emphasis, institutional competence, or specialty. Intense disagreement continues to break out about the relative merits of tight rules and discretionary standards in constraining military—or political—actors. Professionals often assert that only the clearest rules can be effectively implemented in battle, or that statesmen can only be expected to use a vocabulary sufficiently plastic to permit them to express their political interests as conditions change. One often also finds argument the other way — that the military can only be constrained by harnessing its professional judgment about what is "proportional" and "necessary" to humanitarian ends, or that statesmen can only be relied upon to implement treaties which are clear and authoritative.

More significant than these differences, however, is the increasing use of this common vocabulary to speak about the restraint and exercise of military power by statesmen, military strategists, and humanitarians alike. In the last decades, these groups have all come to speak in terms of the new law of force, merging Charter principles with the rules and standards of humanitarian law. One result has been a new conception about the place of institutional arrangements for collective security. No longer a separate world of diplomacy and political deterrence, the United Nations system has increasingly come to be referred to as the repository of a kind of constitutional police power to authorize intervention — by the Security Council, by states, by regional organizations — for legitimate purposes. This constitutional order is managed in the vocabulary of Charter principles and humanitarian law rules.

Intervention can be authorized — even ex post — if consistent with Charter principles, from enforcement of rights or defense of territory through to the implementation of human rights or prevention of genocide. In this new vocabulary, it is possible to speak of "intervention for democracy" and to discuss in federalist terms when intervention is appropriately undertaken at the international, regional, or national level. This complex integration of diplomatic institutions, legal doctrines, and humanitarian principles has supported a growing sense among humanitarian professionals that the "international community" did something "constitutional" in San Francisco by founding the United Nations. The result — a constitutional vision at once realistic, ethically humanist, legally valid, and politically practical — has transformed thinking about the law of force.

This new law of force does not *judge* wars ad hoc — and usually ex post — as just or unjust. Realistically we recognize that among sovereigns, each is judge of his own cause. The function of this vocabulary is another one — to provide a vocabulary in which disputes over the legitimacy of sovereign action can be conducted. At the same time, the traditional effort to limit the *legal status* of warfare by elaborating its doctrinal preconditions is also gone. Those who make war are not worried about what status they occupy. They are looking to accomplish political objectives in ways they feel are legitimate. It would be tempting to say that the new law of force has captured war in a legal vocabulary — war must now be legally justified, force has been linked to the exercise of rights, and the Security Council enforces violations of law. We might also be tempted to say war has become an instrument of the legal order, now that nations may legally use force only to defend their rights. Some international lawyers have interpreted the Charter in these ways. The constitutional vision developed in the last decades, however, is less interested in the imposition of legal norms onto political life. Proponents of this new vision believe they have developed something else entirely — a common vocabulary for both political *and* legal analysis. The United Nations system offers terms of art for both statesmen and lawyers, military strategists and humanitarians, to manage the use of force among nations.

A universal ethic, a political institution linked to the great powers, powers articulated through constitutional standards and limited by legal rules — it is a grand scheme. Realistically, of course, the new law of force will be effective only if used by statesmen to understand their own prerogatives. It is one thing for a lawyer to say that sovereignty is a legal regime or a bundle of rights, or for a humanitarian to articulate the demands of civilization — for these statements to limit sovereign power, the same thing must be said by a statesman. The new vocabulary for force was advanced precisely to meet this test. In 1991, Oscar Schachter put it this way in speaking of self-defense:

A critical question affecting both law and policy on self-defense concerns the degree of uncertainty or indeterminacy that inheres in the proclaimed legal limits. Some indeterminacy results from the key standards of necessity and proportionality, concepts that leave ample room for diverse opinions in particular cases. Other sources of uncertainty can be traced to differing interpretations of the events that would permit forcible defensive action. Varying views have been advanced by governments and scholars. . . .

Notwithstanding its relative indeterminacy, self-defense as a legal norm can have an ascertainable relationship to the policies and actions of governments. The "defensist" principle, namely, that self-defense is the only legitimate reason to use force against another State, has been expressed as the strategic policy of most States. Evidence for this is not only found in governmental statements to international bodies, where they may be expected. Recent studies by political scientists and students of military strategy confirm the practical implication of defensist doctrine. When States proclaim the principle of self-defense as governing the use of force, they have a stake in its credibility to other States and to their own citizens. For such States to be credible, their weapons training and contingent planning must reflect a defensist strategy. . . . Hence, a defensist posture is not merely one of restraint but a source of policy that goes beyond the essentially negative rules of the law.[16]

On its face, it has seemed at least plausible that the modern law of force could become *the* vocabulary of political, legal, and humanitarian legitimacy, rather than a set of rules adding legal or humanitarian imprimatur to what you already want to do for other reasons. The Charter justifications for military action resemble the policy vocabulary used by political actors to describe what they are doing. If you think back on wars of the last century or more, it is hard to think of a war whose political motivation could not be expressed in one or another of these terms: for self-defense, to maintain international peace and security, to promote one or another of the many purposes and principles of the United Nations. Statesmen will have to learn the details of this new vocabulary, to be sure — but there seems little they have wanted to say which could not be said in these terms.

Except perhaps "aggressive" wars of conquest. But it is a rare statesman who launches a war simply to *be aggressive*. There is almost always something else to be said — the province is actually ours; our rights have been violated; our enemy is not, in fact, a state; we were invited to help; they were about to attack us. . . . Something. Of course, other statesmen may well not see things the same way — those on the receiving end generally feel the attack is illegitimate,

---

[16] Schachter, *International Law in Theory and Practice* (1991): 141–46.

unwarranted, aggressive. They are likely to say so; others may agree. These standards might well be interpreted more or less strictly — there is ample room for reasonable disagreement. And, of course, there may be arguments which are simply specious — just as there may be war which simply *is* nothing but aggression. Normally, however, the result will be *an argument* conducted in the *vocabulary* of the Charter.

Something parallel seems to go on with specific applications of military violence. We can easily call to mind historical examples of "wanton violence" in war. And of course they have sometimes been sanctioned by military leadership. But rare is the commander who orders "unnecessary" "wanton violence" "disproportional" to any legitimate military objective. Far more often the tactics employed by *other* forces will seem excessive. The vocabulary in which this charge is made, and defended, is the vocabulary of humanitarian law. Indeed, wherever tactics seem extreme — carpet bombing, siege, nuclear first use, suicide bombing, terrorizing the civilian population — the condemnation and the defense seem to converge on the vocabulary of necessity, proportionality, and so forth. Think of Hiroshima.

Of course, at the beginning, this was simply a possibility, an ambition, for the new law of force. But we might think of its potential in a number of ways. International relations specialists have long debated the relative significance of individual *agents* and broader institutional or ideological *structures* in international affairs. As the new constitutional vocabulary comes to be used by statesmen and military strategists as well as humanitarians eager to restrict the use of force, the significance of the agent/structure debate should diminish. If the program succeeds, the limits and potentials of this common *language* should be more significant than either the interests of agents or the limits of institutional structure. Or, perhaps better formulated, the interests of agents and the limits of institutions will themselves be defined in this new vocabulary.

As this catches on, statesmen might be able to be *argued* into more restrictive conceptions of their prerogatives. Military professionals might be able to be argued into more limited freedom of action on the battlefield. As humanitarians, we will need to put power behind our arguments — just as statesmen do when they back up assertions of right with military force. Moreover, this vocabulary will itself need to be managed, developed, promoted. Someone will be needed to distinguish plausible from specious arguments. International humanitarian lawyers cast themselves for this role — a professional repository of rhetorical innovation, an invisible college of good sense and argumentative skill. The goal was clear — to replace martial combat with argument is what it means to beat swords into ploughshares.

A Vocabulary for Argument about Force

In a way, the modern law of force resembles the pre-1850 world of just war doctrine. It is not surprising that just war theories have had a resurgence in the last years among academicians. Just war also provided a vocabulary for dispute — opposing princes often thought their war just — and a profession for commentators. Like today's legal standards, just war doctrine was too malleable to provide a definitive guide for statesmen or scholars. It was as common for scholars solemnly to recommend statesmen seek their advice beforehand as it was to treat a successful outcome afterwards as evidence of a just cause.

The modern law of force offers a vocabulary for disputation, rather than an external point of judgment. The idea that a constitutional order can rest on a professional vocabulary for argument — rather than on a set of external rules embodied in a sacred text — can be difficult to understand, although it is now a familiar strand of thinking about many domestic constitutional schemes, perhaps most notably in the United States. Professionals using the modern law of force recognize that reasonable people may differ about the application of the Charter's broad standards. When an international lawyer voices a professional opinion about war, however forcefully, he does so as an *argument*. At some level he knows he does not have access to a truth which can be articulated to those in power. At the same time, it is not just argument — somewhere there is also the intuition of commitment. When using the vocabulary of the modern law of force, people often have the simultaneous experience of presenting what they know is simply an argument and of expressing a deeper or larger commitment — to humanitarian values, to victory, to one or another political objective.

Most significantly, this new vocabulary is spoken by military, political, and humanitarian professionals alike. A partnership between humanitarian and military leaders was first embraced by those who initially codified the law in war, among them the early professionals of the International Committee of the Red Cross. Their willingness to accept war as a fact and to work with the military to humanize its conduct often seemed something of a scandal to other humanitarians. The new law of force provides a new basis for partnerships of this type. The law of force now permits humanitarians, military professionals, and statesmen to speak about decisions to go to war and the conduct of war in the same — humanitarian — terms. For humanitarians, the nineteenth-century split between a professional tactic of engagement with the military and a broader commitment to humanism is no longer necessary. Similarly, humanitarianism is no longer a distinct perspective, in tension with how military strategists think, needing to be asserted *against* them. Or, perhaps more accurately, these tensions have become part of the experience of speaking a common vocabulary.

Once military strategists and humanitarians speak the same language, their cooperation no longer seems scandalous. No professional military commander would order the unnecessary or disproportional use of force against targets of no military value — if for no other reason than that doing so might waste ammunition or divert resources from the strategic objective. Doing so would contravene his identity as a professional. At the same time, no professional humanitarian advocate would categorically preclude the use of force for humanitarian objectives. We could say that the professional military has given up the claim to mayhem as the humanitarian has abandoned an absolute pacifism. Both are someplace in between, perhaps agreeing, perhaps disagreeing, about the precise requirements of best military practice for legitimate ends.

For humanitarians, this seems to have come with secularism, with the loss of just war ideas, with the entry into policy making, and with a broader transformation in legal consciousness toward a more

pragmatic mode of analysis. To bend international affairs to humanitarian objectives, it seems unavoidable to think of force, at least
sometimes, as a tool. To participate in a living constitutional order, it
now seems necessary to interpret legal rules by weighing and balancing in instrumental terms. For humanitarians, this new shared vocabulary promises access, clarity and power. No longer standing outside
looking in, no longer tethered blindly to formal commitments, able
to participate in *making policy*, in governing, in rulership.

Pacifist voices remain, to be sure. One sometimes also encounters
international lawyers who interpret the standards of humanitarian
law so narrowly that no use of force seems legitimate. Just as one
still hears echoes of the ancient maxim that in war, law is silent. Or
that humanitarianism should preserve its outsider status and ethical
vision. Such voices may return to prominence — but since at least
1945 they have been on the defensive among humanitarian international lawyers concerned with force.

On the military side, the embrace of this vocabulary accompanied
the emergence of the national professional military as a standard
component of the modern state. The military profession links its embrace of today's humanitarian vocabulary to ancient ideas of military
honor, virtue, and chivalry. But these have all been transformed by
the emergence of mass citizen armies, enormous bureaucratic command structures, complex logistic and technological operating procedures, civilian control. All these encouraged the embrace of a humanitarian vocabulary shared by civilian and political leadership,
and cast in the flexible terms of modern policy science. It is not surprising that the first codification of modern law in war — the Lieber
Code — was promulgated by the American North during the Civil
War. It was not only Francis Lieber who had a son in both the Union
and Confederate armies, and it was not surprising that the Union
government adopted the code unilaterally after having proposed it to
the Confederacy for joint adoption and having been rebuffed. As a
tactic, the Lieber Code communicated something to Northern armies
about what the war was for, about how they might hope to be treated,
and about how one should feel in battle against soldiers from an
indivisible nation. It also promised something to the South about
what defeat would bring.

It may well all be fig leaves and propaganda and obfuscation — and yet, these new humanitarian standards do seem to call modern military leaders to their own best practice. In this sense, at least, the practice of warfare has been, in a sense, civilized — modern humanitarian law provides a vocabulary through which the civilized can discuss military violence. It is a professional vocabulary — about legitimate objectives and proportional means. Indeed, we might say that this broad humanitarian vocabulary now defines the boundaries of civilization. The distinction between belligerents and neutrals makes less sense once the use of force has become the instrument of the international community itself. And indeed, the status of neutrality has withered. The more appropriate distinction seems to be between the international community and outlaws or rogue states who would countenance wanton violence or aggressive war — even if no state perceives *itself* in these terms.

The new humanitarian vocabulary responds to an experience common to military strategists and humanitarians — the apparent necessity of trade-offs, of balancing harms, of accepting costs to achieve benefits, which now seems an inevitable part of getting anything done. The status of "civilians" provides a classic case. In the traditional law, war was to be fought only between combatants, and anyone not part of the enemy armed force was not to be targeted. This idea continues to provide the starting point for the law in war. But civilians *will* be killed in war. As this fact pressed upon the law in war, humanitarians transformed the rule into the "principle of distinction" between civilians and combatants. They did so both to recognize the inevitable — and to provide a vocabulary to limit what they could not — indeed, did not wish to — change. As a principle, the distinction between combatants and noncombatants can align itself with best military practice. Civilian damage, when it does collaterally occur, must be an unavoidable or "necessary" by-product of a permissible use of force. One may not inflict "unnecessary suffering" on enemy soldiers — or civilians.

One will, of course, sometimes know in advance of a strike that civilian casualties will occur, and in this sense, one could say that civilians will be targeted. Here, the measure will also be proportionality — one must target in a way proportional to the military objective. In such a calculation, damage to civilians must be *weighted* more heavily than damage to combatants. In the early days of the 2003 Iraq war, coalition forces were frustrated by Iraqi soldiers who advanced in the company of civilians. Corporal Mikael McIntosh reported that he and a colleague had declined several times to shoot soldiers in fear of harming civilians. "It's a judgment call. If the risks outweigh the losses, then you don't take the shot." He offered an example: "There was one Iraqi soldier, and twenty-five women and children, I didn't take the shot." His colleague, Sergeant Eric Schrumpf, chipped in to describe facing one soldier among two or three civilians, opening fire, and killing civilians: "We dropped a few civilians, but what do you do. I'm sorry, but the chick was in the way."[17]

Civilians, moreover, are also part of the war machinery—they man factories, repair communications infrastructure, provide political and economic support for the regime. Where the shortest road to a military objective runs through civilian casualties, they may also be directly the target of hostility. During the NATO bombardment of Belgrade—justified by the international community's humanitarian objectives in Kosovo—humanitarians and military strategists discussed the targeting of the urban and suburban civilian elites most strongly supporting the Milosevic regime's war efforts. Supposing that bombing the bourgeoisie would have been more effective than a long march inland toward the capital; it was difficult to see the humanitarian or military justification for placing the burden of the war on young draftees in the field rather than upon the civilian population who sent them there. Some humanitarians—and some military strategists—argued that targeting civilians supporting an outlaw regime, at least to the extent their support is effective in prolonging the war, would render civilians responsible for the consequences of their action, extending the Nuremberg principle of individual responsibility. Other strategists and humanitarians thought differently—deliberate civilian casualties in Belgrade would undermine the legitimacy of the campaign and could not be justified.

Each of these propositions about civilian death in war is disput-

---

[17] Quoted in the *New York Times*, March 29, 2003 in Dexter Filkins, "Either Take a Shot or Take a Chance," pp. A1 and B4.

able. Just because military, humanitarian, and political leaders increasingly speak the same language does not mean they say the same thing. One finds a wide range of more or less restrictive and permissive legalists among all three groups, just as one finds broad and narrow readings of the ethical and legal standards embodied in the new law of force spread throughout debate about the limits and legitimacy of warfare. It is not unusual for individual professionals, whether humanitarian or military, to feel ambivalence about how precisely to apply the new vocabulary to particular situations.

The key point is that the framework for these differences has become, in this case, the "necessary" and "proportional" damage which may be inflicted on civilians. Old debates which pitched desirable military objectives against legal prohibitions are gone. Debate about the status or binding effect of the legal rule — once a staple of international legal argument — is also reduced to insignificance. Of course, one can always claim that this or that rule is not yet custom, that one did not agree to this or that treaty or acquiesce in this interpretation. But the new vocabulary for evaluating force has drifted free of these strictly legal roots. It is difficult to ignore the force of a vocabulary which has become the hallmark of civilization, of participation in a shared community of ethical and professional common sense.

In tactical discussions leading up to the recent Iraq War, military strategists, intelligence officials, and representatives of humanitarian organizations in the United States all shared this language. Indeed, it was often hard to tell just who was speaking. The common vocabulary has led to something of a merger of military and humanitarian roles. Perhaps contrary to expectations, the military professional cannot be relied upon for an expansive reading of justifications for warfare or a narrow reading of limits. The humanitarian professional, eager both to legitimate intervention for humanitarian purposes and to demonstrate his or her bona fides as a partner in statecraft or participation in government, will often read limits more permissively.

Some weeks before the Iraq campaign began, I jotted the following rough transcript of a discussion between a military specialist in urban warfare and the representative of a well-known humanitarian nongovernmental organization. Although about half the sentences were spoken by each, it is difficult to guess which ones.

> Baghdad poses the key challenge. Urban warfare can be the most brutal, working your way across the grid. What about a siege? Very high cost for civilians. Not sure that's what we'd want to do — what if it took months, we're sitting there, let's say 500,000 Iraqi civilians without food, could we sustain that? The key today is bringing the mobility of field war into the city — just go after what you need, strategic nodes. That's what the troops are trained for. The key is training. Fighting in the city is so much more intense — civilians will die. A lot depends on the resistance, the speed. When you close in on your target, you don't clear a room by throwing a grenade in first. We used to do that. The best training now secures and dominates a space without killing or wounding everyone in it.

To understand this common vocabulary as a humanitarian advance requires a new idea about how the international system works — about the nature of international affairs. In the traditional conception, political power operated in its own sphere and with its own logic. The traditional humanitarian ambition was to judge that power from another sphere — from religious conviction, natural right, positive law. This vision continues to inspire much humanitarian advocacy and activism. At least since 1945, humanitarians seeking to control the use of force have taken another route. Like the early Red Cross pioneers, they have joined hands with military professionals. But they have also gone further, developing a common language for statecraft and ethics. Henceforth, the ambition to speak from an external viewpoint will need to be realized in a vocabulary common to humanitarians and to the military or political leadership they seek to restrain.

Conversation, Legitimacy, and Progress toward Fairness

Since the Second World War, it is increasingly common to understand the global legal and political environment as an extremely broad and ongoing *conversation* among a wide range of players—national states, private actors, intergovernmental organizations, courts, legislatures, military figures. International law, it is said, is more conversation than trial. Made by the people who use it, international law catalogs the arguments people have used to assess the legitimacy of state behavior. People will differ about what it means, and will make all sorts of diverse claims in its terms. International law reminds us to pay attention to opinion elsewhere in the world, to think about consistency over time, to remember that what we do today may come back to haunt us. A way to discuss what is appropriate in world affairs, international law only rarely offers a definitive judgment on who is right. Disputes do sometimes get resolved in courts—national or international—but far more often they are resolved, or not resolved, diplomatically.

In this conception, the most important court is the court of world public opinion. People are understood to take action against a backdrop of expectations about their prerogatives. When they exceed the authority they were thought to have, they pay a price—the action will be more difficult and might generate negative consequences because it is perceived by a relevant and potentially powerful constituency of other actors to be inappropriate. When states are perceived to have violated international law, it can affect the legitimacy of what they do. Of course, an actor might also get away with it, in which case the expectations of other actors would change, and this new action would become part of their understood prerogative. State behavior can also affect the legitimacy and change the terms of international law.

In such a world, it becomes important for states to defend their prerogatives—and back up assertions of their authority with action to maintain their credibility. A great many military campaigns have been undertaken for credibility in just this sense. Missiles have become missives—communicating claims about one's legitimate prerogatives and contesting the claims of others. The vocabulary used to define these prerogatives becomes significant—not because it represents an external limit, but precisely because it does not. It represents the judgments of *others in the conversation*—others whose views will affect the difficulty of the whatever one seeks to achieve. There is a puzzle here, however. Although modern humanitarian law need not be determinate to be effective—flexibility may indeed be the secret of its success—in any given iteration, it appeals outward, to the Charter, to law, or to a universal ethical understanding. There is a split, in other words, between the way the vocabulary is widely understood to function—flexibly, openly, interactively—and the way one expresses oneself in it—ethically, self-confidently, definitively, judgmentally.

The key to power in such an ongoing conversation is *legitimacy*. Actors who use force in ways which support or are sanctioned by shared expectations seem legitimate, and those which do not, do not. When states take military action outside the framework of the law of force, they may draw down their legitimacy account in the eyes of other actors. When they use force to support the United Nations, offer peacekeeping forces to the United Nations, or hold their military to the professional standards of the modern law in war, they make deposits in their legitimacy account. In this way, international humanitarianism becomes the vocabulary of legitimate statecraft.

Everything depends on audience reaction. Of course, a statesman might simply say, "I'm doing this because it is in our national interest," and, if powerful enough, might get away with it. For modern internationalists, it is significant that an element of what we mean by "powerful" is having a large stockpile of legitimacy to draw down. But one could, of course, imagine a state so powerful in simple military terms as to be beyond the need for such an account. Here, the contemporary vision depends on faith in the historical fact of pluralism. Other powers will emerge; illegitimate statecraft will be unsustainable. It would be foolhardy to fail to present one's case to the world in terms they will find persuasive. In recent years, internationalists developing this vision have also stressed the significance of democracy and fragmented power *within* nations. Although great powers may sometimes be able to press their will in foreign affairs, national authorities who do so will also need to face elections, where their uses of force can be criticized in the vocabulary of humanitarian virtue and good sense. For this system to fail, one would need a state with a leadership whose ethical self-confidence and political authority were both secure and articulated in completely different terms—religious terms, perhaps.

Even here, one may be able to rely on the long run — and on the realism of the legitimacy idea. It is simply easier to exercise power in ways widely regarded as legitimate. Others will find it easier to acquiesce to your action. Rules which seem legitimate in the eyes of the military will be enforced. Military actions whose purpose and conduct can be defended in an internationally acceptable vocabulary will find the road to victory smoother and the peace easier to win. In this conception, faith in *progress* within an open society is very significant. An open-ended conversation, conducted in the vocabulary of legitimacy, will bring the progressive virtues of an open society to international affairs. As the conversation proceeds, things will get more and more humanitarian. Once statesmen must give reasons, the audience before whom they must justify their actions broadens, and their reasons will in turn need to become more humane. What began as legitimacy will become *fairness*.[18]

Writ small, the same progress will ratchet up the standards by which the use of force is judged legitimate. At first, standards which reflect military best practice will be followed — and when followed, the military which follows them will itself be legitimated. The reciprocal convergence of military and humanitarian thinking legitimates the vocabulary itself. As more people come to think of the legitimacy of force in these terms — was it sanctioned by the United Nations? was it an act of self-defense? was it proportional? necessary? — the more their assessment will feed back into the realist assessments of military planners themselves. The result is an upward spiral — as military commanders and humanitarians come to assess acts of violence from a similar vantage point, they reinforce one another's professionalism, and strengthen the humanitarian vocabulary itself.

Take the effect of civilian casualties. In contemplating a potential target, precisely *how much more heavily* should one weigh civilian than military casualties in assessing the proportionality and necessity of the target? From the military point of view, as much more heavily as their death would delegitimate our campaign. If relevant pub-

---

[18] The most sophisticated exponent of these ideas has been Thomas Franck. See, e.g., Tom Franck, *Word Politics: Verbal Strategy among Superpowers* (New York: Cambridge University Press, 1972); Thomas Franck, *The Power of Legitimacy among Nations* (New York: Oxford University Press, 1990); Thomas Franck, *Fairness in International Law and Institutions* (Oxford: Clarendon, 1995).

lics — within the enemy society, at home, in third countries — will view the strike as illegitimate, this may harden the enemy's resolve, strengthen opposition elsewhere, or undermine support for our campaign at home or among our allies. We can imagine calculating a "CNN effect," in which the additional opprobrium resulting from civilian deaths, discounted by the probability of it becoming known to relevant audiences, multiplied by the ability of that audience to hinder the continued prosecution of the war, will need to be added to the probable costs of the strike in calculating its proportionality and necessity.

Of course, military strategists might themselves have humanitarian commitments. They might restrain themselves for ethical reasons, just as humanitarians may seek to deploy force to their ends. The interesting point is that the common vocabulary promises to be attractive — and to develop in a humanist direction — even for participants whose identity and objectives do not align: for military strategists who think *only* in professional and strategic terms about accomplishing their mission and for humanitarians who are absolutely committed to making their ethics real in the world. Or, more precisely, this common vocabulary permits all who speak it to express and experience both their convergence and their distinct identities as humanitarian and military professionals.

For the humanitarian giving voice to universal human values, civilian deaths will seem weightier to the extent they seem weightier to world public opinion. Speaking this vocabulary, professional humanitarians become stand-ins for this broader public, offering assessments the professional military can use as proxies for the CNN effect. The humanitarian international lawyer can participate in deciding how many civilians to kill — and what he says will affect how many are in fact killed by altering, subtly perhaps, the legitimacy of different military tactics.

The professional humanitarian assessment remains a poor proxy for the CNN effect as long as the universal values they voice are not, in fact, shared universally by the public whose views are relevant to the military strategist. Humanitarian assessments lose their legitimacy when they depart from the actual views of those who can influence the success of a military campaign. We can imagine the

American military being concerned about the reaction of U.S. public opinion, opinion among elites in allied nations, and reactions by the civilian population of our enemy. Each will have some potential to make the military campaign easier or more difficult. These may be relevant reference groups for international humanitarians — but we can also imagine humanitarians making implicit reference rather to the views of the "international community," a loose consortium of civilian and governmental elites. In some ways, of course, this "international community" remains a collective fantasy *of* humanitarian policy makers — a way of referring to their own heightened ethical sensibility as the perspective of a larger world.

A Humanitarian Vocabulary of Virtue and Effective Force

As a result, the ambition of the humanitarian must be larger — to make the modern law of force not only the vocabulary of military strategy, but also the dominant vernacular among all who deposit or withdraw from the military's legitimacy stockpile. We must promote the vocabulary among civilian populations, more so even than among the military themselves. Or we must strengthen the legitimacy of professional humanitarians as the voice of a universal ethics, credibly able to *speak for* the world's citizens as arbiter of effectiveness for military action. Harmonic convergence between the military and humanitarian sensibility will only be achieved once the humanitarian vocabulary becomes a dominant global ideology of legitimacy.

Not all humanitarians would express their objective this ambitiously — but many do. Humanitarians who have spent a lifetime feeling marginal to power often find it difficult to imagine that they could inherit the earth in quite this way. Since at least the end of the Cold War, however, many humanitarian voices have become more comfortable speaking about the completion of their realist project.

The most striking examples, until now, come from the field of human rights, rather than from the law of force. For example, the editors of the latest edition of the classic American textbook on international law ostentatiously moved their chapter on human rights sharply toward the front of the book. Human rights would no longer be taught as one application of international law among many. It had become foundational — central to the "constitution" of international affairs.

> The second half of the 20th century has been described as the "Age of Rights." That characterization reflects the view that, with the end of the Second World War, the idea of human rights has become a universal political ideology and a central aspect of an ideology of constitutionalism.[19]

Against a parallel ambition for humanitarian law, the existence of *other* vocabularies to assess the use of force — religious conceptions of just war, more traditional legal ideas — can be seen only as threats. It is not surprising that humanitarian policy makers have struggled to occupy the field — to make of their vocabulary an ideology not only of governance, but of force. Between *using* humanitarian law to assess potential acts of violence and *promoting* it as a vocabulary of statecraft, the latter can easily seem more important, particularly if using

---

[19] Lori Damrosch, et al., *International Law: Cases and Materials* (St. Paul, MN: West Group, 2001), p. 586. These professional international lawyers are not alone. Here is Kofi Annan:

> The Universal Declaration of Human Rights is the product of the untiring efforts and resolute will of men and women from all parts of the world. Today, the principles enshrined in the Declaration are the yardsticks by which we measure human progress. . . . Human rights are foreign to no culture and intrinsic to all nations. They belong not to a chosen few, but to all people. It is this universality that endows human rights with the power to cross any border and defy any force.

Kofi A. Annan, Foreword, to Yael Danieli, Elso Stamatopoulou, and Clarence J. Dias eds., *The Universal Declaration of Human Rights: Fifty Years and Beyond* (Amityville, NY: Baywood Publishers, 1999), p. v. Or Elie Wiesel:

> The defense of human rights has, in the last fifty years, become a kind of worldwide secular religion. It has attracted millions of members and sympathizers. . . . Young and old, white or black, well-established citizens or recently arrived refugees: let their rights as human beings be violated and there will always be a person, a group who will rise in their defense.

Elie Wiesel, "A Tribute to Human Rights," in Yael Danieli, Elso Stamatopoulou, and Clarence J. Dias, eds., *The Universal Declaration of Human Rights: Fifty Years and Beyond* (Amityville: NY: Baywood Publishers, 1999), p. 3.

the vocabulary might delegitimate it as the unrivaled global measure of military legitimacy by entangling it in the pros and cons of a contentious military campaign. We could say that the idea is precisely to enchant humanitarian tools. As a result, we might also say that to *promote* humanitarianism is to be humanitarian. Indeed, it might seem a sensible long-term strategy to *forgo* decisive evaluation of particular acts of violence so as to encourage an upward spiral for humanitarianism as the vocabulary of statecraft.

As a result, the specific consequences of a given act of statecraft would often seem less relevant, from a humanitarian point of view, than the impact of the action on the legitimacy of the long-term regime of humanitarian policy making itself. For a time, whether the United States campaign against Iraq was ultimately a humanitarian act seemed less significant than that the dispute over its legitimacy be held in the United Nations and conducted in the language of the Charter. That an international court exists to evaluate war crimes allegations can seem more significant than whether using it after any particular massacre would promote — or retard — the taking of political responsibility, the emergence of a more humanitarian public consciousness or other humanitarian objectives.

There is no doubt that such long-term calculations may turn out to be correct — it would be foolish for policy makers, humanitarian or otherwise, to focus single-mindedly on immediate consequences rather than on the long haul. One must weigh and balance as carefully as one can the long and the short term — and must be ready to defend the discount rate applied to future costs and benefits. It is here that the humanitarian has the most difficulty. Belief in the humanitarian project, in the upward spiral, in the institutions and tools of humanitarian law too often substitutes for this type of careful calculation. Current costs are discounted, future benefits promised, less as pragmatic calculation of policy than as expression of ideology.

Nevertheless, the deliberation continues to be carried on as if it were a pragmatic assessment of means and ends. Humanitarians concerned to limit force are as attentive to their own strategy as other humanitarian policy makers we have seen. As they write commentary on the meaning of military necessity, promote institutions to enforce humanitarian law, negotiate more precise rules limiting weaponry, there is a constant internal debate — save the vocabulary or use it? build our legitimacy or spend it? interpret humanitarian standards broadly or narrowly? gains now or gains for the longer-term humanitarian campaign? The metric is the expected reaction of various publics — will a strict interpretation alienate statesmen and military planners? Will it please our humanitarian constituency? The strategic choices faced by humanitarian policy makers struggling to promote their vocabulary are strikingly similar to those faced by military planners.

We might calculate a reverse CNN effect to assess the impact of interpreting humanitarian obligations more strictly than the military. The additional opprobrium resulting from the perception that we are unrealistic, discounted by the probability that this will become known to relevant audiences, multiplied by the ability of those audiences to deny support to our ongoing institutional efforts to promote humanitarianism will need to be weighed against our own ability to delegitimate this particular military action. In short, we, like the military planner, must decide when to draw down and when to pay into our legitimacy stockpile — and therefore, when to accept civilian casualties as necessary for longer-term objectives.

Despite this parallel, however, there remains an imbalance. We have a vocabulary for judging the longer-term military objective — the principled justifications for the use of force provided by the Charter. But there is no similar vocabulary for judging the longer-term humanitarian objective — nothing to weigh *against* expansion of humanitarian institutions and ideas. More humanitarianism is always a good thing. We might say that the humanitarian policy maker's pragmatism rests on a foundation of absolute belief — while the military strategist's pragmatism is pragmatic all the way down.

As a result, we need to qualify the observation that both military and humanitarian policy makers have abandoned absolutes for pragmatism. It is true that the professional military strategists do reject wanton violence and aggressive war. And the humanitarian does reject an absolute pacifism — but a deeper belief in the *absolute virtue* of the humanitarian project remains, and can often interrupt what would otherwise seem a completely pragmatic assessment of costs and benefits — for example, by encouraging overestimation of long-run benefits and underestimation of short-term costs for keeping the humanitarian powder dry.

Even when using this new law of force to assess particular military tactics, both the humanitarian and the military planner also often suggest that they might just give it the slip — and be aggressive or be pacifist. Each holds out the possibility of refusing to sacrifice short-term effectiveness for long-term legitimacy. On the military side, this idea came to strategic studies illustrated by Nixon's famous insistence that his adversaries *should* think him just a bit crazy. Uncertainty lengthens the spear — and intensifies the deterrence. In talking about targeting strikes on Iraq, military planners routinely described keeping pilots tightly disciplined by rules of engagement until that last moment in battle when the "tip of the spear must be unleashed," his margin for maneuver loosened. In that moment, the views of others are to be set aside in the interests of victory.

Humanitarians, having assessed costs and benefits, announce their conclusions in the absolute language of judgment — bombing the civilian market failed to respect the principle of distinction: not "on balance failed" — just failed. The moral authority of humanitarianism is strengthened — the pen lengthened, if you will — when articulated with ethical self-confidence. We might say that humanitarian policy making expresses itself in the voice of advocacy. In the moment of articulation, the judgments of others are to be set aside in the interests of humanitarian authority.

For both players, these are tactics. As such, they are limited in different ways. For the military professional, it may be helpful to look crazy, it may feel good to say you're crazy — but it is hard to imagine that it would ever make sense, in fact, to be crazy. When the pilot strikes, his attack must remain proportional, must continue to focus on what is necessity for victory — after all, the tip of the spear must be as effective as the shaft. If, on the last run to the target, he fires wildly to announce "what a violent and crazy guy I am," the strike will fail. It is precisely in the heat of battle that the pilot must remain disciplined — must discipline himself in the name of effectiveness. It would be more accurate to say that the military disciplines the pilot up the last moment so that it will not have to as he bears down for the strike. The pilot must discipline himself, must continue to do what is proportional and necessary, to carry out the mission.

The humanitarian is in a slightly different position. Having completed his calculations of long- and short-term costs, he might well decide to forgo persuasion, saying simply "see how virtuous I am." Being virtuous remains a plausible independent goal, and can feel terrific. Of course, in the moment of articulation, the humanitarian speaks to persuade. This objective will sometimes require that the urge to moral clarity be set to one side. But not often. More often, abandoning the rhetoric of pragmatic assessment for the moral high ground of certainty will help deter the military and also persuade — and it will also feel good. It is not surprising that humanitarians can be tempted to misjudge the long- and short-term costs of doing so.

The humanitarian seems to reserve the right to exit the conversation, to depart the vocabulary of pragmatism about consequences, while the military planner must remain within it. Watching discussions between students with military and humanitarian backgrounds, one often feels the military's frustration after walking through a lengthy analysis of costs and benefits and proportionality and necessity, only to be denounced as inhumane — "these civilians can just say *anything*." They lack discipline.

We might say, to paraphrase a cliché, that humanitarians and military planners are divided by a common language. The terms are common — proportionality, necessity, self-defense, and all the other terms of art coined by the new law of force. As humanitarians and military planners argue about the legitimacy of particular uses of force, they will do so by interpreting these common terms more or less strictly. Both eschew extreme positions — promoting aggressive war and wanton destruction for the military, invoking an absolute religious or pacifist opposition to war for the humanitarian. Both invoke rules, both rely on standards, both interpret strictly and more broadly. Those promoting military action easily present their objectives as humanitarian virtue — just as those arguing for restraint have learned to speak the language of effectiveness in the cause of victory.

Still, we often can tell who is speaking. Their arguments sound different somehow — as if a tune were being played in slightly different keys. We can hear the voice of victory and the voice of virtue. We might say that their different identities, as military professional and humanitarian, are effects of the way they use this common vocabulary. Dropping the voice of strategic engagement for the universal rhetoric of ethical certainty signifies "humanitarian." There is something off when humanitarians speak in the name of strategic calculation. Weighing and balancing signify a relaxation of humanitarian virtue and announce the presence of military policy making. There remains something scandalous about a humanitarian speaking a pragmatic language of costs and benefits.

As they speak, each will focus on their rising and falling legitimacy in the eyes of various publics. These legitimacy effects are extremely difficult to predict. As a starting point, we might expect agreement to legitimate and disagreement to delegitimate each in the other's eyes. When they disagree, each may feel the other has abandoned their common vocabulary. The humanitarian may think the pilot wanton, the military aggressive — the military may think the humanitarian pacifist. In either case, the vocabulary of standards will *itself* seem more legitimate, fueling the upward spiral of convergence of humanitarian and military assessments.

The humanitarian policy maker and military strategist are watched, supported, legitimated by third parties. Some of these others will not speak this vocabulary — may not understand it. For them, both professionals will need to speak more simply — each might chose the simple language of victory or of virtue. It will be difficult, however, for outsiders to join the conversation. If they are unable to translate their pacifism or aggression into the careful assessment of costs and benefits, for either virtue or victory, they will seem naïve. In this sense, the conversation is designed to perfect judgments that can be presented to others in ways our humanitarian and military strategist have learned are *not* persuasive.

Nevertheless, the views of third parties may swamp the calculations of either — for each is ultimately wagering on the legitimacy of his position. Much will depend on public trust that the military planner *does* represent victory, or that the United Nations spokesman *does* represent virtue. This was the essence of President Bush's argument to the United Nations over Iraq — failure to embrace the Iraq campaign would do more to weaken the United Nations than to impugn the war. With multiple publics in mind, we could game this scenario out in numerous ways. The legitimacy of force turns out to be a by-product of an ongoing interactive and social calculation which has no particular moment of decision any more than it has an external vantage point of evaluation.

Faith in an upward spiral is important here. Since the Second World War, humanitarians have predicted that once placed in this ongoing conversation, the military planner and humanitarian analyst would converge, their common vocabulary would come to dominance among third parties — and the world would move toward ever more humane, rather than ever more violent, warfare. Since 1945, they have grounded their optimism in a general hope that the broader the public involved in debate, the more humanitarian the point of consensus. This hope is buttressed by faith in a progressive history — increasing interdependence, commerce, economic prosperity, education, modernity all have softened the human heart; it remains only to provide the words, the institutions, the professional practices which can express the coming enlightenment.

Let us hope so — but we should remember, that this is precisely the constellation of hopes which Freud warned may be illusory:

> Our mortification and our grievous disillusionment regarding the uncivilized behavior of our world compatriots in this war are shown to be unjustified. They were based on an illusion to which we had abandoned ourselves. In reality our fellow citizens have not sunk so low as we feared, because they had never risen so high as we believed. . . . [With war], life has, in truth, become interesting again; it has regained its full significance.[20]

HUMANITARIANISM IN THE WAR MACHINE

Whatever its limitations, the idea that the humanitarianism of the new law of force could become the vocabulary for statecraft and military strategy was an audacious — and astonishingly successful — conception. The modern military is also proud of its relationship to

[20] Freud, "Thoughts for the Times on War and Death," p. 300.

law—submitting to regulation means good discipline, enhances the legitimacy and effectiveness of military operations, and is an ever-present sign of the civilian control—all signs of the military's professionalism. Indeed, nothing was as striking about the military culture I encountered on the aircraft carrier USS *Independence* in the Persian Gulf than its intensely *regulated* feel. It is not exaggerating to say that in the American military today no ship moves, no weapon is fired, no target selected without review for compliance with regulations. But it is more than that.

Imagine the complexity of an aircraft carrier—five thousand sailors, thousands of miles from base, managing complex technologies, deploying all manner of aircraft, delivering all sorts of weaponry, at the center of a fleet of supporting vessels, at the end of an enormous logistics tail, coordinated through complex communications technologies with a global navy, air force, and army operating in dozens of different political and military jurisdictions. Imagine the constant turnover and flux—different ports, new sailors, new officers, new pilots, changing missions, rotating political and civilian leadership. It was absolutely clear that even if you could afford to buy one, you could not possibly operate it—the aircraft carrier is also a social system, depending upon an entrenched culture of standard practices and shared experience.

You can't forget the ship is a machine for war—bullet-proof glass in the tower, guns, missiles, weapons, and planes everywhere. Activity all the time—men hurrying here and there, planes launched and returning, practicing, planning, monitoring. But then again, the ship is also a small town. I met a guy selling Chevys in the mess hall, deliverable when the ship reached port. In the midst of preparations for a massive strike on Baghdad, one guy was lining men up to take photos for the ship's yearbook. The nurse was working on his body building, oiling his muscles after a morning workout. The war room had been moved below deck—up in the tower, officers traded off on a Lifecycle and treadmill.

It is a culture of discipline, as visitors quickly learn. The staging area in Bahrain where you catch the mail run to the carrier resembles any small town airstrip with lots of easy banter among personnel coming and going, waiting to take a plane up to train, catching up on gossip. When my flight was ready, a young crewman rounded up the three of us who would make the trip out, handed out helmets and safety jackets, and briefed us on safety procedures for the flight. His tone was friendly, routine — much like the safety briefing on any commercial airline. I strapped the vest loosely around me, placed the helmet on — aiming for an air of easy nonchalance. But this was not to be — he carefully leaned forward and tightened the straps — and I noticed my two co-passengers, naval officers who had made the flight innumerable times, quite sharp in their attention to the briefing, exact in their compliance.

Something was off, culturally. In my civilian world, the confident professional man is slightly diffident about the rules around him — if ultimately also compliant. You wait to cinch up the helmet until just before takeoff, you fasten the seat belt but are less careful about pulling it tight. You josh with the cabin attendants while the safety video plays. Here, the opposite. The officers who flew with me chalked it up to turnover — processing so many new young men and women through the military each year with safety and efficiency requires an intense culture of rule-following. In my civilian world, this much rule-following would seem compulsive, emasculating — would take the fun and flexibility out of life. But this was not the case either, as soon became clear. Passengers sit strapped in facing backward on the mail flight — the rear of the aircraft swings open for loading and unloading. The crewman who briefed us rode at the back, and as we approached the carrier, he opened the rear hatch and laid down on the open floor in the sun, watching the gulf spin below him as we circled for landing. He was clearly having a great time, enjoying the pleasures of the body, the fleet spread out beneath us.

In this culture, the relationship between swagger and rules was simply different. When popular culture represents the military — take the movie *Top Gun* — they make much of the military's macho culture. For civilian humanitarians like myself, it is easy to think these guys need rules, need to be tamed. There is something intensely macho about the life of navy pilots — but it is easy to misread the relationship between this macho and rules. In one sense, the rules create the swagger. When naval pilots "patrolled the no-fly zone" over

Iraq, they were not simply flying around, watching what was happening. Each flight was planned, placed in a package with other planes, coordinated with allies and fueling planes, supported by backup intelligence flights. Every move of the flight is measured, the takeoff and landing carefully scored and evaluated — and the pilots are obsessed about the scores, are ranked constantly with one another, competitive about exact compliance with specifications for the flight.

Strange as it may sometimes seem to humanitarian policy makers, there is something intensely submissive about men in the military. I expected the ship to be a nightmare of junior-high-school machismo — and there was a lot of horsing around. For all their swagger, however, they live in very tiny spaces, subject to thousands of rules and to the absolute authority of those higher in the chain of command. As the one civilian onboard, I felt sharply distinct — not only as the admiral's guest, but as the only man on board who could not be ordered about — and as a representative of all civilians, an embodiment of the culture which ordered the whole boat about. Sitting up late one night with a member of the Admiral's staff in his cramped office, I asked about his wife and kids, whose photos lined his bookshelf. He spoke about them wistfully, distantly — he had clearly not been home for much of their marriage, and civilian life seemed abstract and far away. He was simply more comfortable knocking about the world in the company of other men. But he was less playboy of the Western world than monastic celibate, having chosen to knock about the world in the navy — under discipline, routine, and rule.

Or take the confusing matter of uniforms — in popular images of the military the uniform is often presented as a barely disguised fetish, emboldening men to fight and kill. Perhaps — but as the only man not wearing a uniform on board, it did not feel that way to me. Of course, there were all sorts of relationships to various uniforms onboard — officers, cooks, janitors, pilots; all had different degrees of dress, casual, and working attire. One officer estimated that more than fifty different outfits were used on board for different tasks, grades, and levels of formality. The flight deck was a kaleidoscope of jumpsuits — green, yellow, blue. The most numerous turned out to be people whose sole job was ensuring the safety of the rest on a loud platform of moving jet planes. While some — the Admiral's eager young aide — seemed to revel in the neat press of their shirt and snappy jacket, others carried their uniform like any well-worn work gear. But for all these differences, the uniform also marked rank and role and belonging, and in some way all of these men seemed to like being told what to wear. In the manner of a priest's collar advertising his chastity, military attire announces a man's subordination, brings him out of the closet as subject to discipline and rule.

On the first overseas flight I took with the military, I was careful to pack light — small carry-on, only the barest essentials in my toilet kit. On arrival, in the crush of third world customs, I discovered each of the four officers on the trip had immense cases, filled with dress uniforms, hats, innumerable bits of paraphernalia. We would have a number of meetings, at the Embassy, with foreign colleagues, in the field — each seemed to require a different outfit. From junior high school, I expected the officers from different services to give one another a hard time for their fancy dress — but quite the reverse. They liked having to wear, or thinking they had to wear, something dramatic and special — even heavy wool in sweltering heat. Jokes were reserved for the guy who had forgotten a couple of key pieces and couldn't seem to get it right.

The significance of military discipline is difficult for civilians to grasp. It is instrumentalism, bureaucratic necessity, central to the effectiveness of the mission and to the safety of colleagues. All this is wrapped in honor, integrity, in a culture set off from civilian life, a higher calling. Although the military discipline of both necessity and virtue is a social production, it is also, and perhaps more importantly, a work on the self. The U.S. Army runs a recruitment commercial that pictures soldiers silhouetted in the middle distance, moving in groups across a shifting terrain, dropping from helicopters, flying over the landscape — repeatedly the camera focuses on an individual face or profile. Near the climax we come close up on one soldier who speaks directly to us — "I am an army of one" — followed by the recruitment pitch "see your recruiter, become an army of one." The promise is power, to be sure, grandiosity of a sort. But also discipline — self-discipline. If you join, you will be transformed inside — *you* will become an army, coordinated, disciplined, your own commanding officer, your own platoon, embodying within yourself the force of hundreds because of the work you will do, and we will do, on you.

The rules that discipline the military have many sources: the technical requirements of equipment and weaponry, the traditions of the corps, safety procedures, the strategic and tactical needs of the particular mission, bureaucratic and institutional necessities of the military command, national law — and of course the rules and standards of international law. The rules of engagement for particular missions or campaigns — when you can fire which weapon, whom you can engage and when — are written to reflect all of these sources. It is difficult to unbraid the skein. From the pilot's point of view, it may not be clear whether a given rule — wait until the enemy locks you in his radar to fire — reflects a technical requirement of the weaponry, a strategic calculation by the command about the risks it seems prudent to allow pilots to take in this operation, and the desirability of a hair trigger response, or broader notions about the meaning of self-defense and military necessity.

Taken together, however, there is no question that international legal norms have been metabolized into the routines of the U.S. Navy patrolling the Gulf. Of course, it's not all submission and rule. There is opportunity for individual judgment and leadership, error, and even rebellion. We remember the pilots who flew beneath the Italian ski lift, slicing the cables. Or the precision guided missile fired in Kosovo with the tail fins put on backward — spinning ever further from its programmed target until it exploded in a crowded civilian marketplace. The American pilots who bombed their Canadian allies. Or, for that matter, My Lai and all the other tales of atrocity in war.

Mistakes — or crimes. Or soldiers run amok — no longer an army of one. Bad judgment, unstable, insane. The tip of the spear must be kept sharp — the soldier must remain disciplined. Absolute power can still corrupt. The memoirs and off-the-cuff reminiscences of front-line marines in the Iraq campaign often make uneasy reading — these guys often do seem to have liked to kill. Still, to step outside the effective and proportional use of force in aid of victory is to be, often literally, crazy. Iraq war reporting was filled with anecdotes about soldiers overcome by remorse at having slaughtered civilians — and being counseled back to duty by their officers, their chaplains, their mental health professionals explaining that what they had done was necessary, proportional, just, and that even their loss of control and perspective was an inevitable part of warfare.

It was not surprising that the investigating officer recommended against a court-martial for the American pilots who mistakenly bombed Canadian troops in Afghanistan. They had been charged with involuntary manslaughter, aggravated assault, and dereliction of duty for "failing to exercise good leadership." Their defense had foregrounded the fog of war, their sense of peril, and the possibility that their judgment had been impaired by a few too many "go-pills." We have tended to treat our pilots gently when they harm foreigners — but their defense would be even easier under the loose standards of international humanitarian law.

Indeed, the standards of self-defense, proportionality, and necessity are so broad that they are routinely invoked to refer to the zone of *discretion* rather than limitation. I have spoken to numerous pilots who describe legal briefings filled with technical rules of engagement and military law. After the lawyer leaves, the commanding officer summarizes in the empowering language of international law: "just don't do anything you don't feel is necessary, and defend yourself — don't get killed out there."

Soldiers fed up with chicken-shit regulations are a staple of wartime literature. One rule of engagement which drew sharp debate among the pilots while I was onboard the USS *Independence* concerned the use of handguns against Iraqi civilians on the ground after bailing from a plane. While awaiting rescue, should pilots wait until being fired upon or until seeing a weapon before firing? Or should they simply use their best judgment, being sure to fire only in self-defense? Most pilots thought the proposed rule of engagement too restrictive and illogical — you mean we can drop bombs on these people but not shoot our pistol if we feel we need to?

No international humanitarian rule restricted these pilots from using their best judgment about the meaning of self-defense. The more restrictive rules came from another source: was it a calculation that pilots would be easier to retrieve if captured? A strategic calculation to avoid the media spectacle of a pilot killing a civilian by hand while enforcing the no-fly zone? It is difficult to speculate. But it was not hard for pilots to warm to the cover of international standards — "if I feel threatened, I'm going to fire." And it is not hard to imagine officers acquiescing in the relaxation permitted by international law, if only for fear pilots would otherwise pull back, dulling the spear, or be sure to bail over Iran instead, increasing the political costs of the campaign.

When I asked the Admiral's staff about the relationship between rules of engagement and pilots' judgment, they described the intense backup command structure — the intelligence planes flying with every package of bombers and fighters, the in-air commanders coordinating and vetting requests for permission to strike. But they would also talk about a tolerated — and expected — residual in battle, of aggressive forward-leaning judgment at the tip of the spear. The point of the rule structure, they explained, was to hold the discipline tight, just up to the point at which it was appropriate to "let them loose out there," a point which could change with different missions. Indeed, the length of the leash and the sensitivity of the hair trigger were focal points for military planning. For pilots patrolling a no-fly zone, for example, one might want a shorter leash than on the day a strike against Iraq began. A coordinated air assault required a shorter leash than close-air-support for ground troops whose needs for air power might constantly change. Fine-tuning was the work of the rules of engagement. Once let loose from these rules, they were on their own in the domain of humanitarian law — proportional, necessary, effective. An army of one.

I was struck by the extent to which the men onboard the USS *Independence* that March debated the wisdom of American policy toward Iraq. Political tensions with Iraq had reached a peak the week before my arrival, and it appeared likely the United States would launch a dramatic strike against Baghdad to persuade the leadership to permit unfettered weapons inspections. Secretary of State Madelaine Albright and Secretary of Defense William Cohen appeared together in a town meeting–style television discussion at Ohio State University — a discussion which did not, from their point of view, go well. Repeatedly challenged with difficult questions, the two appeared unable to explain the foreign policy which had placed the USS *Independence* on alert in the Gulf. Onboard, the show was avidly followed by officers and enlisted men alike. The men onboard received free overseas calling from AT&T, and many called or e-mailed family and friends to discuss the wisdom of the engagement they were planning to launch. The officers had a heated discussion about whether an order to strike Baghdad hard would be legal. This was not a military that aspired to send pilots off to bomb without the confidence that the objective and means were in one or another sense legitimate. It is a military which aspires to be legitimate also in its own eyes.

Of course, it was altogether implausible that the officers, or the enlisted men, would ultimately find in humanitarian law a basis for backing Washington down. It seemed far more likely the conversation would quiet their doubts and confirm their professionalism. Not everyone in a war zone evaluates their role in this language, of course. In the days prior to the invasion of Iraq in 2003, journalists interviewed numerous soldiers at the front about the coming attack. One exchange struck me in particular—a journalist spoke with a group of four young infantrymen who had spent the day readying for battle. He asked them why they were fighting, and the first spoke briefly about the Iraqi regime's humanitarian crimes, the UN resolutions thwarted, the weapons of mass destruction. Then his buddy chimed in, matter of factly, "Actually, I think it's for the oil." Then another, "No, it's cause he tried to off Bush's dad, he's got a thing about Saddam."

It is difficult to know how to interpret all this. We might say that it is simply too early to tell—the humanitarian vocabulary for war has not yet fully colonized the life-world. We might worry that the vocabulary has been corrupted, stretched, or misused and requires tightening. Or we might say that the pragmatic enterprise is right on track. Humanitarians and military officers are speaking the same language—they assess the legitimacy of objectives, the effectiveness and proportionality of means. It is difficult to imagine that we would want them to evaluate the use of force in some other way than pragmatically. They do so with different emphasis and to different effect than humanitarians, but we are halfway there. In an open society, as this goes forward, military men will use the vocabulary in progressively more humanitarian ways. There is already some evidence of that in resources invested between the Gulf War and the 2003 Iraq campaign to improve targeting and protect civilians.

As it turned out, the military men I met in 1998 on the USS *Independence* were by and large not favorable to the strike then planned for Baghdad. The man who had spent the preceding month planning a complex assault, coordinating missiles sited across the region to land within an implausibly narrow time frame ("and make the ground shake") did seem disappointed not to have had the chance to see it happen. But generally, discussion turned to the attitudes of Arab allies, the continued plausibility of deterrence, the extent to which weapons of mass destruction was a "Washington problem." One officer asked pointedly "Who's got the most so-called weapons of mass destruction in the seas we patrol? Libya — and why aren't we worried? Deterrence." Referring to the Ohio State debate, one member of the Admiral's staff remarked, "We've got all this intel, but the college boys just figured it out." Patrolling the Gulf, containing Iraq — yes. Beyond that — the obsession with Weapons of Mass Destruction, the threatened strike, the possibility of war to liberate Iraq — there they saw the meddling hand of civilians and the Clinton foreign policy team. Those were the objectives of political humanitarianism back in the capital — whose commander they served but whose appetite for engagement they did not share. What kept them there was rule, civilian rule.

Of course all this was just one boat, and just one navy, and just one week. The experience of American navy pilots in coalition operations to enforce a no-fly zone over Iraq may well be atypical. In war it might be different; in the army, on the ground, it might be different; in other countries it might be different. In guerrilla war it might be different. The striking thing, however, was how closely this experience seemed to track the highest ambition of humanitarian law — to become the vocabulary of military strategy. The USS *Independence* that March may have been the exception — but if so, it was the exception that embodied the rule.

Modern humanitarian law does seem particularly suited to the highly technical and professional operations of the American navy, and to the broader culture of submission to rule and pragmatic means-ends calculation one finds in such environments. The cornerstone of the modern professional military remains civilian control — military objectives are determined by the political branch. The military's job is to achieve the objective at least cost, avoiding actions which would undermine the broader mission. How else to do this but through careful means-ends strategic evaluations of proportionality and military necessity? And how could a complex military be organized but through the bureaucratic rationality of complex internal rules? Don't target the mosque. Take down the electrical grid only after careful calculation of the military gain and potential costs. It would be strange if avoiding collateral damage were *not* a tactic of modern warfare — alongside trying or threatening to try enemy leaders for war crimes. Or establishing an International Criminal Court. Proportionality, military necessity, self-defense — it is difficult to imagine how *else* one would talk about the use of force.

In 1996, I traveled to Senegal as a civilian instructor with the U.S. Naval Justice School Detachment for International Training to train members of the Senegalese military in the laws of war and human rights. At the time, the training program was operating in fifty-three countries, from Albania to Zimbabwe. It turns out that the American military is by far the world's largest human-rights training institution. Across the globe, engagement with the U.S. military — purchasing our weapons, participating in joint exercises with our forces — comes with training in the international norms and regulatory practices of humanitarian law and human rights. The training message was clear: this is not some humanitarian add-on — a way of being nice or reducing military muscle. We stressed that internalizing humanitarian law and human rights is a way to make the military more effective — and to make your force interoperable with international coalitions, suitable for international peacekeeping missions, or other high-profile assignments. We asserted, with some justification, that it is simply not possible to *use* the sophisticated weapons one purchases or to coordinate with the international military operations in which they would be used without an internal military culture with parallel rules of operation and engagement.

We went over the principles of humanitarian law, and broke into small groups for simulated exercises in strategic thinking. The re-

gional commander of a border area plagued by guerrilla raids repeatedly asked the hard questions — When you capture a guerrilla from a
village, isn't it better to place his head on a stake for deterrence?
Well, no, our officers would patiently explain — this will strengthen
the hostility of villagers to your troops — and imagine what would
happen if CNN were nearby. They would laugh: of course, we must
be sure the press stays away. Ah, but this is no longer possible — and
if the Senegalese wanted to play on the international stage, they
would need to be ready to have CNN constantly at their side. Professional military officers today must imagine their operations to be
transparent — must place an imaginary CNN webcam on their helmet or, better, just over their shoulder. Not because force must be
limited, and not because CNN might show up — but because only
force which can imagine itself to be seen can be effective, complete,
enduring. An act of violence one can stand behind, disclose, be
proud of is ultimately stronger, more forceful, something one can
follow through. By the end of their training in human rights, the
officers had not learned a set of restrictions on the use of force —
they had learned a new vocabulary for strategic thinking, and a new
strategic philosophy for military toughness.

Of course, that is not why the Senegalese had come — they were
there to place their dependence on the French military in a new tri-
angular relationship with the United States, to gain access to peacekeeping assignments with the Organization of African States or
United Nations, to pursue their own political and career ambitions
in the capital. Having seen the American military close only on film,
they were curious how we talked about strategy. Some hoped to increase their chances to be selected for training or assignment abroad,
and some had simply been ordered to participate. But the message
could not be ignored — to participate in the international military
profession, one would need to learn its new humanitarian vocabulary. We had no idea, of course, what it meant in *their* culture for
violence to be legitimate, effective, something one could stand behind proudly. But they had learned something of what that meant in
the culture of global humanitarian and military professionalism. Indeed, the culture I encountered on the USS *Independence* is less significant because it is typical than because it represents the apotheosis
of modern humanitarianism about warfare. In an odd way — and

quite contrary to my expectations — the actions of the U.S. Navy in the Persian Gulf suggest what war would look like were humanitarian policy making fully successful.

THE DARK SIDES OF HUMANITARIAN POLICY MAKING — REVISITED

Problems of implementation remain — the new vocabulary is not yet everywhere as effective as it seemed to be aboard the USS *Independence*. But even there, despite the pragmatic merger of humanitarian law and military strategy, many of the same difficulties I encountered in humanitarian efforts in the fields of refugee policy, development policy, or human rights could be seen. It is worth reviewing those briefly, if only because one would have expected a humanitarianism so attentive to costs and benefits, so deeply and pragmatically engaged in the policy process, both to see through professional blindness or bias and to correct for it through ongoing debate. This was the promise of abandoning an external viewpoint and of participating in an ongoing and open policy conversation.

The new law of force nevertheless still exhibits the dark sides we have seen before. Its institutions are also subject to capture by states, by ideologies, by other agendas. Professional humanitarians here also become victim of their own agendas, place their own interests above the humanitarian objectives they are mandated to further. They can also mistake their own participation for humanitarianism, overestimate the significance of legal pronouncements, mistake legal war for humanitarian war or fealty to norms for enforcement. But the law of force also illustrates difficulties we have not encountered so directly before. The next section picks up the story there — with the dark sides that arise when humanitarian, political, and military policy makers all come to speak the same pragmatic vocabulary.

The Dilemmas of Rules and Standards

Like human rights norms, humanitarian rules may well criticize too little — relying for their implementation on the agreement of the military and political establishments which collectively promulgate them. Waging war within the rules may so little constrain the use of force that adherence to humanitarian rules will do more to legitimate than contain force. It is easy to mistake warfare which follows the rules for humanitarian warfare — rule following can become a substitute for careful humanitarian assessment.

Take land mines. They both kill and maim — to outlaw them seems an unequivocal humanitarian advance. Yet what if formal prohibition drives their use underground? What if their effective elimination encourages tactics — proportional, necessary — designed to deny the enemy access to territory which are more violent? What if land mines are eliminated only after military leaders conclude they do more to frustrate than to advance an effective military campaign? Their persistence is their main defect — other equally ruthless means to deny access to territory have been invented which remain lawful. Land mines pose difficulties for victors — cleaning them up. Better to eliminate them altogether.

Under these conditions, a land-mine prohibition may well make remaining tactics and weapons seem more legitimate by contrast — even where they do gruesome damage. Of course, we would need to ask, in whose eyes and with what results? The over- and underinclusiveness of humanitarian rules call for the balancing of costs and benefits, for a more substantive and case-by-case analysis. Perhaps better a standard — land mines permissible as the least harmful alternative when militarily necessary, proportional. And so forth. Yet it is not at all clear that harnessing our aversion to killing civilians to the requirements of proportionality and military necessity is a helpful advance.

Humanitarian standards seem too vague to restrain those determined to use force, too manipulable to embody humanitarian commitments. In the chaos of war, it seems unlikely that anything other than a clear rule will function. Do we really expect soldiers under fire to settle complex assessments of proportionality? It is easy to imagine such vague standards doing more to legitimate than restrain military violence. Moreover, humanitarianism seems to require a principled affirmation that targeting civilians is inappropriate *regardless* of its usefulness, no matter the consequences for military tactics. Broad standards threaten to blend humanitarian policy making into the strategic logic of warfare itself.

In all my discussions with the navy about their Gulf campaigns, I was unable to identify a military tactic or weapon which they wished they could use were it not for the restrictions of humanitarian law. Rather the opposite. The rules and standards of humanitarian law were routinely the *least* restrictive of the legal, technical, strategic, or political requirements they faced. International law rules — banning chemical weapons, say — prohibited what no American military strategist thought useful. Building a normative fire break between conventional and unconventional weapons was itself a tactic, to protect American soldiers in combat, to prevent a civilian catastrophe which might impede the war effort, and to delegitimate the tactics of guerrilla movements or terrorist groups while building the case for relatively high-tech American weaponry.

Rules call for standards, standards for rules. Modern humanitarian law is a complex blend of the two — a traditional set of rules overlaid with a modern regime of standards, a set of treaty prohibitions placed in a framework of standards for assessing tactics not covered by rules. Yet the two do not blend easily. The move to a modern law of standards was, after all, a criticism of the traditional law of rules — if treating civilians, women, or children as inviolate substantially increases the cost to men or enemy draftees of achieving a legitimate military objective, this will also seem inhumane. In this sense, humanitarianism requires weighing and balancing. But humanitarianism also seems to require rules as escapes to principle from the functional logic of necessity and proportionality. In short, the modern humanitarian is split — between defense of traditional distinctions and proportional comparison of costs and benefits. By combining the two, humanitarian law can seem incoherent, contradictory, ambivalent.

Blind Spots and Biases

In applying standards or rules to combat, the military — like any bureaucracy — develops routine default practices which shortcut a careful pragmatic analysis of costs and benefits. As humanitarians come to speak the same language, they often come to accept the same routines as best humanitarian practices, and find themselves blind to broader consequences. The vocabulary used to justify military tactics can become stuck — difficult to use for humanitarian criticism.

During the Gulf War, coalition forces bombed electrical generators to take down the Iraqi electricity grid. They did so to suppress air defenses by cutting off power at surface-to-air-missile sites, and considered the death of civilians working in or near generators to be necessary and proportional. After the war, this decision was sharply criticized — taking out the generators ended up degrading the electricity grid for months, hampering water treatment and contributing to thousands of Iraqi deaths from infectious diseases. It turned out that there were other ways to knock out electricity, which were later used in the NATO campaign against Serbia. It was a classic case of bureaucratic blame shifting — no one in the chain of command had been tasked with responsibility for thinking about the longer-term consequences or for comparing alternate tactics in these terms.

Nevertheless, military spokesmen defended the decision consistently after the war as having been proportional and necessary. They blamed the long-term consequences — unforeseeable to them, given their bureaucratic structure — on the Iraqi regime. Humanitarian and strategic calculations are tightly woven together in assessments like this. In preparing for Kosovo, military planners may simply have wished to spare civilian lives, or to save civilian infrastructure for postwar reconstruction, or to spare the campaign the criticisms leveled ex post at the Gulf War. They may have learned from their mistakes. For whatever reason, the electrical grid was not so severely damaged. In the 2003 Iraq campaign, coalition forces initially sought to preserve civilian infrastructure, including phone lines and electricity. They had humanitarian reasons, but they also had a different strategic calculation — to preserve civilian infrastructure both to speed reconstruction and build confidence of the civilian population should the Iraqi regime rapidly capitulate.

Military spokesmen are now quite willing to admit that the Gulf War approach was probably a mistake, an unfortunate cost of bureaucracy, a tactical blunder, even ethically unfortunate. What they will *not* do is admit that taking out the electrical generators was disproportional, unreasonable, or unnecessary. Opposing the decision to target the grid seems to require jumping out of the law of force, and in this sense we can say that the law of force legitimates too much, or seems available only for legitimation.

Humanitarians can so enchant an institution like the International Criminal Court as the symbol of humanitarian law that they forgo inquiry into whether the existence and use of the Court — in Yugoslavia or elsewhere, short term and long term — might do more to excuse than condemn the responsible, among the great powers, among Yugoslavian civilians, among international agencies and nongovernmental organizations. It is easy to forget that trying Milosovic *the man* cannot be severed from the workings of his society and culture, for which he is *both* symbol and substitute. The institutions of international humanitarian law easily overestimate their neutrality and disengagement and underestimate the distributive and political effects of their initiatives.

Like the vocabulary of human rights, humanitarian law can crowd out modes of evaluation — by religious leaders or philosopher-kings — which do not share this pragmatic flexibility. Occupying the field, the humanitarian vocabulary can channel attention to a limited range of questions. Something of this sort seems to have happened at the United Nations during the run-up to the 2003 Iraq campaign. Those in the American political and military establishment proposing war with Iraq had a wide mix of objectives. There were internal turf battles and old ideological struggles, economic ideas about the costs and stimulus effects of war, worries about oil, fantasies about the division of spoils after victory. But there were also humanitarian ideas — about human rights, about democracy and market freedom for the Iraqi people. There was a grand vision of remaking societies of the Middle East as stable, open, middle-class countries — to stem terrorism, to promote stability, to ensure a lengthy peace, to link these nations more closely to the West, and even simply to stand up for what seemed "right."

These may have been good or bad ideas, and perhaps no feasible war could achieve them — but they were removed from the debate. Along with them went any international debate about broader policy alternatives. Suppose in the summer of 2002 we had been given a $100 billion and the sustained political attention of the White

House, the media, the United Nations, and the political leadership of the entire globe for a year—all to pursue the humanitarian transformation of unjust Middle Eastern regimes and a decrease in the threat of terror. There might have been much we could have imagined doing—starting with the Israel-Palestine conflict, or with an ambitious agenda of economic development: a Marshall Plan, integration into the European Union, a relaxation of rules governing immigration. We might have started anywhere—Morocco, Jordan, Palestine, Turkey, Egypt, Pakistan, Saudi Arabia, Indonesia.

The Bush administration placed the emphasis on Iraq and selected war as the means. Fair enough—but humanitarians went along. Indeed, many saw the isolation of the issue of Iraqi disarmament and a refusal to discuss broader objectives as a *victory* for humanitarianism. From early in the Bush administration, officials had spoken of the desirability of "regime change" in Iraq. They made no secret of their broader hopes for such a change. In the summer of 2002, as they approached the United Nations to discuss the issue, they retreated sharply. Suddenly regime change was out—they spoke only about enforcing resolutions of the Security Council, disarming Saddam, making the inspections effective.

The United Nations legal and political order simply could not get its mind around a broader discussion. It was not until the United Nations was safely out of the picture that the broader objectives for the campaign came back out of the closet. The taboo on intervention—the mandate that one nation's policy not "interfere" in the domestic affairs of another—made the desire to change the Iraqi regime unspeakable. But humanitarian policy making requires more than deference to sovereign authority. Indeed, it seems the antithesis of unquestioned deference to sovereignty, promising rather the careful evaluation of sovereign acts for their humanitarian consequences.

In the debate which preceded the war, the humanitarian preference for multilateral over unilateral policy making—the equation of "made at the United Nations" for "humanitarian"—focused attention on the fine line between the French demand for two votes in the Security Council and the American assertion that one was plenty. There was something terribly off key about humanitarian voices insisting that the legitimacy of the war would depend upon whether the French went along. Surely such an international law, even if it is the law of the Charter, is not always the best—or even a very good—measure of legitimacy. Suppose the United States had gotten a Security Council vote; would we have been lulled into missing the overwhelming opposition to the war around the world?

The Security Council resolutions which ended the Gulf War seemed to have had something of that effect. The legitimacy of force in the hands of the Security Council placed the earlier United Nations legal ban on Iraqi possession of chemical and biological weapons at the forefront of debate. Once focused on disarmament, the efficacy of the United Nations inspectors became central. The United States and Britain sent more than 100,000 troops to the Gulf, ostensibly to back up the inspections with a credible threat of force. If military force were to become necessary, it seemed natural to assume the invasion should also be focused on disarmament. A neutral invasion, respectful of Iraqi sovereignty, short—once Security Council resolutions were respected, the Americans could, and should, go home. When war came, the British and American governments formally invoked the Security Council's earlier determination—all they were doing was mopping up.

Somehow what started as a pragmatic debate had gotten far off-track. As debate entered the frame of humanitarian law, the vocabulary narrowed sharply—until it became clear that those favoring war were simply not permitted to say why they did so. It is no wonder commentators everywhere speculated about what was "really" going on—and concluded it must be, in some unclear way, oil. Perhaps. And perhaps the goal for humanitarians using the Charter was simply to delay the war until it could not be fought. Although we now know that these efforts were not sufficient to the task, they might have been.

Yet humanitarian policy making is more than conscientious objection—war will sometimes be necessary to prevent great harm. Only by considering the full range of humanitarian policy options, comparing their costs and benefits, could we make a reasoned and pragmatic choice—for either war or peace. The humanitarian objectives beneath the American push for war may well not have been worth the cost. Other avenues to transform the political and economic cultures of the Middle East may well have been more effective and more humane. What was troubling in the run-up to war was that the vocabularies of enlightened humanitarianism made these — humanitarian — issues *more difficult*, rather than less, to get on the table.

Perhaps humanitarians should always prefer the shorter occupation, the intervention not taken, the Security Council resolution respected. Perhaps they did not want to become involved in weighing and balancing. Perhaps they wanted to escape responsibility, complicity, engagement with power. One of the most bizarre humanitarian proposals was the proposal that the U.S. administration say the war is illegal, but that they were going to do it anyway. That way the vocabulary would not be blemished by their action — nor their action limited by the vocabulary. Here we are in the presence of a will to marginality masquerading as a will to power. The whole point of humanitarian policy making was to bring such questions inside the Charter vocabulary and to evaluate military action in its humanitarian terms.

Let us imagine that the British and American leadership was right — that the humanitarian upsides to the war, to the intervention, to a longer occupation, would outweigh the costs. It seems odd for humanitarian policy makers to prefer that the initiative be blocked by the Security Council, unless the prerogatives of the United Nations are always more significant than the outcomes of any particular dispute. Such a presumption suggests rather the enchantment of tools — the substitution of the Security Council's prerogatives for broader humanitarian outcomes.

Indeed, those favoring and opposing the war routinely spoke as if they thought the issue *was* the authority of the United Nations, the desirability of multilateral decision making, the sanctity of sovereignty, the best strategy for ridding Iraq of "weapons of mass destruction." All these were certainly at stake — but so, potentially, were the lives of hundreds of thousands of people, the political and economic futures of an entire region, the political future of American power, and more. To weigh them against one another pragmatically means more than asserting the obvious long-run significance of the United Nations. It means deciding whether, say, a 25 percent decline in the legitimacy of the Security Council for five years in the eyes of a given group is or is not worth, say, 100,000 lives, or the enrichment of these people and the impoverishment of these other people.

Moreover, like other humanitarian policy-making initiatives we have considered, debate about war in Iraq proceeded from the assumption that those who rule — the world, the nation — begin in a posture of repose, high above the struggles of particular places. The question is whether or not *to intervene* in an ongoing national or local situation. It is difficult to remember that nonintervention will also require a complex legal and political regime, which will also have humanitarian costs and benefits. In the Iraqi case, a regime for nonintervention and deterrence would have required complex international agreements to isolate Iraq, promote nonproliferation, just as full normalization would have required a regime for trade, for private commercial and financial relations, and for diplomatic engagement.

In much the same way, it is difficult to remember that in any particular case, decisions will be made in the context of a much longer conversation — which will have already begun. In the Iraqi case, the fact that the United States and other powers had been establishing and removing regimes in the Middle East for more than a century; that today's array of strongmen and princes are partly the ongoing production of Western foreign policy — all this did affect the calculations of numerous publics about the legitimacy of the proposed military campaign. But it was difficult to put this squarely on the table for debate — except as one more reason not to intervene this time. Even the most pragmatic humanitarians, when considering action from the repose of a great height, will often overestimate the costs of action and underestimate the consequences of inaction, and their own responsibility for those consequences. They will also be prone to imagining a form of international intervention — just disarm Iraq — which can seem neutral and temporary. But these tendencies all make it more difficult to achieve the humanitarian upsides of any "intervention" which does take place. Honest humanitarian pragmatism about the use of force begins only after we have disenchanted doctrines of sovereignty and nonintervention, as well as the institutional prerogatives of today's intergovernmental institutions.

A related, and by now equally familiar, bias in humanitarian policy making results from a routine underestimation of the significance of background rules and institutions. By focusing on the law that overtly concerns war — the law of war, humanitarian law — we overlook the far more important contribution made by other legal rules to the incidence of violence. Commercial rules structuring the trade in arms are, after all, far more significant than the thin overlay of disarmament regulations limiting that trade. The rules of state responsibility which structure remedies for violations of international law provide an alternate vocabulary for the calibrated use of pressure — as countermeasures — to encourage settlement of claims and enforce sovereign rights. Rules about jurisdiction — territorial and otherwise — do more to channel warfare than does the traditional distinction of belligerent and neutral. Pilots enforcing no-fly zones over Iraq were careful to refuel along the Saudi Arabian border, forming up their "package" before entering Iraqi airspace. Intelligence aircraft flew over Saudi Arabia. Fighter pilots constantly discussed their preferences — and the rules — about ejecting over Iran, Iraq, or Saudi Arabia. The law of the sea is riddled with rules permitting military use and free passage. Enforcing the embargo in the Gulf required careful planning to avoid interdiction in Iranian waters. And so forth — an unending list of rules and background institutions in whose shadow the military plans and carries out a campaign. These rules facilitate and limit campaigns — and have distributional costs between combatants — and yet all remain outside the normal scope of humanitarian policy-making assessment. By contesting and promoting only the institutions, principles, and rules of the United Nations humanitarian law system, we can make these background rules, whatever their consequences for the incidence of violence, seem matters of fact rather than points of choice.

Like those seeking to extend market democracy to Eastern and Central Europe after 1989, humanitarian policy makers assessing the use of force operate on the basis of an implicit geography which can bias their judgment. As I learned in Senegal, the humanitarian project to infiltrate strategic thought is not complete — it has been more successful at the center than at the periphery, in the U.S. Navy than in the Senegalese military. There is good reason to suspect it has been more successful in highly visible campaigns like the American enforcement of the no-fly zone over Iraq than in purely national campaigns below the radar screen of the international community. There is also a historical direction to the humanitarian conquest of the use of force. Humanitarian law remains a work in progress. As the conversation about legitimacy expands, the strength and number of constituencies pushing for humanism will increase. But only if mankind is also on the move forward. A turn back to primitivism, tribalism, barbarism could undo the entire project of placing legitimacy in the hands of the international community.

As a result, we must develop humanitarian law not only to restrain the military, but also to promote a civilized sensibility about force among the world's public citizens. We might say that in this, the vocabulary of humanitarianism is at the cutting edge of progress, not only for military science, but also for global politics. But this idea introduces all manner of difficulty to our calculations of proportionality and necessity.

Imagine a rich and a poor country undertaking military campaigns of equal legitimacy — both fighting, say, for self-defense. Should we hold the poor country to the same standards of proportionality and necessity? Even if victory requires a far greater sacrifice of human life, civilian life, for the country without the latest technological weaponry? Yet if there is a sliding scale — military necessity measured by the nation's military capacity — we would have far less to say to the regional Senegalese commander who felt it necessary to use terror to maintain control of his sector. Should Russia be held to the same standard of accuracy in bombing Chechnya that the United States observes in Belgrade or Baghdad? And would the United States be justified in pursuing a new war in Iraq using the standards of the Gulf War — now that more accurate weapons are available, if at greater cost? Of course, one could answer these questions in various ways. Once humanitarianism comes to seem a work in progress, however, the question will be how far along more backward peoples have come, how much they may deviate from best practice among advanced peoples. The practices of the center will come to seem the gold standard for humanitarianism — and the question of a military campaign's humanitarianism will be displaced by assessment of its distance from the Persian Gulf practices of the U.S. Navy.

Similar difficulties attend the effort to extend our humanitarianism to conflicts which involve state and nonstate actors — to guerilla warfare, low-intensity conflict, civil war, wars of national liberation — while preserving the illegitimacy of the nonstate actors. In Colombia, international lawyers persistently argued against application of humanitarian law to their internal conflict to avoid recognizing guerrilla sovereignty. Something similar happens when humanitarian law grapples with the novel weaponry and tactics of nonstate actors. Take suicide bombings and collateral damage to civilian villages in the campaign to eradicate terrorism. It may well be that one cause is just and the other unjust. But let us assume a plausible UN Charter–based justification for both sides. Let us assume, for example, that a campaign — which happens to use suicide bombers — is a legitimate expression of the "right to self-determination." A humanitarian policy maker might well want to be able to measure suicide bombings with the same analytic calipers — proportional, necessary — used to measure other uses of force, presuming there is yet no treaty rule prohibiting suicide bombs. Or, from the other direction, a humanitarian policy maker might wish to apply the same level of opprobrium to the "collateral damage" caused by a tank attack on the suicide bomber's headquarters which is directed against the suicide bomber himself. That neither approach seems altogether viable suggests a bias — moral opprobrium at the base and periphery, proportional calculation at the center.

Such a bias can emerge in the calculations which accompany application of a common pragmatic vocabulary. Take the commitment to protect civilians. The U.S. military rules of engagement do embed a commitment to proportionality in the killing of civilians, but in a completely different way for our own and enemy combatants. It seems clear that American soldiers are meant to forgo killing foreign combatants if doing so will kill some number of civilians. The exact exchange rate is unclear, but it seemed to be somewhere in the range of three to ten civilians for each enemy combatant — one should forgo killing the soldier if more than a very small number of civilians would also be likely to be casualties. The exchange rate for American lives seems altogether different — killing a far larger number of civilians seems proportional in reasonable self-defense of even a single American soldier or pilot. The broad vocabulary of "proportionality" can submerge these differences, but they remain apparent to many audiences. As a result, public evaluations of a military action can become *more* rather than less polarized by use of the common vocabulary.

The sense that humanitarian law continues to carry a brief for the civilized against the uncivilized—in ways uncomfortably similar to nineteenth-century international legal principles—can be felt when rogue regimes attempt to mobilize the vocabulary in defense. In a certain way, of course, Saddam Hussein could speak precisely the same humanitarian language as Tony Blair or George Bush. After the outbreak of war, he was quick to reverse the coalition's accusations, labeling the United States a "terrorist regime," dramatizing damage to civilian targets, insisting that Iraqi prisoners were not being given Geneva Convention treatment—just as the Arab League might plausibly argue that Israel is also in long-term violation of Security Council resolutions, possesses weapons of mass destruction, and poses a threat to its neighbors. Were the Arab League to decide on a preemptive strike without the backing of the Security Council, it would be plausible to argue that their action was legal. These are all possible—if highly debatable—uses of the common vocabulary. For some publics, they are highly persuasive.

Yet there is something of parody and presumption in the effort. It is difficult to explain exactly why. There is the clean hands problem—but the modern law of force does not require clean hands. It is a policy vocabulary, a mode of assessing each new action against universal standards. In any event, few have clean hands in the diplomatic world. A vocabulary which requires nuance and sophistication in the assessment of arguments and the measurement of costs—this may seem beyond the ken of a rogue regime, a dictator, a thug. Yet the point of the modern law of force is to transcend such differences, to become a global ideology of rulership. It is difficult to avoid the idea that what is off about these efforts to use the vocabulary against the West is that, in some way, these arguments, terms, tools, judgments simply belong to us. At some point, the effectiveness of Saddam's deployment of these "common" terms rests on his having hoisted us on our own petard—not on the persuasiveness of his argument per se.

All these difficulties are familiar — we have seen them in evaluating other international humanitarian projects. Throughout this volume, I have argued that the remedy is a more thoroughgoing pragmatism. By rooting out bias, disenchanting the doctrines and institutional tools which substitute for analysis, insisting on a rigorous pragmatic analysis of costs and benefits, we might achieve a humanitarianism which could throw light on its own dark sides. The modern law of force was designed precisely to encourage this kind of pragmatism about humanitarian policy making. The enchantment of formal rules and the idolatry of external standpoints on war making were to be set aside. In an open conversation among humanitarian, military and political policy makers before the eyes of the world, all would be encouraged to make the most careful assessments of costs and benefits in a common humanitarian vernacular. So far, this promise has not been met. Humanitarian pragmatics about war has repeated, rather than remedied, the difficulties we saw elsewhere.

THE DARK SIDES OF HUMANITARIAN PRAGMATISM: BAD FAITH AND THE CORROSION OF PRACTICAL REASON

It is difficult to say where the trouble lies. It is tempting to criticize the modern law of force for weakening or abandoning the humanitarian aspiration to develop a critical, external perspective on the use of force. In this view, the virtue of a merged military and humanitarian vocabulary is precisely its vice. The military has taken over the Security Council. War is routinely waged in the vocabulary of the helping professions — as a defense of law, of right, and of the humanitarianism of the international community. What began as a humanitarian vocabulary has been misused, captured, stretched. We were better off when humanitarians, however unpersuasive their rhetoric, stood apart in a culture of ethically self-confident formalism.

The intuition that somehow the pragmatic project went too far is a common one among international lawyers. The principles and standards turned out to be *too* malleable. Even the United States, or perhaps particularly the United States, has stretched "self-defense" and other permissive terms in the modern law of force beyond all reason. People who feel strongly that humanitarianism should speak to power from an external ethical position may feel this even more strongly when they experience what seem to be ethical judgments as having been manipulated by an unspoken strategy. Is he telling us this war is illegal because our common commitments require it? Or is he strategizing about what will promote his objectives, or the legitimacy of the United Nations or of the law of force? If he seems to be manipulating, people who will be persuaded by ethical clarity may not credit him. In this sense, legitimacy cannot simply be strategized into existence. Knowledge that the contemporary humanitarian is strategizing may compromise the upward spiral of humanitarian pragmatism.

Unfortunately, however, our culture has lost access to the sort of transcendental external standpoint which could sustain a sincere humanitarian practice of judgment. In international law, this was the meaning of the turn away from the vocabulary of just war. Since then, all humanitarian efforts to restrain war have been strategic efforts to engage with politics and military planning. We no longer share a professional culture of interpretation which could sustain confidence that we could differentiate a creative from an abusive reading of terms like "self-defense" or "just war." Instead, for almost a century humanitarian professionals have preferred to trust the process by which claims made strategically are evaluated in an open-policy conversation. We may regret it, but there we are.

Judging our new humanitarian vocabulary requires a sociological and historical prediction about the effects of speaking this new pragmatic language over time. How confident can we be in the promise of an upward spiral toward ever more humanitarian outcomes? We should strategize — there may be things we can do within the new vocabulary to hasten that upward momentum. When, for example, should humanitarians press disagreements with military planners over the meaning of "self-defense" or "proportionality?" When will doing so strengthen our legitimacy, weaken that of more aggressive political or military voices, or contribute to the humanitarian tilt of the vocabulary as a whole? These strategic questions will require a careful weighing and balancing of different costs, and a set of sociological predictions about the effects of various approaches on the attitudes of other players about our, and their, legitimacy.

If we follow modern humanitarians into the war room where these strategic decisions are made, however, we can begin to see the difficulties this new vocabulary presents. There is, in fact, very little weighing and balancing of possible legitimation effects going on. People assert that using the United Nations will improve everyone's legitimacy — but they hesitate to measure the costs of doing so in any way that could permit a pragmatic assessment. How should we weigh the costs of leaving the regime in power — for civilians living there, for the international regime — against the costs of removing it militarily? How many civilian deaths should be tolerated to advance the status of the Security Council how far, in whose eyes? It is difficult to find an answer among those who speak the vocabulary of the modern law of force. The various "CNN effects" remain implicit in the new constitutionalism — alluded to, relied upon to explain why the new vocabulary is a pragmatic advance, but never actually calculated.

We can also see this happening when the humanitarian joins the military strategist in conversation. The modern humanitarian develops arguments which are both savvy and principled — which assess the use of force with the cool eye of cost-benefit calculation and invoke the posture of transcendent humanism. Yet there is also often hesitation. If enemy combatants are hiding among the civilian population, how many civilians can you kill to get one combatant? How much risk must there be to the soldier who shoots in such a situation? These are reasonable questions — but ones the humanitarian and the military planner are equally loath to answer. Sometimes, just when pragmatic evaluation is most necessary, one hears instead the invocation of an absolute rule — you just cannot target civilians. Very well, but what happens when they are in the way, when they are not the "target" but their death can be foreseen? When pressed, both humanitarian and military strategist are likely to respond that these are "judgment calls." Fair enough, but suppose it were you, how would you make the judgment? How would you evaluate it?

This tendency to pull back just when the decision point arrives suggests that the modern law of force is not as pragmatic as it seems. Something else is going on. Humanitarians who are worried about violence, using the new United Nations vocabulary to evaluate decisions to use force, certainly mean to *seem* pragmatic, to have merged with the realist perspective they attribute to the military. Military men using the vocabulary mean to seem professional in the conduct of war — even humanitarian in their sensibility. This will to *seem* at once pragmatic and ethical may have altogether different roots than the humanitarian and professional desire to reduce the violence and incidence of warfare.

In my experience, moreover, humanitarians, alongside statesmen, military spokesmen, soldiers, and pilots, do not seem to notice when they pull back in this way. Indeed, when humanitarians insist that the Security Council must be used, they mean it as a pragmatic assessment, a realist conclusion rooted in a theory about legitimacy over time in international affairs. They do not experience it as pulling back from judgment or practical assessment — they experience it as practical judgment itself. When soldiers say that proportionality requires "judgment," they do not experience it as the abandonment of calculation or as a loss of interest in or responsibility for long-term consequences. Just how many civilians will die if we take out the electric generator is precisely the crux for their professional judgment, even if such a calculation also remains above the pay grade of anyone actually tasked with exercising this judgment. Calling the decisions which result exercises of "judgment" nevertheless seems to be experienced as responsible and rational pragmatism.

It is hard to avoid interpreting this, in psychological terms, as a form of denial. Humanitarians, military strategists, and statesmen who use the vocabulary of the new law of force seem out of touch with what they are saying — attributing a kind of calculation to their assessments which they refuse to make. We might call this a form of bad faith or denial — in the sense of a break within their own consciousness between what they believe themselves to be doing and what, if we think about it, they seem in fact to be doing.

It is not at all clear what they are denying, although I have an intuition that they are denying their engagement with power, their participation in the war machine. Lurking somewhere behind the embrace of the modern law of force as a practical vocabulary of judgment seems to lie a desire to deny the harms one finds oneself supporting, legitimating, explaining, or simply not noticing. For humanitarians, this may mean denying the partnership with military and political authority they have sought for more than a century. For those in the military it may mean denying that one weighs life and death in just this pragmatic a spirit. In denial, it is easy to forget one's practical engagement with positions which one announces in a voice of normative clarity — just as one can forget one's responsibility for the consequences that follow.

It is not clear why this denial feels so necessary. The humanitarian vocabulary was designed to make precisely this kind of inattention unnecessary — finally we have a vocabulary for staring down consequences and evaluating the use of force in pragmatic humanitarian terms. The denial which is nevertheless so prevalent may have something to do with a dilemma faced by those speaking in the vernacular of the modern law of force. On the one hand, if a humanitarian is able, in fact, to be pragmatic or strategic, he may forfeit his ethical legitimacy. On the other, if he finds himself pulling back from pragmatic judgment, consciously or unconsciously, his practical legitimacy may be compromised. When discussing the use of force, the humanitarian must manage a kind of split about the vocabulary he uses. He will apply the rules and standards of humanitarian law *as if* they offered external criteria of evaluation, while also being careful to think strategically about his advocacy, assessing its potential to persuade, and the feedback effects of nonpersuasion on the vocabulary itself. He must both husband and spend his stock of legitimacy, but must do so in a vocabulary which presents itself as the voice of humanitarian principle rather than pragmatic calculation. The tensions which result — the distance between his pragmatic consciousness and his principled utterance — may well open the door to denial. The anxiety of managing the tensions within humanitarianism between attention to principle and attention to legitimacy may fuel the experience of thinking oneself more pragmatic than one is.

Humanitarians are often asked — often ask themselves — whether a particular tactic *is or is not* compatible with humanitarian law. This inquiry figures humanitarian law as precisely the sort of answer machine a century of modernization was designed to eliminate. Where the law is a standard, it will be tempting to respond *as if* the response were mandated by a rule. Where the law offers a rule, it is tempting to respond *as if* the rule reflected a pragmatic balancing of humanitarian necessity. In fact, it is so tempting to respond in this way that even the most pragmatic and sophisticated people forget their own pragmatic and critical sensibility. The possibility for this kind of forgetting arises whenever advocacy proceeds on the basis of policy making—when pragmatic assessments, both tactical and strategic, attuned to the feedback loops of reaction from various publics, attentive to the impact on the legitimacy of the humanitarian vocabulary itself, are presented in the voice of deduction or interpretation of a humanitarian truth.

There is something parallel in the professional military's own struggle to blend machismo and submission, to discipline force with the steady hand of effectiveness, while invoking the authority of violence unleashed. On the USS *Independence,* naval officers peppered their conversation with references to unrestrained violence—"unleashing" the pilot, sending in the "ninja guys," "releasing the spear," "letting the snake eaters go at it." It was fun to hear them talk this way. It was quite clear, however, that they had organized their world precisely to prevent just this—they were invoking a violence which would subvert their own goals. If they thought it would occur, they were not at all intending to own it as their own. At the same time, they presented their strategic judgments in the vocabulary of the law of force—proportional, necessary, minimizing collateral damage—when they, no more than the humanitarian, had actually weighed or balanced costs. They would say that each target had been carefully evaluated by lawyers and strategists for necessity and proportionality, and it was true that lawyers and strategists had signed off on each targeting decision. But the word "evaluate" covered a multiplicity of inquiries not undertaken. They did not, in fact, have a metric in mind for comparing enemy civilian lives with those of coalition pilots or for factoring in future deaths from cholera or anything else. They were also forgetting, and denying, saying things which did not add up. I don't think they were trying to pull the wool over my eyes. It was their eyes I was worried about.

In another sense, dialogue about the meaning of humanitarian norms concerns less judgment about uses of force than judgment about the character and identity of those who are engaged in the conversation. Both military planners and humanitarians manage tension between gritty calculation and a more transcendent gaze, oriented to virtue or victory. If you are listening on the radio, it can be hard to tell them apart. To be experienced—by listeners, by themselves—as humanitarian, a person must manage this tension in such a way as to differentiate himself from the military voice. It is not necessary that he take any particular positions—nor that he be more principled or less pragmatic than his military interlocutor. The military person may be quite formal about things, and the humanitarian very practical. For the humanitarian effect to be generated, the audience must come to credit one participant with speaking, whether sincerely or not, from a deeper ethical or political commitment to humanitarian virtue than to military victory. We do this by contrast to what we attribute to the other speakers—a deeper commitment to victory. As a result, we might say that the humanitarianism and pragmatism of the ongoing conversation that is the modern law of force resides not in the positions which are taken or the careful analyses which are made. Rather, humanitarianism and pragmatism are effects of listening to people participate in the language of the law of force in a particular way, regardless of the particular positions taken, intentions of the speakers, or impact in the world.

Once you know that applications of humanitarian standards can be made strategically to legitimate the speaker and the vocabulary of humanitarian law, it is difficult to assume that the standards do, in fact, express normative or military necessity. We might say that the price of pragmatism has been the experience of indeterminacy—the feeling that humanitarian policy pronouncements are open to successful challenge and reinterpretation.

We might worry about this for a variety of reasons. In one sense, the conversation is about itself, rather than outcomes. It is not surprising that participants would enchant their tools or misestimate the consequences of their analysis. The experience of being pragmatic when one is, in fact, not assessing costs and benefits clearly, is very likely to yield blind spots and entrench biases in judgment. Indeed, modern humanitarianism forgets a great deal. At the same time, the pragmatic appearance of judgments may lend them greater weight, get them more deference, than they deserve. In this sense, denial can lead to enchantment.

On the other hand, not everyone who hears the pragmatic performance of the modern humanitarian will be convinced. For some of us in the audience, it will be apparent that the pragmatic evaluation is not, in fact, forthcoming. When we hear humanitarians promoting the modern law of force as a pragmatic instrument for limiting war, we can also see them fumbling in denial. When we do, they will not seem strategic or pragmatic at all. They will seem simply to be proposing the same kinds of political and ethical ideas about how war should be fought which have been proposed for a century from the vantage point of an external humanitarian ethics. If they were speaking ethically, we could engage them directly and agree or disagree. If they were assessing costs and benefits, we could debate their calculations. But to present ethical judgments in policy dress — that is difficult to take seriously. The implausibility of these apparently pragmatic presentations over time should also lead us to be skeptical about the upward humanitarian trajectory predicted for the modern law of force.

NUCLEAR WEAPONS IN THE WORLD COURT: PRAGMATIC HUMANITARIAN JUDGING

These difficulties are well illustrated by the multiyear humanitarian campaign to place the use of nuclear weapons before the International Court of Justice in The Hague for adjudication. The Court is empowered to give advisory opinions on questions of law when requested to do so by various institutional bodies in the United Nations system. Throughout the postwar period, international humanitarians had debated the compatibility of nuclear weapons with the new law of force. Activists proposed numerous arguments against their use — they are so destructive as to be indiscriminate, unavoidably disproportional, incapable of respecting the principle of distinction. Their consequences will outlast and overspread the limits of any legitimate military campaign, violating the sovereignty of all states. In the early 1970s, humanitarian international lawyers began to look to nongovernmental organizations and citizens groups, particularly in the United States, as agents for promoting the humanitarian agenda, often by pursuing litigation in national courts.

About this time, a few international lawyers, loosely networked with one another in the United States, Japan, and Western Europe began a grass-roots campaign to convince one or another intergovernmental organization to ask the Court for an Advisory Opinion on the question. After years of intense work, they were successful, and the World Health Organization voted to do so, on the grounds that use of nuclear weapons would constitute a grave danger to world health. The General Assembly followed suit, and on July 8, 1996, the International Court of Justice issued a opinion on "the legality of the threat or use of nuclear weapons." The response was lengthy and equivocal, a cacophony of dicta and holding, ruling and dissent, which has itself been read in numerous ways.

At first, it seems incongruous that the twentieth-century effort to render humanitarian law pragmatic would end with a turn to the Court. Modern humanitarian law developed, after all, in a repudiation of the formal legalisms of the late-nineteenth-century Hague system. Asking the Court to adjudicate military tactics seems to turn us back to that era. The United Nations, languishing in the chaos of institutional proliferation, nonstop budgetary crises, and internal reforms, bypassed by bilateralism and the great institutions of the private sector, addresses the century's major technological innovation, the most significant transformation in the conditions of war and peace, by asking not the Security Council or the Disarmament Agency, but the International Court, for an advisory opinion.

What was their strategy? The humanitarian campaigners promoting a turn to the Court seemed to have two quite different Courts in mind. Indeed, when today's liberal constitutionalist commentators describe the Court, they do so by blending these quite distinct images in a single pastiche. In one view, the International Court of Justice simply *is* the world court — an adjudicator like any other, empowered to opine, on the basis of law, with some expectation of authority, even of compliance and enforcement. Pleadings and decisions tend to adopt this image. It was the Court's self-image in the 1920s, and remains more common in Europe than in the United States, and in the polemics of advocacy than in academic commentary. This vision suggests a strategy—the Court promises something firmer than the compromises of intergovernmental consultation.

The second image seems a correction to the first—of course the Court is not like that, international law is not like that, even domestic law may not be like that. The Court is one cultural and political institution among others, crafting its decision to enhance its legitimacy and pull toward compliance, the decision one drop in the ocean of world public opinion, part of the *travaux preparatoire* for future interstate behavior as broad as international civil society. This image is more common in the American tradition, where everything legal is process and all the world's a regime. Writing *as if* the Court were a court is simply one posture in a complex theater of persuasion and calculation. We are interested in the effects generated by the opinion, the values advanced, the institutional process followed, and the political strategies of the participants—and also in the strategic effect of commentary which does or does not accept the Court's own fantasy world. In the European tradition, such calculations remain largely offstage, in the private discourse of insiders about what the Court was—wink—actually doing. This vision also suggests a strategy—calling on the Court to participate in our ongoing campaign by pronouncing itself, returning the issue to the intergovernmental body, emboldening them for action.

It is easier to understand humanitarian campaigners as *having a strategy* if we take the second view of the Court. Going to the Court is somewhere on a list of strategies for the General Assembly, like passing a resolution which will never be law in any strong sense, but might shame or mobilize or deter. Or like funding a movie about refugees or hiring a missile to send a message. When we take the first view, it is easier to imagine the campaigners seeking the truth, hoping to *get it right*. There is something noble, if also quixotic, about an effort to find out whether nuclear weapons are or are not legal. At a minimum, we would have to concede that a legal decision prohibiting the use of nuclear weapons seems, if anything, less likely to achieve their elimination than a General Assembly resolution.

For the campaign, it was important to blend these two voices, invoking the law as answer machine, while also enlisting the rhetoric

of law *as a maneuver, as if* we were naïve believers in a world of law
and courts. These two visions are combined differently in different
traditions, but in modern conceptions of humanitarian law they are
both present. There was less enthusiasm among European international lawyers for the advisory opinion campaign than there was in
the United States, precisely because the two humanitarian traditions
combine these elements differently. Humanitarian policy makers in
the United States are more enthusiastic about disaggregating the policy conversation—opening it to all sorts of advocacy groups—and
more optimistic about the impact of the adjudication in the conversation which would result. European international lawyers are more
likely to think the Court a court—worry about opening it to hare-
brained advocacy schemes—while whispering the wisdom of a chastened realpolitik for statecraft. We might say that addressing the
Court as if it would rule is a game for the middle powers—engaging
the Court in a public relations campaign is a game even hegemons
can play.

The Court's opinion in the case was equivocal on every point. Although international law is a complete legal order, it has not worked
out rules for everything. It both covers and does not cover nuclear
weapons—although there are no clear rules covering the use of
nuclear weapons, they must be considered to be covered by international law in general. Their use would therefore be illegal when
it violates international law, but not where it did not. The Court
exhorted the nuclear powers to consider their obligations while remembering their rights, without clarifying what those rights and obligations might be beyond reciting conventional bromides about self-
defense and proportionality and environmental protection and
humanitarianism, norms whose interpretation one might have
thought was precisely the point of the request for an advisory opinion. And the judges decided the case seven to seven.

Yet no one seemed to mind. The parties and advocates, like most
journalists, were willing to take what they could get, reading the
opinion to support a wide variety of positions, simply continuing
their debate in the key of dispute about crucial phrases of the Court's
opinion. The sophisticated commentators were quick to see the wisdom of the Court's maneuver—for the Court also maneuvers, wor-

ries about its legitimacy, its allies and enemies in the game of mutual political regard. If you like doctrine, the decision showed a little doctrine. For those preferring values, there were values. For those who thrill to process, the Court inaugurated an infinite regress of interpretation and commentary, playing its role in the menagerie of international civil society with the elegance of equipoise. The case is a joy to teach—students coming with the naïve idea that the point is to clarify the holding and decide if the case was rightly decided, can easily be brought to higher ground—appreciation of the Court's exquisite sense of strategy.

The Court's nuclear weapons opinion is a well-wrought example of the modern law of force in action. The Court holds that the use of nuclear weapons must be decided *in the language* of the international law of force, rather than offering an external decision about their legitimacy. Yet is it possible to be convinced *both* in the plausibility of the legal project—a world governed by rules interpreted by courts calming the politics of nations—*and* in an interminably malleable process, in which words are acts, deeds transliterated into messages, normativity is relative, and law bleeds off into politics at every turn? Is the modern pragmatic humanitarian voice at once principled and savvy—or schizophrenic? It is difficult to honor the Court's integrity while praising its strategy.

It is here that we encounter problems of good faith: the good faith of judges who flaunt their fealty to positive law while remaining proud of their engagement with the humanist issues of the day, of their national or cultural patriotism, even their participation in internationalist advocacy institutions of one or another stripe; or the good faith of academic commentators split between the voices of earnest advocacy and detached analysis; and also the good faith of humanitarians, understanding themselves as both seekers after truth and participants in cultural politics.

The difficulty is not that these people are strategizing. There is nothing wrong with that—the whole point was to render the law of force pragmatic, and it seems difficult to imagine a persuasive alternative to strategic thinking. The difficulty is that they are seeming—to themselves and to the world—both to be strategic and to sit in judgment, both to be ethically humanitarian and to be realistically pragmatic, allowing the invocation of each to substitute for the firm deployment of either. In creating these effects, they lose track of their own distance from both virtue and calculation — remaining blind to their strategic engagement with power.

In this, the Nuclear Weapons Case exemplifies the modern humanitarian — a modernism of ambivalence and contradiction, of the desire for action and the turn to language. But modernism about nuclear weapons? Even if it were successful, should we see this sort of pragmatism as offering a higher ground? Perhaps in thinking about nuclear war, law, even humanitarian law, with its hedges and equivocations, should simply step aside. Perhaps here we meet the limits of humanitarian efforts to occupy the field.

In one such view, nuclear weaponry properly belongs to the political, its legality not something on which a prudent judge — or humanitarian — should pronounce himself. And yet this is also an argument within the framework of modern humanitarian law — an argument about what particular institutions should do, about the respective limits of principle and strategy, the appropriate moment for effects to overrule the rule. When we hear someone say the matter is political, it seems unavoidable to ask who makes the claim, invoking what transcendent vocabulary — and with what objective, as part of what project, to persuade whom?

It is also tempting to say that nuclear weaponry is better considered in a technical or logical vocabulary of military specialists, a vocabulary of prisoners' dilemmas and games foreign to the rules and values of even the most open-ended legal process. The last thing you want is a lawyer in the clean room. In this vision, humanitarian policy making aims to speak in the transcendent voice of politics or of ethics, when what we need, for deterrence or disarmament, is expertise. Once the legal process becomes subject to capture by one political or social interest after another, becomes enmeshed in a myriad diffused institutions, one hesitates to hand over the button. Yet the expertise of military planners and humanitarian policy makers is no longer so different. The great military machines are also immense bureaucracies whose technical expertise runs parallel to the modern vocabulary of humanitarian policy making about the use of force, and it is difficult to imagine how they would calculate the need for nuclear weapons except in a complex vocabulary of proportionality, necessity and risk.

Or perhaps our complaint against the Court's struggle with nuclear weapons is an ethical one — there is something obscene in the use of legal language to talk about a nuclear strike. The law muddles what is clear. This resonates with calls for the return of formalism, outlawry, principle — if humanitarianism is to stand for anything, it must stand against nuclear weapons. The horrors of warfare, the dead and mangled bodies, the lives and families ripped apart, the intense anxiety and suffering on and off the battlefield, the pain felt by a single wounded child all these do seem harder to remember in the vocabulary of costs and benefits. It is not clear exactly why — they are costs, and the whole point is to remember them — but they do fade from view in the modern humanitarian vocabulary.

Whether prohibiting nuclear weapons outright or providing a humanitarian language of balancing for deciding on their use, the law can only help to make their use seem plausible. Even to say that blowing up the world is illegal somehow speaks the unthinkable — somehow denies what would be a nuclear holocaust. We need, in this view, another vocabulary. The slaughter of the innocents. Holocaust. Armageddon. Hiroshima. Unimaginable death and destruction — the end of civilization, the end of the world as we know it. The end of time. Playing God. The language of religious epiphany, the ethic of life, the intimate testimony of survivors, victims, children. Better pictures, in fact than words. Better art than language. Better even a moment of silence than the cacaphony of the Court's opinion.

Perhaps. And yet, is there an alternative mode of discussion? I am afraid that if we began to speak of nuclear weapons in the language of the "slaughter of the innocents" we would soon find ourselves in the same soup, for nuclear weapons are not simply the "slaughter of the innocents" — they are also a technology, a machinery, a threat, a strategy undeployed, on a continuum with a host of other gadgets and modes of making a point. We would need to account not merely for the horrors of Hiroshima and Nagasaki, but also for their singularity. We will need to take seriously the claims of deterrence, for nuclear weapons have also humanitarian uses in a wicked world.

Soon, we would be back to Corporal McIntosh, "It's a judgment call. If the risks outweigh the losses, then you don't take the shot." And if they don't, you do. It turns out not to be so easy to think outside the vocabulary of humanitarian policy making.

We tend to think of force or war as one of the unyielding consistencies in human history—there has, we think, always been war. The Pentagon pores over satellite maps of the same terrain Alexander the Great conquered on horseback years ago. War has always been with us. So also humanitarianism—an endless human struggle to contain war in the name of civilization. These transcendent claims are also arguments in a contemporary vocabulary of both humanitarian policy makers and military strategists. They work hard to make war and force seem to lie outside the social order, before it, after it, just offstage—constantly threatening the humanitarian laws and civilized practices of the international community. Or deployed as instrument, enforcing the legal order, defending rights, vindicating and implementing policy. The humanitarian—no less than the military strategist—knows that it is not like this at all; that there has long been no outside, that neither the violence of war nor the ethics of humanitarian aspiration give us ground upon which to stand in judgment of the modern law of force. They know it—but they forget it.

PART III What International
Humanitarianism Should
Become

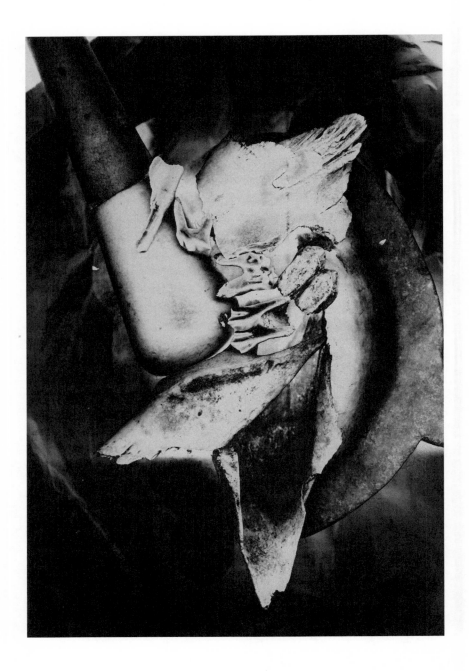

NINE

Humanitarian Power

The impulse to make the world more just, more secure, more fair —
more humane, in short — survives exposure to the dark sides of international humanitarianism. But the dark sides I have described are
also resilient. Aspiring to good, humanitarians too often mute awareness that their best ideas can have bad consequences. When things
do go wrong, rather than facing the darker consequences of humanitarian work, we too often simply redouble our efforts and intensify
our condemnation of whatever other forces we can find to hold
responsible.

It is difficult to work as a human rights activist taking to heart the
dark sides I describe in the first three chapters. To work as a humanitarian policy maker — promoting development or democracy, protecting refugees or limiting the violence and frequency of war — while
conscious of the difficulties I identify in the later chapters is just
as difficult. But why? None of these dark sides is unknown, none of
the criticisms I have developed here is unfamiliar to international
humanitarians.

Indeed, human rights activists and humanitarian policy makers
often identify these same difficulties themselves. Well-known antidotes
seem near at hand. Where our impulse to do good has been betrayed
by the forms of our work or the biases of our professional knowledge, we should be critical of those forms, aware of those biases,
faithful again to our original humanitarian desires. We should clarify

our commitments, confirm their articulation, promote their use as yardsticks to measure the legitimacy of governance — including our own. At the same time, where we have ignored the consequences of our work, mistaking our own involvement — our institutions, adherence to our norms — for humanitarian effects, we should redouble our efforts to be pragmatic, to disenchant our tools and ourselves, to weigh more carefully the benefits and costs of apparent successes and be guided by consequences rather than forms. International humanitarians know all this. What stands in the way of a more thoroughgoing pragmatism, a more aggressively self-critical and aware humanitarian practice?

I am not at all sure. Mine is hardly the first call to renew the practice of international humanitarianism, to reform it for new times. For more than a century, international humanitarians have felt the pull to pragmatism, evaluating their work with a shrewd and strategic eye, rooting their work in practice and expressing their commitments in the vocabularies of statecraft. Along the way, humanitarians have also struggled to reaffirm their values and intentions, articulating them anew for a modern world. The best humanitarian practices today embody these two renewalist ideas — realism about power and clarity about commitment. The international humanitarians I have known over the past twenty-five years are intensely self-critical, calling themselves repeatedly back to values and forward to their pragmatic implementation and expression. The experiences and critical observations I have chronicled here are widely shared among professional humanitarians today.

Humanitarian values have been ever more clearly articulated, and international humanitarianism today is pragmatic, engaged, worldly. Humanitarians have entered the world of policy making. To be sure, the struggle to make humanitarian commitments real in the world of statecraft has not been everywhere equally successful. But human rights are becoming a universal vocabulary of political legitimacy, just as humanitarian law has become the dominant vocabulary for articulating the legitimacy of war. The intensely regulated world of the USS *Independence* is as much apotheosis as outlier, and offers a vision of contemporary humanitarianism realized.

Yet, even the best humanitarian practice loses sight of its darker sides. How does this blindness set in? There are probably as many explanations as there are humanitarians. But I have become convinced that it often begins at the moment the humanitarian averts his eyes from his own power. Even as he struggles to render commitments clear and convincing, to become effective, persuasive and practical, the humanitarian advocate and policy maker remains reluctant to think of himself as a ruler, exercising power, allocating stakes in society. Identifying with the weak and the marginal—perhaps he comes to think of himself also in these terms. But international humanitarians do participate in global governance, both as activists and as policy makers. Their criticisms, strategies, and language all have consequences, allocate stakes, exercise power. When things go wrong, they—we—share responsibility.

I can't remember meeting a humanitarian who did not struggle vigorously to redeem his commitments in effective action. Yet, at the moment of their greatest success, if you say "what does it feel like to rule?" they demur, as if they hit a wall, or encountered a taboo, or had been caught with their hand in the cookie jar.

There is apparently something scandalous about an aircraft carrier sailing off to war as the *realization* of international humanitarianism. Aircraft carriers are the instruments of statesmen. We prefer to think of humanitarians as gentle civilizers, lawyers whispering in the admiral's ear, protesters marching in the streets for peace, scholars documenting the norms and standards of humanitarian law, teachers instructing soldiers in the *limits* to warfare. Pragmatic renewal continues to be necessary because humanitarian rulership is so often rulership denied.

After so many efforts to render international humanitarianism practical, you might think it would be difficult to preserve this sense of innocence. It is difficult not to interpret the recurring cycles of renewal, the extravagant rituals of self-criticism, the repeated calls for a more pragmatic engagement, as symptoms of some sort—practices of denial that humanitarians have crossed the threshold of power.

The puzzling relationship between the normative and practical sides of humanitarian work gives us a clue to how this denial might work. For human rights activists, seeking to speak effectively from the truth of shared ideas, renewal has meant an ever more precise articulation of normative commitments, coupled with efforts to make these norms effective through reporting, shaming, enforcing. For humanitarian policy makers in many fields, renewal has meant setting aside dogmatism about humanitarian values and learning the governance vocabularies of political science, economics, or military science in order to enter the practical world of statesmen. The best modern humanitarian professionals combine fidelity to humanitarian ends with pragmatism about means. They endeavor to speak both from outside statecraft, calling it to humanitarian ideals, and from within statecraft, as a realistic strategist for humanitarian ends. They are, in short, both committed *and* realistic.

But neither activists nor policy makers are committed and strategic in equal measure. For both, fidelity to humanitarian ideals comes before pragmatism about consequences. Human rights activists are proud of their practical wisdom, their street smarts about what governments are really like, their clever insinuations into the halls of power — but these remain secondary to the clear public voice of normative judgment. When the humanitarian policy maker assesses costs and benefits, he focuses on consequences *for his commitments* — will this strengthen multilateralism, the rule of law, the role of international law? He sounds like one who governs — but he carries no general brief for the social consequences of his initiatives. The humanitarian policy maker is but one *interest* among many, clamoring for recognition from a power he imagines elsewhere. As a result, it is not surprising, for example, that the humanitarian who takes up development policy would come to promote the rule of law or the enforcement of human rights as a substitute for assessing the distributional choices necessary for economic development.

These baseline commitments often seem to cut short pragmatic analysis of consequences — occluding the darker sides of humanitarian engagement. Take discussion of acceptable civilian deaths in wartime, which we saw in chapter 8. For a hundred years or more, humanitarians have realized it is neither realistic nor practical to treat civilians as absolutely inviolable or to expect warfare to harm only combatants. Rather, humanitarians have sought to *limit* damage to civilians by promoting respect for the *principle* of distinction, and the standards of necessity and proportionality. To target civilians di-

rectly would be wanton — to know and intend harm to civilians inci-
dental to a legitimate military target is permissible where necessary
and proportional to the military objective.

The proportionality standard places the humanitarian and the military analyst on common ground, assessing the impact of a given
strike on civilians. The language is instrumental and practical —
weighing and balancing civilian casualties against military advantages. The humanitarian will also be attentive to the impact of his
decision on broader humanitarian institutions and commitments —
including the principles of distinction and proportionality themselves. The military strategist will be attentive to the consequences
for the mission, and for the professional status and power of the
military itself. At this point, the discussion seems a model of pragmatism, and it is hard to understand how dark sides of proceeding one
way or the other could not simply be reckoned into the analysis.

As discussion proceeds, however, it often becomes clear that neither humanitarians nor military planners in fact complete the pragmatic analysis they have begun. At the extremes, it is easy — a single
civilian worker in the electric plant, say, or a hundred women and
children for a single artillery emplacement. But how exactly should
military objectives and civilian casualties be weighed in closer cases?
Or what should we think of larger-scale choices, of the sort involved
in the more indiscriminate World War II urban bombing campaigns
on Tokyo, Dresden, or Hiroshima? For such questions — precisely
where pragmatic assessment of consequences would seem most crucial — both humanitarians and military planners are likely to step
outside the rhetoric of weighing and balancing.

The difficulty often seems to arise when the humanitarian would
need to take responsibility for the decision to kill civilians. Perhaps
the strategist will ask precisely how many civilian deaths one should
accept to protect one soldier. In the pragmatic business of targeting,
ultimately one needs to know the exchange rate — a hundred civilians, fifty, twenty-five, a thousand? Or perhaps the military objective
can best be achieved — most easily, with the least loss of life, short
and long term — precisely by attacking civilians rather than troops in
the field.

At this point, the humanitarian is likely to pull back, perhaps reasserting the standard "it must be proportional" rather than applying it, or perhaps returning to the vocabulary of absolute normative commitment: "civilians may never be targeted." At which point he has ceased to speak pragmatically — and it is difficult to see how the strategist can persist in discussing the matter with him at all. "But this is war, I intend to win, that means civilians will be killed, and my forces will kill them. I thought we were having a discussion about how to do that most humanely?" No, for the humanitarian we were not talking about killing civilians. We were talking about strengthening the norm that they not be killed.

The separation of these two objectives — and the priority accorded to humanitarian principle — permits the modern humanitarian to feel innocent of rulership. It is as if their commitments can *only* be articulated — must, in some sense, remain rebukes to those in power, external measures of their legitimacy, rather than guides for action. Or as if pragmatism must remain something humanitarians can only hope to achieve in the future — in the meantime, we will have to settle for being savvy about the power of others. When the rubber meets the road, the humanitarian finds himself sitting on the shoulder, evaluating, judging, condemning, approving

Humanitarians are not alone in experiencing a taboo around the pragmatic assessment of consequences. The military strategist is rarely any more willing to complete the pragmatic analysis called for by the humanitarian law vocabulary. When critics ask how many civilians the military is willing to kill in pursuit of this or that objective, the strategist will also often simply restate the principle — "our soldiers have the right to defend themselves" — or explain that the answer is a matter of "judgment." Like humanitarians, strategists may also step outside to a more absolute vocabulary — here of consequences, invoking the military mission, force protection or simply victory — we will "do our job" or "protect our soldiers."

This imaginary conversation between humanitarian and military voices is echoed in broader debates among foreign policy experts, who seem at first quite eager to participate in statecraft. For most of the last century, American foreign policy was understood as a struggle between the proponents of "idealism" and "realism." Experts in international affairs seemed split between those urging the United States to a larger international role as agent for democracy or freedom and those urging restraint in the name of realpolitik about American interests, the costs of American adventurism, and the dangers of idealist overreaching. Although this simple opposition was never analytically completely satisfactory — was free trade, for example, an idealist commitment or a realpolitik interest? — it did seem to capture something fundamental to much debate about foreign affairs.

Generations of foreign affairs experts were taught to situate themselves on a continuum between these two positions, loosely associated with the left and the right in American politics. For "realists," associated with the right, the world was a Hobbesian place in which states struggled against one another to secure their national interests in territory and wealth. The instruments of power were military, political, and economic. At best, international law and institutions were useful; at worst, a danger or illusion. The United States was a power like any other, which should struggle in the world for its own interests. Its power and wealth defended and enabled isolation. Prosperity required the vigilant defense of free trade, access to economic resources, and the stability necessary for commerce. Beyond that, realists were sympathetic to isolationism, and tended to favor unilateral over multilateral foreign policy. They viewed international affairs through the lenses of diplomatic history and political science.

For "idealists," associated throughout the last century with Woodrow Wilson's campaign for the League of Nations, the world was an interdependent community or society, in which "peoples" and other actors — individuals, corporations, nongovernmental actors, civil society, world public opinion — joined states in the pursuit of self-expression, fulfillment, and social justice. For idealists, the "soft power" of communication, ideas, law, and institutions could be as important as military or political force. Idealists favored multilateral over unilateral initiatives, and sought to strengthen the institutions of international society. To idealists, the United States could be a power unlike all others, taking on an expansionist role in the name of universal values. The expansion of markets and commerce was understood as the vehicle of freedom, rather than of national interest. Idealists viewed international affairs through the lenses of international law, morality, and religion.

Although generations of foreign policy experts were trained to debate these two positions, it was always difficult to find any but straw men at the extremes. If you return to the writings of those remembered for their eloquent defense of "idealism" or "realism" in foreign affairs, you will be disappointed — each defended his program as a recipe to make grand ideals real in the world. Every methodological innovation in the study of international affairs was directed to this same double objective. It was Wilsonian "idealists," after all, who first turned to the study of political science and rejected the old international law of the pre-war Hague as hopelessly out of touch with the realities of the modern era. Functionalism, positivism, policy science — all were enlisted to clarify values and ensure results.

Nevertheless, individual statesmen are still thought to have an orientation to either realism or idealism, and debates about particular foreign policy initiatives are often conducted by claiming the virtues and denouncing the vices of these positions. It would be more accurate to say that every contemporary foreign policy expert situates him or herself between the somewhat imaginary extremes of "realism" and "idealism," rejecting both as simple-minded and inadequate. Nevertheless, it remains far easier to delegitimate a proposal by terming it "idealist" than "realist."

In this sense, we might say that foreign policy elites face a taboo precisely the inverse of that felt by humanitarians. For statesmen, there is something sentimental or scandalous about being too humanitarian or ethical — insufficiently committed to the consequential analytic methods of practical realism. The foreign policy establishment seems confident that it is *normally* dominated by the voices of realism, swinging to embrace a more active idealism only in exceptional moments of crisis or national exuberance. Indeed, idealism is routinely invoked as something one may well have had in the past, but can no longer afford. Or which is good in small doses. Or useful in selling foreign policy initiatives to a reluctant public — but best kept out of the way when decisions are being taken. I have had much less experience talking to statesmen than to humanitarians, but I have noticed when I do that I hear no objection when I say "weren't you a clever and effective ruler." They don't usually mind when you praise their ethical commitment and humane touch. The denial starts when you imply that they are willing to take costs, put the nation at risk, for virtue.

Even this quite modest divergence between realism and idealism — or statecraft and humanitarianism — has been eroded by the emergence of international humanitarianism as a language for statecraft. Statesmen now routinely promote their policies in the language of virtue, while idealists and humanitarians have abandoned dogmatism for the language of pragmatism and practicality. In this new rhetorical situation, it is not surprising that the Democratic Party has developed a muscular humanitarian realism, or that the Republican Party should have reframed its unilateral defense of the national interest as an activist — even multilateral — pursuit of humanitarian ideals, now expanded to include "human security." It has become ever more difficult to distinguish humanitarian ideals from hard-boiled strategic interest. As we have seen, human rights can as well be the second as the first — just as warfare can as well be the first as the second.

This convergence has transformed our understanding of international politics, placing communication and legitimacy in the foreground. Participants in the "foreign policy process" — statesmen and humanitarians alike — now imagine themselves in an ongoing conversation with one another. No one thinks that states are simply billiard balls of self-interest. Over the last twenty years, international law "idealists" and political science "realists" have found themselves converging — the lawyers understanding their norms to be a function of social and political power, the political scientists understanding power to reside in loose "regimes" in which statesmen play against one another's expectations. In more recent years we see the same thing in the literature of political science, as "public choice" proponents of realism bring their empirical and modeling skills to bear to confirm one after another component of what "institutionalists" and "constructivists" have been saying for years about the interactive nature of power in international affairs. Effectiveness and status depend upon good reviews, upon credits and debits paid in the currency of legitimacy. At the same time, it is now common ground that values are also influenced by their *recognition* by those whom they would govern. Idealism and humanitarianism no longer provide a standpoint external to the ebbs and flows of the policy conversation. Action legitimates norms, norms legitimate action. Humanitarians and statesmen — idealists and realists — are in the same game, and are increasingly difficult to distinguish from one another.

It is hard not to share the exuberance of humanitarians who see a constitutional moment of the first order in this convergence — in the emergence of human rights, say, as a global vocabulary of legitimacy. It has long been a commonplace to observe that the techniques of war and peace blend into one another. We need only recall Clausewitz:

> We maintain, on the contrary, that War is nothing but a continuation of political intercourse, with a mixture of other means. We say mixed with other means in order thereby to maintain at the same time that this political intercourse does not cease by the War itself, is not changed into something quite different, but that, in its essence, it continues to exist, whatever may be the form of the means which it uses, and that the chief lines on which the events of the War progress, and to which they are attached, are only the general features of policy which run all through the War until peace takes place. And how can we conceive it to be otherwise? Does the cessation of diplomatic notes stop the political relations between different Nations and Governments? Is not War merely another kind of writing and language for political thoughts? It has certainly a grammar of its own, but its logic is not peculiar to itself.[1]

Clausewitz is usually quoted in a functional or instrumental spirit — war and peace are different *means* to the ends of politics. In this sense, a humanitarian might well insist that peaceful means be exhausted *prior* to the use of force, that war be a *last resort*. Read this way, Clausewitz's aphorism supports the distinction between humanitarian idealism and strategic realism, even as it blends peace into war.

For modern humanitarians, however, it is easy to imagine circumstances in which peaceful means will simply be more costly to hu-

---

[1] Carl von Clausewitz, *On War* (1832; reprint, Penguin Books, 1968), p. 402.

manitarian objectives than war. Appeasing a warlord may lead to famine. One must be strategic also about peace, what peace, when, implemented in what way. Peace is more complicated than humanitarian virtue — costs and benefits must be weighed and balanced. Deterrence has brought force into the communicative domain of peace, and proportionality has brought humanitarian evaluation into the strategic calculations of war.

Humanitarians and statesmen have reimagined the world of statecraft to respond to this merger of legal principle and political calculation. International politics and the use of force has become a series of communicative acts — intended to assert, reinforce, persuade, compel. Measured against the yardstick of legitimacy, every act of state — every demarche and every missile strike — is both a principled assertion and a persuasive strategy. War, like policy, is now aimed at the opponent's *will*, in an effort to gain compliance with our objectives. Where the legitimacy of ends and the persuasiveness of means are measured in the vocabulary of humanitarianism, every act of state is an act of humanitarian policy making and activism. To be legitimate is to be powerful, to be powerful is to be legitimate. Power both principled and realist — humanitarianism realized. In many ways, this *is* a triumph to be celebrated.

When human rights becomes the global ideology for measuring and articulating the legitimacy of governance — or humanitarianism the global ideology for the use of force — we should read Clausewitz differently, with stress on the idea that war is "another kind of writing and language for political thoughts." A common language for *political* thoughts — in which one can communicate either through force or through diplomacy. Participating in this shared vocabulary, humanitarians have become, in a word, *political*.

This can be difficult for both humanitarians and statesmen to accept. We might have hoped that the merger of humanitarian idealism and foreign policy realism would have exorcized both the humanitarian taboo on participating in rulership and the foreign policy maker's taboo on appearing idealist. Sometimes, of course, this does happen. I am afraid that far more often the reverse seems to occur — all participants in the foreign policy process seem to feel the pressure of both taboos. Neither humanitarians nor statesmen seem willing either to speak in a language of virtue, damn the consequences, or to

carry though with the pragmatic weighing and balancing of consequences necessary for responsible practical governance.

Humanitarian policy makers turn back from questions of military
strategy — let us assess together whether to drop this bomb here, or
there, or not at all — preferring to think of themselves as outside of
power, judging the powerful, opposing government, speaking to it
with the truth of law or ethics. Despite a century's worth of pragmatic renewal, humanitarianism still *wants* to be outside of power,
even if ineffective. Or better, wants to seem pragmatic and effective
while continuing to be experienced to be outside power — effective
without responsibility. In a similar way, for all the foreign policy
specialist has come to exercise power in a humanitarian vocabulary,
he continues to shy away from idealism, and we are as likely to
credit his virtuous pronouncements with cynicism as with honor.
Statesmen use the vocabulary of consequential humanitarianism, but
resist pressing its consequentialism to conclusion, as if they wished
to be understood to be the deferential servants of humanism while
continuing to be experienced to be outside the domain of truth or
virtue — decisive without knowing.

As the vocabulary of their articulation merges, the voices of humanitarian virtue and realist strategy remain distinct. To speak as a
humanitarian means to use a common vocabulary in a particular
way — blending principle and strategy while defaulting toward principle and adopting a posture outside power. Speaking as a statesmen
is similar — but it is defaulting toward assertion of results, and
adopting a posture of engagement with power, the voice of necessity
rather than virtue.

Each of these positions is generated by slipping in and out of the
humanitarian vocabulary, if in different ways. Indeed, these voices
can best be distinguished by contrast with one another. We know the
humanitarian as the one who is not a military strategist. For all the
efforts to renew humanitarianism to make it more pragmatic, more
attentive to consequences, the humanitarian voice is also careful to
leave some space between himself and someone else — the strategist,
the statesman — who is *even more* strategic, *even farther* from virtue.
The statesman or military strategist is doing something similar; however cleverly he speaks the language of humanitarian purpose, he is

careful not to be mistaken for those *other* people, who are not realistic. At the same time, they do not want to be too different—when they drift apart, we hear calls for renewal, for a foreign policy worthy of our ideals, for a humanitarianism effective in a modern world.

We must understand international humanitarianism today not only as an effort to make humanitarian values real—but also to speak about foreign affairs in this quite complex rhetorical situation in such a way as to be experienced as humanitarian. To speak about foreign affairs as a humanitarian means to articulate oneself in a way distinguishable from the pragmatic consequentialism of statecraft without seeming to embrace an impractical external ethics. Humanitarian activist and policy-making strategies might be arranged on a continuum of more principled and more practical responses to this common situation. The same could be said about statesmen, however. To speak as a realist means to articulate oneself in a way distinguishable from humanitarianism without seeming to embrace the nihilism of purely practical reason.

These two postures—both situated between the real and the ideal, but differentiated from one another as real and ideal—seem to require a certain holding back from both ethics and instrumentalism. It is therefore not surprising that the pragmatic promise of the new humanitarianism would not be realized—that for all the talk about weighing and balancing, very little of it would be going on. This is no more surprising than that humanitarian virtue seems so often to be invoked but not realized—that so many participants in policy making and advocacy would draw back from clear evaluation of the humanitarian consequences of government. The holding back, the denial, the bad faith, seem to be part of what it means to express oneself as either a humanitarian and a statesman.

Situated in this common rhetorical space, we might imagine the humanitarian and the military strategist, on a good night, dancing beautifully with one another. The one seems effective, the other principled, their steps elegantly coordinated by pragmatism. A century together, they know what they are doing, each allowing the other his moment to shine. The one knows what to do—the other how to do it. Of course, blind spots and biases remain. The humanitarian can always perfect the articulation of his commitments, the strategist his mastery of consequences in the world. Still, we cannot but admire a knowledge which dances so well with power.

This vision of a partnership between humanism and statecraft has been overwhelmingly powerful for my generation of foreign policy specialists. As young adults of the seventies, we largely missed the days of rage and flower power. It sometimes seemed we had been born too late, that the age of ideals lay behind us. We could march on Washington only as a replay, never in the original production. But we also knew the sixties generation had crashed hard—we did not intend to make the same mistakes. Hunkering down in universities and graduate programs and professional schools, we felt that we would be the first to make idealism real, to bring humanitarianism to power. Where they had been sentimental, we would be savvy.

We were not the first to feel this way, of course. Waves of humanitarian pragmatism have followed the crash of numerous idealisms— and realisms. After the First World War, after the failures of The Hague, of the League, of the Cold War, humanitarians have repeatedly felt that they would be the ones to make old ideals real for a new, more down-to-earth world. When American liberals of the sixties looked at Dag Hammarskjöld's United Nations they felt just this twinge—ideals made real by savvy statecraft. In the 1920s, European humanitarians described the "spirit of Geneva" in precisely these terms as they built the League of Nations and the International Labour Organization. I can feel—have felt—the enthusiasm this idea must have generated. If you have read this far, I trust you have felt it too.

When the excitement drains away, however, the feeling can be bitter. Three years after Hammarskjöld's death, international lawyers felt the collapse of the United Nations dream—and indeed, it would never again carry the burden of humanitarian enthusiasm. Likewise the spirit of Geneva, or the thrill of Paris and the Versailles negotiations. Harold Nicolson, looking back on his experiences in the Paris Peace Conference put it this way:

> The [Paris Peace] Conference may, as Mr. Winston Churchill has said, have been a "turbulent collision of embarrassed demagogues."
> I have already indicated some of the causes which led to turbu-

lence, to collision and to demagogic methods. Yet in spite of this, many durable, and some useful things, were accomplished. Many evil things were avoided. None the less, there were few of us who were not disappointed: and in some of us the Conference inculcated a mood of durable disbelief, a conviction that human nature can, like a glacier, move but an inch or two every thousand years. I wish in this concluding chapter to summarise some, at least, of what might be called the psychological factors (or were they symptoms?) of failure; to comment upon the gradual deterioration of our state of mind; to indicate our "change of heart"; and to ascribe, if possible, this decline of thought and feeling to some tangible causes. The historian, with every justification, will come to the conclusion that we were very stupid men. I think we were. Yet I also think that the factor of stupidity is inseparable from all human affairs. It is too often disregarded as an inevitable concomitant of human behaviour; it is too often employed merely as a term of personal affront. What, in the first place, was the nature of this moral and intellectual deterioration? I can speak with assurance only of my own change of heart, yet I believe that the mutations through which I passed were shared by many others, and that my own loss of idealism coincided with a similar loss of idealism on the part of those (and they were many) who had come to the Conference fired by the same certitudes as myself. Our change of heart can be stated as follows. We came to Paris confident that the new order was about to be established; we left it convinced that the new order had merely fouled the old. We arrived as fervent apprentices in the school of President Wilson; we left as renegades. I wish to suggest, in this chapter (and without bitterness), that this unhappy diminution of standard was very largely the fault (or one might say with greater fairness "the misfortune") of democratic diplomacy.[2]

Now, I am afraid, it is our turn. The enthusiasm so many of my generation have felt for the institutions, norms, and professional practices of international humanitarianism must acknowledge their

[2] Harold Nicolson, *Peacemaking, 1919* (New York: Grosset and Dunlap, 1965), pp. 186–87.

dark sides and limitations. It is not that our good works have sometimes been overcome by dark forces — it is that our good work, however principled, however savvy, has itself also had dark sides, has
contributed to the very evils we set out to redress. My objective in
this volume has been to hasten that awareness, give expression to
that disillusionment, and speed the emergence of a new attitude toward our humanitarian commitments, practices, and institutions.

Earlier moments of disillusion were followed by renewal. The international humanitarian project clarified its ideals and improved its
strategy. I wrote this book in that spirit — tracing my own disillusion-
ments with the humanitarian advocacy projects and policy-making
campaigns of the 1980s and 1990s, in the hopes that they might be
renewed. Pragmatism about consequences, vigilance against the betrayal of humanitarian intentions — throughout I argued for the renewal of humanitarianism through self-criticism.

I continue to hope the humanitarian impulse can be made real in
the world. But I am increasingly skeptical that we know how to
renew our humanitarian practices to achieve that end. We can now
look back on renewal efforts launched in precisely the same pragmatic spirit — and see their darker potential. Too many of the dark
sides I have described in these chapters have been the dark sides of
pragmatic renewal itself. To become disenchanted with renewal is a
bitter fruit. My generation may also crash hard. To be disenchanted
with savvyness — one can feel nausea, disorientation, disempower-
ment. It is hard to know what else humanitarianism might become.

Alongside the very real disappointment, however, there is also
something thrilling about the moment when faith in the practices of
humanitarian renewal fades. A brief and exciting vertigo can accompany the loss of the experience of *knowing* what to do or what to
denounce; along with it, an experience of humanitarianism *in power.*
A feeling of responsibility — precisely the heightened responsibility
which comes when one must *decide,* and when one can no longer
simply denounce. When one must decide without knowing, without
having calculated costs and benefits or reached clarity about the requirements of virtue — when one must decide in freedom. As one
international humanitarian, I want to throw in my lot with these
feelings of disenchantment, and this perception of a responsible free-

dom. I hope that you will as well. I hope that international humanitarians will lay down the tools of pragmatic renewal and experience ourselves to be in power, responsible, and uncertain.

The fault line between activists and policy makers often provides the occasion—the flash point—for this experience. Anyone who has spent time in the international humanitarian world will be familiar with the perennial intramural antagonisms between those who seem external to authority, speaking truth or virtue to power, and those who seem instead to struggle for humanitarian outcomes within the institutions of statecraft. Think of human rights activists and good-hearted governmental officials. Or of nongovernmental organizations and the intergovernmental institutions of the United Nations system. Or of civil servants "in the field" and at headquarters. Or of academics and humanitarian statesmen.

These tensions pit two sides of the modern humanitarian project against one another. Those outside power speak the language of virtue and knowledge—of clarity about intentions and commitments. Their style is assertive, clear, direct. Those closer to power speak the language of strategy, realism, and pragmatic accomplishment, remaining attentive to humanitarian objectives. Their posture is less one of clear vision than of careful balance. They are attentive to paradoxical consequences, practical constraints, political compromises, and speak the language of the achievable rather than the virtuous.

The best international humanitarianism blends these voices, speaking to power and as power. There is a voice of principle, of rules, of the traditional law, of ethical commitment, of rights—and a voice of strategy, of standards, cost-benefit calculations, and shrewd participation in statecraft. The tension between these two voices drives us to renewal—to become ever clearer about ideals and ever more practical about consequences. The division of labor between activists and policy makers—or between headquarters and the field—provides a place for each of these vocabularies to thrive. This division might also seem functional—helping each voice find its best articulation, reinforcing one another, disrupting one another, correcting for one another's excesses. When pragmatists in governance lose their edge they need the wake-up call of principle. When principled advocacy drifts toward impracticality, we can rely on the corrections of policy pragmatism.

But we need to push this a step further. If you have spent time along this fault line, you will know that life there is rarely so harmonious. A week spent with human rights advocates — or trying to be one — quickly brings into focus the tension *within* human rights activism between precisely these two voices. The same is true for policy makers. Inside the High Commissioner for Refugees we find the same tension between the Protection and Assistance Divisions, and then again within the Protection Division between headquarters and the field, and within headquarters between formalism about the mandate and pragmatism about solutions, and within discussions about the mandate between strict and loose interpretations. In every act of modern international humanitarianism we find a double movement, back to intentions, forward to consequences.

As this doubled voice proliferates across the field of humanitarian practice, it is easy to lose track of which is which — in part because of a confusion about the place of power. Think for a moment about a human rights activist invoking a clear norm to evaluate a governmental action, and a government official assessing the costs and benefits of the action for humanitarian objectives. It seems appropriate for the activist to speak in a more formal, ethically self-confident vocabulary, just as we think it appropriate for the official to take care for consequences. It is easy to think of the activist as *outside* and the official as *inside* the exercise of power.

Yet, when the activist *affects* the statesman — whether strengthening his hand by approval or weakening it by criticism — it would be puzzling not to conclude that the activist also governs, is also inside power. For the official to orient his margin of maneuver to humanitarian commitments — to govern in the humanitarian spirit, to be an agent for the ideology of human rights — at once makes him less the instrument of governance as it makes humanitarianism the voice of sovereignty.

Indeed, once we see power as a matter of communication and legitimacy, it is no longer clear who is inside and who is outside its exercise. The official assesses the effectiveness of his action in part by predicting the view which will be taken of it by others, including the

activist. The activist affects the policy maker, either directly, by praising, shaming and persuading, or indirectly, by mobilizing others to
view the statesman as more or less legitimate. We can only really
know what happens after the dust settles — if then. Perhaps the activist will delegitimate government action — but perhaps government
action will delegitimate idealistic advocacy. These determinations
will themselves be interpretations, over which we will strategize.
Both voices must be strategic — about one another, and about the
broader world of statecraft and opinion, not only in this round, but
through successive rounds. Humanitarians — whether activists or
policy makers — find themselves split between principled and strategic expression and self-identification, find themselves strategizing
their power in postures of both principal and pragmatism.

In this dynamic conversation, it would be more accurate to say
that power speaks with two quite different voices which express
quite different attitudes toward itself, both addressing itself and
speaking for itself. This doubling complicates the renewalist program. Calling for clarification of ideals and pragmatism about consequences treats them independently, as if they were the province of
different actors, or of each of us at different times. We can imagine
renewing the humanitarian movement by strengthening both. But if
each humanitarian act is a conjuration of both, renewal will be more
difficult. The experience of disenchantment with both will be more
available.

The renewal project is made more complex still once we understand these two parts of the project — fidelity to commitment, realism about consequences — less as real things in the world than as
performances for audiences. For the speaker, fidelity to purpose is a
posture or voice, for the audience it is an attribution or interpretation. Official and activist speak to one another. When we hear them
speaking, we attribute "power" to one and we say about the other
that he is speaking "truth to power." The humanitarian is also staging himself for us, posturing, performing as internal or external to
power. Those watching, evaluating the legitimacy of their performances also judge — speaking to them in the languages of principle
and consequence.

When the humanitarian speaks in the voice of principle, we can say that he is seeking to persuade power, and in that sense to become powerful, to bend power to his commitment. But we can also say that he is *staging himself* outside power. It is not at all clear which "motive" we should attribute to his articulation—a will to power or a will to be seen to be external to power. Something similar goes on for the humanitarian speaking the balanced voice of pragmatism. We can say that he intends to be effective and legitimate, convincing us that he has optimized the mix of principle and outcome—but it is also true that he is staging himself *as* power, external to principle. It is difficult to know whether his is a will to power, or a will to submit to humanitarian principle.

Meanwhile, the humanitarian practices which emerged from the renewalist effort to perfect these voices, render them harmonious, place them in a stable division of labor, both narrow our vision of what humanitarianism might become and render us needlessly complacent about the practice of humanitarian authority. The voice of virtue occupies the field precisely to assert itself as the universal voice of principle. By staging itself outside power, the voice of principle also detaches itself from responsibility—it seems to say "I *know* but I have not *done*." Moreover, as we have repeatedly seen, what it knows is self-consciously narrowed, is renewed precisely by turning back from knowledge of consequences. To remain *truth*, external to power, the voice of virtue abjures appreciation of consequences. To sharpen its spear in the moment of its articulation, it mutes the experience of uncertainty about just what *is* true. When humanitarians adopt the "truth to power" posture, they insulate themselves both from the experience of moral uncertainty—and from responsibility for the consequences of their articulation.

But the voice of strategy fares little better—it has also become a voice of disengagement from responsibility. I did *what could be done* (and knew not). The humanitarian policy maker's sense for the possible is cramped by the shared assumptions of the humanitarian vocabulary. There are shared ideas about geography, and about the direction of progress which I have explored in the previous chapters. The international humanitarian in power imagines himself to act only sporadically, to intervene only intermittently, in a world of facts which preexist his deliberations about what to do. For these facts he has no responsibility, and he all too often fails to attend to the impact of his actions among people, interests, or groups in society. The development specialist who builds the rule of law without confronting the distributional choices it entails, or the humanitarian who joins hands with the military in preparing for war while eschewing responsibility for the carnage which results exemplify this difficulty.

These two voices together — a voice of virtue which insists that it knows what is right but does not act, and a voice of pragmatism oriented to consequences for principles rather than persons — support a humanitarianism which governs — but which governs without the experience of governing, without the experience of responsibility, and without the experience of uncertainty about what will turn out to have been right. As a result, although proud to participate in both virtue and governance, humanitarian policy makers too often flee from the political struggles which go with the exercise of power and with uncertainty over truth. Humanitarian renewal has produced an elite which stages itself to be at once "in power" and "in truth" without feeling the need to take responsibility for uncertainty about truth *or* consequences.

I do hope the humanitarian impulse will continue to mobilize people to seek roles for themselves in the governance professions. That good-hearted people will continue to try to make the world a better place, more just, more humane. To get there, however, we will need to lay down the tools of pragmatic renewal which block our experience of responsibility for rulership, and lead us to false certainty about what humanitarianism can mean. To confront the dark sides of humanitarian policy making, we need a policy-making style which welcomes, rather than obscures, the hard choices of governance. We need to develop a new posture or character for international humanitarianism — informed by the vertiginous experience of disenchantment, of seeing that one is responsible and yet does not already know. That we must act on faith and hope for grace.

Rather than a program of action, I offer a list of suggestions — maxims or heuristics — to help international humanitarians who wish to work to develop such a posture. Can we imagine a humanitarianism which kept these propositions in mind? To work as a humanitarian *as if* these propositions were true might help us develop skepticism about what we know, might prevent us from flinching to acknowledge our participation in power, and might keep alive an awareness of the darker sides of our power.

1. INTERNATIONAL HUMANITARIANISM RULES

There is scarcely a humanitarian practice which does not act as if governance were elsewhere — in government, in congress, in statecraft, in the Member States, the States' Parties, the Security Council, the field, the headquarters, the empire. And yet we do rule, exercise power, affect distributions among people. When we design a regime to protect refugees, we often do protect them. We also make what they are "refugees." We speak as truth to power. Sometimes power listens. But to say what *is* is also to govern. Imagine a humanitarianism comfortable with governance, open to its pleasures, able to accept, suffer, and sometimes also delight in its dark sides. Let us no longer avert our eyes from rulership.

2. INTERNATIONAL HUMANITARIANISM IS POWERFUL

Every international humanitarian practice I know presents itself as weak, needing fealty, barely able to hold its own against the world of power. Take international law — it is customary to imagine the world as a jungle of contending forces, over which international lawyers have succeeded in throwing only the thinnest veil of norms and institutions. In fact, the situation today is more the reverse. A global flood of law, here and there the weakest flicker of politics, and no ark in sight. It nevertheless remains difficult for humanitarian international lawyers to fashion an argument which is not also a plea for more international law. Thinking our humanitarian projects weak and marginal, we hesitate to criticize them, falling easily for the idea that we must refrain from deconstructing what has hardly been built. Thinking we light only a single candle, we fail to look beyond its dim light to see the consequences — also the darker consequences — of our humanitarian work.

We should foster our will to power and embrace the full range of our effects on the world. Thinking of our humanitarianism as force, we will no longer be tempted to nurture it protectively, preserving its knowledge and clarity, that it might one day express itself as counterforce to the power and politics of others. We can turn our attention to building a terrain for politics and political choice, letting go the will to know, but not to do.

3. THE BACKGROUND IS THE FOREGROUND

International humanitarians think we know where politics happens — in the public institutions which host an explicit clash of ideological positions and social interests. The daily newspaper reminds us that it is the sovereign, the President, the Parliament, the government, which decides. Theirs is the vocabulary of politics — we participate in politics when we express our opinions in that vocabulary, when we vote for those people, when we protest the actions of those institutions. An effective humanitarianism carries humanitarian virtues to those heights.

But increasingly the decisions which allocate stakes in global society are not taken there and are not contested in these terms. They are taken by experts, managing norms and institutions in the background of this public spectacle — legal norms and private institutions, decisions rendered in technical vocabularies. They are taken not by the state, but by thousands of decision makers in the economy. We will need to learn the professional vocabularies of these background experts and enter the quotidian places of their deployment, contesting the norms, institutions, and understandings which influence their objectives and bargaining power. Bringing humanitarianism to bear will increasingly mean unearthing the sites and terms experts use to manage these background arrangements and contesting them — translating them into political vocabularies we are accustomed to associating with the clash of interests and ideologies. Even where there is only efficiency, there is distribution.

To hear the workings of these gears, we must mute the clamor calling us to identify power with the foreground sites of conventional politics. We need a humanitarianism which remembers that even when there is no regulation, there is rule — that private rules, customary rules, informal sectors, the miniaturized operations of expertise also govern. Which remembers that public ceremonies, theatrical commitments and magic incantations, even of human rights, do not emancipate, do not bring justice. Justice must be made, by people, in the background vocabularies where life is lived, each time for the first time.

4. WEIGH OUTCOMES, NOT STRUCTURES

Humanitarian pragmatism has focused our attention too often on structures rather than outcomes. Decision-making procedures can be significant; constitutional arrangements can have consequences. But they are also easy to enchant — we too often substitute multilateral decisions for humanitarian decisions, the work of the United Nations for humanitarian work. A long-run increase in the legitimacy of the United Nations may well be worth a bad short-term outcome in this or that case — but we should be suspicious that this is so often asserted and so rarely substantiated. We should be careful to tally the distributional consequences for individuals and groups — rather than the expressive consequences for our principles or the reputational consequences for our institutions and professional vocabularies.

Our focus on structures and procedures has encouraged us to flee from conflict, to smooth our formulations and prefer negotiation, conciliation, mediation, and discussion to contestation. Yet contestation will be necessary to sharpen awareness of all that we do not know, and to bring to the table the dark consequences we are more comfortable leaving in the shadows. We have substituted the forms of politics for the experience of political life. Too often we have opted for electoral form over participation and popular engagement. Let us rather heat up our politics, heightening the experience of uncertainty, of conflict over consequences, and of the necessity for responsible decision.

5. IT'S NOT ABOUT "INTERVENING"

Imagine an international humanitarianism which took a break from preoccupation with the justifications for "intervention." Which no longer imagined the world from high above, on the "international plane," in the "international community." Which saw itself in a location, among others, as an interest among others, as a culture among others. No longer above, looking down, passive, awaiting a justification to act, international humanitarians might develop the habit of acknowledging their ongoing participation in the quotidian, their responsibility for what is. Such a heuristic might also prevent us from overestimating the possibilities for a costless, neutral engagement in far away places, or underestimating our ongoing political role in governance.

6. ASK NOT FOR WHOM THE HUMANITARIAN TOILS

Humanitarian advocates and policy makers routinely think of themselves not only speaking truth to power — but speaking to power as the representative of someone else, the underrepresented, the powerless, the victimized, the voiceless, the public interest, the unborn. Too often we have enchanted our fantasies about these unrepresented, transforming them into truth. We have acted as if speaking *for them* immunized us from challenges to the truth of our positions or removed *us* entirely from responsibility for both truth and power.

Let me propose an exercise, a heuristic, as antidote. Imagine a humanitarianism which spoke in its own name. Imagine articulating what we want to happen — also to them — as *our idea, our interest,* not theirs. To every policy proposal we might attach a "humanitarian impact statement," assessing the consequences for humanitarianism itself, and disclosing the interests which speak rather than those on whose behalf they do so. Speaking in our own voice could make fantasy identifications less common, might help us remember that we — like them — are uncertain where virtue lies, and might center us in governance as people with projects, our feet to the fire of participation in power.

7. TOOLS ARE TOOLS

As human rights advocates, we have too often treated our norms as true — rather than as reminders of what might be made true. As policy makers, we have promoted use of our institutions as surrogates for humanitarian outcomes. We have substituted pragmatism and instrumental reason for responsibility — imagining that if we work pragmatically we can escape uncertainty about both our humanitarian values and about the consequences for our action. But uncertainty remains — and pragmatic renewal has too often become a professional practice of denial.

How difficult it is to disenchant our tools and ourselves. Can we imagine, even heuristically, a humanitarianism *agnostic* about its tools? A refugee officer agnostic about whether the government ratified the protocol, so long as refugees were protected? Agnostic about whether we called them refugees, about whether they were or were not refugees, so long as they were treated humanely? International lawyers agnostic about whether statesmen used the World Court, so long as disputes were resolved, agnostic about whether disputes were resolved so long as outcomes were humanitarian, agnostic about the fate of international law? The idolatry of tools disguises itself as the wisdom of the long run. But let us assess those long term promises with cold and disenchanted eyes.

8. PROGRESS IS NOT PROGRAM

Every humanitarian discipline I have encountered has a shared sense of its own progressive history. These progress narratives are often programs of action — the institutional machinery must be "completed," the developing world must "catch up"; only after an International Jurists' Platform for East Timor has been "established" can action be taken. International law is "primitive" and must be constructed, allowed to mature, before it can bear the scrutiny of criticism. These stories give direction to our work, define what humanitarianism will next become. But they also reinforce the biases and blind spots in our mental map of the terrain on which we work. They deceive us with promises that humanitarianism will be achieved in the final days, if we work now in our own interest, on our own tools, building our own institutions and strengthening our own professions. They reinforce an unwarranted faith in the upward humanitarian spiral of conversations about the legitimacy of government action carried on in our professional vocabularies.

We must unremember these stories, set them aside, demand evidence for their long-term promises. Imagine constructing programs, making proposals, without the metaphors of primitive and mature. Only by forgoing such stories can humanitarians come to live again in history, with all its contingency and possibility — as responsible for what they do next as for what they did before.

9. HUMANITARIANISM AS CRITIQUE

We have used criticism — but we have not been critical. Humanitarians have been self-critical, have deployed criticism of themselves, of one another, in the service of renewal. We have flogged ourselves for ignoring our ideals and misestimating the costs and benefits of our policy activity. Our advocacy and policy making have had blind spots and biases which this self-criticism can help dislodge. But humanitarians have treated criticism as an instrument — to return us to truth, or to perfect our pragmatic assessment of consequences. The point was to *know* — criticism could dislodge idolatry and reveal faith.

Imagine instead a humanitarianism whose *end* was criticism, whose *knowledge* was critique. Imagine a human rights movement which was not the vehicle for what we know justice to be, but a network for criticizing the pretenses of justice as it is. Imagine human rights training in the technologies of critical reasoning, treaty instruments reminding us to ask again what justice requires. Imagine a UNHCR devoted less to identifying and protecting refugees than to opening criticism of the ways national boundaries distort human possibility and of justifications for the incarceration of peoples in states. Imagine a development policy not of best practices—but of capacity building for contestation about the terms, the costs, the winners and losers, the cultural consequences of economic growth.

Such a humanitarianism might find it easier to remember that it does not know—and that it participates in power, contests with others the meaning and requirements of humanism. It might develop our stamina for ambiguity and ambivalence—for victims who are not baby seals and victimizers who are not Adolf Hitler. Such a humanitarianism might make way for apostasy, for heresy about the best practices of international and national governance. With criticism as our objective rather than our tool, we might imagine international humanitarianism—or a human rights movement—as an antiestablishment establishment, invigorating our political life for heterodoxy.

10. DECISION, AT ONCE RESPONSIBLE AND UNCERTAIN

As international humanitarians, we have sought power, but have not accepted responsibility. We have claimed to know when we were unsure. We have advocated and denounced, while remaining content that others should govern. We have made policy while turning our eyes from the darker consequences of our work. Our professional biases and blind spots have eluded our most aggressive efforts to renew the vocabularies which maintain them.

The most difficult heuristic is this—to take responsibility for more than we can see, to make policy as if we did not know more than we do. Imagine a humanitarianism which embraced the act of decision—allocating stakes, distributing resources, making politics, governing, ruling. Which was comfortable intervening because it knew itself always already as a participant in governance. Which exercised power not as humanitarian knowledge imprinting itself on the real, but with all the ambivalence and ignorance and uncertainty we know as human. Such a humanitarianism would reverse the tendency to act *as if* we knew and did not act—would seek instead to *be* as if we acted and did not know.

Ruling, deciding for others when we do not know—there is a freedom which comes when we realize that we are in power but that our expertise no longer guides us. It is the freedom of discretion, of deciding in the exception—a human freedom of the will. It can be pleasurable—but it is also frightening. There is also a terrible responsibility—deciding for others, causing consequences which elude our knowledge but not our power. The darker sides of our nature and our world confronted, embraced, and accepted, rather than denied. I imagine this humanitarianism in the language of spirit and grace—at once uncomfortable and full of human promise.

These heuristic suggestions are rooted in faith that our humanitarian yearnings might yet be realized—even as they have emerged from my own disenchantment with our contemporary international humanitarian practices. For the humanitarianism I imagine, we would need to disenchant our practices, our expertise, and our professional postures, let go attachments to much that humanitarianism has become. I have written about my own experiences of disenchantment because I am convinced that for each of us moments of decision, of responsibility and of freedom in unknowing, will arise from our own moments of disenchantment and will be quite personal, in the ways all human experience ultimately belongs only to each of us alone.

But it is hard to imagine sustaining such a humanitarianism alone. We will need a community and a profession, will need to develop habits, practices, and institutions. Over the years, I have written about these experiences in a community of people as we have struggled with humanitarian promises and possibilities and shared our disenchantments and hopes. This short list of suggestions emerges from those conversations. I hope they will engage others in the work of criticism and disenchantment, and in the search for new humanitarian habits of mind and professional practices.

My generation came into its own as the vocabularies of statecraft and policy making merged with those of humanitarian advocacy. In the 1970s, I thought I was part of a broad generational cohort training to participate in running the country and the world—for good.

At first, we felt distant from the military, suspicious of its piety about mission and macho attachment to violence. We would rule — but we would do no harm. We were skeptical of claims made in the language of ethics and truth, whether by those in power or those we had seen outside our classrooms, holding signs, protesting, and denouncing. We would be realist, and we would be humane.

Over the thirty years which followed, our ideas about the military changed. But the idea that we would rule in virtue thrived, even as we forgot the feeling that we could not tell where virtue lay. After the Cold War, in the years of Bush and Clinton and Bush, people my age began to take control of foreign affairs. We had developed a spirited set of ethical ideas about what to do with military force. Madelaine Albright's retort to Colin Powell — "What's the point of having this superb military that you're always talking about if we can't use it?" — resonated for my generation precisely because it announced this new sensibility. The point was no longer to restrain the military, but to manage it, humanize it, and then to mobilize it to humanitarian ends, to make of the military a humanitarian activist and policy maker. Somehow the passage through relativism had led to ethical commitment, engagement, and to a partnership with the military. Children of the seventies had merged humanitarianism and military strategy.

As I review my experience with international humanitarianism, I realize that I have parted ways with this generational project. As we have entered government, whether as advocates or policy makers, I have come to feel that we have lost our way. Looking back, I should not have been surprised. Although I had registered for the draft as a conscientious objector in 1971, mine was not a strong stand. After Vietnamization, the lottery, we knew it wasn't about whether you were willing to kill people or not. Governance kills, in peacetime, in war — we knew that. A friend or two joined up. Twenty six million men became draft age in America between 1964 and 1973, and sixteen million of us never served. Only 8,800 were imprisoned for conscientious resistance. The one friend I had who really went outside, moved to the Haight, let his hair grow down, performed in the street, married the woman he met out there with daisies in her hair down by the river in the park, barefoot, joined the navy the next day and went to nuclear sub school. I had been his best man, and I visited him in port and we talked about how cool it was. They'd put him through college later, he'd learn something, he'd straighten himself out. The USS *Independence* was in the Gulf because people like me — and him — had put it there.

Modern humanitarianism is a Gordian knot of participation in power and denial, a willful blindness posing as strategic insight. At the same time, humanitarianism is a professional practice in a difficult vocabulary — once learned, it is difficult to set aside. Its defects and imperfections call only for its reinforcement, repetition. It is easy to believe that a return to principle can compensate for strategy run amok — just as careful strategy and hard evaluation of costs and benefits can seem to call us back from the errors of enchantment. This is precisely the genius of humanitarian pragmatism — to harness principle and calculation, packaging them in a single identity, chastening, perfecting, critiquing, reinforcing, legitimating, apologizing for one another.

International humanitarianism could promise more — a heightened experience of freedom and responsibility, a profession committed to the human embrace of action, fallen from knowledge but poised for grace. To realize this promise, we will need new habits and a new sensibility for policy making and advocacy. We will need to recover the pleasures and insights of skeptical — rather than instrumental — reason. But if we do, we might build a new humanitarian community. Forged in disenchantment. Embracing the dark sides. Deciding — at once uncertain and responsible.

Index